Webster's
Spanish-English Dictionary

Webster's Spanish-English Dictionary

Features Latin-American Spanish

Created in cooperation with the Editors of

Merriam-Webster

creative EDGE

This 2008 Edition published by arrangement with Federal Street Press,
a division of Merriam Webster, Incorporated

creative EDGE
118 Seaboard Lane, Franklin, TN 37067
CE10886/0208

ISBN 1-40378-430-2

Printed in the United States of America
10 11 12 CLI 5 4 3

Contents

Preface

This Spanish-English dictionary has been edited with an eye to keeping the vocabulary as concise as possible and yet covering the most essential words in everyday use. There are more than 20,000 boldface entries in all, and each one has a translation. In most cases a single word will serve as a translation; in others, where there is no single word that translates, a phrase is used.

All dictionary entries are printed in **bold** type, followed by an *italicized* part of speech label. **Main entries** follow one another in strict alphabetical order, without regard to intervening spaces or hyphens. The Spanish letter combinations *ch* and *ll* are alphabetized within the letters *C* and *L*. However, the Spanish letter *ñ* is a separate letter of the Spanish alphabet, falling after the letter N and before the letter O, so words that contain the *ñ* are alphabetized accordingly. For example, the Spanish word **mañana** falls alphabetically between the entry word **manzana** and the entry word **mapa**.

Words with identical spellings and differing only in part of speech and derived words and phrases are run into a single entry:

> **back** *n* ... — **back** *adv* ... — **back** *adj* ... — **back** *v* **back up** ... **back down** ... — **backbone** *n* — **background** *n* ...

Words spelled the same but unrelated are given a separate entry with a distinguishing superscript numeral:

> **sobre**[1] *nm* envelope
> **sobre**[2] *prep* on, on top of; over ...

Variant spellings appear at the main entry separated by *or* (as **blond** *or* **blonde** *adj* rubio ... and **cacahuate** *or* **cacahuete** *nm* peanut). For Spanish nouns and adjectives, the main entry by tradition is the masculine form and the feminine ending is shown, usually cut back to the last element, following a comma: (as **campeón, -peona** *n* ... champion).

It is not in the scope of this book to give complete grammatical information. Spanish masculine and feminine nouns and adjectives are noted and part of speech functions are indicated, but inflected forms, such as the plurals of nouns and the principal parts of verbs, are not shown except for the most irregular formations. When they are shown, they are in bold type in parentheses following the part of speech label. Plurals are shown for English nouns where there is an internal spelling change, as **calf** ... (**calves**), or for nouns that end in 'y' and sometimes 'o'. For English verbs the past tense and past participle forms are shown where there is a change in internal spelling, as **break** ... (**broke; broken**). Comparative and superlative forms are generally not shown for adjectives and adverbs. For Spanish nouns, the plural form is shown only when there is a change in spelling, such as the addition or loss of a diacritic on a letter:

> **abdomen** *nm* (**-dómenes**) abdomen
> **abstención** *nf* (**-ciones**) abstention

Where the plural form shown affects only the masculine form, that is indicated by an italic *m* within the parentheses:

bailarín, -rina *n* (**-rines** *m*) dancer

The grammatical functions of entry words, including the traditional parts of speech, are indicated by italic abbreviations. These include indications of plural (*pl*) and masculine (*m*) and feminine (*f*) gender of words as well as the following part of speech labels:

art	article
n	noun (also *nm* masculine noun; *nf* feminine noun; *npl* plural noun)
v	verb
vr	reflexive verb
v impers	impersonal verb
v aux	auxiliary verb
v phr	verb phrase
vr phr	reflexive verb phrase
adj	adjective
adv	adverb
prep	preposition
prep phr	prepositional phrase
pron	pronoun
reflexive pron	reflexive pronoun
conj	conjunction
conj phr	conjunctive phrase
interj	interjection

These labels are also sometimes combined: (*nmpl*) or (*n or adj*).

Spanish-English
Dictionary

A

a¹ *nf* a, first letter of the Spanish alphabet

a² *prep* (**al** when contracted with *el*) to; **a las dos** at two o'clock; **al día siguiente** (on) the following day; **a pie** on foot; **de lunes a viernes** from Monday until Friday; **tres veces a la semana** three times per week

abajo *adv* down, below, downstairs; **hacia ~** downward

abandonar *v* abandon, leave; give up — **abandono** *nm* abandonment, neglect

abanico *nm* fan

abastecer *v* supply, stock — **abastecimiento** *nm* supply, provisions

abdomen *nm* (**-dómenes**) abdomen

abedul *nm* birch

abeja *nf* bee

abertura *nf* opening

abeto *nm* fir tree

abierto, -ta *adj* open

abismo *nm* abyss, chasm

ablandar *v* soften up

abofetear *v* slap

abogado, -da *n* lawyer — **abogacía** *nf* legal profession

abominable *adj* abominable

abonar *v* pay; fertilize — **abonarse** *vr* subscribe — **abonado, -da** *n* subscriber — **abono** *nm* payment, installment; fertilizer; season ticket

abordar *v* approach, deal with; get on board

aborigen *nmf* (**-rígenes**) aborigine — **aborigen** *adj* aboriginal, native

aborrecer *v* abhor, detest

abortar *v* have a miscarriage; abort — **aborto** *nm* abortion, miscarriage

abotonar *v* button

abrazar *v* hug, embrace — **abrazo** *nm* hug, embrace

abrelatas *nms & pl* can opener

abreviar *v* shorten, abridge; abbreviate — **abreviatura** *nf* abbreviation

abrigar *v* dress warmly — **abrigado, -da** *adj* warm, wrapped up — **abrigo** *nm* coat, overcoat

abril *nm* April

abrir *v* open, open up; unlock, undo

abrochar *v* button, fasten

absceso *nm* abscess

absoluto, -ta *adj* absolute, unconditional; **en absoluto** not at all — **absolutamente** *adv* absolutely

absorber *v* absorb; take up, require — **absorbente** *adj* absorbent; absorbing — **absorto, -ta** *adj* absorbed, engrossed

abstenerse *vr* abstain, refrain — **abstención** *nf* (**-ciones**) abstention

abstracto, -ta *adj* abstract — **abstraer** *v* abstract — **abstraerse** *vr* lose oneself in thought

absurdo, -da *adj* absurd, ridiculous — **absurdo** *nm* absurdity

abuelo, -la *n* grandfather, grandmother; **abuelos** *nmpl* grandparents

abundar *v* abound, be plentiful — **abundancia** *nf* abundance — **abundante** *adj* abundant

aburrir *v* bore — **aburrido, -da** *adj* boring — **aburrimiento** *nm* boredom

abusar *v* go too far — **abusivo, -va** *adj* outrageous, excessive — **abuso** *nm* abuse

acá *adv* here, over here

acabar *v* finish, end; **~ con** put an end to — **acabado, -da** *adj* finished, perfect; old, worn-out

academia *nf* academy — **académico, -ca** *adj* academic

acalorar *v* stir up, excite — **acalorado, -da** *adj* emotional, heated

acampar *v* camp

acaparar *v* hoard

acariciar *v* caress

acaso *adv* perhaps, maybe; **por si ∼** just in case

acatarrarse *vr* catch a cold

acaudalado, -da *adj* wealthy, rich

acceder *v* agree; **∼ a** gain access to

acceso *nm* access; entrance

accesorio *nm* accessory

accidentado, -da *adj* eventful, turbulent; injured — **accidentado, -da** *n* accident victim

accidente *nm* accident — **accidentarse** *vr* have an accident

acción *nf* (**-ciones**) action; act, deed; share of stock — **accionista** *nmf* stockholder

aceite *nm* oil — **aceitar** *v* oil — **aceitoso, -sa** *adj* oily

aceituna *nf* olive

acelerar *v* accelerate — **acelerarse** *vr* hurry up — **acelerador** *nm* accelerator

acelga *nf* Swiss chard

acento *nm* accent — **acentuar** *v* accent; emphasize, stress — **acentuarse** *vr* stand out

acepción *nf* (**-ciones**) sense, meaning

aceptar *v* accept — **aceptable** *adj* acceptable

acera *nf* sidewalk

acerca de *prep phr* about, concerning

acercar *v* bring near or closer

acero *nm* steel

acertar *v* guess correctly; be accurate — **acertado, -da** *adj* correct, accurate

achacar *v* attribute, impute

achaque *nm* aches and pains

achicar *v* make smaller

ácido, -da *adj* acid, sour — **acidez** *nf* (**-deces**) acidity — **ácido** *nm* acid

acierto *nm* correct answer; skill; sound judgment

aclamar *v* acclaim

aclarar *v* clarify, explain; clear up — **aclaración** *nf* (**-ciones**) explanation

acné *nm* acne

acobardar *v* intimidate

acoger *v* shelter; receive, welcome —

acogedor, -dora *adj* cozy, welcoming — **acogida** *nf* welcome; refuge

acogerse a *vr phr* resort to

acolchar *v* pad

acólito *nm* altar boy

acometer *v* attack

acomodar *v* adjust; put; make a place for — **acomodarse** *vr* settle in; **acomodarse a** adapt to — **acomodado, -da** *adj* well-to-do

acompañar *v* accompany — **acompañante** *nmf* companion; music accompanist

acondicionar *v* fit out, equip

aconsejar *v* advise

acontecimiento *nm* event

acoplar *v* couple, connect — **acoplarse** *vr* fit together

acordar *v* agree; **acordarse** *vr* remember

acordeón *nm* (**-deones**) accordion

acortar *v* shorten, cut short

acosar *v* hound, harass

acostar *v* put to bed

acostumbrar *v* accustom; **∼ a** be in the habit of

acrecentar *v* increase

acreditar *v* accredit, authorize; prove — **acreditarse** *vr* prove oneself — **acreditado, -da** *adj* reputable; accredited

acreedor, -dora *adj* worthy —**acreedor, -dora** *n* creditor

acribillar *v* riddle, pepper

acrílico *nm* acrylic

acrobacia *nf* acrobatics — **acróbata** *nmf* acrobat

acta *nf* certificate; meeting minutes *pl*

actitud *nf* attitude; posture, position

activar *v* activate; stimulate, speed up — **actividad** *nf* activity — **activo, -va** *adj* active

acto *nm* act, deed; act (in a play)

actor *nm* actor — **actriz** *nf* (**-trices**) actress

actual *adj* present, current — **actualidad** *nf* present time — **actualizar** *v* modernize — **actualmente** *adv* at present, nowadays

actuar *v* act, perform

acuarela *nf* watercolor

acuario *nm* aquarium

acuático, -ca *adj* aquatic, water

acudir *v* go, come; ~ **a** be present at, attend

acueducto *nm* aqueduct

acuerdo *nm* agreement; **de** ~ OK, all right

acumular *v* accumulate

acupuntura *nf* acupuncture

acurrucarse *vr* curl up, nestle

acusar *v* accuse — **acusado, -da** *n* defendant

acústica *nf* acoustics — **acústico, -ca** *adj* acoustic

adaptar *v* adapt; adjust, fit — **adaptación** *nf* (-ciones) adaptation — **adaptador** *nm* electrical adapter

adecuar *v* adapt, make suitable — **adecuado, -da** *adj* suitable, appropriate

adelantar *v* advance, move forward; overtake; pay in advance — **adelantarse** *vr* run fast (of a clock)

adelante *adv* ahead, forward; **más** ~ later on, further on — **¡adelante!** *interj* come in!

adelgazar *v* lose weight

además *adv* besides, furthermore; ~ **de** in addition to, as well as

adentro *adv* inside, within

adherirse *vr* adhere, stick — **adhesión** *nf* (-siones) adhesion; support — **adhesivo, -va** *adj* adhesive — **adhesivo** *nm* adhesive

adición *nf* (-ciones) addition — **adicional** *adj* additional

adicto, -ta *adj* addicted — **adicto, -ta** *n* addict

adiestrar *v* train

adinerado, -da *adj* wealthy

adiós *nm* (**adioses**) farewell **¡adiós!** *interj* good-bye!

adivinar *v* guess; foretell — **adivinanza** *nf* riddle

adjetivo *nm* adjective

adjudicar *v* award — **adjudicarse** *vr* appropriate

administración *nf* (-ciones) administration; management — **administrador, -dora** *n* administrator, manager — **administrar** *v* manage, run; administer (a drug)

admirar *v* admire

admitir *v* admit; accept — **admisión** *nf* (-siones) admission; acceptance

ADN *nm* DNA

adolecer de *v phr* suffer from

adolescente *adj & nmf* adolescent — **adolescencia** *nf* adolescence

adónde *adv* where

adoptar *v* adopt — **adopción** *nf* (-ciones) adoption

adorar *v* adore, worship — **adorable** *adj* adorable

adormecer *v* make sleepy; numb

adornar *v* decorate, adorn — **adorno** *nm* ornament, decoration

adquirir *v* acquire; purchase — **adquisición** *nf* (-ciones) acquisition; purchase

aduana *nf* customs office

aduanero, -ra *adj* customs — **aduanero, -ra** *n* customs officer

adueñarse de *vr phr* take possession of

adular *v* flatter

adulterar *v* adulterate

adulterio *nm* adultery

adulto, -ta *adj & n* adult

adverbio *nm* adverb — **adverbial** *adj* adverbial

adversario, -ria *n* adversary, opponent — **adversidad** *nf* adversity

advertir *v* warn; notice — **advertencia** *nf* warning

adyacente *adj* adjacent

aéreo, -rea *adj* aerial, air

aerolínea *nf* airline

aeronave *nf* aircraft

aeropuerto *nm* airport

afán *nm* (**afanes**) eagerness; effort, hard work — **afanarse** *vr* toil

afección *nf* (**-ciones**) ailment, complaint

afectivo, -va *adj* emotional

afecto *nm* affection — **afectar** *v* affect

afeitar *v* shave

aferrarse *vr* cling, hold on

afianzar *v* secure, strengthen

afiche *nm* poster

afición *nf* (**-ciones**) penchant, fondness; hobby — **aficionado, -da** *n* enthusiast, fan; amateur — **aficionarse a** *vr phr* become interested in

afilar *v* sharpen

afiliarse a *vr phr* join, become a member of — **afiliación** *nf* (**-ciones**) affiliation

afinar *v* tune; perfect, refine

afinidad *nf* affinity, similarity

afirmar *v* state, affirm; strengthen — **afirmación** *nf* (**-ciones**) statement, affirmation

afligir *v* afflict; distress

aflojar *v* loosen, slacken; ease up

afortunado, -da *adj* fortunate, lucky

africano, -na *adj* African

afuera *adv* out; outside, outdoors — **afueras** *nfpl* outskirts

agencia *nf* agency, office — **agente** *nmf* agent, officer

agenda *nf* agenda; notebook

ágil *adj* agile — **agilidad** *nf* agility

agitar *v* agitate; wave, flap; stir up

aglomerar *v* amass

agobiar *v* oppress; overwhelm

agonía *nf* death throes; agony — **agonizar** *v* be dying

agosto *nm* August

agotar *v* deplete, use up; exhaust

agradar *v* be pleasing — **agradable** *adj* pleasant, agreeable

agradecer *v* be grateful for, thank

agrado *nm* taste, liking; **con** ~ with pleasure

agrandar *v* enlarge

agrario, -ria *adj* agrarian, agricultural

agravar *v* make heavier; aggravate, worsen

agredir *v* attack

agregar *v* add, attach

agresión *nf* (**-siones**) aggression, attack — **agresividad** *nf* aggressiveness

agricultura *nf* agriculture, farming — **agricultor, -tora** *n* farmer

agridulce *adj* bittersweet; sweet-and-sour

agrietar *v* crack

agrio, agria *adj* sour

agrupar *v* group together — **agrupación** *nf* (**-ciones**) group, association

agua *nf* water; ~ **oxigenada** hydrogen peroxide; ~**s negras** *or* ~**s residuales** sewage

aguacate *nm* avocado

aguacero *nm* downpour

aguantar *v* bear, withstand; hold; hold out, last — **aguantarse** *vr* restrain oneself

aguardiente *nm* clear brandy

agudo, -da *adj* acute, sharp; shrill, high-pitched — **agudeza** *nf* sharpness; witticism

aguijón *nm* (**-jones**) stinger; goad, stimulus

águila *nf* eagle

aguja *nf* needle; hand (of a clock); church spire

aguzar *v* sharpen; ~ **el oído** prick up one's ears

ahí *adv* there; **por** ~ somewhere, thereabouts

ahínco *nm* eagerness, zeal

ahogar *v* drown; smother — **ahogo** *nm* breathlessness

ahondar *v* deepen; elaborate

ahora *adv* now; ~ **mismo** right now

ahorcar *v* hang, kill by hanging

ahorrar *v* save; save up

ahorro *nm* saving

ahumar *v* smoke, cure

ahuyentar *v* scare away, chase away

airado, -da *adj* irate, angry

aire *nm* air; ∼ **acondicionado** air-conditioning; **al** ∼ **libre** in the open air, outdoors

airear *v* air out

aislar *v* isolate; insulate — **aislamiento** *nm* isolation; insulation

ajedrez *nm* chess

ajeno, -na *adj* someone else's; alien; ∼ **a** foreign to

ají *nm* (**ajíes**) chili pepper

ajo *nm* garlic

ajustar *v* adjust, adapt; agree on — **ajustado, -da** *adj* close, tight; tight-fitting

ajusticiar *v* execute, put to death

ala *nf* wing; brim (of a hat)

alacrán *nm* (**-cranes**) scorpion

alado, -da *adj* winged

alargar *v* extend, lengthen; prolong

alarmar *v* alarm — **alarma** *nf* alarm

alba *nf* dawn

albañil *nm* bricklayer, mason

albedrío *nm* will

albergar *v* house, lodge — **albergue** *nm* lodging; shelter

albóndiga *nf* meatball

álbum *nm* album

alcalde, -desa *n* mayor

alcance *nm* reach; range, scope

alcancía *nf* money box

alcantarilla *nf* sewer, drain

alcanzar *v* reach; catch up with; achieve, attain; suffice, be enough; ∼ **a** manage to

alcaparra *nf* caper

alcoba *nf* bedroom

alcohol *nm* alcohol — **alcohólico, -ca** *adj & n* alcoholic

aleatorio, -ria *adj* random

alegoría *nf* allegory

alegrar *v* make happy, cheer up — **alegre** *adj* glad, happy; colorful, bright — **alegría** *nf* joy, cheer

alejar *v* remove, move away; estrange

alemán, -mana *adj* (**-manes**) German — **alemán** *nm* German language

alentar *v* encourage

alergia *nf* allergy

alerta *adv* on the alert — **alerta** *adj & nf* alert — **alertar** *v* alert

aleta *nf* fin, flipper; small wing

alfabeto *nm* alphabet — **alfabetismo** *nm* literacy — **alfabetizar** *v* teach literacy; alphabetize

alfiler *nm* pin; brooch

alfombra *nf* carpet, rug

alga *nf* seaweed

álgebra *nf* algebra

algo *adv* somewhat, rather — **algo** *pron* something; **algo de** some, a little

algodón *nm* (**-dones**) cotton

alguien *pron* somebody, someone

alguno *pron* one, someone, somebody — **alguno, -na** *adj* (**algún** *before masculine singular nouns*) some, any; (*in negative constructions*) not any, not at all; **algunas veces** sometimes

algunos, -nas *pron pl* some, a few

aliado, -da *n* ally — **aliado, -da** *adj* allied — **alianza** *nf* alliance — **aliarse** *vr* form an alliance

alicates *nmpl* pliers

alienar *v* alienate — **alienación** *nf* (**-ciones**) alienation

aliento *nm* breath; encouragement, strength

aligerar *v* lighten; hasten, quicken

alimentar *v* feed, nourish — **alimentación** *nf* (**-ciones**) feeding; nourishment

alineación *nf* (**-ciones**) alignment; lineup

alinear *v* align, line up — **alinearse con** *vr phr* align oneself with

alisar *v* smooth

alistarse *vr* join up, enlist

aliviar *v* relieve, soothe — **alivio** *nm* relief

allá *adv* there, over there; **más** ∼ farther away; **más** ∼ **de** beyond

allanar *v* smooth, level out; raid — **allanamiento** *nm* raid

allí *adv* there, over there

alma *nf* soul

almacén *nm* (**-cenes**) warehouse; shop, store; **grandes almacenes** department store — **almacenamiento** *nm* storage — **almacenar** *v* store

almanaque *nm* almanac

almendra *nf* almond; kernel

almíbar *nm* syrup

almidón *nm* (**-dones**) starch

almirante *nm* admiral

almohada *nf* pillow

almorzar *v* have lunch; have for lunch — **almuerzo** *nm* lunch

alojar *v* house, lodge — **alojamiento** *nm* lodging, accommodations *pl*

alquilar *v* rent, lease

alrededor *adv* around, about; **~ de** approximately — **alrededor de** *prep phr* around — **alrededores** *nmpl* outskirts

alta *nf* discharge; release

altar *nm* altar

altavoz *nm* (**-voces**) loudspeaker

alterar *v* alter, modify; disturb — **alteración** *nf* (**-ciones**) alteration; disturbance

alternar *v* alternate; **~ con** socialize with — **alternarse** *vr* take turns — **alternativa** *nf* alternative — **alternativo, -va** *adj* alternating, alternative — **alterno, -na** *adj* alternate

altiplano *nm* high plateau

altitud *nf* altitude

altivo, -va *adj* haughty

alto *adv* high; loud, loudly — **alto** *nm* height, elevation; stop, halt — **alto** *interj* halt!, stop!

alto, -ta *adj* tall, high; loud

altruista *adj* altruistic — **altruismo** *nm* altruism

altura *nf* height; altitude; **a la ~ de** near, up by

alucinar *v* hallucinate — **alucinación** *nf* (**-ciones**) hallucination

alud *nm* avalanche

aludido, -da *adj* previously mentioned; **darse por ~** take it personally

aludir *v* allude, refer

alumbrar *v* light, illuminate; **alumbrado** *nm* lighting

alumno, -na *n* pupil, student

alusión *nf* (**-siones**) allusion

aluvión *nm* (**-viones**) flood, barrage

alzar *v* lift, raise — **alza** *nf* rise

amabilidad *nf* kindness — **amable** *adj* kind, nice

amaestrar *v* train

amamantar *v* breast-feed, nurse

amanecer *v impers* dawn — **amanecer** *v* wake up — **amanecer** *nm* dawn, daybreak

amante *adj* loving; **~ de** fond of

amante *nmf* lover

amapola *nf* poppy

amar *v* love

amargo, -ga *adj* bitter — **amargo** *nm* bitterness

amarillo, -lla *adj* yellow — **amarillo** *nm* yellow

amarrar *v* tie up

amasar *v* knead

amateur *adj & nmf* amateur

ambición *nf* (**-ciones**) ambition — **ambicionar** *v* aspire to — **ambicioso, -sa** *adj* ambitious

ambiente *nm* atmosphere; environment, surroundings *pl*

ambigüedad *nf* ambiguity — **ambiguo, -gua** *adj* ambiguous

ambos, -bas *adj & pron* both

ambulancia *nf* ambulance

amén *nm* amen

amenazar *v* threaten — **amenaza** *nf* threat, menace

ameno, -na *adj* pleasant

americano, -na *adj* American

ametralladora *nf* machine gun

amígdala *nf* tonsil — **amigdalitis** *nf* tonsilitis

amigo, -ga *adj* friendly, close — **amigo, -ga** *n* friend

amistad *nf* friendship — **amistoso, -sa** *adj* friendly

amnesia *nf* amnesia

amnistía *nf* amnesty

amo, ama *n* master, mistress; **ama de casa** homemaker, housewife

amoldar *v* adapt, adjust

amontonar *v* pile up

amor *nm* love

amparar *v* shelter, protect

ampliar *v* expand; enlarge — **ampliación** *nf* (**-ciones**) expansion, enlargement

amplio, -plia *adj* broad, wide, ample — **amplitud** *nf* breadth, extent; spaciousness

ampolla *nf* blister; vial

amueblar *v* furnish

añadir *v* add

analfabeto, -ta *adj* & *n* illiterate — **analfabetismo** *nm* illiteracy

analgésico *nm* painkiller, analgesic

analizar *v* analyze — **análisis** *nm* analysis

anaranjado, -da *adj* orange-colored

anatomía *nf* anatomy — **anatómico, -ca** *adj* anatomic, anatomical

anchoa *nf* anchovy

ancho, -cha *adj* wide, broad, ample — **ancho** *nm* width

anchura *nf* width, breadth

anciano, -na *adj* aged, elderly — **anciano, -na** *n* elderly person

andar *v* walk; go, travel; run, work; ~ **en** rummage around in; ~ **por** be approximately

andén *nm* (**-denes**) train platform; sidewalk

andino, -na *adj* Andean

anécdota *nf* anecdote

anemia *nf* anemia — **anémico, -ca** *adj* anemic

anestesia *nf* anesthesia — **anestésico, -ca** *adj* anesthetic — **anestésico** *nm* anesthetic

anexar *v* annex, attach — **anexo, -xa** *adj* attached — **anexo** *nm* annex

anfibio, -bia *adj* amphibious — **anfibio** *nm* amphibian

ángel *nm* angel

angloparlante *adj* English-speaking

angosto, -ta *adj* narrow

ángulo *nm* angle; corner

angustiar *v* anguish, distress; worry — **angustia** *nf* anguish; worry

anhelar *v* yearn for, crave — **anhelo** *nm* longing

anillo *nm* ring

animado, -da *adj* cheerful, animated — **animador, -dora** *n* television host; cheerleader

animal *nm* animal — **animal** *nmf* brute, beast

animar *v* encourage; cheer up — **animarse** *vr* take heart; cheer up; **animarse a** get up the nerve to

ánimo *nm* mood, spirits *pl*; encouragement

anís *nm* anise

aniversario *nm* anniversary

anoche *adv* last night

anochecer *v* get dark — **anochecer** *nm* dusk, nightfall

anónimo, -ma *adj* anonymous

anorexia *nf* anorexia

anormal *adj* abnormal — **anormalidad** *nf* abnormality

anotar *v* annotate — **anotación** *nf* (**-ciones**) annotation, note

ansiedad *nf* anxiety — **ansioso, -sa** *adj* anxious; eager

antártico, -ca *adj* antarctic

ante *prep* before, in front of

anteanoche *adv* the night before last

anteayer *adv* the day before yesterday

antebrazo *nm* forearm

antecedente *adj* previous, prior — **antecedente** *nm* precedent

antelación *nf* (**-ciones**) advance notice; **con** ~ in advance

antena *nf* antenna

anteojos *nmpl* glasses, eyeglasses

antepasado, -da *n* ancestor

antepenúltimo, -ma *adj* third from last

anterioridad *nf* priority; **con ~** beforehand, in advance — **anterior** *adj* previous, earlier; front — **anteriormente** *adv* previously

antes *adv* before, earlier; previously; first; rather

antibiótico *nm* antibiotic

anticipación *nf* (**-ciones**) anticipation; **con ~** in advance

anticipado, -da *adj* advance, early; **por ~** in advance

anticipar *v* move up; pay in advance — **anticiparse** *vr* be early; get ahead

anticonceptivo, -va *adj* contraceptive — **anticonceptivo** *nm* contraceptive

anticuado, -da *adj* antiquated, outdated

antiguo, -gua *adj* ancient, old; former; old-fashioned; **antiguamente** *adv* long ago; formerly — **antigüedad** *nf* antiquity

antihigiénico, -ca *adj* unsanitary

antipatía *nf* aversion, dislike — **antipático, -ca** *adj* unpleasant

antirreglamentario, -ria *adj* unlawful

antirrobo, -ba *adj* antitheft

antisemita *adj* anti-Semitic

antisocial *adj* antisocial

antojo *nm* whim, craving — **antojarse** *vr* crave

antropología *nf* anthropology

anual *adj* annual, yearly — **anuario** *nm* yearbook, annual

anular *v* annul, cancel

anunciar *v* announce; advertise — **anuncio** *nm* announcement; advertisement

año *nm* year; **Año Nuevo** New Year

apachurrar *v* crush

apacible *adj* gentle, mild

apaciguar *v* appease, pacify

apagar *v* switch off; extinguish, put out — **apagado, -da** *adj* off, out

aparato *nm* machine, appliance, apparatus; anatomical system

aparecer *v* appear; show up

aparentar *v* seem — **aparente** *adj* apparent, seeming

apariencia *nf* appearance, look

apartado *nm* section, paragraph; **~ postal** post office box

apartamento *nm* apartment

apartar *v* move away; set aside, separate — **aparte** *adv* apart, separately; besides

apasionar *v* excite, fascinate — **apasionado, -da** *adj* passionate, excited — **apasionante** *adj* exciting

apegado, -da *adj* devoted — **apegarse a** *vr phr* become attached to, grow fond of — **apego** *nm* fondness

apellido *nm* last name, surname — **apellidarse** *vr* have for a last name

apenar *v* sadden — **apenarse** *vr* grieve; become embarrassed

apenas *adv* hardly, scarcely — **apenas** *conj* as soon as

apéndice *nm* appendix — **apendicitis** *nf* appendicitis

aperitivo *nm* appetizer; aperitif

apetecer *v* crave, long for

apetito *nm* appetite — **apetitoso, -sa** *adj* appetizing

apio *nm* celery

aplanar *v* flatten, level

aplastar *v* crush — **aplastante** *adj* overwhelming

aplaudir *v* applaud — **aplauso** *nm* applause; acclaim

aplazar *v* postpone, defer

aplicar *v* apply — **aplicable** *adj* applicable — **aplicado, -da** *adj* diligent

apodo *nm* nickname

aportar *v* contribute — **aportación** *nf* (**-ciones**) contribution

apostar *v* bet, wager

apóstrofo *nm* apostrophe

apoyar *v* support; lean, rest — **apoyo** *nm* support

apreciar *v* appreciate — **apreciable** *adj* considerable — **apreciación** *nf* (**-ciones**) appreciation — **aprecio** *nm* esteem

aprender *v* learn — **aprenderse** *vr* memorize

aprendizaje *nm* apprenticeship

apresurar *v* speed up — **apresuradamente** *adv* hurriedly, hastily — **apresurado, -da** *adj* in a rush

apretar *v* press, push; tighten; squeeze; press (down); fit too tightly — **apretado, -da** *adj* tight

aprisa *adv* quickly

aprobar *v* approve of; pass — **aprobación** *nf* (**-ciones**) approval

apropiación *nf* (**-ciones**) appropriation — **apropiado, -da** *adj* appropriate

apropiarse de *vr phr* take possession of, appropriate

aprovechar *v* take advantage of, make good use of; be of use

aproximar *v* bring closer — **aproximadamente** *adv* approximately

apto, -ta *adj* suitable; capable — **aptitud** *nf* aptitude, capability

apuesta *nf* bet, wager

apuntar *v* aim, point; jot down; point at; prompt — **apuntarse** *vr* sign up; score, chalk up — **apunte** *nm* note

apurar *v* hurry, rush; use up; trouble

aquél, aquélla *pron* (**aquéllos**) that (one), those (ones); the former

aquel, aquella *adj* (**aquellos**) that, those

aquello *pron* that, that matter

aquí *adv* here; now; **por ~** hereabouts

aquietar *v* calm

árabe *adj* Arab, Arabic — **árabe** *nm* Arabic language

araña *nf* spider; chandelier

arañar *v* scratch, claw

arbitrario, -ria *adj* arbitrary — **arbitrio** *nm* (free) will; judgment — **árbitro, -tra** *n* arbitrator; referee, umpire

árbol *nm* tree

arcaico, -ca *adj* archaic

archipiélago *nm* archipelago

archivar *v* file — **archivo** *nm* file; archives *pl*

arco *nm* arch; bow; arc; **~ iris** rainbow

ardilla *nf* squirrel; **~ listada** chipmunk

ardor *nm* burning; passion, ardor

arduo, -dua *adj* arduous

área *nf* area

arena *nf* sand; arena

arete *nm* earring

argentino, -na *adj* Argentinian, Argentine

argolla *nf* hoop, ring

argot *nm* slang

argumentar *v* argue, contend — **argumentación** *nf* (**-ciones**) argument, reason — **argumento** *nm* argument, reasoning; plot, story line

árido, -da *adj* dry, arid

aristocracia *nf* aristocracy

aritmética *nf* arithmetic

arma *nf* arm, weapon; **~ de fuego** firearm — **armada** *nf* navy

armar *v* arm; assemble

armario *nm* closet; cupboard, cabinet

armonía *nf* harmony — **armónica** *nf* harmonica

aroma *nm* aroma, scent

arpa *nf* harp

arquear *v* arch, bend

arqueología *nf* archaeology — **arqueólogo, -ga** *n* archaeologist

arquitectura *nf* architecture — **arquitecto, -ta** *n* architect

arracimarse *vr* cluster together

arraigar *v* take root, become established

arrancar *v* pull out, tear off; start; get going

arranque *nm* engine starter; outburst; **punto de ~** starting point

arrasar *v* destroy; fill to the brim

arrastrar *v* drag; draw, attract; trail — **arrastrarse** *vr* grovel

arrebatar *v* snatch, seize; captivate

arrecife *nm* reef

arreglar *v* fix; tidy up; solve, work out —
    arreglarse *vr* get dressed up

arreglo *nm* agreement

arrendar *v* rent, lease

arrepentirse *vr* regret, be sorry; repent

arriba *adv* above, overhead; up, up-
    wards; upstairs; ∼ **de** more than; **de**
    ∼ **abajo** from top to bottom

arribar *v* arrive; dock, put into port — **arri-
    bista** *nmf* parvenu, upstart — **arribo**
    nm arrival

arriesgar *v* risk, venture

arrobar *v* entrance

arrodillarse *vr* kneel

arrogancia *nf* arrogance

arrojar *v* hurl, cast; give off, spew out;
    yield

arrollar *v* sweep away; crush, over-
    whelm; run over

arroyo *nm* stream; gutter

arroz *nm* (**arroces**) rice

arrugar *v* wrinkle, crease — **arruga** *nf*
    wrinkle, crease

arruinar *v* ruin, wreck — **arruinarse** *vr*
    go bankrupt

arrullar *v* lull to sleep; coo

arte *nmf* (*usually m in singular, f in plu-
    ral*) art; skill; cunning, cleverness

arteria *nf* artery

artesanía *nm* craftsmanship; handicrafts
    pl — **artesanal** *adj* handmade — **arte-
    sano, -na** *n* artisan, craftsman

ártico, -ca *adj* arctic

articular *v* articulate — **articulación** *nf*
    (**-ciones**) articulation; pronunciation;
    joint

artículo *nm* article; ∼**s de primera
    necesidad** essentials; ∼**s de tocador**
    toiletries

artificial *adj* artificial

artista *nmf* artist; actor, actress *f* —
    artístico, -ca *adj* artistic

artritis *nms & pl* arthritis

arveja *nf* pea

asado *nm* roast

asalariado, -da *n* wage earner —
    asalariado, -da *adj* salaried

asaltar *v* assault; mug, rob — **asaltante**
    nmf assailant; mugger, robber —
    asalto *nm* assault; mugging, robbery

asamblea *nf* assembly, meeting

asar *v* roast, grill — **asarse** *vr* feel the
    heat

asbesto *nm* asbestos

ascender *v* ascend, rise up; be pro-
    moted; promote; ∼ **a** amount to — **as-
    censo** *nm* ascent, rise; promotion —
    ascensor *nm* elevator

asco *nm* disgust; **hacer** ∼**s de** turn up
    one's nose at; **me da** ∼ it makes me
    sick

asear *v* clean, tidy up

asegurar *v* assure; secure; insure

asemejarse *vr* be similar; ∼ **a** resemble

aseo *nm* cleanliness

asequible *adj* accessible, attainable

asesinar *v* murder; assassinate — **ase-
    sinato** *nm* murder; assassination —
    asesino, -na *n* murderer; assassin

asesorar *v* advise, counsel — **asesor,
    -sora** *n* advisor, consultant

asfalto *nm* asphalt

asfixiar *v* asphyxiate, suffocate

así *adv* like this, like that, thus; ∼ **de** so,
    that (much); ∼ **que** so, therefore; ∼
    que as soon as; ∼ **como** as well as —
    así *adj* such, like that — **así** *conj* even
    though

asiático, -ca *adj* Asian, Asiatic

asignar *v* assign, allocate; appoint —
    asignación *nf* (**-ciones**) assignment;
    salary, pay — **asignatura** *nf* subject,
    course

asilo *nm* asylum, home; refuge, shelter
    — **asilado, -da** *n* inmate

asimismo *adv* similarly, likewise

asistencia *nf* attendance; assistance

asistente *nmf* assistant; **los** ∼**s** those in
    attendance

asma *nf* asthma

asociar *v* associate — **asociación** *nf* (**-ciones**) association

asociarse a *vr phr* join, become a member of

asombrar *v* amaze, astonish — **asombro** *nm* amazement, astonishment

aspecto *nm* aspect; appearance, look

áspero, -ra *adj* rough, harsh

aspersión *nf* (**-siones**) sprinkling — **aspersor** *nm* sprinkler

aspiración *nf* (**-ciones**) breathing in; aspiration

aspiradora *nf* vacuum cleaner

aspirar *v* inhale, breathe in; ~ **a** aspire to — **aspirante** *nmf* applicant, candidate

aspirina *nf* aspirin

asterisco *nm* asterisk

asteroide *nm* asteroid

astigmatismo *nm* astigmatism

astro *nm* heavenly body; star

astrología *nf* astrology

astronauta *nmf* astronaut

astronomía *nf* astronomy — **astrónomo, -ma** *n* astronomer

astucia *nf* astuteness; cunning, guile — **astuto, -ta** *adj* astute; crafty

asumir *v* assume — **asunción** *nf* (**-ciones**) assumption

asunto *nm* matter, affair; business

asustar *v* scare, frighten

atacar *v* attack — **atacante** *nmf* attacker

atañer a *v phr* concern, have to do with

ataque *nm* attack, assault; fit; ~ **de nervios** nervous breakdown

atar *v* tie up, tie down

atardecer *v impers* get dark — **atardecer** *nm* late afternoon, dusk

ataúd *nm* coffin

ataviar *v* dress up

atención *nf* (**-ciones**) attention; **prestar** ~ pay attention; **llamar la** ~ attract attention — **atención** *interj* attention!, watch out!

atender *v* attend to; look after; heed; pay attention

atentado *nm* attack — **atentar contra** *v phr* make an attempt on

atentamente *adv* attentively; **le saluda** ~ sincerely yours

atento, -ta *adj* attentive, mindful; courteous

ateo, atea *adj* atheistic — **ateo, atea** *n* atheist

aterrador, -dora *adj* terrifying

aterrizar *v* land — **aterrizaje** *nm* landing

atestiguar *v* testify to

atlántico, -ca *adj* Atlantic

atlas *nm* atlas

atleta *nmf* athlete — **atlético, -ca** *adj* athletic — **atletismo** *nm* athletics

atmósfera *nf* atmosphere — **atmosférico, -ca** *adj* atmospheric

átomo *nm* atom — **atómico, -ca** *adj* atomic — **atomizador** *nm* atomizer

atornillar *v* screw

atracción *nf* (**-ciones**) attraction

atraco *nm* holdup, robbery

atractivo, -va *adj* attractive — **atractivo** *nm* attraction, appeal

atraer *v* attract

atrapar *v* trap, capture

atrás *adv* back, behind; before, earlier; **para** ~ *or* **hacia** ~ backwards

atrasar *v* delay; lose time — **atrasado, -da** *adj* late, overdue; backward; slow — **atraso** *nm* delay; backwardness; ~**s** *nmpl* arrears

atravesar *v* cross; pierce; go through — **atravesarse** *vr* be in the way

atreverse *vr* dare — **atrevido, -da** *adj* bold; insolent — **atrevimiento** *nm* boldness; insolence

atribuir *v* attribute; confer — **atribuirse** *vr* take credit for

atributo *nm* attribute

atrocidad *nf* atrocity

atropellar *v* run over; violate, abuse — **atropello** *nm* abuse, outrage

atropellarse *vr* rush — **atropellado, -da** *adj* hasty

atún *nm* (**atunes**) tuna

aturdir *v* stun, shock; bewilder — **aturdido, -da** *adj* dazed, bewildered

audaz *adj* (**-daces**) bold, daring — **audacia** *nf* boldness, audacity

audible *adj* audible

audición *nf* (**-ciones**) hearing; audition

audiencia *nf* audience

audífono *nm* hearing aid; ~**s** *nmpl* headphones, earphones

audiovisual *adj* audiovisual

auditorio *nm* auditorium; audience

auge *nm* peak; boom, upturn

augurar *v* predict, foretell — **augurio** *nm* omen

aula *nf* classroom

aumentar *v* increase, raise; grow — **aumento** *nm* increase, rise

aún *adv* still, yet; **más** ~ furthermore

aun *adv* even; ~ **así** even so

aunque *conj* though, although, even if; ~ **sea** at least

aurora *nf* dawn

ausentarse *vr* leave, go away — **ausencia** *nf* absence — **ausente** *adj* absent — **ausente** *nmf* absentee; missing person

austeridad *nf* austerity

australiano, -na *adj* Australian

austriaco *or* **austríaco, -ca** *adj* Austrian

auténtico, -ca *adj* authentic, genuine

autobiografía *nf* autobiography — **autobiográfico, -ca** *adj* autobiographical

autobús *nm* (**-buses**) bus

autocontrol *nm* self-control

autóctono, -na *adj* indigenous, native

autodefensa *nf* self-defense

autodidacta *adj* self-taught

autodisciplina *nf* self-discipline

autoestop hitchhiking — **autostopista** *nmf* hitchhiker

autografiar *v* autograph — **autógrafo** *nm* autograph

automático, -ca *adj* automatic

automotor, -triz *adj* (**-trices** *f*) self-propelled

automóvil *nm* automobile — **automovilista** *nmf* motorist

autonomía *nf* autonomy — **autónomo, -ma** *adj* autonomous

autopista *nf* expressway, highway

autopsia *nf* autopsy

autoridad *nf* authority — **autoritario, -ria** *adj* authoritarian

autorizar *v* authorize, approve — **autorización** *nf* (**-ciones**) authorization

autor, -tora *n* author; perpetrator

autoservicio *nm* self-service restaurant; supermarket

autosuficiente *adj* self-sufficient

auxiliar *nmf* assistant, helper; ~ **de vuelo** flight attendant — **auxiliar** *v* aid, assist — **auxiliar** *adj* auxiliary

auxilio *nm* aid, assistance; **primeros** ~**s** first aid

avalancha *nf* avalanche

avanzar *v* advance, move forward — **avance** *nm* advance — **avanzado, -da** *adj* advanced

avaro, -ra *adj* miserly — **avaro, -ra** *n* miser — **avaricia** *nf* greed, avarice

ave *nf* bird

avellana *nf* hazelnut

avena *nf* oats *pl*; *or* **harina de** ~ oatmeal

avenida *nf* avenue

aventajar *v* be ahead of, surpass

aventurar *v* venture, risk — **aventura** *nf* adventure; risk; love affair

avergonzar *v* shame, embarrass

averiguar *v* find out; investigate — **averiguación** *nf* (**-ciones**) investigation, inquiry

aversión *nf* (**-siones**) aversion, dislike

avestruz *nm* (**-truces**) ostrich

aviación *nf* (**-ciones**) aviation — **aviador, -dora** *n* aviator

avión *nm* (**aviones**) airplane — **avioneta** *nf* light airplane

aviso *nm* notice; warning; advertisement, ad; **estar sobre** ~ be on the alert — **avisar** *v* notify; warn

avispa *nf* wasp — **avispón** *nm* (**-pones**) hornet

avispado, -da *adj* clever, sharp

axila *nf* underarm, armpit

axioma *nm* axiom

ay *interj* oh!; ouch!, ow!

ayer *adv* yesterday — **ayer** *nm* yesteryear, days gone by

ayuda *nf* help, assistance — **ayudante** *nmf* helper, assistant

ayudar *v* help, assist — **ayudarse de** *vr phr* make use of

azabache *nm* jet

azafata *nf* stewardess *f*

azafrán *nm* (**-franes**) saffron

azalea *nf* azalea

azar *nm* chance; **al ~** at random

azote *nm* whip, lash; scourge

azotea *nf* flat or terraced roof

azteca *adj* Aztec

azúcar *nmf* sugar

azufre *nm* sulphur

azul *adj & nm* blue — **azulado, -da** *adj* bluish

azulejo *nm* ceramic tile; bluebird

B

b *nf* b, second letter of the Spanish alphabet

baba *nf* saliva, drool

babero *nm* bib

babosa *nf* slug

babucha *nf* slipper

bacalao *nm* cod

bachiller *nmf* high school graduate — **bachillerato** *nm* high school diploma

bacteria *nf* bacterium, germ

bagre *nm* catfish

bahía *nf* bay

bailar *v* dance — **bailarín, -rina** *n* (**-rines** *m*) dancer — **baile** *nm* dance; dance party, ball

bajar *v* bring down, lower; go down, come down; descend, drop — **bajarse** *vr* get out of, get off — **bajada** *nf* descent, drop; slope

bajo *adv* low — **bajo** *prep* under, below — **bajo, -ja** *adj* low, lower; short

bala *nf* bullet

balada *nf* ballad

balancear *v* balance; swing, rock — **balancearse** *vr* swing, sway — **balance** *nm* balance — **balanceo** *nm* swaying, rocking

balancín *nm* (**-cines**) seesaw; rocking chair

balanza *nf* scales *pl*, balance

balcón *nm* (**-cones**) balcony

balde *nm* bucket, pail

baldosa *nf* floor tile

ballena *nf* whale

ballet *nm* ballet

balneario *nm* spa

balompié *nm* soccer

balón *nm* (**-lones**) ball — **baloncesto** *nm* basketball

balsa *nf* raft

bambú *nm* (**-búes** *or* **-bús**) bamboo

banal *adj* banal

banana *nf* banana — **banano** *nm* banana

banca *nf* banking; bench — **bancario, -ria** *adj* bank, banking — **banco** *nm* bank; stool, bench, pew

banda *nf* band, strip; band; gang — **bandada** *nf* flock (of birds), school (of fish)

bandeja *nf* tray, platter

bandera *nf* flag, banner

bandido, -da *n* bandit

bando *nm* proclamation, edict; faction, side

banquero, -ra *n* banker

banquete *nm* banquet

baño *nm* bath, swim; ¿**dónde está el** ~**?** where is the bathroom? — **bañar** *v* bathe, wash — **bañera** *nf* bathtub

bar *nm* bar, tavern

baraja *nf* deck of cards

baranda *nf* rail, railing

barato, -ta *adj* cheap — **barato** *adv* cheap, cheaply

barba *nf* beard, stubble

barbaridad *nf* barbarity, cruelty — **bárbaro, -ra** *adj* barbaric

barbero, -ra *n* barber — **barbería** *nf* barbershop

barbilla *nf* chin

barbudo, -da *adj* bearded

barca *nf* boat — **barco** *nm* boat, ship

barman *nm* bartender

barra *nf* bar, rod, stick; counter

barrer *v* sweep

barrera *nf* barrier

barriga *nf* belly

barril *nm* barrel, keg

barrio *nm* neighborhood

barro *nm* mud

basar *v* base

báscula *nf* scales *pl*

base *nf* base; basis, foundation — **básico, -ca** *adj* basic

basquetbol *or* **básquetbol** *nm* basketball

bastante *adv* fairly, rather; enough — **bastante** *adj* enough, sufficient — **bastante** *pron* enough

basto, -ta *adj* coarse, rough

bastón *nm* (**-tones**) cane, walking stick

basura *nf* garbage, rubbish — **basurero, -ra** *n* garbage collector

bata *nf* bathrobe, housecoat; smock

batallar *v* battle, fight — **batalla** *nf* battle, fight, struggle — **batallón** *nm* (**-llones**) battalion

batear *v* bat, hit — **bate** *nm* baseball bat — **bateador, -dora** *n* batter, hitter

batería *nf* battery; drums *pl*

batir *v* beat, whip — **batido** *nm* milk shake — **batidor** *nm* eggbeater, whisk — **batidora** *nf* electric mixer

baúl *nm* trunk, chest

bautismo *nm* baptism — **bautizar** *v* baptize — **bautizo** *nm* baptism, christening

bazar *nm* bazaar

bazo *nm* spleen

bebé *nm* baby

beber *v* drink — **bebida** *nf* drink, beverage — **bebido, -da** *adj* drunk

beca *nf* grant, scholarship

becerro, -rra *n* calf

beige *adj & nm* beige

beisbol *or* **béisbol** *nm* baseball — **beisbolista** *nmf* baseball player

belga *adj* Belgian

belleza *nf* beauty — **bello, -lla** *adj* beautiful; **bellas artes** fine arts

bellota *nf* acorn

bendecir *v* bless — **bendición** *nf* (**-ciones**) benediction, blessing — **bendito, -ta** *adj* blessed, holy

beneficiar *v* benefit, assist — **beneficio** *nm* gain, profit; benefit — **beneficioso, -sa** *adj* beneficial — **benéfico, -ca** *adj* charitable

benigno, -na *adj* benign

berenjena *nf* eggplant

besar *v* kiss — **besarse** *vr* kiss (each other) — **beso** *nm* kiss

bestia *nf* beast, animal — **bestial** *adj* bestial, brutal — **bestialidad** *nf* brutality

betún *nm* (**-tunes**) shoe polish

bianual *adj* biannual

biberón *nm* (**-rones**) baby's bottle

Biblia *nf* Bible

bibliografía *nf* bibliography

biblioteca *nf* library — **bibliotecario, -ria** *n* librarian

bicicleta *nf* bicycle

bicolor *adj* two-tone

bien *adv* well, good; correctly, right; very, quite; willingly; **más** ~ rather — **bien** *adj* all right, well; pleasant, nice;

satisfactory; correct, right — **bien** *nm* good; **bienes** *nmpl* property, goods

bienestar *nm* welfare, well-being

bienhechor, -chora *n* benefactor

bienvenido, -da *adj* welcome — **bienvenida** *nf* welcome

bigote *nm* mustache

bikini *nm* bikini

bilingüe *adj* bilingual

bilis *nf* bile

billar *nm* pool, billiards

billete *nm* bill, banknote; ticket — **billetera** *nf* billfold, wallet

billón *nm* (**-llones**) trillion

bimensual, -suales *adj* twice a month — **bimestral** *adj* every two months

bingo *nm* bingo

binoculares *nmpl* binoculars

biografía *nf* biography

biología *nf* biology — **biológico, -ca** *adj* biological, biologic — **biólogo, -ga** *n* biologist

biombo *nm* folding screen

bis *adv* twice

bisabuelo, -la *n* great-grandfather *m*, great-grandmother *f*

bisagra *nf* hinge

bisexual *adj* bisexual

bisiesto *adj* leap year

bisnieto, -ta *n* great-grandson *m*, great-granddaughter *f*

bisonte *nm* bison, buffalo

bistec *nm* steak

bit *nm* bit (unit of information)

bizco, -ca *adj* cross-eyed

bizcocho *nm* sponge cake

blanco, -ca *adj* white — **blanco, -ca** *n* white person — **blanco** *nm* white; target, bull's-eye; blank (space) — **blancura** *nf* whiteness

blando, -da *adj* soft, tender; weak-willed; lenient — **blandura** *nf* softness, tenderness; weakness; leniency

bloc *nm* (**blocs**) (writing) pad

bloquear *v* block, obstruct; blockade

blusa *nf* blouse — **blusón** *nm* (**-sones**) smock

bobo, -ba *adj* silly, stupid — **bobo, -ba** *n* fool, simpleton

boca *nf* mouth; entrance; ~ **arriba** faceup; ~ **abajo** facedown

bocacalle *nf* entrance (to a street)

bocado *nm* bite, mouthful — **bocadillo** *nm* sandwich

boceto *nm* sketch, outline

bochorno *nm* muggy weather

bocina *nf* horn; mouthpiece

boda *nf* wedding

bodega *nf* wine cellar; warehouse

bofetear *v* slap — **bofetada** *nf or* **bofetón** *nm* slap (in the face)

boga *nf* fashion, vogue

bohemio, -mia *adj & n* bohemian

boina *nf* beret

bola *nf* ball

bolera *nf* bowling alley

boleta *nf* ticket — **boletería** *nf* ticket office

boletín *nm* (**-tines**) bulletin

boleto *nm* ticket

bolígrafo *nm* ballpoint pen

bolillo *nm* bobbin

boliviano, -na *adj* Bolivian

bolsa *nf* bag; — **bolsillo** *nm* pocket — **bolso** *nm* pocketbook, handbag

bomba *nf* bomb

bombardeo *nm* bombing, bombardment

bombero, -ra *n* firefighter

bombilla *nf* lightbulb — **bombillo** *nm* lightbulb

bombo *nm* bass drum

bombón *nm* (**-bones**) candy, chocolate

bonachón, -chona *adj* (**-chones** *m*) good-natured

bonanza *nf* prosperity

bondad *nf* goodness, kindness — **bondadoso, -sa** *adj* kind, good

bonificación *nf* (**-ciones**) bonus, extra; discount

bonito, -ta *adj* pretty, lovely

boquiabierto, -ta *adj* open-mouthed, speechless

bordar *v* embroider — **bordado** *nm* embroidery, needlework

borde *nm* border, edge; — **bordear** *v* border — **bordillo** *nm* curb

bordo *nm* **a** ~ aboard, on board

borracho, -cha *adj & n* drunk — **borrachera** *nf* drunkenness

borrar *v* erase, blot out — **borrador** *nm* rough draft; eraser

borroso, -sa *adj* blurry, smudgy; vague, hazy

bosque *nm* woods, forest

bostezar *v* yawn — **bostezo** *nm* yawn

bota *nf* boot

botánica *nf* botany

botar *v* throw, hurl; throw away; bounce

bote *nm* small boat

botella *nf* bottle

botín *nm* (-tines) ankle boot

botiquín *nm* (-quines) medicine cabinet; first-aid kit

botón *nm* (-tones) button

boutique *nf* boutique

bóveda *nf* vault

boxear *v* box — **boxeador, -dora** *n* boxer — **boxeo** *nm* boxing

bragas *nf* panties

bragueta *nf* fly, pants zipper

braille *adj & nm* braille

brandy *nm* brandy

brasa *nf* ember

brasier *nm* brassiere

brasileño, -ña *adj* Brazilian

bravo, -va *adj* fierce, savage; angry — **bravo, -va** *interj* bravo!, well done!

brazalete *nm* bracelet; armband

brazo *nm* arm; branch (of a river); ~**s** *nmpl* hands, laborers; ~ **derecho** right-hand man; top aide

breve *adj* brief, short; **en** ~ shortly, in short — **brevedad** *nf* brevity, shortness

brigada *nf* brigade

brillar *v* shine, sparkle — **brillante** *adj* brilliant, shiny — **brillante** *nm* dia-

mond — **brillo** *nm* luster, shine; splendor

brinco *nm* jump, skip

brindar *v* drink a toast; offer, provide — **brindarse** *vr* offer one's assistance — **brindis** *nm* drink, toast

brioso, -sa *adj* spirited, lively

brisa *nf* breeze

británico, -ca *adj* British

brocha *nf* paintbrush

broche *nm* fastener, clasp

brócoli *nm* broccoli

bromear *v* joke, fool around — **broma** *nf* joke, prank — **bromista** *adj* fun-loving, joking — **bromista** *nmf* joker, prankster

bronce *nm* bronze — **bronceado, -da** *adj* suntanned — **bronceado** *nm* tan — **broncearse** *vr* get a suntan

bronquitis *nf* bronchitis

brotar *v* bud, sprout — **brote** *nm* outbreak

brujería *nf* witchcraft — **bruja** *nf* witch — **brujo** *nm* warlock, sorcerer — **brujo, -ja** *adj* bewitching

brújula *nf* compass

bruma *nf* haze, mist

brusco, -ca *adj* brusque, rough — **brusquedad** *nf* abruptness, brusqueness

brutal *adj* brutal — **brutalidad** *nf* brutality

bruto, -ta *adj* brutish, stupid

bucal *adj* oral

bucear *v* dive, swim underwater — **buceo** *nm* scuba diving

budismo *nm* Buddhism — **budista** *adj & nmf* Buddhist

bueno, -na *adj* good; kind; appropriate; well, healthy; **buenos días** hello, good day; **buenas noches** good night; **buenas tardes** good afternoon, good evening — **bueno** *interj* OK!, all right!

buey *nm* ox, steer

búfalo *nm* buffalo

bufanda *nf* scarf

bufete *nm* writing desk
búho *nm* owl
buitre *nm* vulture
búlgaro, -ra *adj* Bulgarian
bulto *nm* package, bundle
buñuelo *nm* fried pastry
buque *nm* ship
burbuja *nf* bubble
burdel *nm* brothel
burdo, -da *adj* coarse, rough
burgués, -guesa *adj & n* (-gueses *m*) bourgeois — **burguesía** *nf* bourgeoisie

burlar *v* trick, deceive — **burla** *nf* mockery, ridicule; joke, trick
burlón, -lona *adj* (-lones *m*) mocking
burocracia *nf* bureaucracy
burro, -rra *n* donkey; dunce — **burro, -rra** *adj* stupid
bus *nm* bus
buscar *v* look for, seek; search — **búsqueda** *nf* search
butaca *nf* armchair
buzo *nm* diver
buzón *nm* (-zones) mailbox
byte *nm* byte

C

c *nf* c, third letter of the Spanish alphabet
cabalgar *v* ride — **cabalgata** *nf* cavalcade
caballería *nf* cavalry; horse, mount
caballero *nm* gentleman
caballo *nm* horse; knight (in chess); horsepower
cabaña *nf* cabin, hut
cabaret *nm* (-rets) nightclub, cabaret
cabecilla *nmf* ringleader
cabello *nm* hair
caber *v* fit, go (into)
cabeza *nf* head
cabida *nf* room, capacity
cabina *nf* booth; cabin, cockpit
cable *nm* cable
cabra *nf* goat
cacahuate *or* **cacahuete** *nm* peanut
cacao *nm* cocoa (drink)
cacería *nf* hunt
cacerola *nf* pan, saucepan
cachete *nm* cheek — **cachetada** *nf* slap
cacho *nm* horn
cachorro, -rra *n* puppy
cactus *or* **cacto** *nm* cactus
cada *adj* each, every
cadáver *nm* corpse
cadena *nf* chain

cadera *nf* hip
cadete *nmf* cadet
caducar *v* expire
caer *v* fall, drop; **me cae bien** I like her, I like him — **caerse** *vr* drop, fall (down)
café *nm* coffee; café ~ *adj* brown — **cafetera** *nf* coffeepot — **cafetería** *nf* coffee shop, cafeteria
caída *nf* fall, drop
caimán *nm* (-manes) alligator
caja *nf* box, case; checkout counter; safe; cash register — **cajero, -ra** *n* cashier; teller — **cajón** *nm* (-jones) drawer
cajetilla *nf* pack
calabaza *nf* pumpkin, squash, gourd
calabozo *nm* cell
calamar *nm* squid
calambre *nm* cramp
calavera *nf* skull
calcar *v* trace; copy, imitate
calcetín *nm* (-tines) sock
calcio *nm* calcium
calcomanía *nf* decal
calcular *v* calculate, estimate — **calculadora** *nf* calculator — **cálculo** *nm* calculation; calculus
caldo *nm* broth, stock

calefacción *nf* (**-ciones**) heating, heat
calendario *nm* calendar
calentar *v* heat (up), warm (up) — **calentarse** *vr* get warm, heat up — **calentador** *nm* heater
calidad *nf* quality
cálido, -da *adj* hot, warm
caliente *adj* hot
calificar *v* grade — **calificación** *nf* (**-ciones**) grade
callar *v* keep quiet, be silent; hush — **callarse** *vr* remain silent — **callado, -da** *adj* quiet, silent
calle *nf* street, road — **callejón** *nm* (**-jones**) alley
callo *nm* callus, corn
calma *nf* calm, quiet — **calmante** *nm* tranquilizer — **calmar** *v* calm, soothe
calor *nm* heat, warmth — **caloría** *nf* calorie
caluroso, -sa *adj* warm, enthusiastic
calvo, -va *adj* bald — **calvicie** *nf* baldness
calzada *nf* roadway
calzado *nm* footwear — **calzar** *v* put shoes on (someone)
calzones *nmpl* panties — **calzoncillos** *nmpl* underpants, briefs
cama *nf* bed
cámara *nf* camera
camarero, -ra *n* waiter, waitress *f*
camarón *nm* (**-rones**) shrimp
camarote *nm* cabin, stateroom
cambiar *v* change; exchange — **cambio** *nm* change
camello *nm* camel
camilla *nf* stretcher
caminar *v* walk; cover (a distance)
camino *nm* road, path; way
camión *nm* (**-miones**) truck — **camioneta** *nm* light truck, van
camisa *nf* shirt — **camiseta** *nf* T-shirt, undershirt
campana *nf* bell
campeón, -peona *n* (**-peones** *m*) champion — **campeonato** *nm* championship
campesino, -na *n* peasant, farm laborer — **campestre** *adj* rural, rustic
camping *nm* campsite
campo *nm* field; countryside, country
cana *nf* gray hair
caña *nf* cane, reed; fishing pole
canadiense *adj* Canadian
canal *nm* canal; channel
canario *nm* canary
canasta *nf* basket
cancelar *v* cancel; pay off, settle
cáncer *nm* cancer
cancha *nf* court, field (for sports)
canciller *nm* chancellor
canción *nf* (**-ciones**) song
candado *nm* padlock
candela *nf* candle — **candelabro** *nm* candelabra
candidato, -ta *n* candidate
canela *nf* cinnamon
cangrejo *nm* crab
canguro *nm* kangaroo
canino, -na *adj* canine
canje *nm* exchange, trade
canoa *nf* canoe
cañón *nm* (**-ñones**) cannon
canoso, -sa *adj* gray, gray-haired
cansar *v* tire (out); be tiring — **cansarse** *vr* get tired — **cansado, -da** *adj* tired; tiresome — **cansancio** *nm* fatigue, weariness
cantar *v* sing — **cantar** *nm* song — **cantante** *nmf* singer
cantidad *nf* quantity, amount
cantimplora *nf* canteen, water bottle
canto *nm* singing, song — **cantor, -tora** *adj* singing
caos *nm* chaos
capa *nf* cape, cloak
capacidad *nf* capacity; ability
capacitar *v* train, qualify — **capacitación** *nf* (**-ciones**) training
caparazón *nm* (**-zones**) shell
capaz *adj* (**-paces**) capable, able

capilla *nf* chapel

capital *adj* capital; ∽ *nf* capital (city) — **capitalismo** *nm* capitalism

capitán, -tana *n* (**-tanes** *m*) captain

capítulo *nm* chapter

capricho *nm* whim, caprice — **caprichoso, -sa** *adj* whimsical, capricious

cápsula *nf* capsule

captar *v* grasp

capturar *v* capture, seize — **captura** *nf* capture, seizure

caqui *adj & nm* khaki

cara *nf* face

caracol *nm* snail

carácter *nm* (**-racteres**) character — **característica** *nf* characteristic — **característico, -ca** *adj* characteristic — **caracterizar** *v* characterize

caramba *interj* oh my!, good grief!

caramelo *nm* caramel; candy

carbohidrato *nm* carbohydrate

carbón *nm* (**-bones**) coal

carcajada *nf* loud laugh, guffaw

cárcel *nf* jail, prison

cardenal *nm* cardinal

cardíaco or **cardiaco, -ca** *adj* cardiac, heart

cardiólogo, -ga *n* cardiologist

carecer *vi* lack — **carencia** *nf* lack, want

carestía *nf* high cost

cargar *v* charge; carry — **cargamento** *nm* cargo, load — **cargo** *nm* charge; position, office

caribe *adj* Caribbean

caricatura *nf* caricature

caricia *nf* caress

caridad *nf* charity

cariño *nm* affection, love — **cariñoso, -sa** *adj* affectionate, loving

caritativo, -va *adj* charitable

carnaval *nm* carnival

carne *nf* meat

carnero *nm* ram, sheep

carnet *nm* ID card; ∽ **de conducir** driver's license

carnicería *nf* butcher shop

caro, -ra *adj* expensive; dear — **caro** *adv* dearly

carpa *nf* tent

carpeta *nf* folder

carpintería *nf* carpentry — **carpintero, -ra** *n* carpenter

carrera *nf* running, run; race; course (of studies); career, profession

carretera *nf* highway, road

carril *nm* lane

carro *nm* automobile, car

carrusel *nm* merry-go-round, carousel

carta *nf* letter; playing card; menu

cartel *nm* poster, bill — **cartelera** *nf* billboard

cartera *nf* briefcase; wallet; pocketbook — **carterista** *nmf* pickpocket

cartero, -ra *nm* mail carrier, mailman *m*

cartón *nm* (**-tones**) cardboard

casa *nf* house; home

casar *v* marry — **casado, -da** *adj* married

cascabel *nm* small bell

cascada *nf* waterfall

cáscara *nf* skin, peel, shell

casco *nm* helmet

caseta *nf* booth, stall

casi *adv* almost, nearly

casino *nm* casino

caso *nm* case; pay attention

caspa *nf* dandruff

cassette *nmf* cassette

castaña *nf* chestnut

castaño, -ña *adj* chestnut (color)

castañuela *nf* castanet

castellano *nm* Castilian

castigar *v* punish — **castigo** *nm* punishment

castillo *nm* castle

casual *adj* chance, accidental — **casualidad** *nf* coincidence

catálogo *nm* catalog

catarata *nf* waterfall

catarro *nm* cold

catedral *nf* cathedral

categoría *nf* category; rank; first-rate
católico, -ca *adj & n* Catholic — **catolicismo** *nm* Catholicism
catorce *adj & nm* fourteen — **catorceavo** *nm* fourteenth
caucho *nm* rubber
causar *v* cause, provoke — **causa** *nf* cause; reason
cauteloso, -sa *adj* cautious
cavar *v* dig
caverna *nf* cavern, cave
cavidad *nf* cavity
cazar *v* hunt; go hunting — **caza** *nf* hunt, hunting — **cazador, -dora** *n* hunter
cazuela *nf* casserole
CD *nm* CD, compact disc
cebada *nf* barley
cebolla *nf* onion
cebra *nf* zebra
ceder *v* yield, give way; cede, hand over
cedro *nm* cedar
cédula *nf* document, certificate
ceguera *nf* blindness
ceja *nf* eyebrow
celador, -dora *n* guard, warden
celda *nf* cell
celebrar *v* celebrate — **celebración** *nf* (-ciones) celebration — **célebre** *adj* famous, celebrated
celestial *adj* celestial, heavenly
celo *nm* zeal; **~s** *nmpl* jealousy
célula *nf* cell — **celular** *adj* cellular
cementerio *nm* cemetery
cemento *nm* cement
cena *nf* supper, dinner
cenar *v* have dinner, have supper; have for dinner
cenicero *nm* ashtray
ceniza *nf* ash
centavo *nm* cent; centavo
centenar *nm* hundred
centígrado *adj* centigrade, Celsius
centímetro *nm* centimeter
central *adj* central
centrar *v* center — **centrarse en** *vr phr*

focus on — **centro** *nm* center; downtown
centroamericano, -na *adj* Central American
cepillo *nm* brush; **~ de dientes** toothbrush — **cepillar** *v* brush
cera *nf* wax; beeswax
cerámica *nf* ceramics *pl*; pottery
cerca[1] *nf* fence
cerca[2] *adv* close, near
cerdo *nm* pig, hog
cereal *adj & nm* cereal
cerebro *nm* brain
ceremonia *nf* ceremony
cereza *nf* cherry
cerilla *nf* match
cero *nm* zero
cerrar *v* close, shut; turn off; lock up — **cerrado, -da** *adj* closed — **cerradura** *nf* lock
cerro *nm* hill
certeza *nf* certainty — **certidumbre** *nf* certainty
certificar *v* certify — **certificado, -da** *adj* certified, registered — **certificado** *nm* certificate
cerveza *nf* beer
cesar *v* cease, stop; dismiss, lay off — **cesantía** *nf* unemployment
cesárea *nf* cesarean
césped *nm* lawn, grass
cesta *nf* basket — **cesto** *nm* basket; wastebasket
chal *nm* shawl
chaleco *nm* vest
champaña *or* **champán** *nm* champagne
champiñón *nm* (-ñones) mushroom
champú *nm* (-pús *or* -púes) shampoo
chance *nm* chance, opportunity
chaqueta *nf* jacket
charco *nm* puddle
charlar *v* chat — **charla** *nf* chat, talk
charlatán, -tana *adj* (-tanes *m*) talkative — **charlatán, -tana** *n* chatterbox; charlatan
charol *nm* patent leather

chasis *nms & pl* chassis

chatarra *nf* scrap

chato, -ta *adj* pug-nosed

chaval, -vala *n* kid, boy *m*, girl *f*

checo, -ca *adj* Czech — **checo** *nm* Czech

chef *nm* chef

cheque *nm* check — **chequera** *nf* checkbook

chequear *v* check, inspect, verify; check in — **chequeo** *nm* checkup

chicharrón *nm* (-rrones) pork rind

chichón *nm* (-chones) bump

chicle *nm* chewing gum

chico, -ca *adj* little, small — **chico, -ca** *n* child, boy *m*, girl *f*

chiflar *v* whistle; whistle at, boo — **chiflado, -da** *adj* crazy, nuts — **chiflido** *nm* whistling

chile *nm* chili pepper

chileno, -na *adj* Chilean

chillido *nm* scream; screech, squeal — **chillón, -llona** *adj* (-llones *m*) shrill, loud

chimenea *nf* chimney; fireplace

chimpancé *nm* chimpanzee

chino, -na *adj* Chinese — **chino** *nm* Chinese

chiquillo, -lla *n* kid, child

chiquito, -ta *adj* tiny — **chiquito, -ta** *n* little child, tot

chirriar *v* squeak, creak; screech — **chirrido** *nm* squeak, creak; screech

chismoso, -sa *adj* gossipy — **chismoso, -sa** *n* gossipy person — **chisme** *nm* gossip

chispa *nf* spark

chiste *nm* joke, funny story — **chistoso, -sa** *adj* funny, witty

chivo, -va *n* kid, young goat

chocar *v* crash, collide; clash — **chocante** *adj* striking, shocking; unpleasant, rude

chocolate *nm* chocolate

chofer *or* **chófer** *nm* chauffeur; driver

choque *nm* shock; crash, collision

chorizo *nm* chorizo, sausage

chorrear *v* drip; pour out, gush — **chorro** *nm* stream, jet

choza *nf* hut, shack

chubasco *nm* downpour, squall

chueco, -ca *adj* crooked

chuleta *nf* cutlet, chop

chupar *v* suck; absorb; suckle — **chupete** *nm* pacifier

churro *nm* fried dough

cicatriz *nf* (-trices) scar — **cicatrizar** *v* form a scar, heal

cíclico, -ca *adj* cyclical

ciclismo *nm* cycling — **ciclista** *nmf* cyclist

ciclón *nm* (-clones) cyclone

ciego, -ga *adj* blind — **ciegamente** *adv* blindly

cielo *nm* sky; heaven

ciempiés *nms & pl* centipede

cien *adj* a hundred, hundred — **cien** *nm* one hundred

ciénaga *nf* swamp, bog

ciencia *nf* science

científico, -ca *adj* scientific — **científico, -ca** *n* scientist

ciento *adj* one hundred — **ciento** *nm* hundred, group of a hundred

cierre *nm* closing, closure; fastener, clasp

cierto, -ta *adj* true; certain

ciervo, -va *n* deer, stag *m*, hind *f*

cifra *nf* number, figure; sum; code, cipher

cigarrillo *nm* cigarette

cigüeña *nf* stork

cilantro *nm* cilantro, coriander

cilindro *nm* cylinder — **cilíndrico, -ca** *adj* cylindrical

cima *nf* peak, summit

cimentar *v* cement, strengthen; establish — **cimientos** *nmpl* base, foundation(s)

cinc *nm* zinc

cincel *nm* chisel

cinco *adj & nm* five

cincuenta *adj & nm* fifty

cine *nm* cinema, movies *pl* — **cine-matográfico, -ca** *adj* movie, film

cínico, -ca *adj* cynical — **cínico, -ca** *n* cynic — **cinismo** *nm* cynicism

cinta *nf* ribbon, band; adhesive tape

cintura *nf* waist — **cinturón** *nm* (**-rones**) belt; seat belt

circo *nm* circus

circuito *nm* circuit

circular *v* circulate; drive — **circular** *adj* circular — **circulación** *nf* (**-ciones**) circulation; traffic

círculo *nm* circle

circunferencia *nf* circumference

circunstancia *nf* circumstance

cirio *nm* candle

ciruela *nf* plum; prune

cirugía *nf* surgery — **cirujano, -na** *n* surgeon

cisne *nm* swan

cisterna *nf* cistern

cita *nf* appointment, date; quote, quotation — **citar** *v* quote, cite; make an appointment with

ciudad *nf* city, town — **ciudadano, -na** *n* citizen; resident — **ciudadanía** *nf* citizenship

cívico, -ca *adj* civic

civil *adj* civil — **civil** *nmf* civilian — **civilización** *nf* (**-ciones**) civilization — **civilizar** *v* civilize

clamar *v* clamor, cry out — **clamor** *nm* clamor, outcry

clandestino, -na *adj* clandestine, secret

clara *nf* egg white

claramente *adv* clearly

claridad *nf* clarity, clearness; light

clarificar *v* clarify

clarinete *nm* clarinet

claro *adv* clearly; of course, surely — **claro** *nm* clearing, glade — **claro, -ra** *adj* clear, bright; light; evident

clase *nf* class; sort, kind

clásico, -ca *adj* classic, classical — **clásico** *nm* classic

clasificar *v* classify, sort out — **clasifi-**

carse *vr* qualify — **clasificación** *nf* (**-ciones**) classification; league

cláusula *nf* clause

clausurar *v* close (down)

clavar *v* nail, hammer; drive in, plunge

clave *nf* code; key — **clave** *adj* key

clavel *nm* carnation

clavícula *nf* collarbone

clavo *nm* nail; clove (spice)

clemencia *nf* clemency, mercy — **clero** *nm* clergy

cliente, -ta *n* customer, client — **clientela** *nf* clientele, customers *pl*

clima *nm* climate; atmosphere — **climático, -ca** *adj* climatic

climatizar *v* air-condition — **climatizado, -da** *adj* air-conditioned

clímax *nm* climax

clínica *nf* clinic — **clínico, -ca** *adj* clinical

clip *nm* (**clips**) clip

cloro *nm* chlorine

clóset *nm* (**clósets**) closet, cupboard

club *nm* club

cobarde *nmf* coward — **cobarde** *adj* cowardly — **cobardía** *nf* cowardice

cobertor *nm* bedspread

cobertura *nf* cover; coverage

cobijar *v* shelter — **cobija** *nf* blanket

cobra *nf* cobra

cobrar *v* charge, collect; earn — **cobrador, -dora** *n* collector

cobre *nm* copper

cobro *nm* collection, cashing

cocaína *nf* cocaine

cocer *v* cook; boil

coche *nm* car, automobile; coach (of a train) — **cochecito** *nm* baby carriage, stroller

cochino, -na *n* pig, hog — **cochino, -na** *adj* dirty, filthy — **cochinillo** *nm* piglet

cocido, -da *adj* boiled, cooked

cocina *nf* kitchen; stove; cooking, cuisine — **cocinar** *v* cook — **cocinero, -ra** *n* cook, chef

coco *nm* coconut

cocodrilo *nm* crocodile

coctel *or* **cóctel** *nm* cocktail; cocktail party

código *nm* code; zip code

codo *nm* elbow

codorniz *nf* (**-nices**) quail

cofre *nm* chest, coffer

coger *v* take; catch; pick up

coherencia *nf* coherence — **coherente** *adj* coherent — **cohesión** *nf* (**-siones**) cohesion

cohete *nm* rocket

coincidir *v* coincide — **coincidencia** *nf* coincidence

cojear *v* limp — **cojera** *nf* limp

cojín *nm* (**-jines**) cushion

cojo, -ja *adj* lame — **cojo, -ja** *n* lame person

col *nf* cabbage

cola *nf* tail; line

colaborar *v* collaborate — **colaboración** *nf* (**-ciones**) collaboration — **colaborador, -dora** *n* collaborator; contributor

colador *nm* colander, strainer

colar *v* strain, filter — **colarse** *vr* sneak in, gate-crash

colcha *nf* bedspread, quilt — **colchón** *nm* (**-chones**) mattress — **colchoneta** *nf* mat

colección *nf* (**-ciones**) collection — **coleccionar** *v* collect — **coleccionista** *nmf* collector

colega *nmf* colleague

colegio *nm* school — **colegial, -giala** *n* schoolboy *m*, schoolgirl *f*

colesterol *nm* cholesterol

colgar *v* hang; hang up

colibrí *nm* hummingbird

cólico *nm* colic

coliflor *nf* cauliflower

colilla *nf* (cigarette) butt

colina *nf* hill

coliseo *nm* coliseum

collar *nm* necklace; collar

colocar *v* place, put; find a job for —

colocación *nf* (**-ciones**) placement, placing; position, job

colombiano, -na *adj* Colombian

columna *nf* column; ~ **vertebral** spine, backbone

columpiar *v* push

combinar *v* combine; put together, match — **combinación** *nf* (**-ciones**) combination; connection (in travel)

combustible *nm* fuel — **combustible** *adj* combustible — **combustión** *nf* (**-tiones**) combustion

comedia *nf* comedy

comedor *nm* dining room

comentar *v* comment on, discuss; mention — **comentario** *nm* comment; commentary

comenzar *v* begin, start

comer *v* eat; eat up; eat into; feed

comercio *nm* commerce, trade; business — **comerciante** *nmf* merchant, dealer

cometer *v* commit; make a mistake

comicios *nmpl* elections

comida *nf* food; lunch; dinner

comité *nm* committee

como *conj* as, since; if — **como** *prep* like, as; as well as — **como** *adv* as; around, about

cómo *adv* how; by all means; **¿~ te llamas?** what's your name?

cómodo, -da *adj* comfortable; handy, convenient

compadecer *v* feel sorry for

compañero, -ra *n* companion, partner

compañía *nf* company

comparar *v* compare — **comparación** *nf* (**-ciones**) comparison

compartir *v* share

compensar *v* compensate for

competir *v* compete — **competencia** *nf* competition, rivalry — **competente** *adj* competent

complacer *v* please

complejo, -ja *adj* complex — **complejo** *nm* complex

complementar *v* complement

completar *v* complete — **completo, -ta** *adj* complete; perfect; full

complicar *v* complicate; involve — **complicación** *nf* (**-ciones**) complication

cómplice *nmf* accomplice — **cómplice** *adj* conspiratorial, knowing

componer *v* make up; compose, write (a song); fix, repair

comportamiento *nm* behavior

composición *nf* (**-ciones**) composition — **compositor, -tora** *n* composer, songwriter

comprar *v* buy, purchase — **compra** *nf* purchase

comprender *v* comprehend, understand; cover, include — **comprensión** *nf* (**-siones**) understanding

comprobar *v* check; prove — **comprobante** *nm* proof; receipt, voucher

comprometer *v* compromise; jeopardize; commit — **comprometerse** *vr* get engaged to

computadora *nf or* **computador** *nm* computer; laptop computer

común *adj* (**-munes**) common; ordinary; generally

comunicar *v* communicate — **comunicarse** *vr* get in touch with

con *prep* with; in spite of; (*before an infinitive*) by; so long as

concebir *v* conceive

conceder *v* grant, bestow; concede

concentrar *v* concentrate — **concentración** *nf* (**-ciones**) concentration

concepto *nm* concept; opinion

concertar *v* arrange, coordinate; (*used before an infinitive*) agree; harmonize

conciencia *nf* conscience; consciousness, awareness — **concientizar** *v* make aware

concierto *nm* concert; concerto

conciliar *v* reconcile — **conciliación** *nf* (**-ciones**) reconciliation

concluir *v* conclude — **conclusión** *nf* (**-siones**) conclusion

concordar *v* agree; reconcile — **concordancia** *nf* agreement

concretar *v* make concrete, specify

concurrir *v* come together, meet; ~ **a** take part in

concursar *v* compete, participate — **concursante** *nmf* competitor — **concurso** *nm* competition; gathering; help, cooperation

condenar *v* condemn, damn; sentence — **condena** *nf* condemnation; sentence

condición *nf* (**-ciones**) condition, state; capacity, position — **condicional** *adj* conditional

condimento *nm* condiment, seasoning

condolerse *vr* sympathize — **condolencia** *nf* condolence

condominio *nm* joint ownership; condominium

conducir *v* direct, lead; drive; lead to — **conducirse** *vr* behave

conducta *nf* behavior, conduct

conductor, -tora *n* driver

conectar *v* connect; plug in

conejo, -ja *n* rabbit

confabularse *vr* conspire, plot

confeccionar *v* make (up), prepare — **confección** *nf* (**-ciones**) making, preparation; tailoring, dressmaking

conferencia *nf* lecture; conference

conferir *v* confer, bestow

confesar *v* confess — **confesión** *nf* (**-siones**) confession; religion, creed

confiar *v* trust; entrust — **confiado, -da** *adj* confident; trusting — **confianza** *nf* trust; confidence

confidencia *nf* confidence, secret — **confidencial** *adj* confidential

configuración *nf* (**-ciones**) configuration, shape

confirmar *v* confirm — **confirmación** *nf* (**-ciones**) confirmation

confiscar *v* confiscate

conflagración *nf* (**-ciones**) war, conflict; fire

conflicto *nm* conflict

conformar *v* shape, make up — **conformarse** *vr* content oneself with — **confortable** *adj* comfortable

confrontar *v* confront; compare; border — **confrontación** *nf* (**-ciones**) confrontation

confundir *v* confuse, mix up — **confusión** *nf* (**-siones**) confusion — **congelar** *v* freeze — **congelador** *nm* freezer

congestión *nf* (**-tiones**) congestion

congregar *v* bring together

congreso *nm* congress — **congresista** *nmf* member of congress

conjugar *v* conjugate — **conjugación** *nf* (**-ciones**) conjugation

conjunción *nf* (**-ciones**) conjunction

conjunto, -ta *adj* joint — **conjunto** *nm* collection; outfit; band

conmemorar *v* commemorate — **conmemoración** *nf* (**-ciones**) commemoration

conmigo *pron* with me

conmover *v* move, touch; shake (up)

conmutador *nm* switch; switchboard

conocer *v* know; meet; recognize — **conocimiento** *nm* knowledge; consciousness

conque *conj* so

consciente *adj* conscious, aware

consecuencia *nf* consequence; **en** ~ accordingly

consecutivo, -va *adj* consecutive

conseguir *v* get, obtain

consejo *nm* advice, counsel; council

consenso *nm* consensus

consentir *v* allow, permit; pamper, spoil; consent — **consentimiento** *nm* consent, permission

conservar *v* preserve; keep, conserve — **conservación** *nf* (**-ciones**) conservation, preservation — **conservador, -dora** *adj & n* conservative — **conservatorio** *nm* conservatory

considerar *v* consider; respect

consigna *nf* slogan; assignment; checkroom

consigo *pron* with her, with him, with you, with oneself

consiguiente *adj* consequent; **por** ~ consequently

consistir *v* consist of; lie in, consist in

consolar *v* console, comfort

consolidar *v* consolidate — **consolidación** *nf* (**-ciones**) consolidation

consonante *adj* consonant, harmonious — **consonante** *nf* consonant

consorcio *nm* consortium

constancia *nf* record, evidence; perseverance — **constante** *adj* constant

constar *v* be evident, be clear; consist of

constatar *v* verify; state, affirm

constituir *v* constitute, form; establish, set up — **constituirse** *vr* set oneself up as — **constitución** *nf* (**-ciones**) constitution — **constitucional** *adj* constitutional — **constituyente** *adj & nm* constituent

construir *v* build, construct — **construcción** *nf* (**-ciones**) construction, building

consultar *v* consult — **consulta** *nf* consultation — **consultorio** *nm* office (of a doctor or dentist)

consumar *v* consummate, complete; commit

consumidor, -dora *n* consumer — **consumo** *nm* consumption

contabilidad *nf* accounting, bookkeeping; accountancy

contacto *nm* contact

contagiar *v* infect; transmit — **contagio** *nm* contagion, infection

contaminar *v* contaminate, pollute — **contaminación** *nf* (**-ciones**) contamination, pollution

contar *v* count; tell; rely on

contemplar *v* look at, behold; contemplate

contemporáneo, -nea *adj & n* contemporary

contener *v* contain; restrain, hold back — **contenido** *nm* contents *pl*

contentar *v* please, make happy — **contentarse con** *vr phr* be satisfied with

contestar *v* answer; reply

contexto *nm* context

contigo *pron* with you

continuar *v* continue — **continuación** *nf* (**-ciones**) continuation; next, then — **continuidad** *nf* continuity

contra *prep* against — **contra** *nm* opposition, opponent

contradecir *v* contradict — **contradicción** *nf* (**-ciones**) contradiction

contraer *v* contract; ~ **matrimonio** get married — **contraerse** *vr* tighten up

contralto *nmf* contralto

contrariar *v* oppose; vex, annoy

contraseña *nf* password

contrastar *v* check, verify; resist

contratar *v* contract for; hire

contrato *nm* contract — **contratista** *nmf* contractor

contribuir *v* contribute; pay taxes — **contribución** *nf* (**-ciones**) contribution; tax — **contribuyente** *nmf* contributor; taxpayer

controlar *v* control; monitor, check — **control** *nm* control; inspection, check

controversia *nf* controversy

contundente *adj* blunt; forceful, convincing

convalecencia *nf* convalescence

convencer *v* convince, persuade

convención *nf* (**-ciones**) convention — **convencional** *adj* conventional

convenir *v* be suitable, be advisable; agree on — **conveniencia** *nf* convenience; suitability (of an action, etc.) — **conveniente** *adj* convenient; suitable, advisable; useful — **convenio** *nm* agreement, pact

conversar *v* converse, talk — **conversación** *nf* (**-ciones**) conversation

convertir *v* convert

convexo, -xa *adj* convex

convicción *nf* (**-ciones**) conviction — **convicto, -ta** *adj* convicted

convincente *adj* convincing

convivir *v* live together

convocar *v* convoke, call together

cónyuge *nmf* spouse, partner

cooperar *v* cooperate — **cooperación** *nf* (**-ciones**) cooperation — **cooperativa** *nf* cooperative, co-op

coordinar *v* coordinate — **coordinación** *nf* (**-ciones**) coordination — **coordinador, -dora** *n* coordinator

copa *nf* glass, goblet; cup

copiar *v* copy

copioso, -sa *adj* copious, abundant

coquetear *v* flirt

Corán *nm* the Koran

corazón *nm* (**-zones**) heart; core; **mi** ~ my darling

corbata *nf* tie, necktie

corchete *nm* hook and eye, clasp; square bracket

corcho *nm* cork

cordero *nm* lamb

cordial *adj* cordial

cordillera *nf* mountain range

cordón *nm* (**-dones**) cord; (police) cordon; **cordones** *nmpl* shoelaces

cordura *nf* sanity

coro *nm* chorus; choir

corporación *nf* (**-ciones**) corporation

corporal *adj* corporal, bodily

corporativo, -va *adj* corporate

corpulento, -ta *adj* stout

corrección *nf* (**-ciones**) correction; correctness, propriety — **correcto, -ta** *adj* correct, right; polite

corredor, -dora *n* runner, racer; agent, broker — **corredor** *nm* corridor, hallway

corregir *v* correct

correo *nm* mail; airmail

correr *v* run, race; flow; travel over

corresponder *v* correspond; belong; fit; reciprocate, repay — **corresponderse**

vr write to each other — **correspondencia** *nf* correspondence; connection
corriente *nf* current, draft; tendency, trend; **al ~** up-to-date; informed — **corriente** *adj* current; common, ordinary; running
corroborar *v* corroborate
cortar *v* cut; cut out; cut off — **cortarse** *vr* curdle; have one's hair cut
cortauñas *nms & pl* nail clippers
corte *nm* cutting; cut, style; haircut
cortejo *nm* entourage; courtship; funeral procession
cortés *adj* courteous, polite — **cortesía** *nf* courtesy, politeness
corto, -ta *adj* short; scarce; timid, shy; nearsighted — **cortocircuito** *nm* short circuit
cosa *nf* thing; matter, affair; **poca ~** nothing much
cosechar *v* harvest, reap — **cosecha** *nf* harvest, crop; vintage
cosmético, -ca *adj* cosmetic
cosmopolita *adj* cosmopolitan
cosquillas *nfpl* tickling; tickle
costa¹ *nf* cost; **a toda ~** at any cost
costa² *nf* coast, shore
costarricense *or* **costarriqueño, -ña** *adj* Costa Rican
costumbre *nf* custom, habit; usual
costura *nf* sewing, dressmaking; seam
cotidiano, -na *adj* daily
cotizar *v* quote, set a price on — **cotización** *nf* (**-ciones**) quotation, price
coyuntura *nf* joint; situation, moment
cráneo *nf* cranium, skull
cráter *nm* crater
crear *v* create — **creación** *nf* (**-ciones**) creation — **creador, -dora** *n* creator
crecer *v* grow; increase — **crecimiento** *nm* growth; increase
crédito *nm* credit
creer *v* believe; suppose, think — **creerse** *vr* regard oneself as — **creencia** *nf* belief
cremación *nf* (**-ciones**) cremation

cremallera *nf* zipper
cremoso, -sa *adj* creamy
creyente *nmf* believer
crimen *nm* (**crímenes**) crime — **criminal** *adj & nmf* criminal
criollo, -lla *adj & n* Creole
crisis *nf* crisis; nervous breakdown
cristal *nm* crystal; glass, piece of glass — **cristalería** *nf* glassware — **cristalino, -na** *adj* crystalline — **cristalino** *nm* lens — **cristalizar** *v* crystallize
cristiano, -na *adj & n* Christian — **cristianismo** *nm* Christianity — **Cristo** *nm* Christ
criterio *nm* criterion; judgment, opinion
crítico, -ca *adj* critical — **crítico, -ca** *n* critic, reviewer — **criticar** *v* criticize — **crítica** *nf* criticism; review, critique
crónica *nf* chronicle; (news) report
crónico, -ca *adj* chronic
cronista *nmf* reporter, newscaster
cronología *nf* chronology — **cronológico, -ca** *adj* chronological
cronometrar *v* time, clock — **cronómetro** *nm* chronometer, stopwatch
cruce *nm* crossing; crossroads, intersection; crosswalk
crucero *nm* cruise; cruiser (ship)
crucial *adj* crucial
crucificar *v* crucify — **crucifijo** *nm* crucifix
crucigrama *nm* crossword puzzle
crudo, -da *adj* harsh, crude; raw — **crudo** *nm* crude oil
cruel *adj* cruel — **crueldad** *nf* cruelty
cruz *nf* (**cruces**) cross — **cruzar** *v* cross; exchange — **cruzarse** *vr* pass each other
cuaderno *nm* notebook
cuadra *nf* stable; (city) block
cuadrado, -da *adj* square
cuadrar *v* conform, agree; tally; square — **cuadrarse** *vr* stand at attention
cuadrilátero *nm* quadrilateral; (boxing) ring

cuadro *nm* square; painting; picture, description; staff, management; check

cuadrúpedo *nm* quadruped

cual *pron* who, whom, which; which; everyone, everybody — **cual** *prep* like, as

cuál *pron* which (one), what (one) ∼ *adj* which, what

cualidad *nf* quality, trait

cualquiera (**cualquier** *before nouns*) *adj* (**cualesquiera**) any, whatever ∼ *pron* (**cualesquiera**) anyone, whatever

cuán *adv* how

cuando *conj* when; since, if; ∼ **más** at the most; from time to time — **cuando** *prep* during, at the time of

cuándo *adv* when; since when?

cuanto *adv* as much as; ∼ **antes** as soon as possible; **en** ∼ as soon as; **en** ∼ **a** as for, as regards

cuánto *adv & pron* how much, how many — **cuánto, -ta** *adj* how much, how many

cuanto, -ta *adj* as many, whatever — **cuanto, -ta** *pron* as much as, all that, everything; **unos cuantos, unas cuantas** a few

cuarenta *adj & nm* forty

Cuaresma *nf* Lent

cuartel *nm* barracks *pl*; headquarters; mercy

cuarteto *nm* quartet

cuarto, -ta *adj* fourth — **cuarto, -ta** *n* fourth one — **cuarto** *nm* quarter, fourth part

cuatro *adj & nm* four — **cuatrocientos, -tas** *adj* four hundred — **cuatrocientos** *nms & pl* four hundred

cubano, -na *adj* Cuban

cúbico, -ca *adj* cubic, cubed

cubierta *nf* cover, covering; tire; deck — **cubierto** *nm* cutlery, place setting; under cover

cubrecama *nm* bedspread

cubrir *v* cover — **cubrirse** *vr* cloud over

cuchara *nf* spoon

cuchilla *nf* (kitchen) knife; razor blade — **cuchillo** *nm* knife

cuello *nm* neck; collar

cuenca *nf* river basin; (eye) socket

cuenta *nf* calculation, count; account; check, bill

cuento *nm* story, tale; fairy tale

cuerda *nf* cord, rope, string; ∼**s vocales** vocal cords

cuerdo, -da *adj* sane, sensible

cuero *nm* leather, hide

cuerpo *nm* body; corps

cuervo *nm* crow

cuesta *nf* slope; **a** ∼**s** on one's back

cuestión *nf* (-tiones) matter, affair — **cuestionar** *v* question — **cuestionario** *nm* questionnaire; quiz

cueva *nf* cave

cuidar *v* take care of, look after; pay attention to — **cuidado** *nm* care; worry, concern — **¡cuidado!** *interj* watch out!, careful!

culebra *nf* snake

culinario, -ria *adj* culinary

culminar *v* culminate — **culminación** *nf* (-ciones) culmination

culpa *nf* fault, blame; sin; **tener la** ∼ be at fault — **culpar** *v* blame

culpable *adj* guilty — **culpable** *nmf* culprit, guilty party

cultivar *v* cultivate — **cultivo** *nm* farming, cultivation; crops

culto, -ta *adj* cultured, educated — **culto** *nm* worship; cult — **cultura** *nf* culture

cumpleaños *nms & pl* birthday

cumplido, -da *adj* complete, full; courteous — **cumplido** *nm* compliment, courtesy

cumplir *v* accomplish, carry out; keep; reach; fall due — **cumplirse** *vr* come true — **cumplimiento** *nm* performance

cuna *nf* cradle; birthplace

cuñado, -da *n* brother-in-law *m*, sister-in-law *f*

cuota *nf* fee, dues; quota; installment, payment

cupo *nm* quota, share; capacity
curar *v* cure; dress; tan
curiosidad *nf* curiosity — **curioso, -sa** *adj* curious, inquisitive; strange
currículum *nm* (**-lums**) *or* **currículo** *nm* résumé, curriculum vitae
cursar *v* take, study; send, pass on
cursiva *nf* italics *pl*

curso *nm* course; school year
curva *nf* curve, bend — **curvo, -va** *adj* curved, bent
cutáneo, -nea *adj* skin
cutis *nms & pl* skin, complexion
cuyo, -ya *adj* whose, of whom, of which

D

d *nf* d, fourth letter of the Spanish alphabet
dados *nmpl* dice
dama *nf* lady; ∼**s** *nfpl* checkers
dañar *v* damage, harm — **daño** *nm* damage, harm
danés, -nesa *adj* Danish — **danés** *nm* Danish
danzar *v* dance — **danza** *nf* dance, dancing
dar *v* give; yield, produce
dardo *nm* dart
dátil *nm* date (fruit)
dato *nm* fact
de *prep* of
debajo *adv* underneath
debate *nm* debate
deber *v* owe — *v aux* have to, should; must
débil *adj* weak, feeble — **debilidad** *nf* weakness — **débilmente** *adv* weakly, faintly
década *nf* decade
decena *nf* ten, about ten
decencia *nf* decency
decente *adj* decent
decidir *v* decide, determine — **decidirse** *vr* make up one's mind — **decidido, -da** *adj* determined, resolute
decimal *adj* decimal
décimo, -ma *adj & n* tenth
decir *v* say; tell; **¿comó se dice . . . ?** how do you say . . . ?

decisión *nf* (**-siones**) decision — **decisivo, -va** *adj* decisive
declarar *v* declare; testify — **declaración** *nf* (**-ciones**) statement
decoración *nf* (**-ciones**) decoration — **decorado** *nm* stage set — **decorar** *v* decorate — **decorativo, -va** *adj* decorative
decretar *v* decree — **decreto** *nm* decree
dedicar *v* dedicate — **dedicación** *nf* (**-ciones**) dedication
dedo *nm* finger
deducir *v* deduce; deduct — **deducción** *nf* (**-ciones**) deduction
defecto *nm* defect — **defectuoso, -sa** *adj* defective, faulty
defender *v* defend — **defensa** *nf* defense — **defensor, -sora** *n* defender
definir *v* define — **definición** *nf* (**-ciones**) definition — **definitivo, -va** *adj* definitive
deforme *adj* deformed — **deformidad** *nf* deformity
dejar *v* leave; abandon; allow
delantal *nm* apron
delante *adv* ahead
delantero, -ra *adj* front, forward — **delantero, -ra** *n* forward (in sports)
delegación *nf* (**-ciones**) delegation — **delegado, -da** *n* delegate, representative
deletrear *v* spell out
delfín *nm* (**-fines**) dolphin

delgado, -da *adj* thin
delicadeza *nf* delicacy, daintiness; gentleness; tact — **delicado, -da** *adj* delicate; sensible; tactful
delicia *nf* delight — **delicioso, -sa** *adj* delightful; delicious
delincuencia *nf* delinquency, crime — **delincuente** *adj & nmf* delinquent, criminal
delito *nm* crime
demandar *v* sue; demand
demás *pron* **lo (la, los, las)** ~ the rest, others — **demás** *adj* rest of the, other
demasiado *adv* too — **demasiado** *adj* too much, too many
democracia *nf* democracy — **democrático, -ca** *adj* democratic
demonio *nm* devil, demon
demorar *v* delay — **demorarse** *vr* take a long time — **demora** *nf* delay
demostrar *v* demonstrate; — **demostración** *nf* (**-ciones**) demonstration
denominador *nm* denominator
dentadura *nf* teeth; ~ **postiza** dentures *pl* — **dentífrico** *nm* toothpaste — **dentista** *nmf* dentist
dentro *adv* in, inside
denunciar *v* denounce — **denuncia** *nf* accusation
departamento *nm* department
depender *v* depend — **dependencia** *nf* dependence, dependency; branch office — **dependiente** *adj* dependent — **dependiente, -ta** *n* clerk, salesperson
deporte *nm* sport, sports *pl* — **deportista** *nmf* sportsman; sportswoman — **deportivo, -va** *adj* sporty
depositar *v* put, place; deposit — **depósito** *nm* deposit; warehouse
deprimir *v* depress — **depresión** *nf* (**-siones**) depression
derecha *nf* right side — **derecho** *nm* right; law — **derecho** *adv* straight — **derecho, -cha** *adj* right, right-hand; upright; straight
derramar *v* spill

derretir *v* melt, thaw
derrotar *v* defeat — **derrota** *nf* defeat
derrumbar *v* demolish, knock down — **derrumbarse** *vr* collapse, break down — **derrumbamiento** *nm* collapse — **derrumbe** *nm* collapse
desabotonar *v* unbutton, undo
desabrochar *v* unbutton, undo
desafiar *v* defy, challenge — **desafiante** *adj* defiant
desafío *nm* challenge, defiance
desafortunadamente *adv* unfortunately
desagradar *v* displease — **desagradable** *adj* disagreeable, unpleasant
desagradecido, -da *adj* ungrateful
desahogar *v* relieve; give vent to — **desahogarse** *vr* let off steam, unburden oneself — **desahogo** *nm* relief
desalentar *v* discourage — **desaliento** *nm* discouragement
desanimar *v* discourage — **desanimarse** *vr* get discouraged — **desanimado, -da** *adj* downhearted, despondent
desaparecer *v* disappear — **desaparecido, -da** *n* missing person — **desaparición** *nf* (**-ciones**) disappearance
desapercebido, -da *adj* unnoticed
desarrollar *v* develop — **desarrollarse** *vr* take place — **desarrollo** *nm* development
desastre *nm* disaster
desatar *v* undo, untie; unleash — **desatarse** *vr* come undone; break out, erupt
desayunar *v* have breakfast; have for breakfast — **desayuno** *nm* breakfast
descafeinado, -da *adj* decaffeinated
descalificar *v* disqualify — **descalificación** *nf* (**-ciones**) disqualification
descalzo, -za *adj* barefoot
descansar *v* rest — **descanso** *nm* rest; landing; intermission, halftime
descargar *v* unload; discharge — **descarga** *nf* unloading; discharge — **des-**

cargo *nm* unloading; discharge; defense

descender *v* go down; lower; be descended from — **descendiencia** *nf* descendants *pl*; lineage, descent — **descendiente** *nmf* descendant — **descenso** *nm* descent; drop, fall

desconfiar *v* distrust — **desconfiado, -da** *adj* distrustful — **desconfianza** *nf* distrust

desconocer *v* not know, fail to recognize — **desconocido, -da** *adj* unknown — **desconocido, -da** *n* stranger

descontar *v* discount

descortés *adj* (**-teses**) rude — **descortesía** *nf* discourtesy, rudeness

descremado, -da *adj* nonfat, skim

describir *v* describe — **descripción** *nf* (**-ciones**) description — **descriptivo, -va** *adj* descriptive

descubierto, -ta *adj* exposed, uncovered — **descubierto** *nm* deficit, overdraft

descubrir *v* discover; reveal

descuento *nm* discount

descuidar *v* neglect — **descuidarse** *vr* be careless; let oneself go

desde *prep* from, since; ~ **luego** of course

desdén *nm* scorn, disdain — **desdeñar** *v* scorn

desear *v* wish, want

desempeñar *v* play (a role); redeem, reclaim

desempeñarse *vr* get out of debt

desempleo *nm* unemployment

desenlace *nm* ending, outcome

deseo *nm* desire

desequilibrar *v* throw off balance — **desequilibrio** *nm* imbalance

desesperar *v* exasperate; lose hope — **desesperarse** *vr* become exasperated — **desesperación** *nf* (**-ciones**) desperation, despair

desfallecer *v* weaken; faint

desfavorable *adj* unfavorable

desgracia *nf* misfortune

deshacer *v* undo; destroy, ruin; dissolve; break, cancel — **deshacerse** *vr* come undone

deshonesto, -ta *adj* dishonest

desidia *nf* indolence; sloppiness

designar *v* designate — **designación** *nf* (**-ciones**) appointment

desigual *adj* unequal; uneven — **desigualdad** *nf* inequality

desilusionar *v* disappoint, disillusion — **desilusión** *nf* (**-siones**) disappointment, disillusionment

desinhibido, -da *adj* uninhibited

desistir *v* stop, desist; ~ **de** give up

desleal *adj* disloyal

desmayar *v* lose heart — **desmayarse** *vr* faint — **desmayo** *nm* faint

desmedido, -da *adj* excessive

desmesurado, -da *adj* excessive

desnudar *v* undress, strip — **desnudarse** *vr* get undressed — **desnudo, -da** *adj* nude, naked — **desnudo** *nm* nude

desnutrición *nf* (**-ciones**) malnutrition

desocupar *v* empty, vacate — **desocupado, -da** *adj* vacant, unoccupied; unemployed

desodorante *adj* & *nm* deodorant

desorden *nm* (**desórdenes**) disorder, mess — **desordenado, -da** *adj* untidy

desorganizar *v* disorganize — **desorganización** *nf* (**-ciones**) disorganization

despacio *adv* slowly

despectivo, -va *adj* pejorative; contemptuous

despedir *v* see off; dismiss, fire; emit — **despedirse** *vr* say good-bye — **despedida** *nf* farewell, good-bye

despeinar *v* ruffle (hair) — **despeinado, -da** *adj* disheveled, unkempt

despertar *v* awaken, wake up; rouse — **despertador** *nm* alarm clock

despierto, -ta *adj* awake
desplazar *v* displace — **desplazarse** *vr* travel
desprender *v* detach, remove; give off — **desprenderse** *vr* come off; be inferred, follow
desprovisto, -ta *adj* ~ **de** lacking in; devoid of
después *adv* afterward; then, next
destacar *v* emphasize; stand out — **destacado, -da** *adj* outstanding
destapar *v* open, uncover
destinar *v* assign, allocate; appoint — **destinado, -da** *adj* destined — **destinatario, -ria** *n* addressee — **destino** *nm* destiny; destination
destreza *nf* skill, dexterity
destrozar *v* destroy, wreck
destrucción *nf* (-**ciones**) destruction — **destructivo, -va** *adj* destructive — **destruir** *v* destroy
desusado, -da *adj* obsolete; unusual — **desuso** *nm* disuse
desvanecer *v* make disappear — **desvanecerse** *vr* vanish; faint
desventaja *nf* disadvantage
desvestir *v* undress — **desvestirse** *vr* get undressed
desviación *nf* (-**ciones**) deviation; detour — **desviar** *v* divert, deflect — **desviarse** *vr* branch off; stray — **desvío** *nm* diversion, detour
detener *v* arrest, detain; stop; delay — **detenerse** *vr* stop; linger
detergente *nm* detergent
deteriorar *v* damage — **deteriorarse** *vr* wear out, deteriorate — **deterioro** *nm* deterioration, damage
determinar *v* determine; bring about; decide — **determinarse** *vr* decide — **determinación** *nf* (-**ciones**) determination — **determinado, -da** *adj* determined; specific
detrás *adv* behind
detrimento *nm* harm; **en** ~ **de** to the detriment of

deuda *nf* debt — **deudor, -dora** *n* debtor
devaluar *v* devalue — **devaluarse** *vr* depreciate
devenir *v* come about
devolver *v* give back; refund, pay back; bring up, vomit — **devolverse** *vr* return, come back
diagnosticar *v* diagnose — **diagnóstico, -ca** *adj* diagnostic — **diagnóstico** *nm* diagnosis
diagonal *adj & nf* diagonal
diagrama *nm* diagram
dialecto *nm* dialect
dialogar *v* have a talk — **diálogo** *nm* dialogue
diario, -ria *adj* daily — **diario** *nm* diary; newspaper
dibujar *v* draw; portray — **dibujante** *nmf* draftsman, draftswoman — **dibujo** *nm* drawing
diccionario *nm* dictionary
diciembre *nm* December
dictar *v* dictate; pronounce, deliver — **dictado** *nm* dictation
diecinueve *adj & nm* nineteen
dieciocho *adj & nm* eighteen
dieciséis *adj & nm* sixteen
diecisiete *adj & nm* seventeen
diente *nm* tooth; prong, tine
diestra *nf* right hand — **diestro, -tra** *adj* right; skillful
dieta *nf* diet — **dietético, -ca** *adj* dietetic, dietary
diez *adj & nm* (**dieces**) ten
diferencia *nf* difference — **diferenciar** *v* distinguish between — **diferenciarse** *vr* differ — **diferente** *adj* different
diferir *v* postpone; differ
difícil *adj* difficult — **dificultad** *nf* difficulty — **dificultar** *v* hinder, obstruct
difundir *v* spread (out); broadcast
difusión *nf* (-**siones**) spreading
digerir *v* digest — **digerible** *adj* digestible — **digestión** *nf* (-**tiones**) digestion

dígito *nm* digit — **digital** *adj* digital

digresión *nf* (**-ciones**) digression

dilatar *v* expand, dilate; prolong; postpone

dilema *nm* dilemma

dimensión *nf* (**-siones**) dimension

diminuto, -ta *adj* minute, tiny

dimitir *v* resign — **dimisión** *nf* (**-siones**) resignation

dinámico, -ca *adj* dynamic

dinero *nm* money

dios, diosa *n* god, goddess *f* — **Dios** *nm* God

diploma *nm* diploma — **diplomado, -da** *adj* qualified, trained

diplomacia *nf* diplomacy — **diplomático, -ca** *adj* diplomatic — **diplomático, -ca** *n* diplomat

diputado, -da *n* delegate

dirección *nf* (**-ciones**) address; direction; management; steering — **direccional** *nf* turn signal, blinker — **directivo, -va** *adj* managerial — **directivo, -va** *n* manager, director — **directo, -ta** *adj* direct; straight — **director, -tora** *n* director, manager; conductor — **directorio** *nm* directory — **directriz** *nf* (**-trices**) guideline

dirigir *v* direct, lead; address; aim; conduct — **dirigirse a** *vr phr* go towards

disciplinar *v* discipline — **disciplina** *nf* discipline

discípulo, -la *n* disciple, follower

disco *nm* disc, disk; discus

discoteca *nf* disco, discotheque

discreción *nf* (**-ciones**) discretion

discreto, -ta *adj* discreet

discriminar *v* discriminate against; distinguish — **discriminación** *nf* (**-ciones**) discrimination

disculpar *v* excuse, pardon — **disculparse** *vr* apologize — **disculpa** *nf* apology; excuse

discurrir *v* pass, go by; ponder, reflect

discurso *nm* speech, discourse

discutir *v* discuss; dispute; argue — **dis-cusión** *nf* (**-siones**) discussion; argument

diseñar *v* design — **diseñador, -dora** *n* designer — **diseño** *nm* design

disertación *nf* (**-ciones**) lecture; dissertation

disfrutar *v* enjoy; have a good time

disgustar *v* upset, annoy — **disgustarse** *vr* get annoyed; fall out — **disgusto** *nm* annoyance, displeasure; quarrel

disimular *v* conceal, hide; pretend — **disimulo** *nm* pretense

disipar *v* dispel; squander

diskette *nm* floppy disk, diskette

dislexia *nf* dyslexia — **disléxico, -ca** *adj* dyslexic

disminuir *v* reduce; decrease, drop — **disminución** *nf* (**-ciones**) decrease

disociar *v* dissociate

disolver *v* dissolve — **disolverse** *vr* dissolve

dispensar *v* dispense, distribute; excuse

dispersar *v* disperse, scatter — **dispersarse** *vr* disperse, scatter — **dispersión** *nf* (**-siones**) scattering

disponer *v* arrange, lay out; decide, stipulate — **disponerse a** *vr phr* be ready to — **disponibilidad** *nf* availability

disposición *nf* (**-ciones**) arrangement; aptitude; order, provision (in law)

dispositivo *nm* device, mechanism

dispuesto, -ta *adj* prepared, ready

disputar *v* argue; compete — **disputa** *nf* dispute, argument

distanciar *v* space out — **distanciarse** *vr* grow apart — **distancia** *nf* distance — **distante** *adj* distant

distinguir *v* distinguish — **distinguirse** *vr* distinguish oneself, stand out — **distinción** *nf* (**-ciones**) distinction — **distintivo, -va** *adj* distinctive — **distinto, -ta** *adj* different; distinct, clear

distorsión *nf* (**-siones**) distortion

distraer *v* distract; entertain — **distraerse** *vr* get distracted; amuse oneself

— **distracción** *nf* (**-ciones**) amusement; absentmindedness

distribuir *v* distribute — **distribución** *nf* (**-ciones**) distribution — **distribuidor, -dora** *n* distributor

disturbio *nm* disturbance

disuadir *v* dissuade, discourage — **disuasivo, -va** *adj* deterrent

diurno, -na *adj* day, daytime

divagar *v* digress

diversidad *nf* diversity

diversificar *v* diversify

diversión *nf* (**-siones**) fun, entertainment

diverso, -sa *adj* diverse

divertir *v* entertain — **divertirse** *vr* enjoy oneself, have fun

dividendo *nm* dividend

dividir *v* divide; distribute

divisar *v* discern, make out

división *nf* (**-siones**) division — **divisor** *nm* denominator

divorciar *v* divorce — **divorciarse** *vr* get a divorce — **divorciado, -da** *n* divorcé *m*, divorcée *f* — **divorcio** *nm* divorce

divulgar *v* divulge, reveal; spread, circulate

doblar *v* double; fold; turn; dub (a film) — **doblarse** *vr* double over — **dobladillo** *nm* hem — **doble** *adj & nm* double — **doble** *nmf* stand-in, double

doce *adj & nm* twelve — **docena** *nf* dozen

docente *adj* teaching

dócil *adj* docile

doctor, -tora *n* doctor — **doctorado** *nm* doctorate

doctrina *nf* doctrine

documentar *v* document — **documentación** *nf* (**-ciones**) documentation — **documental** *adj & nm* documentary — **documento** *nm* document

dogma *nm* dogma — **dogmático, -ca** *adj* dogmatic

dólar *nm* dollar

doler *v* hurt — **dolerse de** *vr phr* complain about — **dolor** *nm* pain; grief

domicilio *nm* home, residence

dominar *v* dominate, control; master — **dominarse** *vr* control oneself — **dominación** *nf* (**-ciones**) domination

domingo *nm* Sunday — **dominical** *adj* Sunday; **periódico** ~ Sunday newspaper

dominio *nm* authority; mastery; domain

donación *nf* (**-ciones**) donation

donar *v* donate — **donante** *nmf* donor — **donativo** *nm* donation

donde *conj* where ~ *prep* over by

dónde *adv* where

dondequiera *adv* anywhere

doquier *adv* por ~ everywhere

dormir *v* sleep; put to sleep — **dormirse** *vr* fall asleep — **dormitorio** *nm* bedroom; dormitory

dos *adj & nm* two — **doscientos, -tas** *adj* two hundred — **doscientos** *nms & pl* two hundred

dosis *nfs & pl* dose, dosage

dotar *v* provide, equip — **dotación** *nf* (**-ciones**) endowment, funding; personnel

drama *nm* drama — **dramático, -ca** *adj* dramatic — **dramatizar** *v* dramatize — **dramaturgo, -ga** *n* dramatist, playwright

drástico, -ca *adj* drastic

droguería *nf* drugstore

dual *adj* dual

ducha *nf* shower — **ducharse** *vr* take a shower

dudar *v* doubt; ~ **en** hesitate to — **duda** *nf* doubt — **dudoso, -sa** *adj* doubtful; questionable

duelo *nm* duel; mourning

dueño, -na *n* owner; landlord, landlady

dulce *adj* sweet; fresh; mild, gentle — **dulce** *nm* candy, sweet — **dulzura** *nf* sweetness

duplicar *v* double; duplicate, copy —

duplicado, -da *adj* duplicate — **duplicado** *nm* copy
duración *nf* (**-ciones**) duration, length
duradero, -ra *adj* durable, lasting
durante *prep* during

durar *v* endure, last
durazno *nm* peach
duro *adv* hard — **duro, -ra** *adj* hard; harsh — **dureza** *nf* hardness; harshness

E

e¹ *nf* e, fifth letter of the Spanish alphabet
e² *conj* and
echar *v* throw, cast; expel, dismiss
eclipse *nm* eclipse
eco *nm* echo
ecología *nf* ecology — **ecológico, -ca** *adj* ecological — **ecologista** *nmf* ecologist
economía *nf* economy; economics — **economico, -ca** *adj* economic, economical; inexpensive — **economista** *nmf* economist — **economizar** *v* save
ecuatoriano, -na *adj* Ecuadorian, Ecuadorean, Ecuadoran
edad *nf* age; **Edad Media** Middle Ages *pl*
edición *nf* (**-ciones**) publishing, publication; edition
edificar *v* build — **edificio** *nm* building
editar *v* publish — **editor, -tora** *n* publisher — **editorial** *adj* publishing — **editorial** *nm* editorial
educar *v* educate; bring up, raise — **educación** *nf* (**-ciones**) education — **educado, -da** *adj* polite
efectivo, -va *adj* effective; real — **efectivo** *nm* cash — **efectivamente** *adv* really; yes, indeed — **efecto** *nm* effect — **efectuar** *v* bring about, carry out
eficaz *adj* (**-caces**) effective; efficient
egipcio, -cia *adj* Egyptian
egoísmo *nm* egoism — **egoísta** *adj* egoistic — **egoísta** *nmf* egoist
ejecutivo, -va *adj* & *n* executive
ejemplo *nm* example
ejercicio *nm* exercise

ejército *nm* army
el, la *art* (**los, las**) the — **el** *pron* the one
él *pron* he, him
elaborar *v* manufacture, produce
elástico, -ca *adj* elastic — **elástico** *nm* elastic
elección *nf* (**-ciones**) election; choice
electricidad *nf* electricity — **eléctrico, -ca** *adj* electric, electrical — **electricista** *nmf* electrician
electrodoméstico *nm* electric appliance
electrónico, -ca *adj* electronic — **electrónica** *nf* electronics
elefante, -ta *n* elephant
elegante *adj* elegant — **elegancia** *nf* elegance
elegir *v* elect; choose, select
elemento *nm* element — **elemental** *adj* elementary, basic; fundamental
elevar *v* raise, lift — **elevación** *nf* (**-ciones**) elevation
eliminar *v* eliminate — **eliminación** *nf* (**-ciones**) elimination
ella *pron* she, her — **ello** *pron* it — **ellos, ellas** *pron pl* they, them; **de ellos, de ellas** theirs
embajada *nf* embassy — **embajador, -dora** *n* ambassador
embarazada *adj* pregnant — **embarazo** *nm* pregnancy — **embarazar** *v* make pregnant
embarazoso, -sa *adj* embarrassing
embarcar *v* load — **embarcación** *nf* (**-ciones**) boat, craft
embargo *nm* embargo; **sin ~** nevertheless

embarque *nm* loading, boarding

embellecer *v* embellish, beautify

emborracharse *vr* get drunk

embrague *nm* clutch — **embragar** *v* engage the clutch

embriagado, -da *adj* intoxicated, drunk — **embriagarse** *vr* get drunk

embrión *nm* (**-briones**) embryo

embutido *nm* sausage, cold meat

emergencia *nf* emergency

emigrar *v* emigrate; migrate — **emigración** *nf* (**-ciones**) emigration; migration — **emigrante** *adj & nmf* emigrant

emisora *nf* radio station

emoción *nf* (**-ciones**) emotion — **emocionante** *adj* moving, touching; exciting, thrilling — **emocionar** *v* move, touch; excite, thrill — **emocionarse** *vr* be moved; get excited — **emotivo, -va** *adj* emotional; moving

empacar *v* pack

empanada *nf* pie, turnover

empanar *v* bread

empapar *v* soak — **empaparse** *vr* get soaking wet

empaquetar *v* pack, package

emparedado, -da *adj* walled in, confined — **emparedado** *nm* sandwich

empaste *nm* filling

empatar *v* result in a draw, be tied — **empate** *nm* draw, tie

empedernido, -da *adj* inveterate, hardened

empeño *nm* determination, effort

empeorar *v* get worse; make worse

empequeñecer *v* diminish, make smaller

empezar *v* start, begin

empinar *v* raise — **empinarse** *vr* stand on tiptoe

empírico, -ca *adj* empirical

emplear *v* employ, use — **emplearse** *vr* get a job; be used — **empleado, -da** *n* employee — **empleo** *nm* occupation, job

empobrecer *v* impoverish — **empobrecerse** *vr* become poor

empolvarse *vr* powder one's face

empresa *nf* company, firm — **empresario, -ria** *n* businessman, businesswoman

empujar *v* push — **empuje** *nm* impetus, drive — **empujón** *nm* (**-jones**) push, shove

en *prep* in; into, inside (of); on

enamorar *v* win the love of — **enamorarse** *vr* fall in love — **enamorado, -da** *adj* in love — **enamorado, -da** *n* lover, sweetheart

enano, -na *adj & n* dwarf

encabezar *v* head, lead; title

encaje *nm* lace

encarecer *v* increase, raise — **encarecerse** *vr* become more expensive

encargar *v* put in charge of; order — **encargado, -da** *adj* in charge — **encargado, -da** *n* manager, person in charge — **encargo** *nm* errand; assignment, task; order

encender *v* light, set fire to; switch on, start; arouse — **encendido, -da** *adj* lit, on

encerrar *v* lock up, shut away

encestar *v* score

enchufar *v* plug in, connect — **enchufe** *nm* plug, socket

encía *nf* gum

enciclopedia *nf* encyclopedia — **enciclopédico, -ca** *adj* encyclopedic

encima *adv* on top; **por ∼ de** above, beyond

encinta *adj* pregnant

encoger *v* shrink — **encogerse** *vr* shrink; cower, cringe

encontrar *v* find — **encontrarse** *vr* meet

encubrir *v* conceal, cover (up)

encuentro *nm* meeting, encounter

encuestar *v* poll, survey — **encuesta** *nf* investigation, inquiry; survey — **encuestador, -dora** *n* pollster

enderezar *v* straighten (out); put upright, stand on end

endeudarse *vr* go into debt — **endeudado, -da** *adj* indebted, in debt

endosar *v* endorse — **endoso** *nm* endorsement

endulzar *v* sweeten — **endulzante** *nm* sweetener

endurecer *v* harden

enemigo, -ga *adj* hostile — **enemigo, -ga** *n* enemy — **enemistad** *nf* enmity — **enemistar** *v* make enemies of

energía *nf* energy

enero *nm* January

enfadar *v* annoy, make angry — **enfadarse** *vr* get annoyed — **enfado** *nm* anger, annoyance

énfasis *nms & pl* emphasis

enfermar *v* make sick; get sick — **enfermedad** *nf* sickness, disease — **enfermería** *nf* infirmary — **enfermero, -ra** *n* nurse — **enfermo, -ma** *adj* sick — **enfermo, -ma** *n* sick person, patient

enflaquecer *v* lose weight

enfocar *v* focus; consider

enfrentar *v* confront, face; bring face to face — **enfrente** *adv* opposite

enfriar *v* chill, cool — **enfriarse** *vr* get cold

enfurecer *v* infuriate — **enfurecerse** *vr* fly into a rage

enganchar *v* hook, snag, catch

engañar *v* trick, deceive; cheat on, be unfaithful to — **engaño** *nm* deception, deceit — **engañoso, -sa** *adj* deceptive, deceitful

engordar *v* fatten; gain weight

engrasar *v* lubricate, grease — **engrase** *nm* lubrication

engreído, -da *adj* conceited

enigma *nm* enigma — **enigmático, -ca** *adj* enigmatic

enjabonar *v* soap (up), lather

enjaular *v* cage; jail

enjuagar *v* rinse — **enjuague** *nm* rinse

enlace *nm* bond, link

enlatar *v* can

enloquecer *v* drive crazy — **enloquecerse** *vr* go crazy

enmascarar *v* mask

enmudecer *v* silence; become silent

enojar *v* anger; annoy — **enojo** *nm* anger; annoyance

enorme *adj* enormous

enredo *nm* tangle; confusion, mess

enriquecer *v* enrich — **enriquecerse** *vr* get rich

enrojecer *v* redden — **enrojecerse** *vr* blush

enrollar *v* roll up, coil

enroscar *v* roll up; screw in

ensalada *nf* salad

ensanchar *v* widen; expand — **ensanche** *nm* widening

ensangrentado, -da *adj* bloody, bloodstained

ensayar *v* rehearse; try out, test — **ensayo** *nm* essay; trial, test; rehearsal

enseguida *adv* right away, immediately

enseñar *v* teach; show — **enseñanza** *nf* education; teaching

ensordecer *v* deafen; go deaf — **ensordecedor, -dora** *adj* deafening

ensortijar *v* curl

ensuciar *v* soil — **ensuciarse** *vr* get dirty

entender *v* understand — **entendido, -da** *adj* understood

enterar *v* inform — **enterarse** *vr* find out, learn — **enterado, -da** *adj* well-informed

enternecer *v* move, touch

entero, -ra *adj* whole; absolute, total; intact — **entero** *nm* integer, whole number

enterrar *v* bury

entidad *nf* entity; body, organization

entierro *nm* burial; funeral

entonar *v* sing, intone; be in tune

entonces *adv* then

entorpecer *v* hinder, obstruct; numb

entrada *nf* entrance, entry; ticket; inning (in baseball)

entrar *v* enter; begin; introduce, bring in

entre *prep* between; among

entreabrir *v* leave ajar — **entreabierto, -ta** *adj* half-open, ajar

entrecortado, -da *adj* faltering, labored

entregar *v* deliver, hand over — **entregarse** *vr* surrender — **entrega** *nf* delivery; dedication, devotion

entrenar *v* train, drill — **entrenarse** *vr* train — **entrenador, -dora** *n* trainer, coach — **entranamiento** *nm* training

entretanto *adv* meanwhile

entretener *v* entertain; distract — **entretenerse** *vr* amuse oneself — **entretenido, -da** *adj* entertaining — **entretenimiento** *nm* entertainment, amusement; pastime

entrevistar *v* interview — **entrevista** *nf* interview — **entrevistador, -dora** *n* interviewer

entristecer *v* sadden

entrometerse *vr* interfere — **entrometido, -da** *adj* meddling, nosy — **entrometido, -da** *n* meddler

entusiasmar *v* fill with enthusiasm — **entusiasmarse** *vr* get excited — **entusiasmo** *nm* enthusiasm — **entusiasta** *adj* enthusiastic — **entusiasta** *nmf* enthusiast

enumerar *v* enumerate, list — **enumeración** *nf* (**-ciones**) enumeration, count

envasar *v* package; bottle, can — **envase** *nm* packaging; container; jar, bottle, can

envejecer *v* age — **envejecido, -da** *adj* aged, old — **envejecimiento** *nm* aging

envenenar *v* poison — **envenenamiento** *nm* poisoning

enviar *v* send — **enviado, -da** *n* envoy, correspondent

envidiar *v* envy — **envidia** *nf* envy, jealousy — **envidioso, -sa** *adj* jealous, envious

envío *nm* sending, shipment; remittance

enviudar *v* be widowed

envolver *v* wrap — **envoltorio** *nm or* **envoltura** *nf* wrapping, wrapper

enyesar *v* put in a plaster cast

enzima *nf* enzyme

épico, -ca *adj* epic — **épica** *nf* epic

epidemia *nf* epidemic — **epidémico, -ca** *adj* epidemic

episodio *nm* episode

época *nf* epoch, period; season

equilibrar *v* balance — **equilibrado, -da** *adj* well-balanced — **equilibrio** *nm* balance, equilibrium; good sense

equipaje *nm* baggage, luggage

equipar *v* equip

equipo *nm* equipment; team, crew

equitación *nf* (**-ciones**) horseback riding

equivaler *v* be equivalent — **equivalencia** *nf* equivalence — **equivalente** *adj & nm* equivalent

equivocar *v* mistake, confuse — **equivocarse** *vr* make a mistake — **equivocación** *nf* (**-ciones**) error, mistake — **equivocado, -da** *adj* mistaken, wrong

era *nf* era

erección *nf* (**-ciones**) erection

erizo *nm* hedgehog

ermitaño, -ña *n* hermit

erosionar *v* erode — **erosión** *nf* (**-siones**) erosion

erótico, -ca *adj* erotic

erradicar *v* eradicate

errar *v* miss; be wrong, be mistaken; wander — **errado, -da** *adj* wrong, mistaken

error *nm* error — **erróneo, -nea** *adj* erroneous, mistaken

eructar *v* belch, burp — **eructo** *nm* belch, burp

erudito, -ta *adj* erudite, learned

erupción *nf* (**-ciones**) eruption; rash

escalar *v* climb, scale; escalate — **escala** *nf* scale; ladder; stopover (as of an airplane) — **escalador, -dora** *n* mountain climber

escalera *nf* stairs *pl*, staircase; ladder

escalinata *nf* flight of stairs

escalofrío *nm* shiver, chill — **escalofriante** *adj* chilling, horrifying

escalón *nm* (**-lones**) step, rung

escama *nf* scale (as of fish); flake (of skin)

escandalizar *v* scandalize — **escandalizarse** *vr* be shocked — **escándalo** *nm* scandal; scene, commotion — **escandaloso, -sa** *adj* shocking, scandalous; noisy

escandinavo, -va *adj* Scandinavian

escáner *nm* scanner

escapar *v* escape, run away — **escaparse** *vr* escape

escape *nm* leak; exhaust

escarabajo *nm* beetle

escarbar *v* dig, scratch, poke

escarcha *nf* frost

escarpado, -da *adj* steep

escasear *v* be scarce — **escasez** *nf* (**-seces**) shortage, scarcity — **escaso, -sa** *adj* scarce

escena *nf* scene; stage — **escenario** *nm* setting, scene; stage

escepticismo *nm* skepticism — **escéptico, -ca** *adj* skeptical — **escéptico, -ca** *n* skeptic

esclavo, -va *n* slave — **esclavitud** *nf* slavery — **esclavizar** *v* enslave

escoba *nf* broom

escocés, -cesa *adj* (**-ceses** *m*) Scottish; tartan, plaid — **escocés** *nm* (**-ceses**) Scotch (whiskey)

escoger *v* choose — **escogido, -da** *adj* choice, select

escolar *adj* school — **escolar** *nmf* student, pupil

escolta *nmf* escort — **escoltar** *v* escort, accompany

escombros *nmpl* ruins, rubble

esconder *v* hide, conceal — **esconderse** *vr* hide — **escondidas** *nfpl*

hide-and-seek — **escondite** *nm* hiding place; hide-and-seek

escopeta *nf* shotgun

escorpión *nm* (**-piones**) scorpion

escote *nm* (low) neckline

escribir *v* write — **escribirse** *vr* correspond; be spelled — **escrito, -ta** *adj* written — **escritos** *nmpl* writings — **escritor, -tora** *n* writer — **escritorio** *nm* desk — **escritura** *nf* handwriting

escuadra *nf* square (instrument)

escuchar *v* listen; listen to; hear

escudo *nm* shield

escuela *nf* school

escultor, -tora *n* sculptor — **escultura** *nf* sculpture

escupir *v* spit

escurrir *v* drain — **escurrirse** *vr* drain — **escurridor** *nm* dish drainer

ese, esa *adj* (**esos** *m*) that, those

ése, ésa *pron* (**ésos** *m*) that one, those ones *pl*

esencia *nf* essence — **esencial** *adj* essential

esfera *nf* sphere — **esférico, -ca** *adj* spherical

esforzar *v* strain — **esforzarse** *vr* make an effort — **esfuerzo** *nm* effort

esgrima *nf* fencing

eslabón *nm* (**-bones**) link

eslavo, -va *adj* Slavic

eslogan *nm* (**-lóganes**) slogan

esmalte *nm* enamel ~ **de uñas** nail polish

esmerado, -da *adj* careful

esmeralda *nf* emerald

esmerarse *vr* take great care

esnob *nmf* (**esnobs**) snob — **esnob** *adj* snobbish

eso *pron* (*neuter*) that

espaciar *v* space out, spread out — **espacial** *adj* space — **espacio** *nm* space — **espacioso, -sa** *adj* spacious

espada *nf* sword

espagueti *nm* *or* **espaguetis** *nmpl* spaghetti

espalda *nf* back

espantar *v* scare, frighten — **espantarse** *vr* become frightened — **espantapájaros** *nms & pl* scarecrow — **espanto** *nm* fright, fear — **espantoso, -sa** *adj* frightening, horrific; awful, terrible

español, -ñola *adj* Spanish — **español** *nm* Spanish (language)

esparcir *v* scatter, spread

espárrago *nm* asparagus

especia *nf* spice

especial *adj & nm* special — **especialidad** *nf* specialty — **especialista** *nmf* specialist — **especialmente** *adv* especially

especie *nf* species; type, kind

especificar *v* specify — **especificación** *nf* (**-ciones**) specification — **específico, -ca** *adj* specific

espectáculo *nm* show, performance; spectacle, view — **espectacular** *adj* spectacular — **espectador, -dora** *n* spectator

espectro *nm* spectrum; ghost

especulación *nf* (**-ciones**) speculation

espejo *nm* mirror — **espejismo** *nm* mirage; illusion

esperar *v* wait; wait for; expect — **espera** *nf* wait — **esperanza** *nf* hope, expectation — **esperanzado, -da** *adj* hopeful — **esperanzar** *v* give hope to

esperma *nmf* sperm

espesar *v* thicken — **espeso, -sa** *adj* thick, heavy — **espesor** *nm* thickness, density — **espesura** *nf* thickness

espiar *v* spy; spy on — **espía** *nmf* spy

espiga *nf* ear

espina *nf* thorn; (fish) bone; ~ **dorsal** spine, backbone

espinaca *nf* spinach (plant); ~**s** *nfpl* spinach (food)

espinilla *nf* shin; blackhead, pimple

espinoso, -sa *adj* prickly; bony

espionaje *nm* espionage

espiral *adj & nf* spiral

espirar *v* breathe out, exhale

espíritu *nm* spirit — **espiritual** *adj* spiritual — **espiritualidad** *nf* spirituality

espléndido, -da *adj* splendid — **esplendor** *nm* splendor

esponja *nf* sponge — **esponjoso, -sa** *adj* spongy

espontáneo, -nea *adj* spontaneous

esposo, -sa *n* spouse, wife, husband

espuma *nf* foam, froth; head — **espumoso, -sa** *adj* foamy, frothy; sparkling

esqueleto *nm* skeleton

esquema *nf* outline, sketch

esquí *nm* ski; skiing — **esquiador, -dora** *n* skier — **esquiar** *v* ski

esquina *nf* corner

esquivar *v* evade, dodge; avoid — **esquivo, -va** *adj* shy, elusive

estabilizar *v* stabilize

establecer *v* establish — **establecerse** *vr* establish oneself, settle — **establecimiento** *nm* establishment

establo *nm* stable

estación *nf* (**-ciones**) season; ~ **de servicio** gas station — **estacionar** *v* park — **estacionamiento** *nm* parking

estadía *nf* stay

estadio *nm* stadium; phase, stage

estadista *nmf* statesman

estadística *nf* statistics

estado *nm* state; ~ **civil** marital status

estadounidense *adj & nmf* American

estafar *v* swindle, defraud — **estafa** *nf* swindle, fraud — **estafador, -dora** *n* cheat, swindler

estallar *v* explode

estampilla *nf* stamp

estándar *adj & nm* standard

estar *v aux* be — **estar** *v* be; be at home; stay, remain

estatua *nf* statue

estatura *nf* height

estatus *nm* status, prestige

estatuto *nm* statute

este[1], esta *adj* (**estos** *m*) this, these

este² *adj* eastern, east — **este** *nm* east; east wind; **el Este** the Orient

éste, ésta *pron* (**éstos** *m*) this one, these ones *pl*; the latter

estereofónico, -ca *adj* stereophonic

estereotipo *nm* stereotype

estéril *adj* sterile; infertile

estética *nf* aesthetics

estigmatizar *v* stigmatize

estilo *nm* style; fashion, manner — **estilista** *nmf* stylist

estimar *v* esteem, respect; value, estimate; consider

estimular *v* stimulate; encourage — **estimulante** *adj* stimulating — **estimulante** *nm* stimulant — **estímulo** *nm* stimulus

esto *pron* (*neuter*) this

estoico, -ca *adj* stoic, stoical — **estoico, -ca** *n* stoic

estómago *nm* stomach

estornudar *v* sneeze

estrategia *nf* strategy

estrato *nm* stratum

estrechar *v* narrow; strengthen (a bond); embrace — **estrecho, -cha** *adj* tight, narrow; close

estrella *nf* star; destiny

estrellar *v* crash

estremecer *v* cause to shudder; tremble, shake — **estremecerse** *vr* shudder, shiver

estrenar *v* use for the first time; premiere, open — **estrenarse** *vr* make one's debut

estrés *nm* (**estreses**) stress

estricto, -ta *adj* strict

estrofa *nf* stanza, verse

estructura *nf* structure — **estructural** *adj* structural

estudiar *v* study — **estudiante** *nmf* student — **estudio** *nm* study; studio, office; **~s** *nmpl* studies, education

estupendo, -da *adj* stupendous, marvelous

etapa *nf* stage, phase

ética *nf* ethics

etimología *nf* etymology

etíope *adj* Ethiopian

etiqueta *nf* tag, label; etiquette; **de ~** formal, dressy

étnico, -ca *adj* ethnic

Eucaristía *nf* Eucharist, communion

eufemismo *nm* euphemism

europeo, -pea *adj* European

eutanasia *nf* euthanasia

evacuar *v* evacuate, vacate; have a bowel movement — **evacuación** *nf* (**-ciones**) evacuation

evadir *v* evade, avoid

evaluar *v* evaluate

evangelio *nm* gospel

evasivo, -va *adj* evasive

evento *nm* event

eventual *adj* temporary; possible

evidencia *nf* evidence, proof — **evidenciar** *v* demonstrate, show — **evidente** *adj* evident

evitar *v* avoid; prevent

evolución *nf* (**-ciones**) evolution

exacto, -ta *adj* precise, exact

exagerar *v* exaggerate — **exageración** *nf* (**-ciones**) exaggeration

examen *nm* (**exámenes**) examination, test; investigation — **examinar** *v* examine; study, inspect — **examinarse** *vr* take an exam

exceder *v* exceed, surpass — **excederse** *vr* go too far — **excedente** *adj* & *nm* surplus, excess

excelente *adj* excellent

excepción *nf* (**-ciones**) exception — **excepcional** *adj* exceptional

excepto *prep* except (for)

exceso *nm* excess — **excesivo, -va** *adj* excessive

excitar *v* excite, arouse — **excitación** *nf* (**-ciones**) excitement, agitation, arousal

exclamar *v* exclaim — **exclamación** *nf* (**-ciones**) exclamation

excluir *v* exclude — **exclusión** *nf* (**-siones**) exclusion — **exclusivo, -va** *adj* exclusive

excursión *nf* (**-siones**) excursion — **excursionista** *nmf* tourist, sightseer; hiker

excusar *v* excuse; exempt — **excusa** *nf* excuse; apology

exento, -ta *adj* exempt

exequias *nfpl* funeral rites

exhaustivo, -va *adj* exhaustive

exhibir *v* exhibit, show — **exhibición** *nf* (**-ciones**) exhibition

exigir *v* demand, require — **exigencia** *nf* demand, requirement

existir *v* exist — **existencia** *nf* existence; ∼s *nfpl* goods, stock

éxito *nm* success, hit

expectativa *nf* expectation, hope; ∼s *nfpl* prospects

expedición *nf* (**-ciones**) expedition

experiencia *nf* experience

experimentar *v* experiment; experiment with, test out; experience, feel — **experimento** *nm* experiment

experto, -ta *adj & n* expert

explicar *v* explain — **explicarse** *vr* understand

explícito, -ta *adj* explicit

explosión *nf* (**-siones**) explosion; outburst (as of laughter) — **explosivo, -va** *adj* explosive

explotar *v* exploit; operate, run (as a factory), work (a mine); explode — **explotación** *nf* (**-ciones**) exploitation; operating, running

exponer *v* expose; explain, set out; exhibit, display — **exponerse a** *vr phr* expose oneself to, submit oneself to

exportar *v* export

exposición *nf* (**-ciones**) exposure; exhibition; exposition, setting out — **expositor, -tora** *n* exhibitor; exponent

expresar *v* express — **expresión** *nf* (**-siones**) expression — **expresivo, -va** *adj* expressive; affectionate

expulsar *v* expel, eject — **expulsión** *nf* (**-siones**) expulsion

extender *v* spread out; draw up, write out — **extenderse** *vr* extend, spread; last — **extendido, -da** *adj* widespread; outstretched

extensión *nf* (**-siones**) extension; expanse; range, extent — **extenso, -sa** *adj* extensive

exterior *adj* exterior, external; foreign — **exterior** *nm* outside; **en el** ∼ abroad

externo, -na *adj* external

extinguir *v* extinguish; end, wipe out — **extinción** *nf* (**-ciones**) extinction

extra *adv* extra — **extra** *adj* additional; top-quality — **extra** *nmf* extra (in movies); *nm* extra (expense)

extraer *v* extract — **extracción** *nf* (**-ciones**) extraction

extranjero, -ra *adj* foreign — **extranjero, -ra** *n* foreigner — **extranjero** *nm* foreign countries *pl*

extrañar *v* miss — **extrañarse** *vr* be surprised — **extraño, -ña** *adj* foreign; strange, odd — **extraño, -ña** *n* stranger

extraordinario, -ria *adj* extraordinary

extremidad *nf* tip, end; ∼es *nfpl* extremities — **extremista** *adj & nmf* extremist — **extremo, -ma** *adj* extreme; **en caso** ∼ as a last resort — **extremo** *nm* end; **en** ∼ in the extreme, extremely; **en ultimo** ∼ as a last resort

extrovertido -da *adj* extroverted — **extrovertido -da** *n* extrovert

eyacular *v* ejaculate — **eyaculación** *nf* (**-ciones**) ejaculation

F

f *nf* f, sixth letter of the Spanish alphabet

fabricar *v* manufacture; build, construct; fabricate — **fábrica** *nf* factory — **fabricación** *nf* (**-ciones**) manufacture — **fabricante** *nmf* manufacturer

fábula *nf* fable; story, lie

fabuloso, -sa *adj* fabulous

facial *adj* facial

fácil *adj* easy; likely — **facilidad** *nf* facility, ease; **~es** *nfpl* facilities, services — **facilitar** *v* facilitate; provide, supply

facsímil *or* **facsímile** *nm* facsimile, copy; fax

factible *adj* feasible

factor *nm* factor

factura *nf* bill, invoice; making, manufacture — **facturar** *v* bill for; check in (as baggage)

facultad *nf* faculty, ability; authority; school (of a university)

falda *nf* skirt; side, slope (of a mountain)

fallar *v* fail, go wrong; pronounce judgment on; miss — **falla** *nf* flaw, defect; (geological) fault

fallecer *v* pass away, die — **fallecimiento** *nm* demise, death

fallo *nm* error; sentence, verdict

falso, -sa *adj* false, untrue; counterfeit, forged

falta *nf* lack; defect, fault, error; absence; offense, misdemeanor; foul; **hacer ~** be lacking, be needed; **sin ~** without fail — **faltar** *v* be lacking, be needed; be missing; remain, be left; **¡no faltaba más!** don't mention it!

fama *nf* fame; reputation

familia *nf* family — **familiar** *adj* familial, family; familiar; informal (of language) — **familiar** *nmf* relation, relative — **familiaridad** *nf* familiarity

famoso, -sa *adj* famous

fantástico, -ca *adj* fantastic

fascículo *nm* installment, part (of a publication)

fascinar *v* fascinate — **fascinación** *nf* (**-ciones**) fascination — **fascinante** *adj* fascinating

fascismo *nm* fascism — **fascista** *adj* & *nmf* fascist

fase *nf* phase

fatiga *nf* fatigue — **fatigado, -da** *adj* weary, tired — **fatigar** *v* tire

fauna *nf* fauna

favor *nm* favor; **a ~ de** in favor of; **por ~** please — **favorable** *adj* favorable — **favorecer** *v* favor; look well on, suit — **favorito, -ta** *adj* & *n* favorite

fax *nm* fax — **faxear** *v* fax

faz *nf* (**faces**) face, countenance

fe *nf* faith; **dar ~ de** bear witness to; **de buena ~** in good faith

febrero *nm* February

fecha *nf* date

fecundar *v* fertilize (an egg); make fertile

felicidad *nf* happiness — **felicitación** *nf* (**-ciones**) congratulation — **felicitar** *v* congratulate

feliz *adj* (**-lices**) happy; fortunate; **Feliz Navidad** Merry Christmas

femenino, -na *adj* feminine; female — **femenino** *nm* feminine (in grammar) — **feminismo** *nm* feminism

fenómeno *nm* phenomenon

feo, fea *adj* ugly; unpleasant, nasty

féretro *nm* coffin

feria *nf* fair, market; festival, holiday

fermentar *v* ferment — **fermentación** *nf* (**-ciones**) fermentation — **fermento** *nm* ferment

férreo, -rrea *adj* iron; **vía férrea** railroad track

ferretería *nf* hardware store

fértil *adj* fertile, fruitful — **fertilidad** *nf* fertility

festival *nm* festival — **festividad** *nf* festivity — **festivo, -va** *adj* festive; **día festivo** holiday

fiable *adj* reliable — **fiabilidad** *nf* reliability

fiado, -da *adj* on credit — **fiador, -dora** *n* bondsman, guarantor

fianza *nf* bail, bond; **dar** ∼ pay a deposit

fiar *v* guarantee; sell on credit; **ser de** ∼ be trustworthy — **fiarse de** *vr phr* place trust in

fibra *nf* fiber

ficción *nf* (**-ciones**) fiction

ficha *nf* token; index card; counter, chip (in games) — **fichero** *nm* card file; filing cabinet

ficticio, -cia *adj* fictitious

fidelidad *nf* fidelity, faithfulness

fiebre *nf* fever; ∼ **palúdica** malaria

fiel *adj* faithful, loyal; accurate, reliable — **fiel** *nm* pointer (of a scale)

fiesta *nf* party; holiday, feast day

figura *nf* figure; shape, form — **figurar** *v* figure (in), be included; stand out; represent — **figurarse** *vr* imagine

fijar *v* fasten, affix; set, fix — **fijarse** *vr* settle; **fijarse en** notice, pay attention to — **fijo, -ja** *adj* fixed, firm; permanent

fila *nf* line, file, row; **ponerse en** ∼ line up

filantropía *nf* philanthropy

filial *adj* filial — **filial** *nf* affiliate, subsidiary

filigrana *nf* filigree; watermark

filipino, -na *adj* Filipino

filmar *v* film, shoot — **filme** *or* **film** *nm* film, movie

filosofía *nf* philosophy — **filósofo, -fa** *n* philosopher

filtrar *v* filter — **filtrarse** *vr* leak out, seep through — **filtro** *nm* filter

fin *nm* end; purpose, aim; **en** ∼ well, in short; ∼ **de semana** weekend; **por** ∼ finally, at last

final *adj* final — **final** *nm* end, conclusion; *nf* final (in sports) — **finalidad** *nf* purpose, aim — **finalista** *nmf* finalist — **finalizar** *v* finish, end

financiar *v* finance, fund — **financiero, -ra** *adj* financial — **financiero, -ra** *n* financier — **finanzas** *nfpl* finance

finca *nf* farm, ranch; country house

fingir *v* feign, pretend — **fingido, -da** *adj* false, feigned

finito, -ta *adj* finite

finlandés, -desa *adj* Finnish

fino, -na *adj* fine; slender; refined; sharp, keen

firma *nf* signature; (act of) signing; firm, company

firmar *v* sign

firme *adj* firm, resolute; steady, stable — **firmeza** *nf* strength, resolve; firmness, stability

fiscal *adj* fiscal — **fiscal** *nmf* district attorney — **fisco** *nm* (national) treasury

física *nf* physics — **físico, -ca** *adj* physical — **físico, -ca** *n* physicist — **físico** *nm* physique

fisiología *nf* physiology

fisioterapia *nf* physical therapy — **fisioterapeuta** *nmf* physical therapist

fisonomía *nf* features *pl,* appearance

flaco, -ca *adj* thin, skinny; weak

flamenco, -ca *adj* flamenco; Flemish

flauta *nf* flute; ∼ **dulce** recorder — **flautista** *nmf* flutist

flecha *nf* arrow

flexible *adj* flexible — **flexibilidad** *nf* flexibility

flor *nf* flower — **florecer** *v* bloom, blossom; flourish — **florero** *nm* vase

flota *nf* fleet

flotar *v* float — **flotador** *nm* float; life preserver

fluctuar *v* fluctuate — **fluctuación** *nf* (**-ciones**) fluctuation

fluir *v* flow — **fluidez** *nf* fluidity; fluency — **fluido, -da** *adj* fluid; fluent

fluvial *adj* river

fobia *nf* phobia

foca *nf* seal

foco *nm* focus; spotlight, floodlight

fogata *nf* bonfire

folklore *nm* folklore

fomentar *v* promote, encourage — **fomento** *nm* promotion, encouragement

fondo *nm* bottom; rear, back, end; depth; ~**s** *nmpl* funds, resources; **a** ~ thoroughly, in depth; **en el** ~ deep down

fonética *nf* phonetics

foráneo, -nea *adj* foreign, strange

forense *adj* forensic

forjar *v* forge; build up, create

forma *nf* form, shape; manner, way; **en** ~ fit, healthy; ~**s** *nfpl* appearances, conventions — **formación** *nf* (-**ciones**) formation; training

formal *adj* formal; serious; dependable, reliable — **formalidad** *nf* formality; seriousness; reliability

formar *v* form, shape; constitute; train, educate

formidable *adj* tremendous; fantastic, terrific

fórmula *nf* formula

formular *v* formulate, draw up; make, lodge (as a complaint)

formulario *nm* form

foro *nm* forum

fortalecer *v* strengthen

fortuna *nf* fortune, luck; wealth, fortune; **por** ~ fortunately

forzar *v* force; strain (one's eyes)

fosa *nf* pit, ditch; grave; ~**s nasales** nostrils

fósforo *nm* phosphorus; match — **fosforescente** *adj* phosphorescent

fotocopia *nf* photocopy

fotografía *nf* photography; photograph, picture — **fotografiar** *v* photograph — **fotógrafo, -fa** *n* photographer

fracasar *v* fail — **fracaso** *nm* failure

fracción *nf* (-**ciones**) fraction; faction (in politics)

fractura *nf* fracture — **fracturarse** *vr* fracture, break

fragancia *nf* fragrance, scent

frágil *adj* fragile; frail, delicate

fragmento *nm* fragment

francés, -cesa *adj* (-**ceses** *m*) French — **francés** *nm* French (language)

franco, -ca *adj* frank, candid; free (in commerce) — **franco** *nm* franc

frase *nf* phrase; sentence

fraternal *adj* brotherly, fraternal — **fraternidad** *nf* brotherhood, fraternity

frecuencia *nf* frequency; **con** ~ often, frequently — **frecuentar** *v* frequent, haunt

freír *v* fry

frenar *v* brake

freno *nm* brake

frente *nm* front; facade; **al** ~ **de** at the head of; ~ **a** opposite; **de** ~ (facing) forward; **hacer** ~ **a** face up to, brave — **frente** *nf* forehead

fresa *nf* strawberry

fresco, -ca *adj* fresh; cool; insolent, nervy — **fresco** *nm* fresh air; coolness; fresco (painting)

frialdad *nf* coldness; indifference

fricción *nf* (-**ciones**) friction; rubbing, massage — **friccionar** *v* rub

frigidez *nf* frigidity

frijol *nm* bean

frío, fría *adj* cold; cool, indifferent — **frío** *nm* cold; coldness, indifference

frito, -ta *adj* fried; fed up

frívolo, -la *adj* frivolous — **frivolidad** *nf* frivolity

frontera *nf* border, frontier — **fronterizo, -za** *adj* border, on the border

frotar *v* rub

fructífero, -ra *adj* fruitful

fruncir *v* gather (in pleats)

frustrar *v* frustrate — **frustrarse** *vr* fail — **frustración** *nf* (-**ciones**) frustration

fruta *nf* fruit — **fruto** *nm* fruit; result, consequence

fuego *nm* fire; flame, burner; ~**s artifi-ciales** *nmpl* fireworks

fuente *nf* fountain; spring; source; plat-ter, serving dish

fuera *adv* outside, out; abroad, away; ~ **de** outside of, beyond; aside from, in addition to

fuerte strong; bright (of colors), loud (of sounds); intense; hard — **fuerte** *adv* strongly, hard; loudly; abundantly, a lot — **fuerte** *nm* fort; strong point

fuerza *nf* strength; force; power, might; ~**s armadas** *nfpl* armed forces; **a** ~ **de** by dint of; **a la** ~ necessarily

fuga *nf* flight, escape; fugue (in music); leak — **fugarse** *vr* flee, run away — **fugaz** *adj* (**-gaces**) fleeting — **fugi-tivo, -va** *adj & n* fugitive

fumar *v* smoke — **fumador, -dora** *n* smoker

función *nf* (**-ciones**) function; duties; performance, show (in a theater) — **funcional** *adj* functional — **fun-cionamiento** *nm* functioning — **fun-cionar** *v* function, run, work; **no fun-ciona** out of order — **funcionario, -ria** *n* civil servant, official

funda *nf* cover, sheath

fundamento *nm* foundation; ~**s** *nmpl* fundamentals — **fundamental** *adj* fun-damental, basic — **fundamentar** *v* lay the foundations for; base

fundar *v* found, establish; base — **fun-darse en** *vr phr* be based on

fundir *v* melt down, smelt; fuse, merge — **fundirse** *vr* blend, merge; melt; burn out — **fundición** *nf* (**-ciones**) smelting; foundry

fúnebre *adj* funeral; gloomy

funeral *nm* funeral; ~**es** *nmpl* funeral (rites) — **funeral** *adj* funeral, funerary — **funeraria** *nf* funeral home

funesto, ta *adj* terrible, disastrous

furgoneta *nf* van

furia *nf* fury, rage; violence — **furioso, -sa** *adj* furious, irate; intense, violent

fusión *nf* (**-siones**) fusion; union, merger — **fusionar** *v* fuse; merge — **fusionarse** *vr* merge

futbol *or* **fútbol** *nm* soccer; ~ **ameri-cano** football — **futbolista** *nmf* soccer player, football player

futuro, -ra *adj* future — **futuro** *nm* fu-ture

G

g *nf* g, seventh letter of the Spanish al-phabet

gabardina *nf* trench coat, raincoat

gafas *nfpl* eyeglasses

galaxia *nf* galaxy

galleta *nf* (sweet) cookie

gallina *nf* hen — **gallinero** *nm* henhouse, (chicken) coop — **gallo** *nm* rooster, cock

galón *nm* (**-lones**) gallon

galopar *v* gallop

gamuza *nf* chamois (leather), suede

gana *nf* desire, wish; appetite

ganado *nm* cattle livestock — **gana-dería** *nf* livestock

ganador, -dora *adj* winning — **gana-dor, -dora** *n* winner

ganancia *nf* profit

ganar *v* earn; win (as in games)

gancho *nm* hook; hairpin; (clothes) hanger

ganga *nf* bargain

ganso, -sa *n* goose, gander *m*

garaje *nm* garage

garantizar *v* guarantee — **garantía** *nf* guarantee, warranty

garbanzo *nm* chickpea

garganta *nf* throat

garza *nf* heron

gas *nm* gas; ~ **lacrimógeno** tear gas

gasa *nf* gauze

gaseosa *nf* soda, soft drink

gasolina *nf* gasoline — **gasolinera** *nf* gas station, service station

gastar *v* spend; consume, use up; squander, waste — **gasto** *nm* expense, expenditure

gastronomía *nf* gastronomy

gatear *v* crawl, creep

gato, -ta *n* cat — **gato** *nm* (automobile) jack

gaveta *nf* drawer

gaviota *nf* gull, seagull

gay *adj* gay (homosexual)

gelatina *nf* gelatin

gemelo, -la *adj & n* twin

gemir *v* moan, groan, whine — **gemido** *nm* moan, groan, whine

generación *nf* (**-ciones**) generation

general *adj* general — **general** *nmf* general — **generalmente** *adv* usually, generally

género *nm* kind, sort; gender (in grammar)

generoso, -sa *adj* generous, unselfish — **generosidad** *nf* generosity

genial *adj* brilliant; great, terrific

genio *nm* genius; temper, disposition

genital *adj* genital — **genitales** *nmpl* genitals

gente *nf* people

geografía *nf* geography — **geográfico, -ca** *adj* geographic, geographical

geología *nf* geology — **geológico, -ca** *adj* geologic, geological

geometría *nf* geometry

gerencia *nf* management — **gerente** *nmf* manager

gesto *nm* gesture; (facial) expression

gigante *adj & nm* giant

gimnasia *nf* gymnastics — **gimnasio** *nm* gymnasium, gym

ginebra *nf* gin

ginecología *nf* gynecology — **ginecólogo, -ga** *n* gynecologist

gira *nf* tour

girar *v* turn; turn around, revolve; twist, rotate

girasol *nm* sunflower

giro *nm* turn, rotation

glándula *nf* gland

globo *nm* globe; balloon — **global** *adj* global; total, overall

gloria *nf* glory

glorieta *nf* rotary, traffic circle

glotón, -tona *adj* (**-tones** *m*) gluttonous — **glotón, -tona** *n* (**-tones** *m*) glutton

gobernar *v* govern, rule; direct, manage — **gobernador, -dora** *n* governor — **gobierno** *nm* government

gol *nm* goal (in sports)

golf *nm* golf — **golfista** *nmf* golfer

golfo *nm* gulf

golondrina *nf* swallow

golosina *nf* sweet, candy — **goloso, -sa** *adj* fond of sweets

golpe *nm* blow; punch — **golpear** *v* hit, punch; slam, bang (as a door); knock (at a door)

goma *nf* rubber; glue

gordo, -da *adj* fat — **gordo, -da** *n* fat person — **gordo** *nm* fat — **gordura** *nf* fatness

gorila *nm* gorilla

gorra *nf* cap, bonnet

gorrión *nm* (**-rriones**) sparrow

gorro *nm* cap, bonnet

gota *nf* drop

gozar *v* enjoy oneself

grabar *v* record, tape — **grabación** *nf* (**-ciones**) recording — **grabadora** *nf* tape recorder

gracia *nf* grace; humor, wit; ~**s** *nfpl* thanks; ¡(**muchas**) ~**s!** thank you (very much)! — **gracioso, -sa** *adj* funny, amusing

grado *nm* degree; grade (in school)

graduar *v* regulate, adjust; confer a degree on (in education) — **graduarse** *vr* graduate (from a school) — **graduado, -da** *n* graduate

gramática *nf* grammar — **gramatical** *adj* grammatical

gramo *nm* gram

grande *adj* large, big; tall; great (as in quality, intensity); grown-up

granizar *v impers* hail — **granizo** *nm* hail

granja *nf* farm — **granjero, -ra** *n* farmer

grano *nm* grain; seed

grapadora *nf* stapler — **grapar** *v* staple

grasa *nf* grease — **graso, -sa** *adj* fatty, greasy, oily — **grasoso, -sa** *adj* greasy, oily

gratis *adv & adj* free

grato, -ta *adj* pleasant, agreeable

gratuito, -ta *adj* gratuitous, unwarranted; free

grave *adj* grave, serious — **gravedad** *nf* gravity

griego, -ga *adj* Greek — **griego** *nm* Greek (language)

grieta *nf* crack, crevice

grifo *nm* faucet, tap

grillo *nm* cricket

gringo, -ga *adj & n* Yankee, gringo

gripe *or* **gripa** *nf* flu, influenza

gris *adj & nm* gray

gritar *v* shout, scream, cry — **grito** *nm* shout, scream, cry

grosería *nf* vulgar remark; rudeness — **grosero, -ra** *adj* coarse, vulgar; rude

grosor *nm* thickness

grotesco, -ca *adj* grotesque, hideous

grúa *nf* crane, derrick

grueso, -sa *adj* thick — **grueso** *nm* thickness; main body, mass

gruñir *v* growl, grunt — **gruñido** *nm* growl, grunt — **gruñón, -ñona** *adj* (**-ñones** *m*) grumpy, grouchy

grupo *nm* group

guacamole *nm* guacamole

guante *nm* glove

guapo, -pa *adj* handsome, good-looking

guarda *nmf* keeper, custodian; security guard — **guardabarros** *nms & pl* fender(s) — **guardabosque** *nmf* forest ranger — **guardacostas** *nmfs & pl* coast guard vessel(s) — **guardaespaldas** *nmfs & pl* bodyguard(s) — **guardameta** *nmf* goalkeeper — **guardar** *v* keep; guard, protect; save

guardería *nf* nursery, day-care center

guardia *nf* guard, vigilance — **guardián, -diana** *n* (**-dianes** *m*) guardian, keeper; security guard

guatemalteco, -ca *adj* Guatemalan

guayaba *nf* guava

gubernamental *or* **gubernativo, -va** *adj* governmental

guerra *nf* war, warfare; conflict, struggle — **guerrilla** *nf* guerrilla warfare — **guerrillero, -ra** *adj & n* guerrilla

guiar *v* guide, lead; advise — **guía** *nf* guidebook; guidance; *nmf* guide, leader

guiño *nm* wink

guión *nm* (**guiones**) script, screenplay; hyphen, dash (in punctuation)

guisado *nm* stew

guisante *nm* pea

guisar *v* cook — **guiso** *nm* stew, casserole

guitarra *nf* guitar — **guitarrista** *nmf* guitarist

gula *nf* gluttony

gusano *nm* worm; maggot (larva)

gustar *v* taste; like; be pleasing

gusto *nm* taste; pleasure, liking; **mucho ~** pleased to meet you

H

h *nf* h, eighth letter of the Spanish alphabet

haba *nf* broad bean

habanero, -ra *adj* Havanan

haber *v aux* have, has — **haber** *v impers, form is* **hay** there is, there are — **haber** *nm* assets

habichuela *nf* bean

hábil *adj* able, skillful; clever — **habilidad** *nf* ability, skill

habilitar *v* equip, furnish; authorize

habitar *v* inhabit; reside, dwell — **habitación** *nf* (**-ciones**) room, bedroom — **habitante** *nmf* inhabitant, resident

hábito *nm* habit — **habitual** *adj* habitual, usual — **habituar** *v* accustom, habituate

hablar *v* talk, speak; speak (a language) — **habla** *nf* speech; language, dialect — **hablador, -dora** *adj* talkative — **hablante** *nmf* speaker

hacer *v* do, perform; make; force, oblige; act — **hacer** *v impers* to be; ~ **calor/viento** be hot/be windy; **hace mucho tiempo** a long time ago — **hacerse** *vr* become

hacha *nf* hatchet, ax

hacia *prep* toward, towards; near, around, about

hacienda *nf* estate, ranch; property; **Hacienda** department of revenue

halagar *v* flatter — **halagador, -dora** *adj* flattering — **halago** *nm* flattery

halcón *nm* (**-cones**) hawk, falcon

hallar *v* find; discover, find out — **hallarse** *vr* be, find oneself — **hallazgo** *nm* discovery, find

hamaca *nf* hammock

hambre *nf* hunger; starvation, famine — **hambriento, -ta** *adj* hungry, starving

hamburguesa *nf* hamburger

harina *nf* flour

hasta *prep* until, up until (in time); as far as, up to (in space); ¡~ **luego!** see you later! — **hasta** *adv* even

hazaña *nf* feat, exploit

hebilla *nf* buckle

hebreo, -brea *adj* Hebrew — **hebreo** *nm* Hebrew (language)

hechizo *nm* spell

hecho, -cha *adj* made, done; ready-to-wear (of clothing) — **hecho** *nm* fact; event; act, deed

helar *v* freeze — **helarse** *vr* freeze up, freeze over — **helado, -da** *adj* freezing cold; frozen — **helada** *nf* frost — **heladería** *nf* ice-cream parlor — **helado** *nm* ice cream

helecho *nm* fern

hélice *nf* propeller; spiral, helix

helicóptero *nm* helicopter

hembra *nf* female; woman

hemisferio *nm* hemisphere

hemorragia *nf* hemorrhage

hepatitis *nf* hepatitis

heredar *v* inherit — **heredero, -ra** *n* heir, heiress

herencia *nf* inheritance; heredity (in biology)

herir *v* injure, wound; hurt (as feelings, pride) — **herida** *nf* injury, wound — **herido, -da** *adj* injured, wounded; hurt (as feelings, pride) — **herido, -da** *n* injured person, casualty

hermano, -na *n* brother, sister

hermoso, -sa *adj* beautiful, lovely — **hermosura** *nf* beauty

hernia *nf* hernia

héroe *nm* hero — **heroico, -ca** *adj* heroic — **heroína** *nf* heroine; heroin (narcotic) — **heroísmo** *nm* heroism

herradura *nf* horseshoe

herramienta *nf* tool

hervir *v* boil
heterogéneo, -nea *adj* heterogeneous
heterosexual *adj & nmf* heterosexual
hiato *nm* hiatus
hidratante *adj* moisturizing
hielo *nm* ice; coldness
hierba *nf* herb; grass — **hierbabuena** *nf* mint
hierro *nm* iron
hígado *nm* liver
higiene *nf* hygiene — **higiénico, -ca** *adj* hygienic
higo *nm* fig
hijo, -ja *n* son, daughter; **hijos** *nmpl* children, offspring — **hijastro, -tra** *n* stepson, stepdaughter
hilo *nm* thread
himno *nm* hymn
hinchar *v* inflate, blow up — **hincharse** *vr* swell (up) — **hinchado, -da** *adj* swollen
hindú *adj & nmf* Hindu — **hinduismo** *nm* Hinduism
hiperactivo, -va *adj* hyperactive
hipertensión *nf* (**-siones**) hypertension, high blood pressure
hipo *nm* hiccup, hiccups *pl*
hipocondríaco, -ca *adj* hypochondriacal — **hipocondríaco, -ca** *n* hypochondriac
hipocresía *nf* hypocrisy — **hipócrita** *adj* hypocritical — **hipócrita** *nmf* hypocrite
hipopótamo *nm* hippopotamus
hipoteca *nf* mortgage — **hipotecar** *v* mortgage
hipótesis *nfs & pl* hypothesis
hispano, -na *or* **hispánico, -ca** *adj & n* Hispanic — **hispanoamericano, -na** *adj* Latin-American — **hispanoamericano, -na** *n* Latin American — **hispanohablante** *or* **hispanoparlante** *adj* Spanish-speaking
historia *nf* history; story — **historiador, -dora** *n* historian — **historial** *nm* record, background — **histórico, -ca** *adj* historical; historic, important — **historieta** *nf* comic strip
hocico *nm* snout, muzzle
hockey *nm* hockey
hogar *nm* home
hoguera *nf* bonfire
hoja *nf* leaf; sheet (of paper) — **hojaldre** *nm* puff pastry — **hojear** *v* leaf through — **hojuela** *nf* flake
hola *interj* hello!, hi!
holandés, -desa *adj* (**-deses** *m*) Dutch
holocausto *nm* holocaust
hombre *nm* man; **el ~** mankind
hombría *nf* manliness
hombro *nm* shoulder
homenaje *nm* homage
homeopatía *nf* homeopathy
homicidio *nm* homicide, murder — **homicida** *adj* homicidal, murderous — **homicida** *nmf* murderer
homogéneo, -nea *adj* homogeneous
homosexual *adj & nmf* homosexual — **homosexualidad** *nf* homosexuality
hondo, -da *adj* deep — **hondo** *adv* deeply
hondureño, -ña *adj* Honduran
honesto, -ta *adj* decent, honorable — **honestidad** *nf* honesty, integrity
hongo *nm* mushroom; fungus (in botany and medicine)
honor *nm* honor — **honorable** *adj* honorable — **honorario, -ria** *adj* honorary — **honorarios** *nmpl* payment, fee — **honradez** *nf* (**-deces**) honesty, integrity — **honrado, -da** *adj* honest, upright — **honrar** *v* honor
hora *nf* hour; (specific) time; **¿qué ~ es?** what time is it?; **~s extraordinarias** overtime
horario *nm* schedule, timetable
horizonte *nm* horizon — **horizontal** *adj* horizontal
hormiga *nf* ant
hormigón *nm* (**-gones**) concrete
hormiguero *nm* anthill
hormona *nf* hormone

horno *nm* oven (for cooking); small furnace, kiln — **hornear** *v* bake

horóscopo *nm* horoscope

horrible *adj* horrible — **horror** *nm* horror, dread; atrocity — **horrorizar** *v* horrify, terrify

hortaliza *nf* (garden) vegetable

hospedar *v* put up, lodge — **hospedaje** *nm* lodging

hospital *nm* hospital — **hospitalizar** *v* hospitalize

hostia *nf* host (in religion)

hotel *nm* hotel — **hotelero, -ra** *adj* hotel — **hotelero, -ra** *n* hotel manager, hotelier

hoy *adv* today; ~ **(en) día** nowadays

hoyo *nm* hole

hueco *nm* hollow, cavity

huelga *nf* strike — **huelguista** *nmf* striker

huella *nf* footprint; track, mark; fingerprint

huérfano, -na *n* orphan — **huérfano, -na** *adj* orphaned

huerta *nf* truck farm — **huerto** *nm* vegetable garden

hueso *nm* bone

huésped, -peda *n* guest

huesudo, -da *adj* bony

huevo *nm* egg; ~**s revueltos** scrambled eggs

huida *nf* flight, escape

huir *v* escape, flee

humano, -na *adj* human; humane — **humano** *nm* human (being) — **humanidad** *nf* humanity, mankind; ~**es** *nfpl* humanities — **humanismo** *nm* humanism — **humanista** *nmf* humanist — **humanitario, -ria** *adj & n* humanitarian

humedad *nf* dampness; humidity (in meteorology) — **humedecer** *v* moisten, dampen — **humedecerse** *vr* become moist — **húmedo, -da** *adj* moist, damp; humid (in meteorology)

humildad *nf* humility — **humilde** *adj* humble — **humillación** *nf* (**-ciones**) humiliation — **humillar** *v* humiliate — **humillarse** *vr* humble oneself

humo *nm* smoke, steam, fumes

humor *nm* humor — **humorismo** *nm* humor, wit — **humorista** *nmf* humorist, comedian

hundir *v* sink; destroy, ruin (a building, plans, etc.) — **hundirse** *vr* sink; collapse — **hundido, -da** *adj* sunken — **hundimiento** *nm* sinking; collapse

húngaro, -ra *adj* Hungarian

huracán *nm* (**-canes**) hurricane

hurra *interj* hurrah!, hooray!

hurtar *v* steal — **hurto** *nm* theft; stolen property

huy *interj* ow!, ouch!

I

i *nf* i, ninth letter of the Spanish alphabet

ibérico, -ca *adj* Iberian — **ibero, -ra** *or* **íbero, -ra** *adj* Iberian

ida *nf* outward journey; ~ **y vuelta** round-trip

idea *nf* idea; opinion

ideal *adj & nm* ideal — **idealista** *adj* idealistic — **idealista** *nmf* idealist — **idealizar** *v* idealize

idear *v* devise, think up

identidad *nf* identity — **idéntico, -ca** *adj* identical — **identificar** *v* identify — **identificarse** *vr* identify oneself — **identificación** *nf* (**-ciones**) identification

ideología *nf* ideology — **ideológico, -ca** *adj* ideological

idioma *nm* language — **idiomático, -ca** *adj* idiomatic

idiota *adj* idiotic — **idiota** *nmf* idiot — **idiotez** *nf* idiocy

ídolo *nm* idol — **idolatrar** *v* idolize

iglesia *nf* church

iglú *nm* igloo

ignorar *v* ignore; be unaware of — **ignorancia** *nf* ignorance — **ignorante** *adj* ignorant — **ignorante** *nmf* ignorant person

igual *adv* in the same way — **igual** *adj* equal; the same — **igual** *nmf* equal, peer — **igualar** *v* make equal; be equal to — **igualdad** *nf* equality; uniformity — **igualmente** *adv* likewise

iguana *nf* iguana

ilegal *adj* illegal

ilegítimo, -ma *adj* illegitimate

ileso, -sa *adj* unharmed

ilimitado, -da *adj* unlimited

ilógico, -ca *adj* illogical

iluminar *v* illuminate — **iluminación** *nf* (**-ciones**) illumination; lighting

ilusionar *v* excite — **ilusión** *nf* (**-siones**) illusion; hope — **ilusionado, -da** *adj* excited

ilustrar *v* illustrate; explain — **ilustración** *nf* (**-ciones**) illustration; learning

ilustre *adj* illustrious

imagen *nf* (**imágenes**) image, picture

imaginar *v* imagine — **imaginarse** *vr* imagine — **imaginación** *nf* (**-ciones**) imagination — **imaginario, -ria** *adj* imaginary

imán *nm* (**imanes**) magnet

imbécil *adj* stupid, idiotic — **imbécil** *nmf* idiot

imborrable *adj* indelible

imitar *v* imitate, copy; impersonate — **imitación** *nf* (**-ciones**) imitation, copy; impersonation — **imitador, -dora** *n* impersonator

impaciencia *nf* impatience — **impacientar** *v* make impatient, exasperate — **impacientarse** *vr* grow impatient — **impaciente** *adj* impatient

impacto *nm* impact

impar *adj* odd — **impar** *nm* odd number

imparcial *adj* impartial — **imparcialidad** *nf* impartiality

impartir *v* impart, give

impecable *adj* impeccable, spotless

impedir *v* prevent; impede, hinder — **impedido, -da** *adj* disabled — **impedimento** *nm* obstacle, impediment

impenetrable *adj* impenetrable

imperativo, -va *adj* imperative — **imperativo** *nm* imperative

imperceptible *adj* imperceptible

imperdonable *adj* unforgivable

imperfección *nf* (**-ciones**) imperfection — **imperfecto, -ta** *adj* imperfect — **imperfecto** *nm* imperfect (tense)

imperialismo *nm* imperialism — **imperialista** *adj* & *nmf* imperialist

imperio *nm* empire

impermeable *adj* waterproof — **impermeable** *nm* raincoat

impersonal *adj* impersonal

ímpetu *nm* impetus; energy, vigor; force — **impetuoso, -sa** *adj* impetuous

implemento *nm* implement, tool

implicar *v* involve, implicate; imply

implícito, -ta *adj* implicit

imponer *v* impose; command (as respect); be imposing — **imponerse** *vr* assert oneself, command respect — **imponente** *adj* imposing, impressive

impopular *adj* unpopular — **impopularidad** *nf* unpopularity

importación *nf* (**-ciones**) importation; **importaciones** *nfpl* imports — **importado, -da** *adj* imported — **importador, -dora** *adj* importing — **importador, -dora** *n* importer

importancia *nf* importance — **importante** *adj* important — **importar** *v* matter, be important; **no me importa** I don't care

importar *v* import

imposible *adj* impossible — **imposibilidad** *nf* impossibility

impostor, -tora *n* impostor

impotente *adj* powerless, impotent — **impotencia** *nf* impotence

impracticable *adj* impracticable

impreciso, -sa *adj* vague, imprecise — **imprecisión** *nf* (**-siones**) vagueness; inaccuracy

impregnar *v* impregnate

imprenta *nf* printing; printing shop, press

imprescindible *adj* essential, indispensable

impresión *nf* (**-siones**) impression; printing — **impresionante** *adj* impressive — **impresionar** *v* impress; affect, move; make an impression — **impresionarse** *vr* be impressed; be affected

impreso, -sa *adj* printed — **impresora** *nf* (computer) printer

imprimir *v* print

improbable *adj* improbable

impropio, -pia *adj* inappropriate; incorrect

improvisar *v* improvise — **improvisación** *nf* (**-ciones**) improvisation

imprudente *adj* imprudent, rash — **imprudencia** *nf* imprudence, carelessness

impuesto *nm* tax

impulsar *v* propel, drive — **impulsivo, -va** *adj* impulsive — **impulso** *nm* drive, thrust; impulse

impuro, -ra *adj* impure — **impureza** *nf* impurity

inaceptable *adj* unacceptable

inactivo, -va *adj* inactive — **inactividad** *nf* inactivity

inadecuado, -da *adj* inadequate; inappropriate

inalámbrico, -ca *adj* wireless, cordless

inalcanzable *adj* unreachable, unattainable

inanimado, -da *adj* inanimate

inapropiado, -da *adj* inappropriate

inaugurar *v* inaugurate — **inauguración** *nf* (**-ciones**) inauguration

incalculable *adj* incalculable

incandescente *adj* incandescent

incansable *adj* tireless

incapacitar *v* incapacitate, disable — **incapacidad** *nf* incapacity, inability — **incapaz** *adj* (**-paces**) incapable

incendiar *v* set fire to, burn (down) — **incendiarse** *vr* catch fire — **incendio** *nm* fire

incertidumbre *nf* uncertainty

incienso *nm* incense

incierto, -ta *adj* uncertain

incitar *v* incite, rouse

incivilizado, -da *adj* uncivilized

inclinar *v* tilt, lean — **inclinarse** *vr* lean (over) — **inclinación** *nf* (**-ciones**) inclination; incline, tilt

incluir *v* include; enclose — **inclusive** *adv* up to and including — **incluso** *adv* even, in fact — **incluso, -sa** *adj* enclosed

incógnito, -ta *adj* unknown

incoherente *adj* incoherent — **incoherencia** *nf* incoherence

incoloro, -ra *adj* colorless

incomodar *v* inconvenience; bother, annoy — **incomodarse** *vr* take the trouble; get annoyed — **incomodidad** *nf* discomfort — **incómodo, -da** *adj* uncomfortable; inconvenient, awkward

incomparable *adj* incomparable

incompetente *adj* incompetent — **incompetencia** *nf* incompetence

incompleto, -ta *adj* incomplete

incomprendido, -da *adj* misunderstood — **incomprensible** *adj* incomprehensible — **incomprensión** *nf* (**-siones**) lack of understanding

incomunicado, -da *adj* isolated; in solitary confinement

inconcebible *adj* inconceivable

inconcluso, -sa *adj* unfinished

incondicional *adj* unconditional

inconfundible *adj* unmistakable

inconsciente *adj* unconscious, unaware; reckless — **inconsciente** *nm*

(the) unconscious — **inconsciencia** *nf* unconsciousness; thoughtlessness
inconsiderado, -da *adj* inconsiderate
inconstante *adj* changeable, unreliable
inconstitucional *adj* unconstitutional
incontable *adj* countless
inconveniente *adj* inconvenient; inappropriate — **inconveniente** *nm* obstacle, problem
incorrecto, -ta *adj* incorrect; impolite
incrédulo, -la *adj* incredulous
increíble *adj* incredible, unbelievable
incrementar *v* increase
inculto, -ta *adj* uneducated; uncultivated (of land)
incumplimiento *nm* noncompliance
indecisión *nf* (-siones) indecision — **indeciso, -sa** *adj* undecided; indecisive
indefenso, -sa *adj* defenseless, helpless
indefinido, -da *adj* indefinite
independiente *adj* independent — **independencia** *nf* independence
indicar *v* indicate; show — **indicación** *nf* (-ciones) sign, indication; **indicaciones** *nfpl* directions — **indicador** *nm* sign, signal; gauge, dial, meter — **indicativo, -va** *adj* indicative
índice *nm* indication; index (of a book); index finger
indiferente *adj* indifferent
indígena *adj* indigenous, native — **indígena** *nmf* native
indigestión *nf* (-tiones) indigestion
indigno, -na *adj* unworthy
indio, -dia *adj* American Indian; Indian (from India)
indirecto, -ta *adj* indirect
indisciplina *nf* lack of discipline — **indisciplinado, -da** *adj* undisciplined
indiscreto, -ta *adj* indiscreet — **indiscreción** *nf* (-ciones) indiscretion; tactless remark
indiscriminado, -da *adj* indiscriminate
indiscutible *adj* indisputable
indispensable *adj* indispensable

indisponer *v* upset, make ill; set against, set at odds — **indispuesto, -ta** *adj* unwell, indisposed
individual *adj* individual — **individuo** *nm* individual
indivisible *adj* indivisible
índole *nf* nature, character; type, kind
indonesio, -sia *adj* Indonesian
inducir *v* induce; infer
indudable *adj* beyond doubt
industria *nf* industry — **industrial** *adj* industrial — **industrial** *nmf* industrialist, manufacturer
inédito, -ta *adj* unpublished
ineludible *adj* unavoidable, inescapable
inesperado, -da *adj* unexpected
inestable *adj* unstable
inevitable *adj* inevitable
inexperto, -ta *adj* inexperienced, unskilled
inexplicable *adj* inexplicable
infalible *adj* infallible
infancia *nf* infancy — **infantería** *nf* infantry — **infantil** *adj* child's, children's; childish
infarto *nm* heart attack
infectar *v* infect — **infección** *nf* (-ciones) infection — **infeccioso, -sa** *adj* infectious
inferior *adj* & *nmf* inferior
inferir *v* infer; cause (harm or injury)
infiel *adj* unfaithful — **infidelidad** *nf* infidelity
infinitivo *nm* infinitive — **infinito, -ta** *adj* infinite — **infinito** *nm* infinity
inflación *nf* (-ciones) inflation
inflamar *v* inflame — **inflamable** *adj* flammable, inflammable — **inflamación** *nf* (-ciones) inflammation
inflexible *adj* inflexible — **inflexión** *nf* (-xiones) inflection
influir *v* influence — **influjo** *nm* influence — **influyente** *adj* influential
información *nf* (-ciones) information; news; (telephone) directory assistance
informal *adj* informal; unreliable

informar *v* inform — **informática** *nf* information technology — **informativo, -va** *adj* informative

informe *adj* shapeless — **informe** *nm* report

infracción *nf* (**-ciones**) violation, infraction

infraestructura *nf* infrastructure

infructuoso, -sa *adj* fruitless

infundado, -da *adj* unfounded, baseless

infundir *v* instill, infuse

ingeniería *nf* engineering — **ingeniero, -ra** *n* engineer

ingenio *nm* ingenuity; wit; device, apparatus — **ingenioso, -sa** *adj* ingenious; clever, witty

ingenuo, -nua *adj* naive

ingerir *v* ingest, consume

ingle *nf* groin

inglés, -glesa *adj* (**-gleses** *m*) English — **inglés** *nm* English (language)

ingrato, -ta *adj* ungrateful; **ingratitud** *nf* ingratitude

ingrediente *nm* ingredient

ingresar *v* deposit

ingreso *nm* entrance, entry; admission (as into a hospital); **~s** *nmpl* income, earnings

inhabilidad *nf* unskillfulness

inherente *adj* inherent

inhibir *v* inhibit — **inhibición** *nf* (**-ciones**) inhibition

inhóspito, -ta *adj* inhospitable

inhumano, -na *adj* inhuman, inhumane

iniciar *v* initiate, begin — **iniciación** *nf* (**-ciones**) initiation; beginning — **inicial** *adj* & *nf* initial — **iniciativa** *nf* initiative — **inicio** *nm* start, beginning

injusticia *nf* injustice, unfairness — **injusto, -ta** *adj* unfair, unjust

inmaduro, -ra *adj* immature; unripe (of fruit)

inmediaciones *nfpl* surrounding area

inmediato, -ta *adj* immediate; adjoining

inmenso, -sa *adj* immense, vast

inmigración *nf* (**-ciones**) immigration — **inmigrante** *adj* & *nmf* immigrant

inminente *adj* imminent, impending

inmoral *adj* immoral

inmóvil *adj* motionless, still — **inmovilizar** *v* immobilize

inmueble *nm* building, property

inmutable *adj* unchangeable

innato, -ta *adj* innate

innecesario, -ria *adj* unnecessary, needless

innegable *adj* undeniable

innovar *v* introduce; innovate — **innovación** *nf* (**-ciones**) innovation — **innovador, -dora** *adj* innovative — **innovador, -dora** *n* innovator

innumerable *adj* innumerable

inocencia *nf* innocence — **inocente** *adj* & *nmf* innocent

inodoro, -ra *adj* odorless — **inodoro** *nm* toilet

inofensivo, -va *adj* inoffensive, harmless

inolvidable *adj* unforgettable

inoportuno, -na *adj* untimely, inopportune

inquietar *v* disturb, worry — **inquietante** *adj* disturbing, worrisome — **inquieto, -ta** *adj* anxious, worried — **inquietud** *nf* anxiety, worry

insatisfecho, -cha *adj* unsatisfied; dissatisfied

inscribir *v* enroll, register; inscribe, engrave — **inscribirse** *vr* register — **inscripción** *nf* (**-ciones**) inscription; registration

inseguro, -ra *adj* insecure; unsafe; uncertain — **inseguridad** *nf* insecurity; lack of safety; uncertainty

insensible *adj* insensitive, unfeeling; numb (in medicine); imperceptible

inseparable *adj* inseparable

insertar *v* insert

insignificante *adj* insignificant, negligible

insinuar *v* insinuate — **insinuante** *adj* insinuating, suggestive

insistir *v* insist — **insistente** *adj* insistent

insólito, -ta *adj* rare, unusual

insomnio *nm* insomnia

insoportable *adj* unbearable

insospechado, -da *adj* unexpected

inspirar *v* inspire; inhale — **inspiración** *nf* (**-ciones**) inspiration; inhalation

instalar *v* install — **instalación** *nf* (**-ciones**) installation

instancia *nf* request

instantáneo, -nea *adj* instantaneous, instant — **instantánea** *nf* snapshot — **instante** *nm* instant

institución *nf* (**-ciones**) institution — **institucional** *adj* institutional — **instituto** *nm* institute

instruir *v* instruct — **instrucción** *nf* (**-ciones**) instruction; **instrucciones** *nfpl* instructions, directions

instrumento *nm* instrument — **instrumental** *adj* instrumental

insuficiencia *nf* insufficiency, inadequacy; ~ **cardíaca** heart failure — **insuficiente** *adj* insufficient, inadequate

insular *adj* insular, island

insuperable *adj* insurmountable

intacto, -ta *adj* intact

intangible *adj* intangible

integral *adj* integral; **pan** ~ whole grain bread — **íntegro, -gra** *adj* honest, upright; whole, complete — **integridad** *nf* integrity; wholeness

integrar *v* integrate — **integración** *nf* (**-ciones**) integration

intelectual *adj* & *nmf* intellectual

inteligencia *nf* intelligence — **inteligente** *adj* intelligent — **inteligible** *adj* intelligible

intempestivo, -va *adj* untimely, inopportune

intención *nf* (**-ciones**) intention, intent — **intencionado, -da** *adj* intended — **intencional** *adj* intentional

intensidad *nf* intensity — **intensificar** *v* intensify — **intensivo, -va** *adj* intensive — **intenso, -sa** *adj* intense

intentar *v* attempt, try — **intento** *nm* intention; attempt

interactuar *v* interact — **interacción** *nf* (**-ciones**) interaction — **interactivo, -va** *adj* interactive

intercambiar *v* exchange, trade

interceder *v* intercede

interés *nm* (**-reses**) interest — **interesado, -da** *adj* interested; selfish — **interesante** *adj* interesting — **interesar** *v* interest; be of interest

interfaz *nf* (**-faces**) interface

interferir *v* interfere; interfere with — **interferencia** *nf* interference

interior *adj* interior, inner — **interior** *nm* interior, inside

interjección *nf* (**-ciones**) interjection

interlocutor, -tora *n* speaker

intermediario, -ria *adj* & *n* intermediary

intermedio, -dia *adj* intermediate — **intermedio** *nm* intermission

interminable *adj* interminable, endless

intermitente *adj* intermittent — **intermitente** *nm* blinker, turn signal

internacional *adj* international

interponer *v* interpose — **interponerse** *vr* intervene

interpretar *v* interpret; play, perform (in a theater) — **interpretación** *nf* (**-ciones**) interpretation — **intérprete** *nmf* interpreter; performer (of music)

interrogación *nf* (**-ciones**) interrogation; **signo de** ~ question mark — **interrogativo, -va** *adj* interrogative — **interrogatorio** *nm* interrogation, questioning — **interrogar** *v* interrogate, question

interrumpir *v* interrupt — **interrupción** *nf* (**-ciones**) interruption — **interruptor** *nm* (electrical) switch

intersección *nf* (**-ciones**) intersection

intervalo *nm* interval

intervenir *v* take part; intervene; tap (a

telephone); audit; operate on — **intervención** *nf* (**-ciones**) intervention; audit (in business) — **interventor, -tora** *n* inspector, auditor
intimidad *nf* private life; intimacy
íntimo, -ma *adj* intimate, close; private
intolerante *adj* intolerant
intoxicar *v* poison — **intoxicación** *nf* (**-ciones**) poisoning
intransitable *adj* impassable
intransitivo, -va *adj* intransitive
intrascendente *adj* unimportant, insignificant
intrínseco, -ca *adj* intrinsic
introducción *nf* (**-ciones**) introduction — **introducir** *v* introduce; insert — **introductorio, -ria** *adj* introductory
intromisión *nf* (**-siones**) interference
introvertido, -da *adj* introverted *n* introvert
intuir *v* sense — **intuición** *nf* (**-ciones**) intuition — **intuitivo, -va** *adj* intuitive
inundar *v* flood — **inundación** *nf* (**-ciones**) flood
inútil *adj* useless; disabled
invadir *v* invade
invalidez *nf* (**-deces**) invalidity; disability (in medicine) — **inválido, -da** *adj* & *n* invalid
invariable *adj* invariable
invasión *nf* (**-siones**) invasion — **invasor, -sora** *adj* invading *n* invader
inventar *v* invent; fabricate, make up (as a word, an excuse) — **invención** *nf* (**-ciones**) invention; lie, fabrication
inventario *nm* inventory
inventor, -tora *n* inventor
inverosímil *adj* unlikely
inversión *nf* (**-siones**) inversion, reversal; investment (of money, time, etc.)
inverso, -sa *adj* inverse; opposite
invertebrado, -da *adj* invertebrate — **invertebrado** *nm* invertebrate
invertir *v* invert, reverse; invest (as money, time); make an investment
investigar *v* investigate; research — **investigación** *nf* (**-ciones**) investigation; research — **investigador, -dora** *n* investigator, researcher
invicto, -ta *adj* undefeated
invierno *nm* winter
invitar *v* invite — **invitación** *nf* (**-ciones**) invitation — **invitado, -da** *n* guest
involuntario, -ria *adj* involuntary
inyectar *v* inject — **inyección** *nf* (**-ciones**) injection, shot
ir *v* go; work, function; suit — **irse** *vr* go away, be gone
ira *nf* rage, anger
iraní *adj* Iranian
iraquí *adj* Iraqi
iris *nms & pl* iris(es) (of the eye)
irlandés, -desa *adj* (**-deses** *m*) Irish
ironía *nf* irony — **irónico, -ca** *adj* ironic, ironical
irracional *adj* irrational
irradiar *v* radiate, irradiate
irreal *adj* unreal
irrefutable *adj* irrefutable
irregular *adj* irregular — **irregularidad** *nf* irregularity
irrelevante *adj* irrelevant
irrespetuoso, -sa *adj* disrespectful
irresponsable *adj* irresponsible — **irresponsabilidad** *nf* irresponsibility
irreverente *adj* irreverent
irreversible *adj* irreversible
irrevocable *adj* irrevocable
irrigar *v* irrigate — **irrigación** *nf* (**-ciones**) irrigation
irrisorio, -ria *adj* laughable, ridiculous
irritar *v* irritate — **irritarse** *vr* get annoyed — **irritación** *nf* (**-ciones**) irritation — **irritante** *adj* irritating
isla *nf* island
islámico, -ca *adj* Islamic, Muslim
islandés, -desa *adj* (**-deses** *m*) Icelandic
isleño, -ña *n* islander
israelí *adj* Israeli
istmo *nm* isthmus

italiano, -na *adj* Italian — **italiano** *nm* Italian (language)

itinerario *nm* itinerary

izquierda *nf* left — **izquierdista** *adj* & *nmf* leftist — **izquierdo, -da** *adj* left

J

j *nf* j, tenth letter of the Spanish alphabet

jabalina *nf* javelin

jabón *nm* (**-bones**) soap

jacinto *nm* hyacinth

jaguar *nm* jaguar

jaiba *nf* crab

jalea *nf* jelly

jamaicano, -na *or* **jamaiquino, -na** *adj* Jamaican

jamás *adv* never

jamón *nm* (**-mones**) ham

Januká *nmf* Hanukkah

japonés, -nesa *adj* (**-neses** *m*) Japanese — **japonés** *nm* Japanese (language)

jaque *nm* check (in chess); ~ **mate** checkmate

jaqueca *nf* headache, migraine

jarabe *nm* syrup

jardín *nm* (**-dines**) garden; ~ **infantil** *or* ~ **de niños** kindergarten — **jardinería** *nf* gardening — **jardinero, -ra** *n* gardener

jarra *nf* pitcher, jug

jaula *nf* cage

jazmín *nm* (**-mines**) jasmine

jazz *nm* jazz

jeans *nmpl* jeans

jefe, -fa *n* chief, leader; boss

jerarquía *nf* hierarchy; rank — **jerárquico, -ca** *adj* hierarchical

jerez *nm* (**-reces**) sherry

jerga *nf* coarse cloth; jargon, slang

jeringa *or* **jeringuilla** *nf* syringe

jeroglífico *nm* hieroglyphic

jersey *nm* (**-seys**) jersey

jesuita *adj* & *nm* Jesuit

Jesús *nm* Jesus

jinete *nmf* horseman, horsewoman, rider

jirafa *nf* giraffe

jockey *nmf* (**-keys**) jockey

jornada *nf* day's journey; working day

jota *nf* iota, jot

joven *adj* (**jóvenes**) young — **joven** *nmf* (**jóvenes**) young man, young woman, youth

joya *nf* jewel — **joyería** *nf* jewelry store — **joyero, -ra** *n* jeweler — **joyero** *nm* jewelry box

jubilado, -da *adj* retired — **jubilado, -da** *nmf* retiree — **jubilar** *v* retire, pension off

judaísmo *nm* Judaism

judía *nf* bean

judicial *adj* judicial

judío, -día *adj* Jewish — **judío, -día** *n* Jew

judo *nm* judo

juego *nm* game; playing (as by children)

jueves *nms* & *pl* Thursday

juez *nmf* (**jueces**) judge; umpire, referee

jugar *v* play; gamble, bet — **jugarse** *vr* risk, gamble (away) — **jugada** *nf* play, move; (dirty) trick — **jugador, -dora** *n* player; gambler

jugo *nm* juice; substance, essence — **jugoso, -sa** *adj* juicy; substantial, important

juguete *nm* toy — **juguetería** *nf* toy store

juicio *nm* judgment; reason, sense — **juicioso, -sa** *adj* wise, sensible

julio *nm* July

junio *nm* June

junta *nf* board, committee; meeting; (political) junta; joint, gasket — **junto, -ta**

adj joined; close, adjacent; (*also used adverbially*) together

Júpiter *nm* Jupiter

jurar *v* swear — **jurado** *nm* jury; juror, member of a jury — **juramento** *nm* oath

jurídico, -ca *adj* legal

jurisdicción *nf* (**-ciones**) jurisdiction

jurisprudencia *nf* jurisprudence

justicia *nf* justice, fairness

justificar *v* justify; excuse, vindicate — **justificación** *nf* (**-ciones**) justification

justo, -ta *adj* just, fair; exact; tight — **justo** *adv* just, exactly

juvenil *adj* youthful — **juventud** *nf* youth; young people

juzgar *v* try (a case in court); judge, consider — **juzgado** *nm* court, tribunal

K

k *nf* k, eleventh letter of the Spanish alphabet

karate *or* **kárate** *nm* karate

kilo *nm* kilo — **kilogramo** *nm* kilogram

kilómetro *nm* kilometer — **kilometraje** *nm* distance in kilometers, mileage

L

l *nf* l, twelfth letter of the Spanish alphabet

la *pron* her, it

laberinto *nm* labyrinth, maze

labio *nm* lip

labor *nf* work, labor; task — **laborar** *v* work — **laboratorio** *nm* laboratory, lab

labrar *v* cultivate, till — **labrado, -da** *adj* cultivated, tilled

laca *nf* lacquer; hair spray

lacio, -cia *adj* straight (of hair)

ladera *nf* slope, hillside

lado *nm* side; **al ~** next door, nearby; **al ~ de** beside, next to; **de ~** sideways; **por otro ~** on the other hand; **por todos ~s** everywhere, all around

ladrar *v* bark

ladrillo *nm* brick

ladrón, -drona *n* (**-drones** *m*) thief

lagarto *nm* lizard — **lagartija** *nf* (small) lizard

lago *nm* lake

lágrima *nf* tear

laguna *nf* lagoon

laico, -ca *adj* lay, secular — **laico, -ca** *n* layman, layperson

lamentar *v* regret, be sorry about — **lamentarse** *vr* lament — **lamento** *nm* lament, moan

lámpara *nf* lamp

lampiño, -ña *adj* beardless, hairless

lana *nf* wool

lancha *nf* boat, launch

langosta *nf* lobster; locust (insect) — **langostino** *nm* prawn, crayfish

lanudo, -da *adj* woolly

lanzar *v* throw; shoot (a glance), give (as a sigh); launch (a missile, a project) — **lanzamiento** *nm* throwing, launching

lapicero *nm* (mechanical) pencil

lápida *nf* tombstone

lápiz *nm* (**-pices**) pencil; **~ de labios** lipstick

largo, -ga *adj* long — **largo** *nm* length — **largometraje** *nm* feature film

laringe *nf* larynx — **laringitis** *nfs & pl* laryngitis

láser *nm* laser

lastimar *v* hurt — **lástima** *nf* pity

lata *nf* (tin) can

lateral *adj* side, lateral

latido *nm* beat, throb

latín *nm* Latin (language)

latino, -na *adj* Latin; Latin-American — **latino, -na** *n* Latin American — **latinoamericano, -na** *adj* Latin-American — **latinoamericano, -na** *n* Latin American

latir *v* beat, throb

latitud *nf* latitude

lavar *v* wash — **lavabo** *nm* sink — **lavado** *nm* wash, washing — **lavadora** *nf* washing machine — **lavamanos** *nms & pl* washbowl(s) — **lavandería** *nf* laundry (service) — **lavaplatos** *nms & pl* dishwasher(s); kitchen sink(s)

lazo *nm* lasso

le *pron* (to) her, (to) him, (to) it; (*as direct object*) him, you

leal *adj* loyal, faithful — **lealtad** *nf* loyalty, allegiance

lección *nf* (-ciones) lesson; lecture (in a classroom)

leche *nf* milk

lechuga *nf* lettuce

lechuza *nf* owl

lector, -tora *n* reader — **lectura** *nf* reading; reading matter

leer *v* read

legal *adj* legal — **legalidad** *nf* legality — **legalizar** *v* legalize

legislar *v* legislate — **legislación** *nf* (-ciones) legislation — **legislador, -dora** *n* legislator

legítimo, -ma *adj* legitimate; authentic — **legitimidad** *nf* legitimacy

legumbre *nf* vegetable

lejano, -na *adj* distant, far away

lejos *adv* far (away); **a lo ~** in the distance; **de ~** *or* **desde ~** from afar; **~ de** far from

lengua *nf* tongue; language

lenguaje *nm* language

lente *nmf* lens; **~s** *nmpl* eyeglasses

lenteja *nf* lentil

lento, -ta *adj* slow — **lento** *adv* slowly — **lentitud** *nf* slowness

leña *nf* firewood

león, -ona *n* (**leones** *m*) lion, lioness

leopardo *nm* leopard

les *pron* (to) them, (to) you; (*as direct object*) them, you

lesbiano, -na *adj* lesbian — **lesbiana** *nf* lesbian — **lesbianismo** *nm* lesbianism

lesión *nf* (-siones) lesion, wound — **lesionado, -da** *adj* injured, wounded — **lesionar** *v* injure, wound; damage

letra *nf* letter; handwriting; lyrics (of a song); **~ de cambio** bill of exchange; **~s** *nfpl* arts — **letrero** *nm* sign, notice

leucemia *nf* leukemia

levadura *nf* yeast

levantar *v* lift, raise; pick up; erect, put up; rouse, stir up — **levantarse** *vr* rise, stand up; get out of bed; rise up

leve *adj* light, slight; minor, trivial (as of wounds, sins)

léxico *nm* vocabulary, lexicon

ley *nf* law

leyenda *nf* legend

libanés, -nesa *adj* (-neses *m*) Lebanese

libélula *nf* dragonfly

liberación *nf* (-ciones) liberation, deliverance

liberal *adj & nmf* liberal

liberar *v* liberate, free — **libertad** *nf* freedom, liberty; **~ condicional** parole — **libertar** *v* set free

libido *nf* libido

libio, -bia *adj* Libyan

libra *nf* pound

libre *adj* free; unoccupied (of space), spare (of time); **al aire ~** in the open air

libro *nm* book — **librería** *nf* bookstore — **librero, -ra** *n* bookseller — **libreta** *nf* notebook

licencia *nf* license, permit; permission; (military) leave — **licenciado, -da** *n*

graduate; lawyer — **licenciarse** *vr*
graduate — **licenciatura** *nf* degree
lícito, -ta *adj* lawful, legal; just, fair
licor *nm* liquor; liqueur — **licorera** *nf*
decanter
licuadora *nf* blender — **licuar** *v* liquefy
líder *adj* leading — **líder** *nmf* leader —
liderato *or* **liderazgo** *nm* leadership
liga *nf* league — **ligamento** *nm* ligament
ligero, -ra *adj* light, lightweight; slight;
agile; lighthearted, superficial
lija *nf* sandpaper
lila *nf* lilac
lima *n* file **∼ para uñas** nail file —
limar *v* file
limitar *v* limit — **limitación** *nf* (**-ciones**)
limitation, limit — **límite** *nm* limit;
boundary, border; **fecha ∼** deadline —
limítrofe *adj* bordering
limón *nm* (**-mones**) lemon — **limonada**
nf lemonade
limosna *nf* alms — **limosnero, -ra** *n*
beggar
limpiabotas *nmfs & pl* bootblack(s)
limpiaparabrisas *nms & pl* windshield
wiper(s)
limpiar *v* clean, wipe (away) — **limpieza** *nf* cleanliness — **limpio** *adv*
cleanly, fairly — **limpio, -pia** *adj* clean,
neat
lindo, -da *adj* pretty, lovely
línea *nf* line; **guardar la ∼** watch one's
figure — **lineal** *adj* linear
lingüista *nmf* linguist — **lingüística** *nf*
linguistics — **lingüístico, -ca** *adj* linguistic
linterna *nf* lantern; flashlight
liquidar *v* liquidate (as merchandise);
settle, pay off (as a debt) — **liquidación** *nf* (**-ciones**) liquidation;
clearance sale — **líquido, -da** *adj* liquid
lírico, -ca *adj* lyric, lyrical — **lírica** *nf*
lyric poetry
lirio *nm* iris

liso, -sa *adj* smooth; flat; plain; **pelo ∼**
straight hair
lista *nf* stripe; list
listo, -ta *adj* clever, smart; ready
litera *nf* bunk bed, berth
literal *adj* literal
literatura *nf* literature — **literario, -ria**
adj literary
litografía *nf* lithograph (picture)
litoral *adj nm* shore, seaboard
litro *nm* liter
liturgia *nf* liturgy — **litúrgico, -ca** *adj*
liturgical
liviano, -na *adj* light
llama *nf* flame; llama (animal)
llamar *v* call; call up; phone; knock, ring
(at the door) — **llamarse** *vr* be called
— **llamada** *nf* call
llanta *nf* rim (of a wheel); tire
llanto *nm* crying, weeping
llanura *nf* plain
llave *nf* key; **cerrar con ∼** lock; **∼ inglesa** monkey wrench — **llavero** *nm*
key chain
llegar *v* arrive, come; reach; be enough;
∼ a ser become — **llegada** *nf* arrival
llenar *v* fill (up), fill in — **lleno, -na** *adj*
full
llevar *v* take, carry; lead — **llevarse** *vr*
take (away)
llorar *v* cry, weep — **lloroso, -sa** *adj*
tearful
llover *v impers* rain — **llovizna** *nf* drizzle — **lloviznar** *v impers* drizzle
lluvia *nf* rain — **lluvioso, -sa** *adj* rainy
lo *pron* him, it; (*formal, masculine*) you;
∼ que what, that which — **lo** *art* the
lobo, -ba *n* wolf
lóbulo *nm* lobe
local *adj* local — **local** *nm* premises —
localidad *nf* town, locality — **localizar** *v* localize; locate
loción *nf* (**-ciones**) lotion
loco, -ca *adj* crazy, insane — **loco, -ca** *n*
crazy person, lunatic
locución *nf* (**-ciones**) expression, phrase

locura *nf* insanity, madness

locutor, -tora *n* announcer

lodo *nm* mud

lógica *nf* logic — **lógico, -ca** *adj* logical

logotipo *nm* logo

lograr *v* achieve, attain; get, obtain — **logro** *nm* achievement, success

loma *nf* hill, hillock

lombriz *nf* (**-brices**) worm

lomo *nm* back (of an animal); spine (of a book)

longaniza *nf* sausage

longitud *nf* longitude; length

loro *nm* parrot

los, las *pron* them; you

losa *nf* flagstone

lotería *nf* lottery

loto *nm* lotus

lubricar *v* lubricate — **lubricante** *adj* lubricating — **lubricante** *nm* lubricant

lucero *nm* bright star

luchar *v* fight, struggle; wrestle (in sports) — **lucha** *nf* struggle, fight; wrestling (sport) — **luchador, -dora** *n* fighter, wrestler

lucidez *nf* (**-deces**) lucidity — **lúcido, -da** *adj* lucid

lucido, -da *adj* magnificent, splendid

luciérnaga *nf* firefly, glowworm

luego *adv* then; later (on); **desde ∼** of course; **¡hasta ∼!** see you later! — **luego** *conj* therefore

lugar *nm* place; space, room; **en ∼ de** instead of

lujo *nm* luxury — **lujoso, -sa** *adj* luxurious

luminoso, -sa *adj* shining, luminous

luna *nf* moon; mirror; **∼ de miel** honeymoon — **lunar** *adj* lunar — **lunar** *nm* mole, beauty spot

lunes *nms & pl* Monday(s)

lupa *nf* magnifying glass

luto *nm* mourning

luz *nf* (**luces**) light; lighting (in a room); electricity

M

m *nf* m, 13th letter of the Spanish alphabet

maceta *nf* flowerpot

macho *adj* male; macho — **macho** *nm* male — **machista** *nm* male chauvinist

macizo, -za *adj* solid

madera *nf* wood; lumber

madre *nf* mother — **madrastra** *nf* stepmother

madrina *nf* godmother; bridesmaid

madrugada *nf* dawn, daybreak

madurar *v* mature; ripen (of fruit) — **madurez** *nf* (**-reces**) maturity; ripeness (of fruit) — **maduro, -ra** *adj* mature; ripe

maestría *nf* mastery, skill — **maestro, -tra** *adj* masterly, skilled — **maestro, -tra** *n* teacher (in grammar school); expert, master

magisterio *nm* teachers, teaching profession

magistrado, -da *n* magistrate, judge

magistral *adj* masterful; magisterial (as of an attitude)

magnífico, -ca *adj* magnificent

mago, -ga *n* magician; **los Reyes Magos** the Magi

mahometano, -na *adj* Islamic, Muslim — **mahometano, -na** *n* Muslim

maicena *nf* cornstarch

maíz *nm* corn

mal *adv* badly, poorly; incorrectly; with difficulty, hardly — **mal** *nm* evil; harm, damage; illness

malasio, -sia *adj* Malaysian

malayo, -ya *adj* Malay, Malayan

maldad *nf* evil; evil deed

maleable *adj* malleable

maleducado, -da *adj* rude

malentendido *nm* misunderstanding

malestar *nm* discomfort; uneasiness

maleta *nf* suitcase — **maletero, -ra** *n* porter — **maletero** *nm* trunk (of an automobile) — **maletín** *nm* (**-tines**) briefcase; overnight bag

malo, -la *adj* bad; poor (in quality); unwell — **malo, -la** *n* villain, bad guy (as in movies)

maltratar *v* mistreat

mamá *nf* mom, mama

mamífero, -ra *adj* mammalian — **mamífero** *nm* mammal

manantial *nm* spring; source

manchar *v* stain, spot, mark — **mancharse** *vr* get dirty — **mancha** *nf* stain

manco, -ca *adj* one-armed, one-handed

mandar *v* command, order; send; hurl, throw; be in charge — **mandamiento** *nm* order, warrant; commandment (in religion)

mandarina *nf* mandarin orange, tangerine

mandato *nm* term of office; mandate — **mandatario, -ria** *n* leader (in politics); agent (in law)

mandíbula *nf* jaw, jawbone

mando *nm* command, leadership

manecilla *nf* hand (of a clock), pointer

manejar *v* handle, operate; manage (as a business); drive (a car) — **manejo** *nm* handling, use; management

manera *nf* way, manner

manga *nf* sleeve

mango *nm* hilt, handle; mango (fruit)

manguera *nf* hose

maní *nm* (**-níes**) peanut

manía *nf* mania, obsession; craze, fad

manicomio *nm* insane asylum

manifestar *v* demonstrate, show; express, declare — **manifestarse** *vr* become evident; demonstrate (in politics) — **manifestación** *nf* (**-ciones**) manifestation, sign; demonstration (in politics) — **manifestante** *nmf* protester, demonstrator

manija *nf* handle

manipular *v* manipulate; handle — **manipulación** *nf* (**-ciones**) manipulation

maniquí *nmf* (**-quíes**) mannequin, model — **maniquí** *nm* mannequin, dummy

manjar *nm* delicacy, special dish

mano *nf* hand

mansión *nf* (**-siones**) mansion

manso, -sa *adj* gentle; tame (of an animal)

manta *nf* blanket

mantel *nm* tablecloth

mantener *v* support; preserve; keep up, maintain (as relations, correspondence); affirm — **mantenimiento** *nm* maintenance; sustenance

mantequilla *nf* butter

manual *adj* manual — **manual** *nm* manual, handbook

manubrio *nm* handle, crank; handlebars

manzana *nf* apple; (city) block

mañana *adv* tomorrow — **mañana** *nf* morning

mapa *nm* map — **mapamundi** *nm* map of the world

maquillaje *nm* makeup — **maquillarse** *vr* put on makeup

máquina *nf* machine; locomotive — **maquinaria** *nf* machinery; mechanism, works (as of a watch)

mar *nmf* sea

maraca *nf* maraca

maratón *nm* (**-tones**) marathon

maravilla *nf* wonder, marvel — **maravillar** *v* astonish — **maravillarse** *vr* be amazed — **maravilloso, -sa** *adj* marvelous

marca *nf* mark; brand (on livestock); record (in sports) — **marcador** *nm* scoreboard; marker, felt-tipped pen

marcar *v* mark; brand (livestock); indicate, show; dial (as a telephone); score (in sports)

marchar *v* go; walk; work, run — **marcharse** *vr* leave, go — **marcha** *nf* march; pace, speed

marco *nm* frame; setting, framework

marea *nf* tide — **marear** *v* make nauseous or dizzy — **marearse** *vr* become nauseated or dizzy — **mareado, -da** *adj* sick, nauseous; dazed, dizzy

maremoto *nm* tidal wave

mareo *nm* nausea, seasickness; dizziness

margarina *nf* margarine

margarita *nf* daisy

margen *nm* (**márgenes**) edge, border; margin (as of a page) — **marginado, -da** *adj* alienated — **marginado, -da** *n* outcast — **marginal** *adj* marginal

marido *nm* husband

marimba *nf* marimba

marina *nf* coast

marinero, -ra *adj* sea, marine; seaworthy (of a ship) — **marinero** *nm* sailor — **marino, -na** *adj* marine — **marino** *nm* seaman, sailor

marioneta *nf* puppet, marionette

mariposa *nf* butterfly

marisco *nm* shellfish; ∼**s** *nmpl* seafood

marítimo, -ma *adj* maritime, shipping

mármol *nm* marble

marquesina *nf* marquee, (glass) canopy

marrano, -na *n* pig, hog

marrón *adj & nm* (**-rrones**) brown

marroquí *adj* Moroccan

Marte *nm* Mars

martes *nms & pl* Tuesday(s)

martillo *nm* hammer — **martillar** *or* **martillear** *v* hammer

mártir *nmf* martyr

marxismo *nm* Marxism — **marxista** *adj & nmf* Marxist

marzo *nm* March

mas *conj* but

más *adv* more; **el/la/lo** ∼ (the) most — **más** *adj* more; most — **más** *prep* plus

masa *nf* mass, volume; dough (in cooking); ∼**s** *nfpl* people, masses

masaje *nm* massage

mascar *v* chew

máscara *nf* mask (as ceremonial, decorative) — **mascarilla** *nf* mask (as cosmetic, protective)

mascota *nf* mascot

masculino, -na *adj* masculine, male; manly; masculine (in grammar)

masivo, -va *adj* mass, large-scale

masticar *v* chew

matador *nm* matador, bullfighter

matar *v* kill; slaughter (animals) — **matarse** *vr* be killed; commit suicide

matemáticas *nfpl* mathematics — **matemático, -ca** *adj* mathematical — **matemático, -ca** *n* mathematician

materia *nf* matter; material — **material** *adj* material — **material** *nm* material; equipment, gear

maternidad *nf* motherhood; maternity hospital — **materno, -na** *adj* maternal; **lengua materna** native language, mother tongue

matrícula *nf* list, roll, register; registration; license plate (of an automobile) — **matricular** *v* register

matrimonio *nm* marriage; (married) couple

matriz *nf* (**-trices**) uterus, womb

maullar *v* meow

maxilar *nm* jaw, jawbone

máxima *nf* maxim

máximo, -ma *adj* maximum, highest

maya *adj* Mayan

mayo *nm* May

mayonesa *nf* mayonnaise

mayor *adj* bigger, larger, greater, older; biggest, largest, greatest, oldest ∼ **de edad** of (legal) age — **mayor** *nmf* major (in the military); adult; ∼**es** *nmfpl* grown-ups

mayoría *nf* majority

mayorista *adj* wholesale — **mayorista** *nmf* wholesaler

mayúscula *nf* capital letter — **mayúsculo, -la** *adj* capital, uppercase

mazapán *nm* (**-panes**) marzipan

mazorca *nf* spike (of a plant) ∼ **de maíz** corncob

me *pron* me; to me, for me, from me; myself, to myself, for myself, from myself

mecánica *nf* mechanics — **mecánico, -ca** *adj* mechanical — **mecánico, -ca** *n* mechanic

mecanismo *nm* mechanism

mecedora *nf* rocking chair

mecer *v* rock; push (on a swing) — **mecerse** *vr* rock, swing

media *nf* stocking

mediano, -na *adj* medium, average

medianoche *nf* midnight

mediante *prep* through, by means of

medicación *nf* (**-ciones**) medication — **medicamento** *nm* medicine — **medicar** *v* medicate — **medicina** *nf* medicine — **medicinal** *adj* medicinal

medición *nf* (**-ciones**) measurement

médico, -ca *adj* medical — **médico, -ca** *n* doctor, physician

medida *nf* measurement, measure

medio, -dia *adv* half — **medio, -dia** *nm* half; means, way; ∼ **ambiente** environment — **medio, -dia** *adj* half; **la clase media** the middle class

mediodía *nm* noon, midday

medir *v* measure; weigh, consider — **medirse** *vr* be moderate

meditar *v* meditate, contemplate; think over, consider; plan, work out — **meditación** *nf* (**-ciones**) meditation

mediterráneo, -nea *adj* Mediterranean

megabyte *nm* megabyte

mejilla *nf* cheek

mejillón *nm* (**-llones**) mussel

mejor *adv* better; best — **mejor** *adj* better; best

mejorar *v* improve; get better

melancolía *nf* melancholy — **melancólico, -ca** *adj* melancholic, melancholy

mellizo, -za *adj & n* twin

melocotón *nm* (**-tones**) peach

melodía *nf* melody

melón *nm* (**-lones**) melon

memoria *nf* memory; remembrance; report — **memorizar** *v* memorize

mencionar *v* mention, refer to — **mención** *nf* (**-ciones**) mention

mendigar *v* beg

menopausia *nf* menopause

menor *adj* smaller, lesser, younger; smallest, least, youngest — **menor** *nmf* minor, juvenile

menos *adv* less; least — **menos** *adj* less, fewer; least, fewest — **menos** *prep* minus; except ∼ *pron* less, fewer

mensaje *nm* message — **mensajero, -ra** *n* messenger

menstruar *v* menstruate — **menstruación** *nf* menstruation

mensual *adj* monthly — **mensualidad** *nf* monthly payment; monthly salary

menta *nf* mint, peppermint

mental *adj* mental — **mentalidad** *nf* mentality

mente *nf* mind

mentir *v* lie — **mentira** *nf* lie — **mentiroso, -sa** *adj* lying — **mentiroso, -sa** *n* liar

mentón *nm* (**-tones**) chin

menú *nm* (**-nús**) menu

menudo, -da *adj* small, insignificant

meñique *adj* little — **dedo meñique** *nm* little finger, pinkie

mercado *nm* market

mercancía *nf* merchandise, goods — **mercantil** *adj* commercial

Mercurio *nm* Mercury (planet)

merecer *v* deserve; be worthy

merienda *nf* afternoon snack, tea

mérito *nm* merit, worth — **mérito** *n* intern, trainee

mermelada *nf* marmalade, jam

mes *nm* month

mesa *nf* table

Mesías *nm* Messiah

mestizo, -za *adj* of mixed ancestry; hybrid — **mestizo, -za** *n* person of mixed ancestry

meta *nf* goal, objective

metáfora *nf* metaphor — **metafórico, -ca** *adj* metaphoric, metaphorical

metal *nm* metal — **metálico, -ca** *adj* metallic, metal

metamorfosis *nfs & pl* metamorphosis

meteorología *nf* meteorology — **meteorólogo, -ga** *adj* meteorological, meteorologic — **meteorólogo, -ga** *n* meteorologist

meter *v* put (in); place (as in a job); involve; make, cause — **meterse** *vr* get in, enter

método *nm* method — **metódico, -ca** *adj* methodical — **metodología** *nf* methodology

metro *nm* meter; subway (train)

metrópoli *nf or* **metrópolis** *nfs & pl* metropolis(es) — **metropolitano, -na** *adj* metropolitan

mexicano, -na *adj* Mexican

mezcla *nf* mixture; mortar — **mezclar** *v* mix, blend; mix up, muddle; involve — **mezclarse** *vr* get mixed up

mezquita *nf* mosque

mi *adj* my

mí *pron* me

mico *nm* (long-tailed) monkey

microbio *nm* microbe, germ — **microbiología** *nf* microbiology

micrófono *nm* microphone

microonda *nf* microwave (radiation); **un horno de** ∼**s** *nms & pl* microwave (oven)(s)

microscopio *nm* microscope

miedo *nm* fear — **miedoso, -sa** *adj* fearful

miel *nf* honey

miembro *nm* member; limb, extremity

mientras *conj* while, as — **mientras** *adv or* ∼ **tanto** meanwhile, in the meantime

miércoles *nms & pl* Wednesday(s)

migración *nf* (**-ciones**) migration

migraña *nf* migraine

mil *adj & nm* thousand

milagro *nm* miracle

milenio *nm* millennium

milímetro *nm* millimeter

militar *adj* military — **militar** *nmf* soldier — **militarizar** *v* militarize

milla *nf* mile

millar *nm* thousand

millón *nm* (**-llones**) million — **millonario, -ria** *n* millionaire

mímica *nf* mime, sign language; mimicry

mimo *nm* pampering, indulgence; ∼ *nmf* mime

mina *nf* mine; lead (for pencils)

mineral *adj* mineral — **mineral** *nm* mineral; ore

minería *nf* mining — **minero, -ra** *adj* mining — **minero, -ra** *n* miner

minifalda *nf* miniskirt

minimizar *v* minimize

mínimo, -ma *adj* minimum; minute — **mínimo** *nm* minimum

ministerio *nm* ministry — **ministro, -tra** *n* minister, secretary

minoría *nf* minority

minoritario, -ria *adj* minority

minusválido, -da *adj* disabled

minuto *nm* minute — **minutero** *nm* minute hand

mío, mía *adj* mine

miope *adj* nearsighted

mirar *v* look; look at; watch; consider — **mirarse** *vr* look at oneself; look at each other — **mirada** *nf* look

misa *nf* Mass

misión *nf* (**-siones**) mission

mismo *adv* right, exactly — **mismo, -ma** *adj* same; very — **mismo** *pron* self **yo** ∼ myself, etc. (used reflexively)

misterio *nm* mystery — **misterioso, -sa** *adj* mysterious

mística *nf* mysticism — **místico, -ca** *adj* mystic, mystical — **místico, -ca** *n* mystic

mitad *nf* half; middle

mitin *nm* (**mítines**) (political) meeting

mito *nm* myth — **mitología** *nm* mythology

mixto, -ta *adj* mixed, joint; coeducational (of a school)

mocasín *nm* (**-sines**) moccasin

mochila *nf* backpack, knapsack

moco *nm* mucus

moda *nf* fashion, style — **modales** *nmpl* manners

modelo *adj* model — **modelo** *nm* model, pattern; *nmf* model, mannequin

módem *or* **modem** *nm* modem

moderar *v* moderate; reduce (as speed)

moderno, -na *adj* modern — **modernismo** *nm* modernism

modesto, -ta *adj* modest

modificar *v* modify, alter — **modificación** *nf* (**-ciones**) alteration

modismo *nm* idiom

modo *nm* way, manner

mojar *v* wet, moisten — **mojado, -da** *adj* wet, damp

molestar *v* annoy, bother; be a nuisance — **molestarse** *vr* bother; take offense — **molestia** *nf* annoyance, nuisance; discomfort — **molesto, -ta** *adj* annoyed; annoying; in discomfort

molinillo *nm* grinder, mill

momento *nm* moment, instant; (period of) time

moneda *nf* coin; currency (of a country)

monetario, -ria *adj* monetary

monja *nf* nun

mono, -na *n* monkey — **mono, -na** *adj* lovely, cute

monografía *nf* monograph

monolingüe *adj* monolingual

monólogo *nm* monologue

monosílabo *nm* monosyllable

monoteísta *adj* monotheistic

montaje *nm* assembly; staging (in theater), editing (of films)

montaña *nf* mountain — **montañero, -ra** *n* mountain climber — **montañoso, -sa** *adj* mountainous

montar *v* mount; establish; assemble, put together

monte *nm* mountain; woodland

montura *nf* mount (horse); saddle; frame (of eyeglasses)

monumento *nm* monument

monzón *nm* (**-zones**) monsoon

moño *nm* bun (of hair); bow (knot)

mora *nf* mulberry; blackberry

morado, -da *adj* purple — **morado** *nm* purple

moral *adj* moral — **moral** *nf* ethics, morals; morale — **moraleja** *nf* moral (of a story)

morder *v* bite

moreno, -na *adj* dark-haired, brunette; dark-skinned — **moreno, -na** *n* brunette; dark-skinned person

morfina *nf* morphine

morir *v* die; die out, go out

moroso, -sa *adj* delinquent, in arrears

morral *nm* backpack

mortal *adj* mortal; deadly (as of a wound, an enemy) — **mortal** *nmf* mortal — **mortalidad** *nf* mortality

mosca *nf* fly

mostaza *nf* mustard

mostrador *nm* counter (in a store)

mostrar *v* show

motín *nm* (**-tines**) riot, uprising; mutiny (of troops)

motivo *nm* motive, cause; motif (as in art, music) — **motivación** *nf* (**-ciones**) motivation — **motivar** *v* cause; motivate

motocicleta *nf* motorcycle — **motociclista** *nmf* motorcyclist

motor, -triz *or* **-tora** *adj* motor (biology, technology) — **motor** *nm* motor, engine

mover *v* move, shift; shake (the head) — **moverse** *vr* move (over)

móvil *adj* mobile — **móvil** *nm* motive; mobile — **movilidad** *nf* mobility

movimiento *nm* movement, motion

muchacho, -cha *n* kid, boy, girl

mucho *adv* very much, a lot; long, a long time — **mucho, -cha** *adj* a lot of, many, much — **mucho, -cha** *pron* a lot, many, much

mudo, -da *adj* mute; silent

mueble *nm* piece of furniture

muela *nf* tooth, molar

muerte *nf* death — **muerto, -ta** *adj* dead; dull (as of colors) — **muerto, -ta** *nm* dead person, deceased

muestra *nf* sample; sign, show

mujer *nf* woman; wife

mulato, -ta *adj & n* mulatto

muleta *nf* crutch; prop, support

multa *nf* fine — **multar** *v* fine

multimedia *adj* multimedia

multinacional *adj* multinational

multiplicar *v* multiply — **multiplicarse** *vr* multiply, reproduce — **múltiple** *adj*

multiple — **multiplicación** *nf* (-ciones) multiplication — **múltiplo** *nm* multiple

multitud *nf* crowd, multitude

mundo *nm* world — **mundial** *adj* world, worldwide

municipal *adj* municipal — **municipio** *nm* municipality; town council

muñeca *nf* wrist; doll — **muñeco** *nm* boy doll; dummy, puppet

mural *adj & nm* mural — **muralla** *nf* wall, rampart

murciélago *nm* bat (animal)

muro *nm* wall

músculo *nm* muscle — **muscular** *adj* muscular — **musculoso, -sa** *adj* muscular

museo *nm* museum

música *nf* music — **musical** *adj* musical — **músico, -ca** *adj* musical — **músico, -ca** *n* musician

muslo *nm* thigh

musulmán, -mana *adj & n* (-manes *m*) Muslim

mutuo, -tua *adj* mutual

muy *adv* very, quite; too

N

n *nf* n, 14th letter of the Spanish alphabet

nacer *v* be born; arise, spring up

nacido, -da *adj* born —**nacido, -da** *n* **recién** ~ newborn — **nacimiento** *nm* birth

nación *nf* (-ciones) nation, country — **nacional** *adj* national — **nacional** *nmf* national, citizen — **nacionalidad** *nf* nationality — **nacionalizar** *v* nationalize; naturalize (as a citizen) — **nacionalizarse** *vr* become naturalized

nada *pron* nothing; **de** ~ you're welcome — **nada** *adv* not at all

nadar *v* swim — **nadador, -dora** *n* swimmer

nadie *pron* nobody, no one

naipe *nm* playing card

nalgas *nfpl* buttocks, bottom

naranja *adj & nm* orange (color) — **naranja** *nf* orange (fruit)

narciso *nm* narcissus, daffodil

narcótico, -ca *adj* narcotic — **narcótico** *nm* narcotic — **narcotraficante** *nmf* drug trafficker — **narcotráfico** *nm* drug trafficking

nariz *nf* (-rices) nose

narrar *v* narrate, tell — **narración** *nf* (-ciones) narration — **narrador, -dora** *n* narrator — **narrativa** *nf* narrative, storytelling

nasal *adj* nasal

natación *nf* (-ciones) swimming

natal *adj* native, birth — **natalidad** *nf* birthrate

nativo, -va *adj & n* native

natural *adj* natural; normal; ~ **de** native of, from — **natural** *nm* native — **naturaleza** *nf* nature — **naturalidad** *nf* naturalness — **naturalmente** *adv* naturally; of course

naufragio *nm* shipwreck — **náufrago, -ga** *adj* shipwrecked

náusea *nf* nausea

navaja *nf* pocketknife, penknife

naval *adj* naval

nave *nf* ship; ~ **espacial** spaceship

navegar *v* navigate, sail — **navegable** *adj* navigable — **navegación** *nf* (**-ciones**) navigation — **navegante** *adj* sailing, seafaring — **navegante** *nmf* navigator

Navidad *nf* Christmas; **feliz** ~ Merry Christmas

neblina *nf* mist

necesario, -ria *adj* necessary — **necesariamente** *adv* necessarily — **necesidad** *nf* need, necessity; poverty — **necesitado, -da** *adj* needy — **necesitar** *v* need

necio, -cia *adj* silly, dumb

neerlandés, -desa *adj* (**-deses** *m*) Dutch — **neerlandés** *nm* Dutch (language)

negar *v* deny; refuse — **negarse** *vr* refuse — **negación** *nf* (**-ciones**) denial; negative (in grammar) — **negativa** *nf* denial; refusal — **negativo, -va** *adj* negative

negociar *v* negotiate; deal, do business — **negociable** *adj* negotiable — **negociación** *nf* (**-ciones**) negotiation — **negociante** *nmf* businessman, businesswoman — **negocio** *nm* business; deal; ~**s** business, commerce

negro, -gra *adj* black, dark — **negro, -gra** *n* dark-skinned person — **negro** *nm* black (color)

nene, -na *n* baby, small child

neoyorquino, -na *adj* of or from New York

Neptuno *nm* Neptune

nervio *nm* nerve — **nerviosismo** *nf* nervousness — **nervioso, -sa** *adj* nervous, anxious; **sistema nervioso** nervous system

neumático *nm* tire

neumonía *nf* pneumonia

neurólogo, -ga *n* neurologist

neurosis *nfs & pl* neurosis (-roses) — **neurótico, -ca** *adj & n* neurotic

neutral *adj* neutral — **neutro, -tra** *adj* neutral; neuter (in biology, grammar)

nevar *v impers* snow — **nevada** *nf* snowfall — **nevado, -da** *adj* snow-covered, snowy; snow-white

nevera *nf* refrigerator

ni *conj* neither, nor; ~ **siquiera** not even

nicaragüense *adj* Nicaraguan

nicotina *nf* nicotine

nido *nm* nest

niebla *nf* fog, mist

nieto, -ta *n* grandson, granddaughter; **nietos** *nmpl* grandchildren

nieve *nf* snow

nigeriano, -na *adj* Nigerian

nilón *or* **nilon** *nm* (**-lones**) nylon

ninguno, -na *adj* no, not any — **ninguno, -na** *pron* neither, none; no one, nobody

niño, -ña *n* child, boy, girl ~ *adj* young — **niñero, -ra** *n* baby-sitter, nanny — **niñez** *nf* (**-ñeces**) childhood

nipón, -pona *adj* Japanese

nitrógeno *nm* nitrogen

nivel *nm* level, height; ~ **de vida** standard of living — **nivelar** *v* level (out)

no *adv* not; no

noche *nf* night, evening; **buenas** ~**s** good evening, good night; **de** ~ *or* **por la** ~ at night — **Nochebuena** *nf* Christmas Eve — **Nochevieja** *nf* New Year's Eve

noción *nf* (**-ciones**) notion, concept; **nociones** *nfpl* rudiments

nocturno, -na *adj* night; nocturnal (as of animals) — **nocturno** *nm* nocturne

nogal *nm* walnut tree

nómada *nmf* nomad

nombrar *v* appoint; mention — **nombrado, -da** *adj* famous, well-known — **nombramiento** *nm* appointment, nomination — **nombre** *nm* name; noun

nordeste *or* **noreste** *adj* northeastern — **nordeste** *or* **noreste** *nm* northeast

nórdico, -ca *adj* Scandinavian

norma *nf* rule, norm, standard — **normal** *adj* normal — **normalidad** *nf* normality — **normalizar** *v* normalize; standardize — **normalmente** *adv* ordinarily, generally

noroeste *adj* northwestern — **noroeste** *nm* northwest

norte *adj* north, northern — **norte** *nm* north

norteamericano, -na *adj* North American

noruego, -ga *adj* Norwegian — **noruego** *nm* Norwegian (language)

nos *pron* us; to us, for us, from us; ourselves; each other, one another

nosotros, -tras *pron* we; us

nostalgia *nf* nostalgia

nota *nf* note; grade, mark (in school)

notario, -ria *n* notary (public)

noticia *nf* news item, piece of news — **noticiero** *nm* newscast

notorio, -ria *adj* obvious; well-known

novecientos, -tas *adj* nine hundred — **novecientos** *nms & pl* nine hundred

novedad *nf* newness, innovation — **novedoso, -sa** *adj* original, novel

novela *nf* novel; soap opera — **novelista** *nmf* novelist

noveno, -na *adj* ninth — **noveno** *nm* ninth

noventa *adj & nm* ninety

noviazgo *nm* engagement

noviembre *nm* November

novio, -via *n* boyfriend, girlfriend; bridegroom, bride (at a wedding)

nube *nf* cloud — **nubarrón** *nm* (-rrones) storm cloud — **nublado, -da** *adj* cloudy — **nublado** *nm* storm cloud — **nublar** *v* cloud — **nublarse** *vr* get cloudy

nuca *nf* nape, back of the neck

nuclear *adj* nuclear

nudillo *nm* knuckle

nudismo *nm* nudism — **nudista** *adj & nmf* nudist

nudo *nm* knot

nuera *nf* daughter-in-law

nuestro, -tra *adj* our — **nuestro, -tra** *pron* (*with definite article*) **el/la/lo** ～ ours, our own

nuevamente *adv* again, anew

nueve *adj & nm* nine

nuevo, -va *adj* new; **de nuevo** again, once more

nuez *nf* (**nueces**) nut

nulo, -la *adj* null, invalid; useless, inept ～ **y sin efecto** null and void

numerar *v* number — **numeración** *nf* (-**ciones**) numbering; numbers, numerals — **numeral** *adj* numeral — **número** *nm* number, numeral; issue (of a publication) — **numérico, -ca** *adj* numerical — **numeroso, -sa** *adj* numerous

nunca *adv* never, ever

nupcial *adj* nuptial, wedding — **nupcias** *nfpl* nuptials, wedding

nutria *nf* otter

nutrir *v* feed, nourish; fuel, foster — **nutrición** *nf* (-**ciones**) nutrition — **nutritivo, -va** *adj* nourishing, nutritious

Ñ

ñ *nf* 15th letter of the Spanish alphabet

O

o[1] *nf* o, 16th letter of the Spanish alphabet

o[2] *conj* or, either; ∼ **sea** in other words

obedecer *v* obey — **obediencia** *nf* obedience — **obediente** *adj* obedient

obeso, -sa *adj* obese — **obesidad** *nf* obesity

obispo *nm* bishop

objeto *nm* object — **objetivo, -va** *adj* objective — **objetivo** *nm* objective, goal

oblicuo, -cua *adj* oblique

obligar *v* require, oblige — **obligarse** *vr* commit oneself (to do something) — **obligación** *nf* (**-ciones**) obligation — **obligatorio, -ria** *adj* mandatory

obra *nf* deed; work (as of art, literature); construction work — **obrar** *v* work, produce; act, behave — **obrero, -ra** *adj* working; **la clase obrera** the working class — **obrero, -ra** *n* worker, laborer

obsequiar *v* give, present — **obsequio** *nm* gift, present

observar *v* watch; notice; keep, observe (as a custom, ritual) — **observación** *nf* (**-ciones**) observation — **observador, -dora** *adj* observant — **observador, -dora** *n* observer — **observatorio** *nm* observatory

obsesionar *v* obsess — **obsesión** *nf* (**-siones**) obsession — **obsesivo, -va** *adj* obsessive

obstaculizar *v* hinder — **obstáculo** *nm* obstacle

obstar *v* hinder — **no obstante** *conj phr* nevertheless, however — **no obstante** *prep phr* in spite of, despite

obstinarse *vr* be stubborn — **obstinado, -da** *adj* obstinate, stubborn; persistent

obtener *v* obtain, get

obvio, -via *adj* obvious

ocasión *nf* (**-siones**) occasion; opportunity; bargain — **ocasional** *adj* occasional; accidental, chance — **ocasionar** *v* cause

ocaso *nm* sunset

occidente *nm* west — **occidental** *adj* western, Western

océano *nm* ocean

ochenta *adj* & *nm* eighty

ocho *adj* & *nm* eight — **ochocientos, -tas** *adj* eight hundred — **ochocientos** *nms* & *pl* eight hundred

ocio *nm* free time, leisure — **ocioso, -sa** *adj* idle, inactive; useless

octágono *nm* octagon

octavo, -va *adj* & *n* eighth

octubre *nm* October

ocular *adj* ocular, eye — **oculista** *nmf* ophthalmologist

ocultar *v* conceal, hide — **ocultarse** *vr* hide — **oculto, -ta** *adj* hidden, occult

ocupar *v* occupy; hold (as a position); provide work for — **ocuparse** *vr* concern oneself with; ∼ **de** take care of (as children) — **ocupación** *nf* (**-ciones**) occupation; job — **ocupado, -da** *adj* busy; occupied (of a place) — **ocupante** *nmf* occupant

ocurrir *v* occur, happen — **ocurrirse** *vr* occur to

odiar *v* hate — **odio** *nm* hatred — **odioso, -sa** *adj* hateful

odontología *nf* dentistry, dental surgery — **odontólogo, -ga** *n* dentist, dental surgeon

oeste *adj* west, western — **oeste** *nm* west

ofender *v* offend — **ofenderse** *vr* take offense — **ofensa** *nf* offense, insult

oferta *nf* offer; **de ~** on sale

oficial *adj* official; officer (in the military)

oficina *nf* office — **oficinista** *nmf* office worker

oficio *nm* trade, profession

ofrecer *v* offer; provide, present (as an opportunity) — **ofrecerse** *vr* volunteer — **ofrecimiento** *nm* offer

oftalmología *nf* ophthalmology — **oftalmólogo, -ga** *n* ophthalmologist

ogro *nm* ogre

oír *v* hear; listen to — **oído** *nm* ear; (sense of) hearing

ojal *nm* buttonhole

ojalá *interj* I hope so!, if only!

ojear *v* eye, look at — **ojeada** *nf* glimpse, glance

ojo *nm* eye — **¡ojo!** *interj* look out!, pay attention!

ola *nf* wave — **oleaje** *nm* swell (of the sea)

olé *interj* bravo!

oleada *nf* wave, swell

oler *v* smell

olfatear *v* sniff; sense, sniff out — **olfato** *nm* sense of smell

Olimpiada *or* **Olimpíada** *nf* Olympics, Olympic Games — **olímpico, -ca** *adj* Olympic

oliva *nf* olive — **olivo** *nm* olive tree

olla *nf* pot

olmo *nm* elm

olor *nm* smell — **oloroso, -sa** *adj* fragrant

olvidar *v* forget; leave behind; omit — **olvidarse** *vr* forget — **olvidadizo, -za** *adj* forgetful — **olvido** *nm* forgetfulness

ombligo *nm* navel

omitir *v* omit — **omisión** *nf* (**-siones**) omission

omnipotente *adj* omnipotent

once *adj & nm* eleven

onda *nf* wave — **ondear** *v* ripple — **ondulación** *nf* (**-ciones**) undulation — **ondulado, -da** *adj* wavy — **ondular** *v* wave (hair); undulate, ripple

onza *nf* ounce

opaco, -ca *adj* opaque; dull

opción *nf* (**-ciones**) option — **opcional** *adj* optional

ópera *nf* opera

operar *v* operate; operate on; deal, do business — **operarse** *vr* have an operation — **operación** *nf* (**-ciones**) operation; transaction, deal — **operador, -dora** *n* operator

opinar *v* think; express an opinion — **opinión** *nf* (**-niones**) opinion

opio *nm* opium

oponer *v* raise, put forward (as arguments) — **oponerse** *vr* oppose, be against — **oponente** *nmf* opponent

oportunidad *nf* opportunity — **oportunista** *nmf* opportunist — **oportuno, -na** *adj* opportune, timely

opositor, -tora *n* opponent — **oposición** *nf* (**-ciones**) opposition

oprimir *v* press, squeeze — **opresión** *nf* (**-siones**) oppression

optar *v* apply for

óptica *nf* optics; optician's (shop) — **óptico, -ca** *adj* optical — **óptico, -ca** *n* optician

optimismo *nm* optimism — **optimista** *adj* optimistic — **optimista** *nmf* optimist

optometría *nf* optometry

opuesto *adj* opposite

oración *nf* (**-ciones**) prayer; sentence, clause

orador, -dora *n* speaker

oral *adj* oral

orar *v* pray

órbita *nf* orbit (in astronomy)

orden *nm* (**órdenes**) order; **orden** *nf* (**órdenes**) order (of food)

ordenar *v* order, command; put in order

ordeñar *v* milk

ordinal *adj & nm* ordinal

ordinario, -ria *adj* ordinary; common, vulgar

oreja *nf* ear

orgánico, -ca *adj* organic

organismo *nm* organism; agency, organization

organizar *v* organize — **organizarse** *vr* get organized — **organización** *nf* (**-ciones**) organization

órgano *nm* organ

orgasmo *nm* orgasm

orgullo *nm* pride — **orgulloso, -sa** *adj* proud

orientación *nf* (**-ciones**) orientation; direction; guidance

oriental *adj* eastern; oriental — **oriental** *nmf* Oriental, Asian

orientar *v* orient, position; guide, direct

oriente *nm* east, East

origen *nm* (**orígenes**) origin — **original** *adj & nm* original — **originar** *v* give rise to

originario, -ria *adj* original; ~ **de** native to

orilla *nf* border, edge

orinar *v* urinate — **orina** *nf* urine

oro *nm* gold

orquesta *nf* orchestra

orquídea *nf* orchid

ortografía *nf* spelling

orzuelo *nm* sty (in the eye)

os *pron pl* you, (to) you; yourselves, (to) yourselves; each other, (to) each other

osado, -da *adj* bold, daring — **osadía** *nf* boldness, daring

oscuro, -ra *adj* dark — **oscurecer** *v* darken — **oscurecer** *v impers* get dark — **oscurecerse** *vr* grow dark — **oscuridad** *nf* darkness

oso, osa *n* bear

osteoporosis *nf* osteoporosis

ostra *nf* oyster

otoño *nm* autumn, fall

otorgar *v* grant, award

otro, otra[1] *adj* another, other; **otra vez** again

otro, otra[2] *pron* another (one), other (one)

óvalo *nm* oval — **oval** *or* **ovalado, -da** *adj* oval

ovario *nm* ovary

oveja *nf* sheep, ewe

overol *nm* overalls

ovni *or* **OVNI** *nm* UFO

ovular *v* ovulate — **ovulación** *nf* (**-ciones**) ovulation

oxígeno *nm* oxygen

oyente *nmf* listener

P

p *nf* p, 17th letter of the Spanish alphabet

pabellón *nm* (**-llones**) pavilion; block, building (as in a hospital complex)

paciencia *nf* patience — **paciente** *adj & nmf* patient

pacificar *v* pacify, calm — **pacífico, -ca** *adj* peaceful, pacific — **pacifista** *adj & nmf* pacifist

pacto *nm* pact, agreement

padecer *v* suffer, endure

padre *nm* father; ~**s** *nmpl* parents — **padrastro** *nm* stepfather — **padrino** *nm* godfather; best man (at a wedding)

paella *nf* paella

pagar *v* pay, pay for

página *nf* page

pago *nm* payment

país *nm* country, nation; region, land —
paisaje *nm* scenery, landscape
paja *nf* straw
pájaro *nm* bird; ∼ **carpintero** woodpecker
pala *nf* shovel, spade
palabra *nf* word; speech
palacio *nm* palace, mansion; ∼ **de justicia** courthouse
paladar *nm* palate
palanca *nf* lever, crowbar; leverage, influence; ∼ **de cambio** *or* ∼ **de velocidades** gearshift
palco *nm* box (in a theater)
palestino, -na *adj* Palestinian
pálido, -da *adj* pale — **palidecer** *v* turn pale
palillo *nm* toothpick
palma *nf* palm (of the hand); palm (tree or leaf) — **palmada** *nf* pat, slap
palmera *nf* palm tree
palo *nm* stick
paloma *nf* pigeon, dove
palomitas *nfpl* popcorn
palpar *v* feel, touch
palpitar *v* palpitate, throb — **palpitación** *nf* (**-ciones**) palpitation
paludismo *nm* malaria
pampa *nf* pampa
pan *nm* bread
pana *nf* corduroy
panadería *nf* bakery, bread shop — **panadero, -ra** *n* baker
panameño, -ña *adj* Panamanian
pancarta *nf* placard, banner
páncreas *nms & pl* pancreas
pandilla *nf* gang
pánico *nm* panic
panorama *nm* panorama
panqueque *nm* pancake
pantalla *nf* screen; lampshade
pantalón *nm* (**-lones**) *or* **pantalones** *nmpl* pants, trousers; **pantalones vaqueros** jeans
pantera *nf* panther
pantorrilla *nf* calf (of the leg)

pantufla *nf* slipper
pañuelo *nm* handkerchief
panza *nf* belly, paunch
pañal *nm* diaper
paño *nm* cloth
papa[1] *nm* pope
papa[2] *nf* potato; ∼**s fritas** potato chips, french fries
papá *nm* dad, pop; ∼**s** *nmpl* parents, folks
papagayo *nm* parrot
papaya *nf* papaya
papel *nm* paper, sheet of paper; ∼ **higiénico** *or* ∼ **de baño** toilet paper — **papelera** *nf* wastebasket — **papelería** *nf* stationery store
papilla *nf* baby food, pap
paquete *nm* package, parcel
paquistaní *adj* Pakistani
par *nm* pair, couple — **par** *adj* even (in number) — **par** *nf* par
para *prep* for; towards; (in order) to; around, by (a time)
parabrisas *nms & pl* windshield(s)
paracaídas *nms & pl* parachute(s) — **paracaidista** *nmf* parachutist; paratrooper
parada *nf* stop — **paradero** *nm* bus stop — **parado, -da** *adj* standing (up)
parafrasear *v* paraphrase
paraguas *nms & pl* umbrella(s)
paraguayo, -ya *adj* Paraguayan
paraíso *nm* paradise
parálisis *nfs & pl* paralysis (-lyses) — **paralítico, -ca** *adj* paralytic — **paralizar** *v* paralyze
páramo *nm* barren plateau
parapléjico, -ca *adj & n* paraplegic
parar *v* stop; stand, prop — **pararse** *vr* stop; stand up
pararrayos *nms & pl* lightning rod(s)
parasol *nm* parasol
parcial *adj* partial
pardo, -da *adj* brownish grey
parecer *v* seem, look; look like, seem like — **parecerse a** *vr phr* resemble

parecido, -da *adj* similar — **parecido** *nm* resemblance, similarity

pared *nf* wall

pareja *nf* couple, pair; partner

parentesco *nm* relationship, kinship

paréntesis *nms & pl* parenthesis (-theses)

pariente *nmf* relative, relation

parlamentario, -ria *adj* parliamentary — **parlamentario, -ria** *n* member of parliament — **parlamento** *nm* parliament

paro *nm* stoppage, shutdown; strike; ~ **cardíaco** cardiac arrest

párpado *nm* eyelid — **parpadear** *v* blink — **parpadeo** *nm* blink

parque *nm* park; ~ **de atracciones** amusement park

parqué *nm* parquet

parquear *v* park

parquímetro *nm* parking meter

párrafo *nm* paragraph

parrilla *nf* broiler, grill

párroco *nm* parish priest — **parroquia** *nf* parish; parish church

parte[1] *nm* report; ~ **meteorológico** weather forecast

parte[2] *nf* part; share; side; **de** ~ **de** on behalf of

partición *nf* (**-ciones**) division, sharing

participar *v* participate, take part — **participación** *nf* (**-ciones**) participation

participio *nm* participle

particular *adj* particular; private ~ *nm* matter; individual

partido *nm* (political) party; game, match (in sports)

partir *v* split, divide; break, crack; depart; ~ **de** start from; **a** ~ **de** as of, from — **partida** *nf* departure — **partidario, -ria** *n* follower, supporter

parto *nm* childbirth

pasa *nf* raisin

pasado, -da *adj* past — **pasado** *nm* past

pasaje *nm* ticket, fare — **pasajero, -ra** *n* passenger

pasamanos *nms & pl* handrail(s), banister(s)

pasaporte *nm* passport

pasar *v* cross; pass, go (by); come in; happen; **¿qué pasa?** what's the matter?; what's happening?

pasatiempo *nm* pastime, hobby

Pascua *nf* Easter; Passover; Christmas

pasear *v* go for a ride; take a walk; take for a walk — **paseo** *nm* walk, ride

pasillo *nm* passage, corridor

pasión *nf* (**-siones**) passion

pasivo, -va *adj* passive

paso *nm* step; **de** ~ in passing

pasta *nf* paste; pasta

pastel *nm* pie — **pastelería** *nf* pastry shop

pastilla *nf* pill, tablet

pasto *nm* pasture; grass, lawn — **pastor, -tora** *n* shepherd; pastor (in religion)

pata *nf* paw, leg (of an animal); foot, leg (of furniture) — **patada** *nf* kick

patata *nf* potato

patear *v* kick

paternal *adj* fatherly, paternal — **paternidad** *nf* fatherhood; paternity — **paterno, -na** *adj* paternal

patillas *nfpl* sideburns

patinar *v* skate — **patín** *nm* (**-tines**) skate — **patinador, -dora** *n* skater — **patinaje** *nm* skating

patio *nm* courtyard, patio

pato, -ta *n* duck

patria *nf* native land

patrimonio *nm* inheritance; heritage

patriota *adj* patriotic — **patriota** *nmf* patriot

patrocinador, -dora *n* sponsor — **patrocinar** *v* sponsor

patrón, -trona *n* (**-trones** *m*) patron; boss

patrulla *nf* patrol — **patrullar** *v* patrol

pausa *nf* pause, break

pavimento *nm* pavement — **pavimentar** *v* pave

pavo, -va *n* turkey; **pavo real** peacock

pavor *nm* dread, terror

payaso, -sa *n* clown

paz *nf* (**paces**) peace

peaje *nm* toll

peatón *nm* (**-tones**) pedestrian

peca *nf* freckle

pecado *nm* sin — **pecador, -dora** *adj* sinful — **pecador, -dora** *n* sinner — **pecar** *v* sin

pecho *nm* chest; breast — **pechuga** *nf* breast (of fowl)

pedagogía *nf* education, pedagogy — **pedagogo, -ga** *n* educator, teacher

pedal *nm* pedal — **pedalear** *v* pedal

pedazo *nm* piece, bit

pediatra *nmf* pediatrician

pedir *v* ask; ask for, request; order (as food, merchandise)

pegar *v* stick, glue, paste; hit, strike; hit — **pegarse** *vr* hit oneself, hit each other; stick, adhere — **pegamento** *nm* glue

peinar *v* comb — **peinado** *nm* hairstyle, hairdo — **peine** *nm* comb

pelar *v* cut the hair of (a person); peel (fruit)

pelear *v* fight; quarrel — **pelea** *nf* fight; quarrel

pelícano *nm* pelican

película *nf* movie, film

peligro *nm* danger; risk

pelirrojo, -ja *adj* red-haired — **pelirrojo, -ja** *n* redhead

pellizcar *v* pinch — **pellizco** *nm* pinch

pelo *nm* hair; fur

pelota *nf* ball

peluca *nf* wig

peluche *nm* plush

peludo, -da *adj* hairy, furry

peluquería *nf* hairdresser's shop, barber shop — **peluquero, -ra** *n* barber, hairdresser

pelvis *nfs & pl* pelvis(es)

pena *nf* sorrow; suffering, pain; embarrassment

penal *adj* penal

penalty *nm* penalty (in sports)

penar *v* punish; suffer

pendiente *adj* pending — **pendiente** *nm* earring

penetrar *v* pierce; penetrate; ~ **en** go into — **penetración** *nf* (**-ciones**) penetration; insight — **penetrante** *adj* penetrating; sharp (as of odors), piercing (of sounds)

penicilina *nf* penicillin

península *nf* peninsula

penitencia *nf* penitence; penance

penoso, -sa *adj* painful, distressing; difficult; shy

pensar *v* think — **pensamiento** *nm* thought; pansy (flower) — **pensativo, -va** *adj* pensive, thoughtful

pensión *nf* (**-siones**) boarding house; (retirement) pension

pentágono *nm* pentagon

penúltimo, -ma *adj* next to last, penultimate

peón *nm* (**peones**) laborer, peon; pawn (in chess)

peor *adv* worse; worst — **peor** *adj* worse; worst

pepino *nm* cucumber — **pepinillo** *nm* pickle, gherkin

pepita *nf* seed, pip

pequeño, -ña *adj* small, little — **pequeñez** *nf* (**-ñeces**) smallness

pera *nf* pear — **peral** *nm* pear tree

percepción *nf* (**-ciones**) perception

percibir *v* perceive

percusión *nf* (**-siones**) percussion

perder *v* lose; miss (as an opportunity); waste (time) — **perderse** *vr* get lost; disappear; be wasted — **perdedor, -dora** *n* loser

perdón *nm* (**-dones**) forgiveness, pardon — **perdón** *interj* sorry! — **perdonar** *v* forgive; pardon

perecer *v* perish, die

perejil *nm* parsley

pereza *nf* laziness — **perezoso, -sa** *adj* lazy

perfección *nf* (**-ciones**) perfection — **perfeccionar** *v* perfect; improve — **perfeccionista** *nmf* perfectionist — **perfecto, -ta** *adj* perfect

perfil *nm* profile; outline

perforar *v* perforate; drill, bore (a hole) — **perforadora** *nf* (paper) punch

perfume *nm* perfume, scent — **perfumar** *v* perfume — **perfumarse** *vr* put perfume on

periferia *nf* periphery, outskirts — **periférico, -ca** *adj* peripheral

periódico, -ca *adj* periodic — **periódico** *nm* newspaper — **periodismo** *nm* journalism — **periodista** *nmf* journalist

período *or* **periodo** *nm* period

perjudicar *v* harm, damage — **perjudicial** *adj* harmful

perla *nf* pearl

permanecer *v* remain — **permanente** *adj* permanent

permitir *v* permit, allow — **permiso** *nm* permission; permit, license (document); leave (in the military); **con** ～ excuse me

pero *conj* but — **pero** *nm* fault; objection

perpendicular *adj & nf* perpendicular

perro, -rra *n* dog; **perro caliente** hot dog

perseguir *v* pursue, chase; persecute — **persecución** *nf* (**-ciones**) pursuit, chase; persecution

persiana *nf* (venetian) blind

persona *nf* person — **personaje** *nm* character (as in literature); important person, celebrity — **personal** *adj* personal — **personal** *nm* personnel, staff — **personalidad** *nf* personality — **personificar** *v* personify

perspectiva *nf* perspective; view; prospect, outlook

persuadir *v* persuade

pertenecer *v* belong to — **perteneciente** *adj* belonging to

peruano, -na *adj* Peruvian

pesa *nf* weight; ～**s** weights (as for exercise, fitness) — **pesadez** *nf* (**-deces**) heaviness

pesadilla *nf* nightmare

pesado, -da *adj* heavy; tough, difficult

pésame *nm* condolences

pesar *v* weigh; be heavy; carry weight (as in importance)

pescado *nm* fish — **pesca** *nf* fishing; fish *pl*; catch (of fish) — **pescadería** *nf* fish market — **pescador, -dora** *n* (**-dores** *m*) fisherman — **pescar** *v* fish; fish for; catch, nab

pesebre *nm* manger

pesimista *adj* pessimistic — **pesimista** *nmf* pessimist

peso *nm* weight; burden; peso (currency)

pestaña *nf* eyelash

pétalo *nm* petal

petición *nf* (**-ciones**) petition, request

petróleo *nm* oil, petroleum — **petrolero, -ra** *adj* oil — **petrolero** *nm* oil tanker

peyorativo, -va *adj* pejorative

pez *nm* (**peces**) fish; ～ **gordo** big shot

piano *nm* piano — **pianista** *nmf* pianist, piano player

picado, -da *adj* perforated; minced, chopped (as of meat); decayed (of teeth); choppy (of the sea) — **picada** *nf* bite, sting; sharp descent — **picadura** *nf* sting, bite; (moth) hole

picante *adj* hot, spicy

picar *v* bite; peck at, nibble on (food); prick, puncture; chop, mince; take the bait; sting, itch; be spicy (of food) — **picarse** *vr* get a cavity

picnic *nm* (**-nics**) picnic

pico *nm* beak; peak; (sharp) point; pick, pickax (tool)

pie *nm* foot (in anatomy); base, bottom, stem; **al** ～ **de la letra** word for word; **de** ～ standing (up)

piedad *nf* pity, mercy; piety

piedra *nf* stone; flint (of a lighter); hailstone

piel *nf* skin; leather; fur, pelt
pierna *nf* leg
pieza *nf* piece, part; room
pijama *nm* pajamas
pila *nf* battery; pile; sink; basin (as of a fountain)
píldora *nf* pill
piloto *nmf* pilot
pimienta *nf* pepper (condiment) — **pimentón** *nm* (**-tones**) paprika; cayenne pepper
pincel *nm* paintbrush
pino *nm* pine (tree)
pintar *v* paint — **pintarse** *vr* put on makeup — **pintor, -tora** *n* (**-tores** *m*) painter — **pintura** *nf* paint; painting
pinza *nf* clothespin; claw, pincer (as of a crab); **~s** *nfpl* tweezers
piña *nf* pine cone; pineapple
piñata *nf* piñata
piñón *nm* (**-ñones**) pine nut
pío, pía *adj* pious; piebald (of a horse)
pionero, -ra *n* pioneer
pipa *nf* pipe (for smoking); seed, pip
piropo *nm* (flirtatious) compliment
pisar *v* step, tread; step on; walk all over, abuse
piscina *nf* swimming pool; (fish) pond
piso *nm* floor, story; floor (of a room); apartment
pista *nf* trail, track; clue; **~ de aterrizaje** runway, airstrip; **~ de baile** dance floor
pistola *nf* pistol, gun; spray gun
pistón *nm* (**-tones**) piston
pito *nm* whistle; horn — **pitar** *v* blow a whistle; beep, honk (of a horn); whistle at — **pitillo** *nm* cigarette
pizza *nf* pizza — **pizzería** *nf* pizzeria
placa *nf* sheet, plate; plaque; (police) badge
placenta *nf* placenta
placer *v* please — **placer** *nm* pleasure — **placentero, -ra** *adj* pleasant, agreeable
plagio *nm* plagiarism
plan *nm* plan

plancha *nf* iron (for ironing clothes); grill (for cooking); sheet, plate — **planchar** *v* iron (clothes)
planear *v* plan; glide
planeta *nm* planet
planificar *v* plan — **planificación** *nf* (**-ciones**) planning
planilla *nf* list, roster
plano, -na *adj* flat — **plano** *nm* map, plan; plane (surface); level
planta *nf* plant; floor, story; sole (of the foot)
plantear *v* expound, set forth; raise (a question); create, pose (a problem) — **plantearse** *vr* think about, consider
plantel *nm* staff, team; educational institution
plantilla *nf* insole; pattern, template; staff (as of a business)
plástico, -ca *adj* plastic
plata *nf* silver; money
plátano *nm* banana; plantain
platea *nf* orchestra seating area (in a theater)
platillo *nm* saucer; cymbal; dish, course
plato *nm* plate, dish; course (of a meal)
platónico, -ca *adj* platonic
playa *nf* beach, seashore
plaza *nf* square, plaza; seat (in transportation); post, position; market, marketplace
plazo *nm* period, term; installment
pleno, -na *adj* full, complete — **plenitud** *nf* fullness, abundance
pliego *nm* sheet (of paper) — **pliegue** *nm* crease, fold; pleat (in fabric)
plomero, -ra *n* plumber
pluma *nf* feather; (fountain) pen
plural *adj* & *nm* plural — **pluralidad** *nf* plurality
Plutón *nm* Pluto
población *nf* (**-ciones**) city, town, village; population
pobre *adj* poor — **pobreza** *nf* poverty
poco, -ca *adj* little, not much, (a) few — **poco, -ca** *pron* little, few

poder[1] *v aux* be able to, can; might, may; can, may — **poder** *v* be possible

poder[2] *nm* power; possession — **poderoso, -sa** *adj* powerful

poema *nm* poem — **poesía** *nf* poetry; poem — **poeta** *nmf* poet

polaco, -ca *adj* Polish

polarizar *v* polarize

polémica *nf* controversy — **polémico, -ca** *adj* controversial

policía *nf* police; *nmf* police officer, policeman, policewoman

politécnico, -ca *adj* polytechnic

política *nf* politics; policy — **político, -ca** *adj* political; **hermano político** brother-in-law — **político, -ca** *n* politician

pollo, -lla *n* chicken, chick; chicken (for cooking)

polo *nm* pole; polo (sport); ~ **norte** North Pole

polución *nf* (**-ciones**) pollution

polvo *nm* powder; dust — **pólvora** *nf* gunpowder

pómulo *nm* cheekbone

poner *v* put; add; contribute; suppose; arrange, set out; give (a name), call; turn on; set up, establish; lay (eggs) — **ponerse** *vr* move (into a position); put on (as clothing); set (of the sun)

pontífice *nm* pontiff

popular *adj* popular; colloquial — **popularidad** *nf* popularity

póquer *nm* poker (card game)

por *prep* for; around, during; about; through, along; because of; per; ~ *or* ~ **medio de** by means of; times (in mathematics); as for, according to; ~ **ciento** percent; ~ **favor** please; ~ **lo tanto** therefore; **¿por qué?** why?

porcelana *nf* porcelain, china

porcentaje *nm* percentage

porción *nf* (**-ciones**) portion, piece

porque *conj* because; ~ *or* **por que** in order that — **porqué** *nm* reason

portada *nf* facade; title page (of a book), cover (of a magazine)

portador, -dora *n* bearer

portaequipajes *nms & pl* luggage rack(s)

portafolio *or* **portafolios** *nm* (**-lios**) portfolio; briefcase

portal *nm* doorway; hall, vestibule

portar *v* carry, bear — **portarse** *vr* behave

portátil *adj* portable

portavoz *nmf* (**-voces**) spokesperson, spokesman; spokeswoman

porteño, -ña *adj* of or from Buenos Aires

portería *nf* superintendent's office; goal, goalposts (in sports) — **portero, -ra** *n* goalkeeper, goalie; janitor, superintendent

portugués, -guesa *adj* (**-gueses** *m*) Portuguese — **portugués** *nm* Portuguese (language)

porvenir *nm* future

posar *v* pose; place, lay — **posarse** *vr* settle, rest

poseer *v* possess, own — **posesionarse de** *vr phr* take possession of, take over — **posesivo, -va** *adj* possessive

posguerra *nf* postwar period

posibilidad *nf* possibility — **posible** *adj* possible

posición *nf* (**-ciones**) position

positivo, -va *adj* positive

posponer *v* postpone; put behind, subordinate

postal *adj* postal — **postal** *nf* postcard

poste *nm* post, pole

postergar *v* pass over; postpone

posteridad *nf* posterity — **posterior** *adj* later, subsequent; back, rear

postre *nm* dessert

postular *v* advance, propose; nominate

póstumo, -ma *adj* posthumous

postura *nf* position, stance

potable *adj* drinkable, potable

potencia *nf* power — **potente** *adj* powerful

práctica *nf* practice — **practicar** *v* practice; perform, carry out — **practicar** *v* practice — **práctico, -ca** *adj* practical

precaución *nf* (**-ciones**) precaution; caution, care

precedente *adj* preceding, previous — **precedente** *nm* precedent

precio *nm* price, cost — **precioso, -sa** *adj* beautiful; precious

precipitar *v* hasten, speed up; hurl — **precipitarse** *vr* rush; act rashly; throw oneself — **precipitación** *nf* (**-ciones**) precipitation; haste — **precipitado, -da** *adj* hasty

preciso, -sa *adj* precise; necessary — **precisar** *v* specify, determine; require — **precisión** *nf* (**-siones**) precision; necessity

precoz *adj* (**-coces**) early; precocious (of children)

predecir *v* foretell, predict

predicado *nm* predicate

predicar *v* preach

predicción *nf* (**-ciones**) prediction; forecast

predilección *nf* (**-ciones**) preference — **predilecto, -ta** *adj* favorite

predominar *v* predominate — **predominante** *adj* predominant, prevailing

prefacio *nm* preface

preferir *v* prefer — **preferido, -da** *adj* favorite

prefijo *nm* prefix; area code

pregunta *nf* question — **preguntar** *v* ask — **preguntarse** *vr* wonder

prehistórico, -ca *adj* prehistoric

prejuicio *nm* prejudice

preliminar *adj & nm* preliminary

prematrimonial *adj* premarital

prematuro, -ra *adj* premature

premio *nm* prize; reward

premisa *nf* premise

prenda *nf* piece of clothing; pledge; forfeit (in a game)

prender *v* pin, fasten; capture; light (as a match); turn on (as a light) catch, burn (of fire); take root — **prenderse** *vr* catch fire

preocupar *v* worry — **preocupación** *nf* (**-ciones**) worry

preparar *v* prepare — **prepararse** *vr* get ready — **preparación** *nf* (**-ciones**) preparation — **preparado, -da** *adj* prepared, ready

preposición *nf* (**-ciones**) preposition

presentar *v* present; offer, give; show; introduce (persons) — **presentarse** *vr* show up; arise, come up (as a problem); introduce oneself — **presentación** *nf* (**-ciones**) presentation; introduction (of persons); appearance — **presentador, -dora** *n* presenter, host (as of a television program)

presente *adj* present; **tener** ~ keep in mind — **presente** *nm* present

presentimiento *nm* premonition

presidente, -ta *n* president; chair, chairperson (of a meeting) — **presidencia** *nf* presidency; chairmanship

presión *nf* (**-siones**) pressure — **presionar** *v* press; put pressure on

preso, -sa *adj* imprisoned — **preso, -sa** *n* prisoner

prestar *v* lend, loan; give (aid) — **prestado, -da** *adj* borrowed, on loan — **préstamo** *nm* loan

prestigio *nm* prestige

presupuesto *nm* budget, estimate; assumption

pretender *v* try to; claim; court, woo — **pretensión** *nf* (**-siones**) intention, aspiration; claim (to a throne, etc.)

pretérito *nm* past (in grammar)

pretexto *nm* pretext, excuse

prevenir *v* prevent; warn — **prevención** *nf* (**-ciones**) prevention; precaution; prejudice — **prevenido, -da** *adj* prepared, ready; cautious

prima *nf* bonus; (insurance) premium

primario, -ria *adj* primary

primavera *nf* spring (season); primrose (flower)

primero, -ra *adj* first; top, leading; main, basic — **primero, -ra** *n* first one — **primero** *adv* first; rather, sooner

primitivo, -va *adj* primitive

primo, -ma *n* cousin

principal *adj* main, principal

principio *nm* principle; beginning, start; origin

prioridad *nf* priority

prisa *nf* hurry, rush

prisión *nf* (-**siones**) prison; imprisonment — **prisionero, -ra** *n* prisoner

privar *v* deprive; forbid; knock out — **privación** *nf* (-**ciones**) deprivation — **privado, -da** *adj* private

privilegio *nm* privilege

probabilidad *nf* probability

probar *v* try, test; try on (clothing); prove; taste — **probarse** *vr* try on (clothing)

problema *nm* problem

proceder *v* proceed, act; be appropriate — **procedimiento** *nm* procedure, method; proceedings (in law)

procesar *v* prosecute; process (data) — **procesador** *nm* processor; ~ **de textos** word processor — **proceso** *nm* process; trial, proceedings *pl* (in law)

procurar *v* try, endeavor; obtain, procure — **procurador, -dora** *n* attorney

producir *v* produce; cause; yield, bear (as interest, fruit) — **producirse** *vr* take place — **producción** *nf* (-**ciones**) production — **producto** *nm* product

profesar *v* practice (a profession) — **profesión** *nf* (-**siones**) profession — **profesional** *adj* & *nmf* professional — **profesor, -sora** *n* teacher; professor — **profesorado** *nm* teaching profession; faculty

profundo, -da *adj* deep; profound (as of thoughts) — **profundidad** *nf* depth — **profundizar** *v* study in depth

programa *nm* program; curriculum —

programación *nf* (-**ciones**) programming — **programador, -dora** *n* programmer — **programar** *v* schedule; program (as a computer)

progreso *nm* progress — **progresar** *v* (make) progress

prohibir *v* prohibit, forbid — **prohibición** *nf* (-**ciones**) ban, prohibition — **prohibido, -da** *adj* forbidden

proletariado *nm* proletariat

prólogo *nm* prologue, foreword

prolongar *v* prolong; lengthen — **prolongarse** *vr* last, continue

promesa *nf* promise — **prometer** *v* promise; show promise — **prometerse** *vr* get engaged

promocionar *v* promote — **promoción** *nf* (-**ciones**) promotion

promover *v* promote; cause — **promotor, -tora** *n* promoter

pronombre *nm* pronoun

pronóstico *nm* prediction, forecast; (medical) prognosis

pronto, -ta *adj* quick, prompt; ready — **pronto** *adv* soon; quickly, promptly; **de** ~ suddenly; **tan** ~ **como** as soon as

pronunciar *v* pronounce; give, deliver (a speech) — **pronunciarse** *vr* declare oneself; revolt — **pronunciación** *nf* (-**ciones**) pronunciation

propiedad *nf* property; ownership, possession — **propietario, -ria** *n* owner, proprietor

propio, -pia *adj* own; proper, appropriate; characteristic, typical; himself, herself, oneself

proponer *v* propose; nominate (a person) — **proponerse** *vr* propose, intend

proporción *nf* (-**ciones**) proportion — **proporcional** *adj* proportional — **proporcionar** *v* provide; adapt, proportion

proposición *nf* (-**ciones**) proposal, proposition

propósito *nm* purpose, intention; **a** ~ incidentally, by the way

propuesta *nf* proposal; offer (as of employment)

prosa *nf* prose

prosperar *v* prosper, thrive — **prosperidad** *nf* prosperity — **próspero, -ra** *adj* prosperous, fluorishing

prostituta *nf* prostitute

protagonista *nmf* protagonist

proteger *v* protect — **protección** *nf* (-ciones) protection — **protector, -tora** *adj* protective — **protector, -tora** *n* protector

protestar *v* protest — **protesta** *nf* protest

provecho *nm* benefit, advantage

provisional *adj* provisional

provocar *v* provoke, cause; irritate — **provocación** *nf* (-ciones) provocation — **provocativo, -va** *adj* provocative

próximo, -ma *adj* near; next — **proximidad** *nf* proximity; ~**es** *nfpl* vicinity

proyectar *v* plan; throw, hurl; cast (light); show (a film) — **proyección** *nf* (-ciones) projection — **proyecto** *nm* plan, project — **proyector** *nm* projector

prudente *adj* prudent, sensible

prueba *nf* proof, evidence; test (as in education, medicine); event (in sports)

psicología *nf* psychology — **psicológico, -ca** *adj* psychological — **psicólogo, -ga** *n* psychologist

psiquiatra *nmf* psychiatrist

pubertad *nf* puberty

publicar *v* publish; divulge, disclose — **publicación** *nf* (-ciones) publication

publicidad *nf* publicity; advertising (in marketing) — **publicista** *nmf* publicist

público, -ca *adj* public — **público** *nm* public; audience (in a theater), spectators (in sports)

pudín *nm* (-dines) pudding

pueblo *nm* town, village; people, nation

puente *nm* bridge

puerta *nf* door, gate

puerto *nm* port; (mountain) pass; haven

puertorriqueño, -ña *adj* Puerto Rican

pues *conj* since, because; so, therefore; well, then — **puesto, -ta** *adj* put, set; dressed — **puesto** *nm* place; position, job; stand, stall (in a market)

pulga *nf* flea

pulgada *nf* inch — **pulgar** *nm* thumb; big toe

pulir *v* polish; touch up, perfect

pulmón *nm* (-mones) lung

pulsar *v* press (a button), strike (a key); play (music) — **pulsación** *nf* (-ciones) beat, throb; keystroke

pulsera *nf* bracelet

pulso *nm* pulse; steadiness (of hand)

punta *nf* tip, end; point (of a needle, etc.)

puntilla *nf* lace edging

punto *nm* dot, point; period (in punctuation); item, question; spot, place; moment; point (in a score); stitch; **dos** ~**s** colon; ~ **de partida** starting point; ~ **muerto** deadlock; ~ **y coma** semicolon

puntuación *nf* (-ciones) punctuation; scoring, score (in sports)

puntual *adj* prompt, punctual; accurate, detailed — **puntualidad** *nf* punctuality; accuracy

puño *nm* fist; cuff (of a shirt); handle, hilt

pupila *nf* pupil (of the eye)

pupitre *nm* desk

puré *nm* purée

pureza *nf* purity

purificar *v* purify — **purificación** *nf* (-ciones) purification

puro[1], -ra *adj* pure; plain, simple; only, just

puro[2] *nm* cigar

Q

q *nf* q, 18th letter of the Spanish alphabet

que *conj* that; than; so that, or else — **que** *pron* who, whom; that, which

qué *adv* how, what — **qué** *adj* what, which — **qué** *pron* what

quedar *v* remain, stay; be; appear; turn out to be; be left — **quedarse** *vr* stay; **quedarse con** remain

queja *nf* complaint — **quejarse** *vr* complain

quemar *v* burn — **quemarse** *vr* burn oneself; burn (up); get sunburned — **quemado, -da** *adj* burned — **quemadura** *nf* burn

querer *v* want; love — **querer** *nm* love

queso *nm* cheese

quiebra *nf* break

quien *pron* (**quienes**) who; whom; whoever, anyone, some people

quién *pron* (**quiénes**) who; whom

quieto, -ta *adj* calm, quiet; still — **quietud** *nf* stillness

quijada *nf* jaw, jawbone (of an animal)

química *nf* chemistry

quince *adj & nm* fifteen — **quincena** *nf* two-week period, fortnight

quinientos, -tas *adj* five hundred — **quinientos** *nms & pl* five hundred

quinto, -ta *adj & n* fifth — **quinto** *nm* fifth

quiosco *nm* kiosk, newsstand

quiste *nm* cyst

quitar *v* remove, take away; take off (clothes) — **quitarse** *vr* withdraw, leave — **quitaesmalte** *nm* nail-polish remover — **quitamanchas** *nms & pl* stain remover

quizá *or* **quizás** *adv* maybe, perhaps

R

r *nf* r, 19th letter of the Spanish alphabet

rabia *nf* rage, anger

rabo *nm* tail

racionamiento *nm* rationing

racismo *nm* racism — **racista** *adj & nmf* racist

radio *nmf* radio

raíz *nf* (**raíces**) root

rallar *v* grate — **rallador** *nm* grater

rama *nf* branch

rana *nf* frog

rapar *v* shave; crop (hair)

rápido, -da *adj* rapid, quick — **rápidamente** *adv* rapidly, fast — **rapidez** *nf* speed — **rápido** *adv* quickly, fast

raqueta *nf* racket (in sports)

raro, -ra *adj* rare; odd, strange — **raramente** *adv* rarely, infrequently — **rareza** *nf* rarity

rascacielos *nms & pl* skyscraper(s)

rascar *v* scratch; scrape — **rascarse** *vr* scratch oneself

rasgar *v* rip, tear

rasgo *nm* stroke (of a pen); trait, characteristic; **~s** *nmpl* features

rasguñar *v* scratch — **rasguño** *nm* scratch

raspar *v* scrape; file down, smooth; be rough

rasurar *v* shave

rata *nf* rat

ratero, -ra *n* thief

rato *nm* while

ratón *nm* (**-tones**) mouse

raya *nf* line; stripe — **rayar** *v* scratch

rayo *nm* ray, beam

raza *nf* (human) race

razón *nf* (**-zones**) reason; **tener** ～ be right

reacción *nf* (**-ciones**) reaction — **reaccionar** *v* react

real *adj* real, true

realidad *nf* reality; **en** ～ actually, in fact

realismo *nm* realism — **realista** *adj* realistic — **realista** *nmf* realist

realizar *v* carry out; achieve (a goal) — **realización** *nf* (**-ciones**) execution, realization

realmente *adv* really, actually

rebajar *v* lower, reduce — **rebaja** *nf* reduction; discount; **rebajas** *nfpl* sales

rebanada *nf* slice

rebaño *nm* herd; flock (of sheep)

rebelarse *vr* rebel — **rebelde** *adj* rebellious — **rebelde** *nmf* rebel — **rebeldía** *nf* rebelliousness

rebuznar *v* bray

recaída *nf* relapse

recargar *v* overload; recharge (a battery); reload (as a firearm) — **recargo** *nm* surcharge

recepción *nf* (**-ciones**) reception — **recepcionista** *nmf* receptionist

receta *nf* recipe; prescription (in medicine)

rechazar *v* reject, refuse; repel — **rechazo** *nm* rejection

recibir *v* receive; welcome; receive visitors — **recibimiento** *nm* reception, welcome — **recibo** *nm* receipt

reciclar *v* recycle — **reciclaje** *nm* recycling

recién *adv* newly, recently; ～ **casados** newlyweds — **reciente** *adj* recent — **recientemente** *adv* recently

recipiente *nm* container, receptacle; ～ *nmf* recipient

recitar *v* recite — **recital** *nm* recital

reclamar *v* demand, ask for; complain

reclinar *v* rest, lean

recoger *v* collect, gather; pick up; clean up, tidy (up) — **recogerse** *vr* retire, withdraw — **recogedor** *nm* dustpan — **recogido, -da** *adj* quiet, secluded

recolección *nf* (**-ciones**) collection; harvest

recomendar *v* recommend — **recomendación** *nf* (**-ciones**) recommendation

recompensar *v* reward — **recompensa** *nf* reward

reconocer *v* recognize; admit

récord *nm* (**-cords**) record

recordar *v* remember; remind

recorrer *v* travel through; cover (a distance) — **recorrido** *nm* journey, trip; route, course

recortar *v* reduce; cut (out) — **recorte** *nm* cut, cutting

recostar *v* lean, rest

recreativo, -va *adj* recreational — **recreo** *nm* recreation, amusement; recess, break (at school)

rectángulo *nm* rectangle — **rectangular** *adj* rectangular

rectificar *v* rectify, correct; straighten (out) — **rectitud** *nf* straightness; (moral) rectitude — **recto, -ta** *adj* straight; upright, honorable

rector, -tora *adj* governing, managing — **rector, -tora** *n* rector — **rectoría** *nf* rectory

recuerdo *nm* memory; souvenir, remembrance (of a journey, etc.); ～**s** *nmpl* regards

recuperar *v* recover, retrieve — **recuperación** *nf* (**-ciones**) recovery

recurso *nm* recourse, resort; ～**s** *nmpl* resources

red *nf* net; network, system; **la Red** the Internet

redactar *v* write (up), draft — **redacción** *nf* (**-ciones**) writing, drafting; editing (as of a newspaper) — **redactor, -tora** *n* editor

redondo, -da *adj* round

reducir *v* reduce — **reducido, -da** *adj* reduced, limited; small

reembolso *nm* refund, reimbursement

reemplazar *v* replace — **reemplazo** *nm* replacement

referencia *nf* reference

reflejar *v* reflect — **reflejarse** *vr* be reflected — **reflejo** *nm* reflection; (physical) reflex; **reflejos** *nmpl* highlights (in hair)

reflexionar *v* reflect, think — **reflexión** *nf* (**-xiones**) reflection, thought — **reflexivo, -va** *adj* reflective, thoughtful; reflexive (in grammar)

reforma *nf* reform; ∼s *nfpl* renovations — **reformar** *v* reform; renovate, repair (as a house) — **reformarse** *vr* mend one's ways

reforzar *v* reinforce

refrán *nm* (**-franes**) proverb, saying

refrendar *v* approve, endorse

refrescar *v* cool, turn cooler; refresh; brush up on (knowledge) — **refrescante** *adj* refreshing

refuerzo *nm* reinforcement

refugiar *v* shelter — **refugio** *nm* refuge, shelter

regadera *nf* watering can; shower head, shower

regalar *v* give (as a gift)

regalo *nm* gift, present; pleasure, delight

regañar *v* scold; grumble; quarrel

régimen *nm* (**regímenes**) regime; diet

región *nf* (**-giones**) region, area — **regional** *adj* regional

regir *v* rule; manage, run; govern, determine; apply, be in force

registrar *v* register; record, tape; search (as a house), frisk (a person) — **registrarse** *vr* register; be recorded — **registro** *nm* registration; register (book); registry (office); range (as of a voice); search

regla *nf* rule, regulation; ruler (for measuring); period — **reglamento** *nm* regulations, rules

regresar *v* return, come back, go back; give back — **regreso** *nm* return

regular *adj* regular; medium, average — **regular** *v* regulate, control — **regulación** *nf* (**-ciones**) regulation, control

rehabilitar *v* rehabilitate; reinstate (in a position); renovate (as a building)

rehén *nm* (**-henes**) hostage

reimpresión *nf* (**-siones**) reprinting, reprint

reincidir *v* backslide, relapse

reintegrar *v* reinstate; refund (money), reimburse (as expenses) — **reintegro** *nm* reimbursement

reír *v* laugh; laugh at

reiterar *v* repeat, reiterate

reivindicar *v* claim; restore

reja *nf* grille, grating

rejuvenecer *v* rejuvenate

relación *nf* (**-ciones**) relation, connection; relationship, relations; account; list; **con** ∼ **a** *or* **en** ∼ **a** in relation to — **relacionar** *v* relate, connect

relámpago *nm* flash of lightning

relatar *v* relate, tell

relativo, -va *adj* relative — **relatividad** *nf* relativity

relato *nm* account, report; story, tale

relevante *adj* outstanding, important

relevar *v* relieve, take over from — **relevo** *nm* relief, replacement; **carrera de** ∼**s** relay race

relieve *nm* relief (in art); prominence, importance

religión *nf* (**-giones**) religion — **religioso, -sa** *adj* religious — **religioso, -sa** *n* monk, nun

reloj *nm* clock; ∼ **de arena** hourglass; **como un** ∼ like clockwork

remar *v* row

rematar *v* conclude, finish up; finish off; sell off cheaply; auction; shoot (in sports) — **remate** *nm* shot (in sports); end

remediar *v* remedy, repair; solve (a

problem); avoid — **remedio** *nm* remedy, cure; solution; **sin** ~ hopeless

remesa *nf* remittance; shipment (of merchandise)

remisión *nf* (**-siones**) remission

remitir *v* send, remit; subside, let up — **remite** *nm* return address — **remitente** *nmf* sender

remolacha *nf* beet

remoto, -ta *adj* remote

remover *v* stir; move around, turn over (as earth); bring up again; fire, dismiss

remunerar *v* remunerate

renacer *v* be reborn, revive — **renacimiento** *nm* rebirth, revival; **el Renacimiento** the Renaissance

renacuajo *nm* tadpole, pollywog

rencor *nm* rancor, hostility

rendido, -da *adj* submissive; exhausted

rendir *v* render, give; yield, produce; exhaust; make progress, go a long way — **rendimiento** *nm* performance; yield, return (as in finance)

renglón *nm* (**-glones**) line (of writing); line (of products)

renovar *v* renew, restore; renovate (as a building)

rentar *v* produce, yield; rent — **renta** *nf* income; rent; **impuesto sobre la renta** income tax — **rentable** *adj* profitable

renunciar *v* resign — **renuncia** *nf* renunciation; resignation

reorganizar *v* reorganize

reparar *v* repair, fix; make amends for

repartir *v* allocate; distribute; spread — **reparto** *nm* allocation; delivery; cast (of characters)

repente *nm* fit, outburst; **de** ~ suddenly — **repentino, -na** *adj* sudden

repercutir *v* reverberate — **repercusión** *nf* (**-siones**) repercussion

repertorio *nm* repertoire

repetir *v* repeat; have a second helping of (food) — **repetirse** *vr* repeat oneself; recur (as an event)

réplica *nf* reply; replica, reproduction

reponer *v* replace; reply — **reponerse** *vr* recover

reportar *v* yield, bring; report — **reportaje** *nm* article, (news) report — **reporte** *nm* report — **reportero, -ra** *n* reporter

reposar *v* rest; stand, settle (as liquids, dough) — **reposado, -da** *adj* calm, relaxed — **reposición** *nf* (**-ciones**) replacement; rerun, repeat

representar *v* represent; perform (as a play); look, appear as — **representación** *nf* (**-ciones**) representation; performance — **representante** *nmf* representative; performer

reprimir *v* repress; suppress

reproducir *v* reproduce — **reproducirse** *vr* breed, reproduce; recur (as an event) — **reproducción** *nf* (**-ciones**) reproduction

reptil *nm* reptile

república *nf* republic

repuesto *nm* spare (auto) part

reputación *nf* (**-ciones**) reputation

requerir *v* require; summon, send for (a person)

requisito *nm* requirement

res *nf* beast, animal; ~ **or carne de** ~ beef

resaltar *v* stand out; emphasize

resbalar *v* slip, slide; skid (of an automobile) — **resbaloso, -sa** *adj* slippery

rescatar *v* rescue, ransom; recover, get back — **rescate** *nm* rescue; ransom (money); recovery

reseco, -ca *adj* dry, dried-up

reseñar *v* review; describe — **reseña** *nf* review, report; description

reservar *v* reserve; keep, save — **reserva** *nf* reservation; reserve; **de reserva** spare, in reserve — **reservación** *nf* (**-ciones**) reservation — **reservado, -da** *adj* reserved; confidential (as of a document)

resfriar *v* cool — **resfriado** *nm* cold

residencia *nf* residence; ~ *or* ~ **universitaria** dormitory — **residencial** *adj* residential — **residente** *adj & nmf* resident — **residir** *v* reside, live

residuo *nm* residue; ~**s** *nmpl* waste

resignación *nf* (**-ciones**) resignation

resistir *v* stand, bear; withstand; resist — **resistencia** *nf* resistance; endurance, stamina — **resistente** *adj* resistant, strong, tough

resma *nf* ream

resolver *v* resolve; decide — **resolverse** *vr* make up one's mind — **resolución** *nf* (**-ciones**) resolution; decision; determination, resolve

respaldar *v* back, endorse — **respaldarse** *vr* lean back — **respaldo** *nm* back (as of a chair); support, backing

respetar *v* respect — **respeto** *nm* respect — **respetuoso, -sa** *adj* respectful

respirar *v* breathe — **respiración** *nf* (**-ciones**) respiration, breathing — **respiratorio, -ria** *adj* respiratory

responder *v* answer, reply; answer back

responsable *adj* responsible

respuesta *nf* answer, reply; response

resta *nf* subtraction

restablecer *v* reestablish, restore — **restablecerse** *vr* recover

restar *v* deduct, subtract; minimize; be left

restaurante *nm* restaurant

restaurar *v* restore

resto *nm* rest, remainder; ~**s** *nmpl* leftovers; ~**s** *or* ~**s mortales** mortal remains

restringir *v* restrict, limit — **restricción** *nf* (**-ciones**) restriction, limitation

resuelto, -ta *adj* determined, resolved

resultar *v* succeed, work out; turn out (to be) — **resultado** *nm* result, outcome

resumen *nm* (**-súmenes**) summary; **en** ~ in short — **resumir** *v* summarize, sum up

resurgir *v* reappear, revive — **resurgimiento** *nm* resurgence

retener *v* retain, keep; withhold (as funds); detain — **retención** *nf* (**-ciones**) retention; deduction, withholding

retina *nf* retina

retirar *v* remove, take away; withdraw (as funds, statements) — **retirarse** *vr* retreat, withdraw; retire — **retiro** *nm* retreat; retirement; withdrawal

reto *nm* challenge, dare

retórico, -ca *adj* rhetorical

retrasar *v* delay, hold up; postpone; set back (a clock) — **retrasarse** *vr* be late; fall behind — **retrasado, -da** *adj* retarded; in arrears; backward; slow (of a clock) — **retraso** *nm* delay; backwardness; **retraso mental** mental retardation

retratar *v* portray; photograph; paint a portrait of — **retrato** *nm* portrayal; portrait; photograph

retroactivo, -va *adj* retroactive

retroceder *v* go back, turn back; back down — **retroceso** *nm* backward movement; backing down

retrovisor *nm* rearview mirror

reumatismo *nm* rheumatism

reunir *v* unite, join; have, possess; gather, collect — **reunirse** *vr* meet, gather — **reunión** *nf* (**-niones**) meeting; (social) gathering, reunion

revelar *v* reveal, disclose; develop (film) — **revelación** *nf* (**-ciones**) revelation — **revelador, -dora** *adj* revealing

reventar *v* burst, blow up

reversa *nf* reverse (gear)

reverso *nm* back, reverse

revés *nm* (**-veses**) back, wrong side; setback; slap; backhand (in sports); **al** ~ the other way around, upside down, inside out

revisar *v* examine, inspect; check over, overhaul (as machinery); revise —

revisión *nf* (**-siones**) revision; inspection, check

revista *nf* magazine, journal; revue (in theater); **pasar** ∼ review, inspect

revivir *v* revive, come alive again; relive

revocar *v* revoke

revolución *nf* (**-ciones**) revolution — **revolucionario, -ria** *adj & n* revolutionary

revolver *v* mix, stir; upset (one's stomach); mess up — **revolverse** *vr* toss and turn; turn around

revuelto, -ta *adj* choppy, rough; messed up; **huevos revueltos** scrambled eggs

rezar *v* pray; say; recite

ribera *nf* bank, shore

rico, -ca *adj* rich, wealthy; abundant; rich, tasty — **rico, -ca** *n* rich person

riesgo *nm* risk

rifa *nf* raffle

rígido, -da *adj* rigid, stiff; harsh, strict

rigor *nm* rigor, harshness; precision — **riguroso, -sa** *adj* rigorous

rima *nf* rhyme; ∼**s** *nfpl* verse, poetry

rincón *nm* (**-cones**) corner, nook

rinoceronte *nm* rhinoceros

riña *nf* fight, brawl; dispute, quarrel

riñón *nm* (**-ñones**) kidney

río *nm* river; torrent, stream

riqueza *nf* wealth; richness; ∼**s naturales** natural resources

risa *nf* laughter, laugh; **morirse de la** ∼ die laughing

ritmo *nm* rhythm; pace, speed — **rítmico, -ca** *adj* rhythmical

rito *nm* rite, ritual

rival *adj & nmf* rival — **rivalidad** *nf* rivalry, competition

rizado, -da *adj* curly; choppy (of water) — **rizo** *nm* curl; ripple (in water); loop (in aviation)

róbalo *nm* bass (fish)

robar *v* steal; burglarize; kidnap — **robo** *nm* robbery, theft

roble *nm* oak

robot *nm* (**-bots**) robot — **robótica** *nf* robotics

robusto, -ta *adj* robust, sturdy

roca *nf* rock, boulder

rocoso, -sa *adj* rocky

rodar *v* roll, roll down, roll along; turn, go around; travel (of a vehicle); shoot, film (as movies); break in (a vehicle) — **rodaje** *nm* filming, shooting; breaking in

rodear *v* surround, encircle; round up (cattle)

rodilla *nf* knee

rodillo *nm* roller; rolling pin

rogar *v* beg, request; pray

rojo, -ja *adj* red; **ponerse** ∼ blush — **rojo** *nm* red

rollo *nm* roll, coil; boring speech, lecture

romance *nm* romance; Romance (language)

romano, -na *adj & n* Roman

romántico, -ca *adj* romantic — **romanticismo** *nm* romanticism

rompecabezas *nms & pl* puzzle(s)

romper *v* break; rip, tear; break off (relations), break (a contract)

ron *nm* rum

roncar *v* snore — **ronco, -ca** *adj* hoarse

ronda *nf* rounds, patrol; round (of drinks)

ropa *nf* clothes, clothing; ∼ **interior** underwear — **ropero** *nm* wardrobe, closet

rosa *nf* rose (flower); ∼ *nm* rose (color) — **rosa** *adj* rose-colored — **rosado, -da** *adj* pink — **rosado** *nm* pink (color)

rosbif *nm* roast beef

rosca *nf* thread (of a screw); ring, coil

roseta *nf* rosette

rostro *nm* face

rotación *nf* (**-ciones**) rotation — **rotativo, -va** *adj* rotary, revolving

roto, -ta *adj* broken, torn

rótulo *nm* heading, title; label, sign

rozar *v* graze, touch lightly; touch on, border on; rub against — **rozarse** *vr* rub, chafe

rubio, -bia *adj & n* blond

rubor *nm* flush, blush

rúbrica *nf* flourish (in writing); title, heading

rudimentos *nmpl* rudiments, basics — **rudimentario, -ria** *adj* rudimentary

rueda *nf* wheel; circle, ring; (round) slice; **ir sobre ~s** go smoothly

ruido *nm* noise

ruina *nf* ruin, destruction; collapse; **~s** *nfpl* ruins, remains

rumano, -na *adj* Romanian, Rumanian

rumba *nf* rumba

rumbo *nm* direction, course; lavishness

rumor *nm* rumor; murmur

ruptura *nf* break, rupture; breach (of a contract); breaking off (of relations)

rural *adj* rural

ruso, -sa *adj* Russian — **ruso** *nm* Russian (language)

rústico, -ca *adj* rural, rustic; **en rústica** in paperback

ruta *nf* route

rutina *nf* routine — **rutinario, -ria** *adj* routine

S

s *nf* s, 20th letter of the Spanish alphabet

sábado *nm* Saturday

sábana *nf* sheet

saber *v* know; know how to, be able to; learn, find out; taste — **saber** *nm* knowledge — **sabiduría** *nf* wisdom — **sabio, -bia** *adj* learned; wise, sensible

sabor *nm* flavor, taste — **saborear** *v* savor

sabroso, -sa *adj* delicious, tasty

sacacorchos *nms & pl* corkscrew(s)

sacapuntas *nms & pl* pencil sharpener(s)

sacar *v* take out; get, obtain; extract, withdraw; take (photos), make (copies); remove

sacerdote, -tisa *n* priest; priestess

saco *nm* bag, sack; jacket

sacrificar *v* sacrifice — **sacrificarse** *vr* sacrifice oneself — **sacrificio** *nm* sacrifice

sacudir *v* shake; beat — **sacudirse** *vr* shake off

sagrado, -da *adj* sacred, holy

sal *nf* salt

sala *nf* room, hall; living room

salar *v* salt — **salado, -da** *adj* salty; witty

salario *nm* salary, wage

salchicha *nf* sausage — **salchichón** *nf* (**-chones**) salami-like cold cut

saldo *nm* balance (of an account); **~s** *nmpl* remainders, sale items — **saldar** *v* settle, pay off; sell off

salero *nm* saltshaker

salir *v* go out, come out; leave; appear; turn out; rise (of the sun); **~ con** date — **salirse** *vr* leave; leak out, escape; come off — **salida** *nf* exit; (action of) leaving, departure; **salida de emergencia** emergency exit

saliva *nf* saliva

salmón *nm* (**-mones**) salmon

salón *nm* (**-lones**) lounge, sitting room; **~ de belleza** beauty salon; **~ de clase** classroom

salpicar *v* splash, spatter

salsa *nf* sauce; salsa (music)

saltamontes *nms & pl* grasshopper(s)

saltar *v* jump, leap; bounce; jump (over)

salto *nm* jump, leap

salud *nf* health — **¡salud!** *interj* here's to your health!; bless you! (when someone sneezes) — **saludable** *adj* healthy

saludar *v* greet, say hello to — **saludo**

nm greeting; (military) salute; **saludos** best wishes, regards

salvación *nf* (**-ciones**) salvation

salvadoreño, -ña *adj* (El) Salvadoran

salvaje *adj* wild; savage, primitive — **salvaje** *nmf* savage

salvar *v* save, rescue — **salvarse** *vr* save oneself — **salvavidas** *nms & pl* life preserver(s)

salvo, -va *adj* safe

samba *nf* samba

sanar *v* heal, cure; recover

sanción *nf* (**-ciones**) sanction — **sancionar** *v* sanction

sandalia *nf* sandal

sandía *nf* watermelon

sandwich *nm* (**-wiches**) sandwich

sangrar *v* bleed — **sangre** *nf* blood — **sangriento, -ta** *adj* bloody — **sanguíneo, -nea** *adj* blood

sano, -na *adj* healthy — **sanitario** toilet

santo, -ta *adj* holy; **Santo, Santa** Saint (as in a name) — **santo, -ta** *n* saint

sapo *nm* toad

sarampión *nm* measles

sardina *nf* sardine

sargento *nmf* sergeant

sartén *nmf* (**-tenes**) frying pan

sastre, -tra *n* tailor — **sastrería** *nf* tailoring; tailor's shop

satélite *nm* satellite

satisfacer *v* satisfy; fulfill, meet; pay — **satisfacerse** *vr* be satisfied — **satisfacción** *nf* (**-ciones**) satisfaction — **satisfactorio, -ria** *adj* satisfactory — **satisfecho, -cha** *adj* satisfied

Saturno *nm* Saturn

sauce *nm* willow

sauna *nmf* sauna

sazón *nf* (**-zones**) seasoning — **sazonar** *v* season

se *pron* himself, herself, itself, oneself, yourself, yourselves, themselves; (to) him, (to) her, (to) you, (to) them; each other, one another

secar *v* dry — **secarse** *vr* dry (up) —

secador *nm* hair dryer — **secadora** *nf* (clothes) dryer

sección *nf* (**-ciones**) section

seco, -ca *adj* dry; dried (as of fruits)

secretario, -ria *n* secretary — **secretaría** *nf* secretariat

secreto, -ta *adj* secret — **secreto** *nm* secret; **en secreto** in confidence

sector *nm* sector

secuencia *nf* sequence

secuestrar *v* kidnap — **secuestrador, -dora** *n* kidnapper — **secuestro** *nm* kidnapping

secundario, -ria *adj* secondary

sed *nf* thirst

seda *nf* silk

sedante *adj & nm* sedative

sede *nf* seat, headquarters

sedentario, -ria *adj* sedentary

sediento, -ta *adj* thirsty

sedoso, -sa *adj* silky, silken

seducir *v* seduce; captivate, charm — **seducción** *nf* (**-ciones**) seduction — **seductor, -tora** *adj* seductive; charming — **seductor, -tora** *n* seducer

seglar *adj* lay, secular — **seglar** *nm* layperson; layman; laywoman

segmento *nm* segment

seguir *v* follow; go on, continue — **seguido** *adv* straight (ahead) — **en seguida** *adv phr* right away

según *prep* according to — **según** *adv* it depends — **según** *conj* as, just as

segundo, -da *adj* second — **segundo, -da** *n* second (one) — **segundo** *nm* second (of time)

seguro, -ra *adj* safe; secure; sure, certain; reliable — **seguramente** *adv* for sure, surely — **seguridad** *nf* safety; security; certainty; confidence — **seguro** *adv* certainly — **seguro** *nm* insurance; safety (device)

seis *adj & nm* six — **seiscientos, -tas** *adj* six hundred — **seiscientos** *nms & pl* six hundred

selección *nf* (**-ciones**) selection — **seleccionar** *v* select, choose

sellar *v* seal; stamp — **sello** *nm* seal; stamp

selva *nf* jungle; forest

semáforo *nm* traffic light

semana *nf* week — **semanal** *adj* weekly

semántica *nf* semantics

sembrar *v* sow

semejar *v* resemble — **semejarse** *vr* look alike — **semejante** *adj* similar — **semejanza** *nf* similarity

semen *nm* semen

semestre *nm* semester

semifinal *nf* semifinal

semilla *nf* seed

seminario *nm* seminary; seminar, course

senado *nm* senate — **senador, -dora** *n* senator

sencillo, -lla *adj* simple; single — **sencillez** *nf* simplicity

seno *nm* breast, bosom

sensación *nf* (**-ciones**) feeling, sensation — **sensacional** *adj* sensational

sensato, -ta *adj* sensible

sensible *adj* sensitive — **sensibilidad** *nf* sensitivity

sensual *adj* sensual, sensuous

sentar *v* seat, sit — **sentarse** *vr* sit (down)

sentido *nm* sense

sentimiento *nm* feeling, emotion — **sentimental** *adj* sentimental

sentir *v* feel; be sorry for — **sentirse** *vr* feel

seña *nf* sign

señal *nf* signal; sign — **señalar** *v* indicate, point out; mark; fix, set

señor, -ñora *n* gentleman, man; lady, woman; Sir; Madam; Mr.; Mrs.; **señora** wife — **señorita** *nf* young lady, young woman; Miss

separar *v* separate; move away — **separarse** *vr* separate — **separación** *nf* (**-ciones**) separation — **separado, -da** *adj* separate

septiembre *nm* September

séptimo, -ma *adj* seventh — **séptimo, -ma** *n* seventh

sepultar *v* bury

sequedad *nf* dryness

ser *v* be; **a no ~ que** unless; **~ de** belong to; **~ de** come from; **son las diez** it's ten o'clock — **ser** *nm* being; **ser humano** human being

serbio, -bia *adj* Serb, Serbian

serenar *v* calm — **serenarse** *vr* calm down — **serenata** *nf* serenade — **serenidad** *nf* serenity — **sereno, -na** *adj* serene, calm

serie *nf* series

serio, -ria *adj* serious; reliable; **en serio** seriously — **seriedad** *nf* seriousness

sermón *nm* (**-mones**) sermon

serpiente *nf* serpent, snake

serrucho *nm* saw, handsaw

servicio *nm* service; **los ~s** *nmpl* restroom — **servicial** *adj* obliging, helpful

servilleta *nf* napkin

servir *v* serve; work, function; be of use

sesenta *adj & nm* sixty

sesión *nf* (**-siones**) session; showing (of a film), performance (of a play)

setecientos, -tas *adj* seven hundred — **setecientos** *nms & pl* seven hundred

setenta *adj & nm* seventy

seudónimo *nm* pseudonym

severo, -ra *adj* harsh, severe; strict

sexo *nm* sex — **sexismo** *nm* sexism — **sexista** *adj & nmf* sexist

sexto, -ta *adj & n* sixth

sexual *adj* sexual — **sexualidad** *nf* sexuality

si *conj* if; whether

sí[1] *adv* yes — **sí** *nm* consent

sí[2] *reflexive pron* **de por ~** *or* **en ~** by itself, in itself, per se; **para ~ (mismo)** to himself, to herself, for himself, for herself

SIDA *or* **sida** *nm* AIDS

sidra *nf* (hard) cider
siembra *nf* sowing
siempre *adv* always
sien *nf* temple
sierra *nf* saw; mountain range
siervo, -va *n* slave
siesta *nf* nap, siesta
siete *adj & nm* seven
sigla *nf* acronym, abbreviation
siglo *nm* century
significar *v* mean, signify; express — **significado, -da** *adj* well-known — **significado** *nm* meaning
signo *nm* sign; ~ **de admiración** exclamation point; ~ **de interrogación** question mark
siguiente *adj* next, following
sílaba *nf* syllable
silbar *v* whistle — **silbido** *nm* whistle, whistling
silencio *nm* silence — **silencioso, -sa** *adj* silent, quiet
silla *nf* chair; ~ *or* ~ **de montar** saddle; ~ **de ruedas** wheelchair — **sillón** *nm* (**-llones**) armchair, easy chair
símbolo *nm* symbol — **simbólico, -ca** *adj* symbolic
similar *adj* similar, alike
simio *nm* ape
simpatía *nf* liking, affection; friendliness — **simpático, -ca** *adj* nice, likeable; pleasant, kind — **simpatizar** *v* get along, hit it off
simple *adj* simple — **simplificar** *v* simplify
simular *v* simulate
simultáneo, -nea *adj* simultaneous
sin *prep* without
sincero, -ra *adj* sincere — **sinceramente** *adv* sincerely — **sinceridad** *nf* sincerity
sindicato *nm* (labor) union
sinfonía *nf* symphony
singular *adj* exceptional, outstanding;

peculiar; singular (in grammar) — **singular** *nm* singular (one)
sino *conj* but, rather; except, save
sinónimo, -ma *adj* synonymous — **sinónimo** *nm* synonym
sintaxis *nfs & pl* syntax(es)
síntesis *nfs & pl* synthesis (-theses)
síntoma *nm* symptom
sintonía *nf* tuning in (of a radio) — **sintonizar** *v* tune (in) to
sinvergüenza *nmf* scoundrel
siquiera *adv* at least; **ni** ~ not even — **siquiera** *conj* even if
sirena *nf* siren
sirio, -ria *adj* Syrian
sistema *nm* system
sitio *nm* place, site; room, space
situar *v* situate, place — **situarse** *vr* be located — **situación** *nf* (**-ciones**) situation, position
smoking *nm* tuxedo
soberbia *nf* pride, arrogance
sobornar *v* bribe — **soborno** *nm* bribe
sobrar *v* be more than enough; be left over — **sobrado, -da** *adj* more than enough
sobre[1] *nm* envelope
sobre[2] *prep* on, on top of; over, above; about; ~ **todo** especially, above all
sobredosis *nfs & pl* overdose(s)
sobregiro *nm* overdraft
sobremesa *nf* **de** ~ after-dinner
sobrepasar *v* exceed
sobresalir *v* protrude; stand out — **sobresaliente** *adj* outstanding
sobretodo *nm* overcoat
sobrevivir *v* survive; outlive
sobriedad *nf* sobriety; restraint
sobrino, -na *n* nephew, niece
sobrio , -bria *adj* sober
social *adj* social — **socialismo** *nm* socialism — **socialista** *adj & nmf* socialist
sociedad *nf* society; company; ~ **anónima** incorporated company

socio, -cia *n* partner; member — **sociología** *nf* sociology

soda *nf* soda (water)

sodio *nf* sodium

sofá *nm* couch, sofa

sofocar *v* suffocate, smother; put out (a fire), stifle (as a rebellion)

sol *nm* sun

solamente *adv* only, just

solapa *nf* lapel (of a jacket); flap (of an envelope)

soldado *nm* soldier

soleado, -da *adj* sunny

soledad *nf* loneliness, solitude

solicitar *v* request, solicit; apply for (as a job) — **solicitud** *nf* concern; request; application

solidaridad *nf* solidarity

sólido, -da *adj* solid; sound (as of an argument)

solista *nmf* soloist

solitario, -ria *adj* solitary; lonely, deserted — **solitario, -ria** *n* recluse

solo, -la *adj* alone; lonely — **solo** *nm* solo

sólo *adv* just, only

soltar *v* release; let go of, drop; unfasten, undo — **soltarse** *vr* break free; come undone

soltero, -ra *adj* single, unmarried — **soltero, -ra** *n* bachelor, single woman

soltura *nf* looseness; fluency (in language); agility, ease

solución *nf* (**-ciones**) solution — **solucionar** *v* solve, resolve

sombra *nf* shadow; shade; ~**s** *nfpl* darkness, shadows

sombrero *nm* hat

sombrilla *nf* parasol, umbrella

someter *v* subjugate; subordinate; subject (as to treatment); submit, present — **someterse** *vr* submit, yield

somnífero *nm* sleeping pill

sonajero *nm* (baby's) rattle

sonar *v* sound; ring (as a bell); look or sound familiar

sondeo *nm* sounding, probing; survey, poll

sonido *nm* sound

sonoro, -ra *adj* resonant, sonorous; loud

sonreír *v* smile

soñar *v* dream — **soñador, -dora** *adj* dreamy — **soñador, -dora** *n* dreamer

sopa *nf* soup

soplar *v* blow; blow out, blow off, blow up — **soplo** *nm* puff, gust

soportar *v* support; bear

sorber *v* sip; absorb; suck up — **sorbete** *nm* sherbet — **sorbo** *nm* sip, swallow

sordera *nf* deafness

sordo, -da *adj* deaf; muted (of a sound) — **sordomudo, -da** *n* deaf-mute

sorprender *v* surprise — **sorprendente** *adj* surprising — **sorpresa** *nf* surprise

sortear *v* raffle off, draw lots for; dodge

sortija *nf* ring; ringlet (of hair)

sospechoso, -sa *adj* suspicious — **sospechoso, -sa** *n* suspect

sostener *v* support; hold; sustain, maintain — **sostenerse** *vr* stand (up); remain; support oneself — **sostén** *nm* (**-tenes**) support; sustenance; brassiere, bra — **sostenido, -da** *adj* sustained; sharp (in music)

soya *nf* soy

Sr. *nm* Mr. — **Sra.** *nf* Mrs., Ms. — **Srta.** or **Srita.** *nf* Miss, Ms.

su *adj* his, her, its, their, one's; your

suave *adj* soft; smooth; gentle, mild

subasta *nf* auction

subcampeón, -peona *n* (**-peones** *m*) runner-up

subcomité *nm* subcommittee

subconsciente *adj* & *nm* subconscious

subdesarrollado, -da *adj* underdeveloped

subdirector, -tora *n* assistant manager

subir *v* climb, go up; bring up, take up; raise; come up; ~ **a** get in (a car), get on (a bus, etc.) — **subida** *nf* ascent, climb; rise; slope — **subido, -da** *adj* bright, strong

subjetivo, -va *adj* subjective

subjuntivo *nm* subjunctive (case)

sublevar *v* stir up, incite to rebellion

submarino, -na *adj* underwater — **submarino** *nm* submarine

subrayar *v* underline; emphasize, stress

subsanar *v* rectify, correct; make up for (a deficiency), overcome (an obstacle)

subsidio *nm* subsidy, benefit

subsistir *v* live, subsist; survive

subterráneo, -nea *adj* underground, subterranean — **subterráneo** *nm* underground passage

subtítulo *nm* subtitle

subversivo, -va *adj & n* subversive

subyacente *adj* underlying

suceder *v* happen, occur — **suceso** *nm* event; incident

sucio, -cia *adj* dirty, filthy

sucursal *nf* branch (of a business)

sudadera *nf* sweatshirt

sudafricano, -na *adj* South African

sudamericano, -na *adj* South American

sudar *v* sweat

sudeste *adj* southeast, southeastern; southeasterly (as of wind) — **sudeste** *nm* southeast, Southeast

sudoeste *adj* southwest, southwestern; southwesterly (as of wind) — **sudoeste** *nm* southwest, Southwest

sudor *nm* sweat

sueco, -ca *adj* Swedish — **sueco** *nm* Swedish (language)

suegro, -gra *n* father-in-law, mother-in-law; **suegros** *nmpl* in-laws

suela *nf* sole (of a shoe)

sueldo *nm* salary, wage

suelo *nm* ground; floor (in a house); soil, land

suelto, -ta *adj* loose, free

sueño *nm* dream

suerte *nf* luck, fortune; chance; fate

suéter *nm* sweater

suficiente *adj* enough, sufficient; smug

sufijo *nm* suffix

sufragio *nm* suffrage, vote

sufrir *v* suffer; bear, stand — **sufrido, -da** *adj* long-suffering — **sufrimiento** *nm* suffering

sugerir *v* suggest — **sugerencia** *nf* suggestion — **sugestivo, -va** *adj* suggestive; interesting, stimulating

suicidio *nm* suicide — **suicida** *adj* suicidal — **suicida** *nmf* suicide (victim) — **suicidarse** *vr* commit suicide

suite *nf* suite

suizo, -za *adj* Swiss

sujetar *v* hold (on to); fasten; subdue — **sujeto, -ta** *adj* fastened — **sujeto** *nm* individual; subject (in grammar)

suma *nf* sum, total; addition — **sumar** *v* add (up); add up to, total

sumario *nm* summary; indictment (in law)

sumergir *v* submerge, plunge

suministrar *v* supply, provide — **suministro** *nm* supply, provision

superar *v* surpass, outdo; overcome — **superarse** *vr* improve oneself

superficie *nf* surface; area — **superficial** *adj* superficial

superior *adj* superior; upper (floor) — **superior** *nm* superior (one)

superlativo, -va *adj* superlative — **superlativo** *nm* superlative

supermercado *nm* supermarket

supervivencia *nf* survival — **superviviente** *adj* surviving — **superviviente** *nmf* survivor

suplente *adj & nmf* substitute

suponer *v* suppose, assume; mean; involve, entail

supositorio *nm* suppository

suprimir *v* suppress, eliminate; delete

supuesto, -ta *adj* supposed, alleged; **por supuesto** of course — **supuesto** *nm* assumption

sur *nm* south, South; south wind

sureño, -ña *adj* southern, Southern — **sureño, -ña** *n* Southerner

surf *or* **surfing** *nm* surfing

surgir *v* arise; appear — **surgimiento** *nm* rise, emergence

surtir *v* supply, provide — **surtido, -da** *adj* assorted, varied; stocked (with merchandise)

susceptible *adj* susceptible, sensitive

suscribir *v* sign; endorse — **suscribirse a** *vr phr* subscribe to — **suscripción** *nf* (**-ciones**) subscription

suspender *v* suspend; hang; fail (as an exam)

suspirar *v* sigh

sustancia *nf* substance

sustantivo *nm* noun

sustentar *v* support; sustain, nourish; maintain — **sustentación** *nf* (**-ciones**) support

susto *nm* fright, scare

sustraer *v* remove, take away; subtract — **sustracción** *nf* (**-ciones**) subtraction

susurrar *v* whisper; murmur (of water); rustle (of leaves)

sutil *adj* delicate, fine; subtle (of fragrances, differences, etc.)

suyo, -ya *adj* his, her, its, one's, theirs; yours — **suyo, -ya** *pron* his, hers, its (own), one's own, theirs; yours

switch *nm* switch

T

t *nf* t, 21st letter of the Spanish alphabet

tabaco *nm* tobacco

tabique *nm* thin wall, partition

tabla *nf* board, plank; table, list — **tablero** *nm* bulletin board; (game) board; blackboard

tableta *nf* tablet, pill

tabú *adj* taboo — **tabú** *nm* (**-búes** or **-bús**) taboo

tacaño, -na *adj* stingy, miserly

tachar *v* cross out, delete; ～ **de** accuse of, label as

tachón *nm* (**-chones**) stud, hobnail

tácito, -ta *adj* tacit

tacón *nm* (**-cones**) heel (of a shoe)

táctica *nf* tactic, tactics

tacto *nm* (sense of) touch, feel; tact

tailandés, -desa *adj* Thai

tajar *v* cut, slice — **tajada** *nf* slice

tal *adj* such, such a; ～ **vez** maybe, perhaps — **tal** *adv* so, in such a way — **tal** *pron* such a one, such a thing

taladrar *v* drill — **taladro** *nm* drill

talco *nm* talcum powder

talla *nf* size (in clothing)

tallarín *nf* (**-rines**) noodle

taller *nm* workshop; studio (of an artist)

tallo *nm* stalk, stem

talón *nm* (**-lones**) heel (of the foot)

tamaño, -ña *adj* such a, such a big — **tamaño** *nm* size

también *adv* too, as well, also

tambor *nm* drum

tampoco *adv* neither, not either

tampón *nm* (**-pones**) tampon

tan *adv* so, so very

tanque *nm* tank

tanto *adv* so much; so long — **tanto** *nm* certain amount — **tanto, -ta** *adj* so much, so many; as much, as many — **tanto, -ta** *pron* so much, so many

tapa *nf* cover, top, lid; snack

tapar *v* cover, put a lid on

tapete *nm* small rug, mat; cover (for a table)

tapón *nm* (**-pones**) cork; (bottle) cap

taquilla *nf* box office

tardar *v* take a long time, be late — **tarde** *adv* late — **tarde** *nf* afternoon, evening; ¡buenas ～s! good afternoon!, good evening!

tarea *nf* task, job; (school) homework

tarifa *nf* fare, rate; price list

tarjeta *nf* card; ~ **de crédito** credit card; ~ **postal** postcard

tarro *nm* jar, pot

tasa *nf* rate; tax

taxi *nm* (**taxis**) taxi, taxicab — **taxista** *nmf* taxi driver

taza *nf* cup; (toilet) bowl

te *pron* you; for you, to you, from you; yourself, for yourself, to yourself, from yourself

té *nm* tea

teatro *nm* theater

techo *nm* roof; ceiling

tecla *nf* key (of a musical instrument or a machine)

técnica *nf* technique, skill; technology — **técnico, -ca** *adj* technical — **técnico, -ca** *n* technician

tecnología *nf* technology

teja *nf* tile — **tejado** *nm* roof

tejer *v* knit, crochet

tejido *nm* fabric, cloth; tissue (of the body)

tela *nf* fabric, material — **telar** *nm* loom — **telaraña** *nf* spiderweb, cobweb

telefonear *v* telephone, call — **telefónico, -ca** *adj* telephone — **telefonista** *nmf* telephone operator — **teléfono** *nm* telephone; **teléfono celular** *m* cell phone, cellular phone

telenovela *nf* soap opera

telescopio *nm* telescope

televidente *nmf* (television) viewer

televisión *nf* (**-siones**) television, TV — **televisar** *v* televise — **televisor** *nm* television set

tema *nm* theme

temblar *v* tremble, shiver; shake (as of a building, the ground) — **temblor** *nm* shaking, trembling — **tembloroso, -sa** *adj* trembling, shaky

temer *v* fear, dread; be afraid — **temeroso, -sa** *adj* fearful — **temor** *nm* fear, dread

temperamento *nm* temperament

temperatura *nf* temperature

tempestad *nf* storm

templo *nm* temple, synagogue

temporada *nf* season, time; period, spell — **temporal** *adj* temporal; temporary — **temporal** *nm* storm

temprano, -na *adj* early — **temprano** *adv* early

tenaz *adj* (**-naces**) tenacious — **tenaza** *nf or* **tenazas** *nfpl* pliers

tendencia *nf* tendency, trend

tender *v* spread out, stretch out; ~ **a** have a tendency towards

tendón *nm* (**-dones**) tendon

tenebroso, -sa *adj* gloomy, dark; sinister

tenedor *nm* table fork

tener *v* have, possess; hold; take; ~ **... años**> be ... years old; ~ **frío** (**hambre,** *etc.*) be cold (hungry, etc.) — **tenerse** *vr* stand up

teniente *nmf* lieutenant

tenis *nms & pl* tennis; ~ *nmpl* sneakers — **tenista** *nmf* tennis player

tensión *nf* (**-siones**) tension; ~ **arterial** blood pressure — **tenso, -sa** *adj* tense

tentación *nf* (**-ciones**) temptation

teoría *nf* theory — **teórico, -ca** *adj* theoretical

terapia *nf* therapy — **terapeuta** *nmf* therapist — **terapéutico, -ca** *adj* therapeutic

tercermundista *adj* third-world

tercero, -ra *adj* third; **el Tercer Mundo** the Third World — **tercero, -ra** *n* third (in a series)

terco, -ca *adj* obstinate, stubborn

terminar *v* conclude, finish; come to an end — **terminarse** *vr* run out; come to an end — **terminación** *nf* (**-ciones**) termination, conclusion — **terminal** *adj* terminal, final — **terminal** *nf* terminal, station — **término** *nm* end; period, term — **terminología** *nf* terminology

termómetro *nm* thermometer

ternero, -ra *n* calf (animal) — **ternera** *nf* veal

ternura *nf* tenderness

terquedad *nf* obstinacy, stubbornness

terraza *nf* terrace; balcony

terremoto *nm* earthquake

terreno *nm* terrain; earth, ground; plot, tract of land — **terreno, -na** *adj* earthly — **terrestre** *adj* terrestrial

terrible *adj* terrible

territorio *nm* territory — **territorial** *adj* territorial

terrón *nm* (**-rones**) lump

terror *nm* terror — **terrorismo** *nm* terrorism — **terrorista** *adj* & *nmf* terrorist

terso, -sa *adj* smooth; polished, flowing (of a style) — **tersura** *nf* smoothness

tertulia *nf* gathering, group

tesis *nfs* & *pl* thesis (theses)

tesoro *nm* treasure — **tesorero, -ra** *n* treasurer

testamento *nm* testament, will

testículo *nm* testicle

testificar *v* testify — **testigo** *nmf* witness — **testimoniar** *v* testify — **testimonio** *nm* testimony

tetera *nf* teapot

tetilla *nf* teat, nipple (of a man)

textil *adj* & *nm* textile

texto *nm* text — **textual** *adj* textual; literal, exact

textura *nf* texture

tez *nf* (**teces**) complexion

ti *pron* you; ~ **mismo,** ~ **misma** yourself

tibio, -bia *adj* lukewarm

tiburón *nm* (**-rones**) shark

tic *nm* tic

tiempo *nm* time; age, period; weather; halftime (in sports); tense (in grammar)

tienda *nf* store, shop

tierno, -na *adj* tender, fresh, young; affectionate

tierra *nf* land; ground, earth; **la Tierra** the Earth; **por** ~ overland

tieso, -sa *adj* stiff, rigid

tigre, -gresa *n* tiger, tigress

tijera *nf or* **tijeras** *nfpl* scissors

tilde *nf* tilde; accent mark

timbre *nm* bell

tímido, -da *adj* timid, shy — **timidez** *nf* timidity, shyness

timón *nm* (**-mones**) rudder

tímpano *nm* eardrum

tina *nf* bathtub

tinieblas *nfpl* darkness

tinta *nf* ink

tinto, -ta *adj* red (of wine)

tintura *nf* dye, tint

tío, tía *n* uncle, aunt

tiovivo *nm* merry-go-round

típico, -ca *adj* typical

tiple *nm* soprano

tipo *nm* type, kind; figure (of a woman), build (of a man) — **tipo, -pa** *n* guy, gal

tique *or* **tíquet** *nm* ticket

tira *nf* strip, strap

tirante *adj* brace, strut; ~**s** *nmpl* suspenders

tirar *v* throw; throw away; pull

tiritar *v* shiver

tiro *nm* shot, gunshot; shot, kick (in sports)

tiroides *nmf* thyroid (gland)

tirón *nm* (**-rones**) pull, yank

tirotear *v* shoot at — **tiroteo** *nm* shooting

títere *nm* puppet

titubear *v* hesitate

titular[1] *v* title, call — **titularse** *vr* be called, be titled; receive a degree

titular[2] *adj* titular, official — **titular** *nm* headline; ~ *nmf* holder, incumbent — **título** *nm* title; degree, qualification (in education)

tiza *nf* chalk

toalla *nf* towel — **toallero** *nm* towel rack

tobillo *nm* ankle

tobogán *nm* (**-ganes**) toboggan, sled; slide (as on a playground)

tocador *nm* dressing table

tocar *v* touch, feel; touch on, refer to;

play (a musical instrument); knock, ring

tocino *nm* bacon; salt pork — **tocineta** *nf* bacon

todavía *adv* still; even; ~ **no** not yet

todo, -da *adj* all; every, each; **a toda velocidad** at top speed; **todo el mundo** everyone, everybody — **todo, -da** *pron* everything, all; **todos, -das** *pl* everybody, everyone, all — **todo** *nm* whole

tolerar *v* tolerate — **tolerancia** *nf* tolerance — **tolerante** *adj* tolerant

toma *nf* inlet; outlet; ~ **de corriente** (electrical) wall outlet

tomar *v* take; have (food or drink); drink (alcohol); ~ **el sol** sunbathe

tomate *nm* tomato

tomillo *nm* thyme

tomo *nm* volume

tonel *nm* barrel, cask

tonelada *nf* ton

tono *nm* tone; shade (of colors)

tontería *nf* silly thing or remark; foolishness — **tonto, -ta** *adj* stupid, silly — **tonto, -ta** *n* fool, idiot

tópico *nm* cliché

topo *nm* mole (animal)

torbellino *nm* whirlwind

torcer *v* turn; twist, bend; turn (a corner); wring (out) — **torcerse** *vr* twist, sprain; go wrong; go astray — **torcedura** *nf* twisting; sprain — **torcido, -da** *adj* twisted, crooked

torear *v* fight (bulls); dodge, sidestep — **toreo** *nm* bullfighting — **torero, -ra** *n* bullfighter

tormenta *nf* storm — **tormento** *nm* torture; torment, anguish — **tormentoso, -sa** *adj* stormy

tornado *nm* tornado

torneo *nm* tournament

tornillo *nm* screw

torno *nm* winch, turning device; **en** ~ **a** around, about

toro *nm* bull; ~**s** *nmpl* bullfight

toronja *nf* grapefruit

torpe *adj* clumsy, awkward; stupid, dull

torpeza *nf* clumsiness, awkwardness; slowness, stupidity

torre *nf* tower; turret (on a ship); rook, castle (in chess)

torrente *nm* torrent; ~ **sanguíneo** bloodstream — **torrencial** *adj* torrential

torsión *nf* (**-siones**) twisting

torta *nf* torte, cake

tortícolis *nfs & pl* stiff neck(s)

tortilla *nf* tortilla

tortuga *nf* turtle, tortoise; ~ **de agua dulce** terrapin

tortura *nf* torture — **torturar** *v* torture

tosco, -ca *adj* rough, coarse

toser *v* cough — **tos** *nf* cough

tostar *v* toast — **tostada** *nf* piece of toast; tostada — **tostador** *nm* toaster

total *adj & nm* total — **total** *adv* so, after all — **totalidad** *nf* whole — **totalizar** *v* total, add up to

tóxico, -ca *adj* toxic, poisonous — **tóxico** *nm* poison

trabajar *v* work; work on, work at; act, perform (as in theater) — **trabajador, -dora** *adj* hard-working — **trabajador, -dora** *n* worker — **trabajo** *nm* work; job; task; effort; **costar trabajo** be difficult; **trabajo en equipo** teamwork; **trabajos** *nmpl* hardships, difficulties — **trabajoso, -sa** *adj* hard, laborious

trabalenguas *nms & pl* tongue twister

trabar *v* join, connect; impede

tracción *nf* traction

tractor *nm* tractor

tradición *nf* (**-ciones**) tradition — **tradicional** *adj* traditional

traducir *v* translate — **traducción** *nf* (**-ciones**) translation — **traductor, -tora** *n* translator

traer *v* bring; cause, bring about; carry, have — **traerse** *vr* bring along

traficar *v* trade, deal; ~ **en** traffic in — **traficante** *nmf* dealer, trafficker —

tráfico *nm* trade (of merchandise); traffic (of vehicles)

tragar *v* swallow

tragedia *nf* tragedy — **trágico, -ca** *adj* tragic

trago *nm* swallow, swig; drink, liquor; ~ *nmf* glutton

traicionar *v* betray — **traición** *nf* (-**ciones**) betrayal; treason (in law) — **traidor, -dora** *adj* traitorous, treacherous — **traidor, -dora** *n* traitor

traje *nm* dress, costume; (man's) suit; ~ **de baño** bathing suit

trajinar *v* rush around — **trajín** *nm* (-**jines**) hustle and bustle

trama *nf* plot

tramitar *v* negotiate — **trámite** *nm* procedure, step

tramo *nm* stretch, section

trampa *nf* trap; **hacer** ~**s** cheat

trampolín *nm* (-**lines**) diving board; trampoline

tramposo, -sa *adj* crooked, cheating — **tramposo, -sa** *n* cheat, swindler

tranquilo, -la *adj* calm, tranquil — **tranquilidad** *nf* tranquility, peace — **tranquilizante** *nm* tranquilizer — **tranquilizar** *v* calm, soothe — **tranquilizarse** *vr* calm down

transacción *nf* (-**ciones**) transaction

transatlántico, -ca *adj* transatlantic — **transatlántico** *nm* ocean liner

transbordo *nm* transfer; **hacer** ~ change (as trains)

transcurrir *v* elapse, pass — **transcurso** *nm* course, progression

transferir *v* transfer — **transferencia** *nf* transfer, transference

transformar *v* transform, change; convert — **transformarse** *vr* be transformed — **transformación** *nf* (-**ciones**) transformation — **transformador** *nm* transformer

transfusión *nf* (-**siones**) transfusion

transición *nf* (-**ciones**) transition

transitar *v* go, travel — **transitable** *adj* passable

transitivo, -va *adj* transitive

tránsito *nm* transit; traffic

transmitir *v* transmit; broadcast (as radio, TV); pass on — **transmisión** *nf* (-**siones**) broadcast; transfer

transparente *adj* transparent

transportar *v* transport, carry — **transportarse** *vr* get carried away — **transporte** *nm* transport, transportation

tranvía *nm* streetcar, trolley

trapear mop

trapecio *nm* trapeze

trapo *nm* cloth, rag

tráquea *nf* trachea, windpipe

trascendental *adj* transcendental; important

trasero, -ra *adj* rear, back — **trasero** *nm* buttocks

trasladar *v* transfer, move; postpone — **trasladarse** *vr* move, relocate — **traslado** *nm* transfer, move

trasnochar *v* stay up all night

trasplante *nm* transplant

trastornar *v* disturb, disrupt — **trastornado, -da** *adj* disturbed, deranged — **trastorno** *nm* disturbance, disruption; (medical or psychological) disorder

tratable *adj* friendly, sociable

tratar *v* deal with; treat; handle — **tratarse de** *vr phr* be about, concern — **tratamiento** *nm* treatment — **trato** *nm* treatment; deal, agreement

trauma *nm* trauma — **traumático, -ca** *adj* traumatic

través *nm* **a** ~ **de** across, through; **de** ~ sideways

travesía *nf* voyage, crossing (of the sea)

travesura *nf* prank; ~**s** *nfpl* mischief — **travieso, -sa** *adj* mischievous, naughty

trayecto *nm* trajectory, path; journey; route — **trayectoria** *nf* path, trajectory

trazar *v* trace, outline; draw up (a plan, etc.)

trébol *nm* clover, shamrock

trece *adj & nm* thirteen

treinta *adj & nm* thirty

tremendo, -da *adj* tremendous, enormous

tren *nm* train; ∼ **de aterrizaje** landing gear

trenza *nf* braid, pigtail

trepar *v* climb; creep, spread (of a plant)

tres *adj & nm* three — **trescientos, -tas** *adj* three hundred

triángulo *nm* triangle — **triangular** *adj* triangular

tribu *nf* tribe

tribunal *nm* court, tribunal

tributar *v* pay, render; pay taxes — **tributo** *nm* tribute; tax

triciclo *nm* tricycle

trigésimo, -ma *adj & n* thirtieth

trigo *nm* wheat

trigonometría *nf* trigonometry

trillizo, -za *n* triplet

trilogía *nf* trilogy

trimestral *adj* quarterly

trío *nm* trio

triple *adj & nm* triple

trípode *nm* tripod

tripulación *nf* (**-ciones**) crew — **tripulante** *nmf* crew member

triste *adj* sad; dismal, gloomy — **tristeza** *nf* sadness, grief

triunfo *nm* triumph, victory

trivial *adj* trivial

trofeo *nm* trophy

trombón *nm* (**-bones**) trombone; trombonist

trombosis *nf* thrombosis

trompa *nf* trunk (of an elephant), snout; horn (musical instrument); tube (in anatomy)

trompeta *nf* trumpet — **trompetista** *nmf* trumpet player

trompo *nm* top (toy)

tronar *v* thunder, rage; shoot — **tronar** *v impers* thunder

tropezar *v* trip, stumble

tropical *adj* tropical

trotar *v* trot; rush about

trucha *nf* trout

trueno *nm* thunder

tu *adj* your

tú *pron* you

tuberculosis *nf* tuberculosis

tubo *nm* tube, pipe; ∼ **de escape** exhaust pipe (of a vehicle); ∼ **de desagüe** drainpipe — **tubería** *nf* pipes, tubing

tuerca *nf* nut (for a screw)

tulipán *nm* (**-panes**) tulip

tumba *nf* tomb, grave

tumor *nm* tumor

túnel *nm* tunnel

turbio, -bia *adj* cloudy, murky; blurred (as of vision)

turco, -ca *adj* Turkish — **turco** *nm* Turkish (language)

turista *nmf* tourist — **turismo** *nm* tourism, tourist industry

turno *nm* turn

tutear *v* address as *tú*

tutela *nf* guardianship (in law)

tuyo, -ya *adj* yours, of yours — **tuyo, -ya** *pron* **el tuyo, la tuya, lo tuyo, los tuyos, las tuyas** yours; **los tuyos** your family, your friends

U

u[1] *nf* u, 22d letter of the Spanish alphabet

u[2] *conj* or

ubicar *v* place, position; find — **ubicarse** *vr* be located

ubre *nf* udder

último, -ma *adj* last; latest, most recent (in time); farthest (in space)

umbilical *adj* umbilical

un, una *art* (**unos** *m*) a, an; **unos** *or*
unas *pl* some, a few; about, approximately
unánime *adj* unanimous — **unanimi-
dad** *nf* unanimity
undécimo, -ma *adj & n* eleventh
único, -ca *adj* only, sole; unique —
único, -ca *n* only one
unidad *nf* unit; unity — **unido, -da** *adj*
united; close (as of friends)
uniforme *adj & nm* uniform
unilateral *adj* unilateral
unir *v* unite, join; combine, mix together
— **unirse** *vr* join together — **unión** *nf*
(**uniones**) union; joint, coupling
universal *adj* universal
universidad *nf* university, college —
universitario, -ria *adj* university, college
universo *nm* universe
uno, una *adj* one — **uno, una** *pron* one;
unos, unas *pl* some; **uno(s) a otro(s)**
one another, each other; **uno y otro**
both — **uno** *nm* one (number)

untar *v* smear, grease; bribe
uña *nf* nail, fingernail; claw, hoof
Urano *nm* Uranus
urbano, -na *adj* urban, city — **urbani-
zación** *nf* (**-ciones**) housing development
urgencia *nf* urgency; emergency — **urgente** *adj* urgent
urinario, -ria *adj* urinary
urna *nf* urn; ballot box
uruguayo, -ya *adj* Uruguayan
usar *v* use; wear — **usarse** be used; be
worn, be in fashion — **usado, -da** *adj*
used; worn, worn-out — **uso** *nm* use;
wear and tear; custom, usage
usted *pron* you; ∼**es** *pl* you (*pl*)
usual *adj* usual
usuario, -ria *n* user
útero *nm* uterus, womb
utilizar *v* use, utilize — **útil** *adj* useful —
útiles *nmpl* implements, tools — **utilidad** *nf* utility, usefulness
uva *nf* grape

V

v *nf* v, 23d letter of the Spanish alphabet
vaca *nf* cow
vacaciones *nfpl* vacation; **estar de** ∼
be on vacation
vacante *adj* vacant — **vacante** *nf* vacancy
vaciar *v* empty (out); hollow out; cast,
mold (a statue, etc.)
vacío *nm* void; vacuum (in physics);
space, gap
vacuna *nf* vaccine
vacuno, -na *adj* bovine
vagina *nf* vagina
vagón *nm* (**-gones**) car (of a train)
vaho *nm* breath; vapor, steam
vainilla *nf* vanilla
vajilla *nf* dishes

vale *nm* voucher; IOU
valentía *nf* courage, bravery
valer *v* be worth; cost; gain, earn; be
equal to; be valid, count; be of use
valeroso, -sa *adj* courageous
válido, -da *adj* valid
valiente *adj* brave; fine, great
valioso, -sa *adj* valuable
valla *nf* fence; hurdle (in sports)
valle *nm* valley
valor *nm* value, worth; courage, valor;
∼**es** *nmpl* values, principles; ∼**es**
nmpl securities, bonds — **valoración**
nf (**-ciones**) valuation — **valorar** *v*
evaluate, assess
vals *nm* waltz
vanagloriarse *vr* boast, brag

vanguardia *nf* vanguard; avant-garde; **a la ~** at/in the forefront

vanidad *nf* vanity — **vanidoso, -sa** *adj* vain, conceited

vapor *nm* steam, vapor; **al ~** steamed

variar *v* vary; change, alter — **variable** *adj & nf* variable — **variante** *nf* variant

varicela *nf* chicken pox

variedad *nf* variety

vario, -ria *adj* varied; **~s** *pl* several

varón *nm* (**-rones**) man, male; boy — **varonil** *adj* manly

vasco, -ca *adj* Basque — **vasco** *nm* Basque (language)

vasija *nf* container, vessel

vaso *nm* glass; vessel (in anatomy)

vecino, -na *n* neighbor; resident, inhabitant — **vecino, -na** *adj* neighboring — **vecindario** *nm* neighborhood; community, residents

vegetal *nm* vegetable, plant — **vegetal** *adj* vegetable — **vegetación** *nf* (**-ciones**) vegetation — **vegetariano, -na** *adj & n* vegetarian

vehículo *nm* vehicle

veinte *adj & nm* twenty — **veinteavo** *nm* twentieth

vejez *nf* old age

vejiga *nf* bladder; blister

vela *nf* candle; sail (of a ship); vigil

velar *v* hold a wake over; watch over; blur (a photograph); veil, mask; stay awake — **velado, -da** *adj* veiled, hidden; blurred

vello *nm* body hair; down, fuzz — **velludo, -da** *adj* hairy

veloz *adj* (**-loces**) fast, quick — **velocidad** *nf* speed, velocity; gear (of an automobile)

vena *nf* vein; grain (of wood); mood

venado *nm* deer; venison

vencer *v* win; beat, defeat; overcome; expire — **vencedor, -dora** *adj* winning — **vencedor, -dora** *n* winner — **vencimiento** *nm* expiration; maturity (of a loan)

vender *v* sell — **venderse** *vr* be sold; **se vende** for sale — **vendedor, -dora** *n* seller; salesman, saleswoman

veneno *nm* poison; venom

venezolano, -na *adj* Venezuelan

vengar *v* avenge — **vengarse** *vr* get even, take revenge — **venganza** *nf* vengeance, revenge

venir *v* come; arrive; be, appear; fit

venta *nf* sale, selling

ventaja *nf* advantage

ventana *nf* window — **ventanilla** *nf* window (of a vehicle or airplane); ticket window, box office

ventilación *nf* (**-ciones**) ventilation — **ventilador** *nm* fan, ventilator

ver *v* see; watch (as television); **a ~** *or* **vamos a ~** let's see — **verse** *vr* see oneself; find oneself; see each other, meet

verano *nm* summer

verbal *adj* verbal

verbo *nm* verb

verdad *nf* truth; **de ~** really, truly; **¿verdad?** right?, isn't that so? — **verdadero, -dera** *adj* true, real

verde *adj* green; unripe; dirty, risqué — **verde** *nm* green (color)

verdura *nf* vegetable(s), green(s)

vergüenza *nf* shame; bashfulness, shyness

verificar *v* verify, confirm; test, check out — **verificarse** *vr* take place; come true (as of a prophecy)

vernáculo, -la *adj* vernacular

verosímil *adj* probable, likely; credible

versátil *adj* versatile; fickle

versión *nf* (**-siones**) version; translation

verso *nm* poem, verse; line (of poetry)

vértebra *nf* vertebra

vertical *adj & nf* vertical

vértice *nm* vertex, apex

vertiente *nf* slope

vértigo *nm* vertigo, dizziness — **vertiginoso, -sa** *adj* dizzy

vesícula *nf* blister; **~ biliar** gallbladder

vestíbulo *nm* vestibule, hall, foyer

vestido *nm* dress; clothing, clothes

vestir *v* dress, clothe; wear — **vestuario** *nm* wardrobe, clothes; dressing room (in a theater), locker room

veterano, -na *adj & n* veteran

veterinario, -ria *adj* veterinary — **veterinario, -ria** *n* veterinarian

veto *nm* veto

vez *nf* (**veces**) time; turn; **a la ~** at the same time; **a veces** sometimes; **de una ~** all at once; **de una ~ para siempre** once and for all; **de ~ en cuando** from time to time; **en ~ de** instead of **una ~** once

vía *nf* way, road, route; means; track, line (of a railroad); (anatomical) tract; **en ~ de** in the process of — **vía** *prep* via

viable *adj* viable, feasible

viaducto *nm* viaduct

viajar *v* travel — **viaje** *nm* trip, journey — **viajero, -ra** *adj* traveling — **viajero, -ra** *n* traveler; passenger

vial *adj* road, traffic

vibrar *v* vibrate — **vibración** *nf* (**-ciones**) vibration

vicepresidente, -ta *n* vice president

vicio *nm* vice; bad habit; defect — **viciado, -da** *adj* corrupt; stuffy, stale (as of air)

víctima *nf* victim

victoria *nf* victory

vida *nf* life; lifetime; **de por ~** for life; **estar con ~** be alive

video *or* **vídeo** *nm* video; VCR, video-cassette recorder

vidrio *nm* glass — **vidriera** *nf* stained-glass window; glass door; shopwindow — **vidrioso, -sa** *adj* delicate (of a subject, etc.)

viejo, -ja *adj* old; **hacerse ~** get old — **viejo, -ja** *n* old man, old woman

viento *nm* wind

vientre *nm* abdomen, belly; womb; bowels

viernes *nms & pl* Friday(s); **Viernes Santo** Good Friday

vietnamita *adj & nm* Vietnamese

vigencia *nf* validity — **vigente** *adj* valid, in force

vigésimo, -ma *adj & n* twentieth

vigilar *v* look after, watch over; keep watch — **vigilancia** *nf* vigilance — **vigilante** *adj* vigilant — **vigilante** *nmf* watchman, guard — **vigilia** *nf* wakefulness; vigil (in religion)

vigor *nm* vigor — **vigoroso, -sa** *adj* vigorous

VIH *nm* HIV

villancico *nm* (Christmas) carol

vinagre *nm* vinegar

vincular *v* tie, link — **vínculo** *nm* link, tie, bond

vino *nm* wine

violar *v* violate (as a law); rape — **violación** *nf* (**-ciones**) violation, offense; rape

violencia *nf* violence, force — **violento, -ta** *adj* violent; awkward, embarrassing

violeta *adj & nm* violet (color) — **violeta** *nf* violet (flower)

violín *nm* (**-lines**) violin — **violinista** *nmf* violinist — **violoncelista** *or* **violonchelista** *nmf* cellist — **violoncelo** *or* **violonchelo** *nm* cello

virar *v* turn, change direction

virginidad *nf* virginity

viril *adj* virile

virtual *adj* virtual

virtud *nf* virtue

viruela *nf* smallpox

virus *nms & pl* virus(es)

visa *nf* visa — **visado** *nm* visa

visera *nf* visor

visible *adj* visible

visión *nf* (**-siones**) eyesight; vision, illusion; view, perspective

visitar *v* visit — **visita** *nf* visit

visón *nm* (**-sones**) mink

vista *nf* vision, eyesight; look, gaze; view, vista; hearing (in court); **a**

primera ∼ *or* **a simple** ∼ at first sight; **perder de** ∼ lose sight of
visto, -ta *adj* clear, obvious; commonly seen
visto bueno *nm* approval
visual *adj* visual
vital *adj* vital — **vitalicio, -cia** *adj* life, for life — **vitalidad** *nf* vitality
vitamina *nf* vitamin
vitrina *nf* showcase, display case; shop-window
viudo, -da *n* widower, widow — **viudo, -da** *adj* widowed
víveres *nmpl* provisions, supplies
vivero *nm* nursery (for plants); (fish) hatchery, (oyster) bed
vivienda *nf* housing; dwelling
vivir *v* experience, live, live (through), be alive; ∼ **de** live on (as an income) — **vivir** *nm* life, lifestyle — **vivo, -va** *adj* alive; intense, bright; lively; sharp, quick
vocabulario *nm* vocabulary
vocación *nf* (**-ciones**) vocation
vocal[1] *adj* vocal — **vocalista** *nmf* singer, vocalist
vocal[2] *nmf* member (as of a committee); ∼ *nf* vowel
volar *v* fly; blow away (as papers); disappear; blow up — **volante** *adj* flying — **volante** *nm* steering wheel; shuttlecock; flounce (of fabric); flier, circular

volcán *nm* (**-canes**) volcano
volcar *v* upset, knock over; empty out; overturn
voleibol *nm* volleyball
voltear *v* turn over, turn upside down
volumen *nm* (**-lúmenes**) volume
voluntad *nf* will; wish; intention — **voluntario, -ria** *adj* voluntary — **voluntario, -ria** *n* volunteer
volver *v* turn, turn over, turn inside out; turn (into); return, come or go back; ∼ **a** return to, do again; ∼ **en sí** come to — **volverse** *vr* turn (around); become
vomitar *v* vomit; spew (out) — **vómito** *nm* (action of) vomiting; vomit
vos *pron* you
vosotros, -tras *pron* you, yourselves
votar *v* vote; vote for — **voto** *nm* vote; vow (in religion)
voz *nf* (**voces**) voice; shout, yell; word, term; rumor
vuelo *nm* flight; (action of) flying; flare (of clothing)
vuelta *nf* turn; circle, revolution; bend, curve; return; round, lap (in sports); walk, drive, ride; back, other side; change
vuestro, -tra *adj* your, of yours — **vuestro, -tra** *pron* yours
vulgar *adj* vulgar; common
vulnerable *adj* vulnerable

W

w *nf* w, 24th letter of the Spanish alphabet

whisky *nm* (**-skys** *or* **-skies**) whiskey

X

x *nf* x, 25th letter of the Spanish alphabet

xenofobia *nf* xenophobia

Y

y[1] *nf* y, 26th letter of the Spanish alphabet

y[2] *conj* and

ya *adv* already; (right) now; later, soon

yegua *nf* mare

yema *nf* bud, shoot; yolk (of an egg); ∼ *or* ∼ **del dedo** fingertip

yerno *nm* son-in-law

yeso *nm* gypsum; plaster (for art, construction)

yo *pron* I; me — **yo** *nm* ego, self

yoga *nm* yoga

yogurt *or* **yogur** *nm* yogurt

yuca *nf* yucca

yugoslavo, -va *adj* Yugoslavian

yugular *adj* jugular

Z

z *nf* z, 27th letter of the Spanish alphabet

zafar *v* loosen, untie — **zafarse** *vr* come undone; get free of (an obligation, etc.)

zafiro *nm* sapphire

zanahoria *nf* carrot

zancudo *nm* mosquito

zapato *nm* shoe — **zapatilla** *nf* slipper; sneaker

zarpar *v* set sail, raise anchor

zigzag *nm* (**-zags**) *or* **-zagues** zigzag

zona *nf* zone, area

zoología *nf* zoology — **zoológico** *nm* zoo — **zoólogo, -ga** *n* zoologist

zorro, -rra *n* fox, vixen — **zorro, -rra** *adj* foxy, sly

zueco *nm* clog (shoe)

zurdo, -da *adj* left-handed — **zurdo, -da** *n* left-handed person

English-Spanish
Dictionary

A

a¹ *n* (**a's** *or* **as**) a *f*, primera letra del alfabeto inglés

a² *art* un *m*, una *f*; por, a la, al

abandon *v* abandonar; renunciar a — **abandonment** *n* abandono *m*

abbreviate *v* abreviar — **abbreviation** *n* abreviatura *f*, abreviación *f*

abdomen *n* abdomen *m*, vientre *m*

ability *n* (**-ties**) aptitud *f*, capacidad *f*; habilidad *f*

able *adj* **abler; ablest** capaz, hábil; competente

abnormal *adj* anormal — **abnormality** *n* (**-ties**) anormalidad *f*

aboard *adv* a bordo — **aboard** *prep* a bordo de

abort *v* abortar — **abortion** *n* aborto *m*

abound *v* ~ **in** abundar en

about *adv* aproximadamente, más o menos; alrededor — **about** *prep* alrededor de; acerca de, sobre

above *adv* arriba — **above** *prep* encima de

abroad *adv* en el extranjero; por todas partes; **go** ~ ir al extranjero

absence *n* ausencia *f* — **absent** *adj* ausente — **absentee** *n* ausente *mf*

absolute *adj* absoluto — **absolutely** *adv* absolutamente

absorb *v* absorber — **absorbent** *adj* absorbente

abstain *v* ~ **from** abstenerse de

abstract *adj* abstracto — **abstract** *n* resumen *m*

absurd *adj* absurdo — **absurdity** *n* absurdo *m*

abundant *adj* abundante — **abundance** *n* abundancia *f*

abuse abuso *m*

abyss *n* abismo *m*

academy *n* (**-mies**) academia *f* — **academic** *adj* académico

accelerate *v* acelerar

accent *v* acentuar — **accent** *n* acento *m*

accept *v* aceptar — **acceptable** *adj* aceptable — **acceptance** *n* aprobación *f*

access *n* acceso *m*

accessory *n* (**-ries**) accesorio *m*

accident *n* accidente *m*; casualidad *f* — **accidentally** *adv* por casualidad; sin querer

acclaim *v* aclamar

accommodate *v* acomodar, adaptar — **accomodations** *npl* alojamiento *m*

accompany *v* acompañar

accomplish *v* realizar, llevar a cabo — **accomplishment** *n* realización *f*; logro *m*, éxito *m*

according to *prep* según

accordion *n* acordeón *m*

account *n* cuenta *f*; relato *m*, informe *m* — **account for** *v phr* dar cuenta de, explicar — **accountable** *adj* responsable — **accountant** *n* contador *m*, **-dora** *f* — **accounting** *n* contabilidad *f*

accumulate *v* acumular; acumularse

accuse *v* acusar

accustomed *adj* **become** ~ **to** acostumbrarse a

ace *n* as *m*

ache *v* doler — **ache** *n* dolor *m*

achieve *v* lograr, realizar — **achievement** *n* logro *m*, éxito *m*

acid *adj* ácido — **acid** *n* ácido *m*

acknowledge *v* admitir; reconocer — **acknowledgment** *n* reconocimiento *m*

acne *n* acné *m*

acorn *n* bellota *f*

acquaint *v* ~ ... **with** poner a algún al corriente de; **be** ~**ed with** conocer a (una persona), saber (un hecho)

acquire *v* adquirir — **acquisition** *n* adquisición *f*

acrobat *n* acróbata *mf*

across *adv* de un lado a otro; a través —
across *prep* a través de

act *v* actuar; interpretar (un papel) — **act**
n acto *m*, acción *f*

action *n* acción *f*

activate *v* activar

active *adj* activo — **activity** *n* (**-ties**) actividad *f*

actor *n* actor *m* — **actress** *n* actriz *f*

actual *adj* real, verdadero — **actually**
adv realmente, en realidad

acupuncture *n* acupuntura *f*

acute *adj* agudo

adapt *v* adaptar — **adaptation** *n*
adaptación *f* — **adapter** *n* adaptador *m*

add *v* añadir; sumar

addict *n* adicto *m*, -ta *f*; ~ *or* **drug** ~
drogadicto *m*, -ta *f* — **addiction** *n* dependencia *f*

addition *n* suma *f* (en matemáticas); **in**
~ además

address *v* dirigirse a (una persona); po-
nerle la dirección a (una carta) — **address** *n* dirección *f*, domicilio *m*

adhere *v* adherirse — **adherence** *n* adhesión *f* — **adhesive** *adj* adhesivo

adjacent *adj* adyacente, contiguo

adjective *n* adjetivo *m*

adjust *v* ajustar, arreglar; adaptarse

administer *v* administrar — **administration** *n* administración *f* — **administrator** *n* administrador *m*, -dora *f*

admiral *n* almirante *m*

admire *v* admirar — **admiration** *n* admiración *f*

admit *v* admitir, dejar entrar — **admission** *n* entrada *f*, admisión *f*

adolescent *n* adolescente *mf* — **adolescence** *n* adolescencia *f*

adopt *v* adoptar — **adoption** *n* adopción
f

adore *v* adorar

adorn *v* adornar

adult *adj* adulto — **adult** *n* adulto *m*, -ta
f

advance *v* adelantar — **advance** *n*
avance *m* — **advancement** *n* adelanto
m, progreso *m*

advantage *n* ventaja *f*; **take** ~ **of**
aprovecharse de

adventure *n* aventura *f*

adverb *n* adverbio *m*

adversary *n* (**-saries**) adversario *m*, -ria
f

adversity *n* (**-ties**) adversidad *f*

advertise *v* anunciar; hacer publicidad
— **advertisement** *n* anuncio *m* — **ad-
vertiser** *n* anunciante *mf* — **advertising** *n* publicidad *f*

advice *n* consejo *m*

advise *v* aconsejar, asesorar — **adviser**
n consejero *m*, -ra *f*; asesor *m*, -sora *f*

aerial *adj* aéreo — **aerial** *n* antena *f*

aerobics *ns & pl* aeróbic *m*

affair *n* asunto *m*, cuestión *f*; ~ *or* **love**
~ amorío *m*, aventura *f*

affect *v* afectar — **affection** *n* afecto *m*,
cariño *m*

affinity *n* (**-ties**) afinidad *f*

affirm *v* afirmar — **affirmative** *adj* afir-
mativo

afflict *v* afligir

afford *v* tener los recursos para, permi-
tirse (el lujo de); brindar

afraid *adj* **be** ~ tener miedo

African *adj* africano

after *adv* después; detrás, atrás — **after**
conj después de (que) — **after** *prep* después de

afternoon *n* tarde *f*

afterward *or* **afterwards** *adv* después,
más tarde

again *adv* otra vez, de nuevo

against *prep* contra, en contra de

age *n* edad *f*; era *f*, época *f* — **age** *v* envejecer — **aged** *adj* anciano, viejo

agency *n* (**-cies**) agencia *f*

agenda *n* orden *m* del día

agent *n* agente *mf*, representante *mf*

aggravate *v* agravar, empeorar

aggression *n* agresión *f* — **aggressive**
adj agresivo

agile *adj* ágil — **agility** *n* agilidad *f*

agitate *v* agitar; inquietar — **agitation** *n* agitación *f*, inquietud *f*

ago *adv* hace; **long** ∼ hace mucho tiempo

agony *n* atormentarse

agree *v* acordar — **agreement** *n* acuerdo *m*

agriculture *n* agricultura *f*

ahead *adv* delante, adelante; por adelantado; a la delantera; **get** ∼ adelantar

aid *v* ayudar — **aid** *n* ayuda *f*, asistencia *f*

AIDS *n* SIDA *m*, sida *m*

aim *v* apuntar (un arma), dirigir (una observación); apuntar — **aim** *n* propósito *m*, objetivo *m*

air *v* ∼ *or* ∼ **out** airear — **air** *n* aire *m* — **air conditioning** *n* aire *m* acondicionado — **airline** *n* aerolínea *f*, línea *f* aérea — **airmail** *n* correo *m* aéreo — **airplane** *n* avión *m* — **airport** *n* aeropuerto *m*

ajar *adj* entreabierto

alarm *n* alarma *f* — **alarm** *v* alarmar, asustar — **alarm clock** *n* despertador *m*

album *n* álbum *m*

alcohol *n* alcohol *m* — **alcoholic** *adj* alcohólico — **alcoholic** *n* alcohólico *m*, -ca *f* — **alcoholism** *n* alcoholismo *m*

alert *adj* alerta, atento — **alert** *n* alerta *f* — **alert** *v* alertar, poner sobre aviso

alga *n* (**-gae**) alga *f*

algebra *n* álgebra *f*

alien *adj* extranjero — **alien** *n* extranjero *m*, -ra *f*

alienation *n* enajenación *f*

align *v* alinear — **alignment** *n* alineación *f*

alike *adv* igual, del mismo modo — **alike** *adj* parecido

alive *adj* vivo, viviente

all *adv* todo, completamente — **all** *adj* todo — **all** *pron* todo, -da; **not at all** de ninguna manera — **all–around** *adj* completo

allergy *n* (**-gies**) alergia *f*

alley *n* (**-leys**) callejón *m*

alliance *n* alianza *f*

alligator *n* caimán *m*

allocation *n* asignación *f*, reparto *m*

allow *v* permitir; dar, conceder

all right *adv* sí, de acuerdo; bien — **all right** *adj* bien, bueno

allusion *n* alusión *f*

ally *v* ∼ **oneself with** aliarse con — **ally** *n* aliado *m*, -da *f*

almanac *n* almanaque *m*

almond *n* almendra *f*

almost *adv* casi

alone *adv* sólo, solamente, únicamente — **alone** *adj* solo

along *adv* adelante; ∼ **with** con, junto con — **along** *prep* por, a lo largo de — **alongside** *adv* al costado

aloud *adv* en voz alta

alphabet *n* alfabeto *m* — **alphabetical** *or* **alphabetic** *adj* alfabético

already *adv* ya

also *adv* también, además

altar *n* altar *m*

alteration *n* alteración *f*, modificación *f*

alternate *v* alternar — **alternative** *adj* alternativo — **alternative** *n* alternativa *f*

although *conj* aunque

altitude *n* altitud *f*

altogether *adv* completamente, del todo; en suma, en general

always *adv* siempre; para siempre

amateur *adj* amateur — **amateur** *n* amateur *mf*; aficionado *m*, -da *f*

amaze *v* asombrar — **amazement** *n* asombro *m* — **amazing** *adj* asombroso

ambassador *n* embajador *m*, -dora *f*

ambiguous *adj* ambiguo

ambition *n* ambición *f*

ambulance *n* ambulancia *f*

amen *interj* amén

American *adj* americano

amiss *adv* **something is** ∼ algo anda mal

amnesia *n* amnesia *f*

among *prep* entre

amount *v* ∼ **to** equivaler a; sumar, ascender a — **amount** *n* cantidad *f*

amphibian *n* anfibio *m* — **amphibious** *adj* anfibio

amuse *v* hacer reír, divertir; entretener — **amusement** *n* diversión *f* — **amusing** *adj* divertido

analyze *v* analizar

anatomy *n* (**-mies**) anatomía *f*

ancestor *n* antepasado *m*, -da *f*

anchor *n* ancla *f* — **anchor** *v* anclar

ancient *adj* antiguo, viejo

and *conj* y

anemia *n* anemia *f*

anesthesia *n* anestesia *f* — **anesthetic** *n* anestésico *m*

angel *n* ángel *m*

anger *v* enojar, enfadar — **anger** *n* ira *f*, enojo *m*, enfado *m*

angle *n* ángulo *m*

Anglo–Saxon *adj* anglosajón

angry *adj* enojado, enfadado

anguish *n* angustia *f*

animal *n* animal *m*

animated *adj* animado, vivo; ∼ **cartoon** dibujos *mpl* animados

ankle *n* tobillo *m*

anniversary *n* (**-ries**) aniversario *m*

annotate *v* anotar — **annotation** *n* anotación *f*

announce *v* anunciar — **announcement** *n* anuncio *m* — **announcer** *n* locutor *m*, -tora *f*

annoy *v* fastidiar, molestar — **annoyance** *n* fastidio *m*, molestia *f* — **annoying** *adj* molesto, fastidioso

annual *adj* anual

anonymous *adj* anónimo

another *adj* otro — **another** *pron* otro, otra

answer *n* respuesta *f*, contestación *f*; solución *f* — **answer** *v* contestar a, responder a

ant *n* hormiga *f*

antarctic *adj* antártico

antenna *n* (**-nae** *or* **-nas**) antena *f*

anthem *n* himno *m*

anthropology *n* antropología *f*

antibiotic *n* antibiótico *m*

anticipate *v* anticipar, prever

antipathy *n* antipatía *f*

antiquity *n* (**-ties**) antigüedad *f*

antisocial *adj* antisocial

antonym *n* antónimo *m*

anxiety *n* (**-eties**) inquietud *f*, ansiedad *f* — **anxious** *adj* ansioso

any *adv* algo, un poco — **any** *adj* alguno; ningún; cualquier — **any** *pron* alguno, -na; ninguno, -na

anyhow *adv* de todas formas; de cualquier modo

anymore *adv* **not** ∼ ya no

anyone *pron* alguien; quienquiera

anything *pron* nada; cualquier cosa, lo que sea

anytime *adv* en cualquier momento

anywhere *adv* en cualquier parte, dondequiera; en algún sitio

apart *adv* aparte; ∼ **from** excepto, aparte de

apartment *n* apartamento *m*

ape *n* simio *m*

apostrophe *n* apóstrofo *m*

apparent *adj* claro, evidente — **apparently** *adv* al parecer, por lo visto

apparition *n* aparición *f*

appear *v* aparecer — **appearance** *n* apariencia *f*, aspecto *m*

appendix *n* (**-dixes** *or* **-dices**) apéndice *m* — **appendicitis** *n* apendicitis *f*

appetite *n* apetito *m* — **appetizer** *n* aperitivo *m* — **appetizing** *adj* apetitoso

applause *n* aplauso *m*

apple *n* manzana *f*

appliance *n* aparato *m*

apply *v* aplicar; ∼ **for** solicitar, pedir — **applicant** *n* solicitante *mf*; candidato *m*, -ta *f* — **application** *n* solicitud *f* (para un empleo, etc.)

appoint *v* fijar, señalar — **appointment** *n* cita *f*

appreciate *v* apreciar; darse cuenta de

apprentice *n* aprendiz *m*, -diza *f*

approach *v* acercarse a; dirigirse a (algún); acercarse — **approach** *n* acercamiento *m*

appropriate *v* apropiarse de — **appropriate** *adj* apropiado

approve *v* aprobar — **approval** *n* aprobación *f*

approximate *adj* aproximado — **approximate** aproximarse a — **approximately** *adv* aproximadamente

apricot *n* albaricoque *m*

April *n* abril *m*

apron *n* delantal *m*

apt *adj* apto, apropiado — **aptitude** *n* aptitud *f*

aquarium *n* (-iums *or* -ia) acuario *m*

aquatic *adj* acuático

aqueduct *n* acueducto *m*

Arab *adj* árabe — **Arabic** *adj* árabe — **Arabic** *n* árabe *m* (idioma)

arch *n* arco *m*

archaeology *or* **archeology** *n* arqueología *f* — **archaeologist** *n* arqueólogo *m*, -ga *f*

archipelago *n* (-goes *or* -gos) archipiélago *m*

architecture *n* arquitectura *f* — **architect** *n* arquitecto *m*, -ta *f*

archives *npl* archivo *m*

arctic *adj* ártico

area *n* área *f*, zona *f*; ~ **code** código *m* de la zona, prefijo *m*

arena *n* arena *f*, ruedo *m*

Argentine *or* **Argentinean** *or* **Argentinian** *adj* argentino

argue *v* discutir; argumentar, sostener — **argument** *n* disputa *f*, discusión *f*

arid *adj* árido

arise *v* (**arose**; **arisen**) levantarse

arithmetic *n* aritmética *f*

arm *n* brazo *m*; arma *f* — **arm** *v* armar — **armament** *n* armamento *m* — **arm**-

chair *n* sillón *m* — **armed** *adj* **armed forces** fuerzas *fpl* armadas

armpit *n* axila *f*, sobaco *m*

army *n* (-mies) ejército *m*

aroma *n* aroma *m*

around *adv* de circunferencia; por ahí; más o menos, aproximadamente; **all** ~ por todos lados, todo alrededor; **turn** ~ voltearse — **around** *prep* alrededor de; por; cerca de

arrange *v* arreglar, poner en orden — **arrangement** *n* arreglo *m*

arrest *v* detener — **arrest** *n* arresto *m*, detención *f*

arrive *v* llegar — **arrival** *n* llegada *f*

arrow *n* flecha *f*

art *n* arte *m*; ~**s** *npl* letras *fpl* (en educación)

artery *n* (-teries) arteria *f*

arthritis *n* (-tides) artritis *f*

artichoke *n* alcachofa *f*

article *n* artículo *m*

articulate *v* articular

artificial *adj* artificial

artillery *n* artillería *f*

artist *n* artista *mf* — **artistic** *adj* artístico

as *adv* tan, tanto; ~ **much** tanto como — **as** *conj* mientras; como; ya que; por más que — **as** *prep* de; como — **as** *pron* que

as for *prep* en cuanto a

ash *n* ceniza *f*

ashamed *adj* avergonzado

ashore *adv* en tierra

ashtray *n* cenicero *m*

Asian *adj* asiático

aside *adv* a un lado; aparte — **aside from** *prep* además de; aparte de, menos

as if *conj* como si

ask *v* preguntar; pedir; invitar

asleep *adj* dormido; **fall** ~ dormirse, quedarse dormido

asparagus *n* espárrago *m*

aspect *n* aspecto *m*

asphalt *n* asfalto *m*

asphyxiate *v* asfixiar — **asphyxiation** *n* asfixia *f*

aspire *v* aspirar — **aspiration** *n* aspiración *f*

aspirin *n* (**-in** *or* **-ins**) aspirina *f*

ass *n* asno *m*; imbécil *mf*; idiota *mf*

assault *n* ataque *m*, asalto *m*

assign *v* designar, nombrar; asignar — **assignment** *n* misión *f*; tarea *f*

assist *v* ayudar — **assistance** *n* ayuda *f* — **assistant** *n* ayudante *mf*

associate *v* asociar; asociarse — **associate** *n* socio *m*, -cia *f* — **association** *n* asociación *f*

as soon as *conj* tan pronto como

assume *v* suponer; asumir — **assumption** *n* suposición *f*

assure *v* asegurar

asterisk *n* asterisco *m*

asthma *n* asma *m*

astonish *v* asombrar — **astonishing** *adj* asombroso — **astonishment** *n* asombro *m*

astrology *n* astrología *f*

astronaut *n* astronauta *mf*

astronomy *n* astronomía *f*

astute *adj* astuto, sagaz — **astuteness** *n* astucia *f*

as well as *conj* tanto como — **as well as** *prep* además de, aparte de

asylum *n* asilo *m*

at *prep* a; **~ night** en la noche, por la noche; **~ two o'clock** a las dos — **at all** *adv* **not at all** en absoluto, nada

atheist *n* ateo *m*, atea *f*

athlete *n* atleta *mf* — **athletic** *adj* atlético — **athletics** *ns & pl* atletismo *m*

atlas *n* atlas *m*

atmosphere *n* atmósfera *f*

atom *n* átomo *m* — **atomic** *adj* atómico

atomizer *n* atomizador *m*

atrocity *n* (**-ties**) atrocidad *f* — **atrocious** *adj* atroz

atrophy *v* atrofiarse

attach *v* sujetar, atar; adjuntar (un documento, etc.) — **attachment** *n* accesorio *m*

attack *v* atacar — **attack** *n* ataque *m*

attempt *v* intentar — **attempt** *n* intento *m*

attend *v* asistir (a) **~ to** ocuparse de — **attendance** *n* asistencia *f* — **attendant** *n* encargado *m*, -da *f*; asistente *mf*

attention *n* atención *f*; **pay ~** prestar atención, hacer caso

attitude *n* actitud *f*; postura *f*

attract *v* atraer — **attraction** *n* atracción *f*; atractivo *m* — **attractive** *adj* atractivo, atrayente

audacity *n* audacia *f*; atrevimiento *m*

audible *adj* audible

audience *n* público *m*

audiovisual *adj* audiovisual

audition *n* audición *f*

August *n* agosto *m*

aunt *n* tía *f*

Australian *adj* australiano

authentic *adj* auténtico

author *n* autor *m*, -tora *f*

authority *n* autoridad *f* — **authorization** *n* autorización *f* — **authorize** *v* autorizar

autobiography *n* (**-phies**) autobiografía *f* — **autobiographical** *adj* autobiográfico

autograph *n* autógrafo *m* — **autograph** *v* autografiar

automatic *adj* automático

autonomy *n* autonomía *f* — **autonomous** *adj* autónomo

autopsy *n* (**-sies**) autopsia *f*

autumn *n* otoño *m*

auxiliary *n* (**-ries**) auxiliar *mf*

available *adj* disponible — **availability** *n* disponibilidad *f*

avenge *v* vengar

avenue *n* avenida *f*; vía *f*

average *n* promedio *m* — **average** *adj* medio; regular, ordinario

aviation *n* aviación *f* — **aviator** *n* aviador *m*, -dora *f*

avocado *n* (**-dos**) aguacate *m*
avoid *v* evitar
awake *v* (**awoke; awoken**) despertar —
  awake *adj* despierto
aware *adj* **be ～ of** estar consciente de
  — **awareness** *n* conciencia *f*

away *adv* de aquí, de distancia; **far ～**
  lejos
awful *adj* terrible, espantoso
awhile *adv* un rato
awkward *adj* torpe
ax *or* **axe** *n* hacha *f*
axis *n* (**axes**) eje *m*

B

b *n* (**b's** *or* **bs**) b, segunda letra del alfabeto inglés
baby *n* (**-bies**) bebé *m;* niño *m*, -ña *f*
baby–sit *v* (**-sat**) cuidar a los niños
bachelor *n* soltero *m*; licenciado *m*, -da *f*
back *n* espalda *f*; reverso *m*, dorso *m*,
  revés *m* — **back** *adv* atrás; **be back**
  estar de vuelta; **go back** volver —
  back *adj* de atrás, trasero; atrasado —
  back *v* **back up** darle marcha atrás a
  (un vehículo); **back down** volverse
  atrás — **backbone** *n* columna *f* vertebral — **background** *n* fondo *m* (de un
  cuadro, etc.), antecedentes *mpl* (de una
  situación); formación *f* — **backpack** *n*
  mochila *f* — **backup** *n* respaldo *m*,
  apoyo *m*; copia *f* de seguridad (para
  computadoras) — **backward** *or* **backwards** *adv* hacia atrás — **backward**
  adj hacia atrás
bacon *n* tocino *m*, tocineta *f*, bacon *m*
bacteria bacterias *fpl*
bad *adj* (**worse; worst**) malo; **too ～!**
  ¡qué lástima!
badly *adv* mal; gravemente
bag *n* bolsa *f*, saco *m*; bolso *m*, cartera *f*;
  maleta *f* — **bag** *v* poner en una maleta
baggage *n* equipaje *m*
bail *n* fianza *f* — **bail out** *v phr* poner en
  libertad bajo fianza
bake *v* cocer al horno; cocerse (al horno)
  — **baker** *n* panadero *m*, -ra *f* — **bakery**
  n (**-ries**) panadería *f*
balance *n* balanza *f*; equilibrio *m*; **bank**

～ saldo *m* — **balance** *v* hacer el balance de (una cuenta); equilibrar
balcony *n* (**-nies**) balcón *m*
bald *adj* calvo
ball *n* pelota *f*, bola *f*, balón *m*; **～ of
  string** ovillo *m* de cuerda
ballad *n* balada *f*
ballerina *n* bailarina *f*
ballet *n* ballet *m*
balloon *n* globo *m*
ballpoint pen *n* bolígrafo *m*
bamboo *n* bambú *m*
banana *n* plátano *m*, banana *f*, banano *m*
band *n* banda *f*; grupo *m*, conjunto *m*
bandage *n* vendaje *m*, venda *f* — **bandage** *v* vendar
bandit *n* bandido *m*, -da *f*
bang *v* golpear; cerrar de un golpe por-
  tazo *m*
bangle *n* brazalete *m*, pulsera *f*
banister *n* pasamanos *m*, barandal *m*
bank *n* banco *m* — **banker** *n* banquero
  m, -ra *f* — **banking** *n* banca *f*
banner *n* bandera *f*, pancarta *f*
banquet *n* banquete *m*
baptize *v* bautizar — **baptism** *n* bautismo *m*
bar *n* barra *f*; mostrador *m*; bar *m*
barbarian *n* bárbaro *m*, -ra *f*
barbecue *v* asar a la parrilla — **barbecue** *n* barbacoa *f*
barber *n* barbero *m*, -ra *f*
bare *adj* desnudo — **barefaced** *adj*
  descarado — **barefoot** *or* **barefooted**

adv & *adj* descalzo — **barely** *adv* apenas, por poco

bargain *n* ganga *f* — **bargain** *v* regatear, negociar

bark *v* ladrar

barley *n* cebada *f*

barracks *ns* & *pl* cuartel *m*

barrel *n* barril *m*, tonel *m*

barrier *n* barrera *f*

bartender *n* camarero *m*, -ra *f*

base *n* base *f* — **base** *v* basar, fundamentar

baseball *n* beisbol *m*, béisbol *m*

basement *n* sótano *m*

basic *adj* básico, fundamental — **basically** *adv* fundamentalmente

basil *n* albahaca *f*

basis *n* (**bases**) base *f*

basket *n* cesta *f*, cesto *m* — **basketball** *n* baloncesto *m*, basquetbol *m*

bat[1] *n* murciélago *m* (animal)

bat[2] *n* bate *m* — **bat** *v* batear

batch *n* hornada *f* (de pasteles, etc.), lote *m* (de mercancías), montón *m* (de trabajo), grupo *m* (de personas)

bath *n* baño *m*; cuarto *m* de baño; **take a ~** bañarse — **bathe** *v* bañar, lavar; bañarse — **bathrobe** *n* bata *f* (de baño) — **bathroom** *n* baño *m*, cuarto *m* de baño — **bathtub** *n* bañera *f*, tina *f* (de baño)

baton *n* batuta *f*

battalion *n* batallón *m*

battery *n* (**-teries**) batería *f*, pila *f* (de electricidad)

battle *n* batalla *f*; lucha *f* — **battle** *v* luchar — **battlefield** *n* campo *m* de batalla

bay[1] *n* bahía *f*

bay[2] *n* or **~ leaf** laurel *m*

bazaar *n* bazar *m*; venta *f* benéfica

be *v* (**was, were; been; being; am, is, are**) ser; (*expressing location*) estar; (*expressing existence*) ser, existir; (*expressing a state of being*) estar, tener — **be** *v impers* (*indicating time*) ser; (*indi-*

cating a condition) hacer, estar — **be** *v aux* (*expressing occurrence*) ser; (*expressing possibility*) poderse; (*expressing obligation*) deber; (*expressing progression*) estar

beach *n* playa *f*

beak *n* pico *m*

beam *v* brillar; transmitir, emitir

bean *n* habichuela *f*, frijol *m*; **string ~** judía *f*

bear[1] *n* (**bears** *or* **bear**) oso *m*, osa *f*

bear[2] *v* (**bore; borne**) portar; soportar

beard *n* barba *f*

bearing *n* comportamiento *m*; relacíon *f*, importancia *f*

beast *n* bestia *f*

beat *v* (**beat; beaten** *or* **beat**) golpear; batir (huevos, etc.); derrotar; latir (dícese del corazón) — **beat** *n* golpe *m*; latido *m* (del corazón); ritmo *m*, tiempo *m* — **beating** *n* paliza *f*; derrota *f*

beauty *n* (**-ties**) belleza *f* — **beautiful** *adj* hermoso, lindo — **beautifully** *adv* maravillosamente — **beautify** *v* embellecer

beaver *n* castor *m*

because *conj* porque — **because of** *prep* por, a causa de, debido a

become *v* (**-came; -come**) hacerse, ponerse — **becoming** *adj* apropiado

bed *n* cama *f*; **go to ~** irse a la cama — **bedclothes** *npl* ropa *f* de cama — **bedroom** *n* dormitorio *m* — **bedspread** *n* colcha *f* — **bedtime** *n* hora *f* de acostarse

bee *n* abeja *f*

beech *n* (**beeches** *or* **beech**) haya *f*

beef *n* carne *f* de vaca, carne *f* de res — **beefsteak** *n* bistec *m*

beeline *n* **make a ~ for** irse derecho a

beep *n* pitido *m* — **beep** *v* pitar

beer *n* cerveza *f*

beet *n* remolacha *f*

beetle *n* escarabajo *m*

before *adv* antes — **before** *prep* (*in space*) delante de, ante; (*in time*) antes de — **before** *conj* antes de que — **beforehand** *adv* antes

beg *v* pedir, mendigar; suplicar; pedir limosna

begin *v* (**-gan; -gun**) empezar, comenzar — **beginner** *n* principiante *mf* — **beginning** *n* principio *m,* comienzo *m*

behalf *n* **on ∼ of** de parte de, en nombre de

behave *v* comportarse, portarse — **behavior** *n* comportamiento *m,* conducta *f*

behind *adv* detrás; **fall ∼** atrasarse — **behind** *prep* atrás de, detrás de

behold *v* (**-held**) contemplar

beige *adj & nm* beige

being *n* ser *m;* **come into ∼** nacer

belated *adj* tardío

Belgian *adj* belga

belie *v* contradecir, desmentir

belief *n* confianza *f;* creencia *f,* convicción *f;* fe *f* — **believable** *adj* creíble — **believe** *v* creer — **believer** *n* creyente *mf*

Belizean *adj* beliceño *m,* -ña *f*

bell *n* campana *f;* timbre *m* (de teléfono, de la puerta, etc.)

belly *n* (**-lies**) vientre *m*

belong *v* **∼ to** pertenecer a, ser propiedad de; ser miembro de (un club, etc.) — **belongings** *npl* pertenencias *fpl,* efectos *mpl* personales

beloved *adj* querido, amado — **beloved** *n* querido *m,* -da *f*

below *adv* abajo — **below** *prep* abajo de, debajo de

belt *n* cinturón *m;* cinta *f,* correa *f* — **belt** *v* ceñir con un cinturón

bench *n* banco *m;* mesa *f* de trabajo

bend *v* (**bent**) doblar, torcer; torcerse; **∼ over** inclinarse — **bend** *n* curva *f,* ángulo *m*

beneath *adv* abajo, debajo — **beneath** *prep* bajo, debajo de

benediction *n* bendición *f*

benefit *n* ventaja *f,* provecho *m* — **benefit** *v* beneficiar

berry *n* (**-ries**) baya *f*

beside *prep* al lado de, junto a — **besides** *adv* además — **besides** *prep* además de

best *adj or adv* mejor

bestow *v* otorgar, conceder

bet *n* apuesta *f* — **bet** *v* (**bet**) apostar

betray *v* traicionar — **betrayal** *n* traición *f*

better *adj* mejor; **get ∼** mejorar — **better** *adv* mejor

between *prep* entre — **between** *adv* **in ∼** en medio

beverage *n* bebida *f*

beware *v* **∼ of** tener cuidado con

bewitch *v* hechizar, encantar

beyond *adv* más allá, más lejos (en el espacio), más adelante (en el tiempo) — **beyond** *prep* más allá de

bib *n* babero *m* (para niños)

Bible *n* Biblia *f*

bibliography *n* (**-phies**) bibliografía *f*

bicycle *n* bicicleta *f* — **bicycle** *v* ir en bicicleta

big *adj* grande

bike *n* bici *f;* moto *f*

bikini *n* bikini *m*

bile *n* bilis *f*

bill *n* cuenta *f,* factura *f;* billete *m* — **bill** *v* pasarle la cuenta a — **billboard** *n* cartelera *f*

billiards *n* billar *m*

billion *n* (**billions** *or* **billion**) mil millones *mpl*

bind *v* (**bound**) atar; unir; vendar — **binder** *n* carpeta *f*

bingo *n* (**-gos**) bingo *m*

binoculars *npl* binoculares *mpl,* gemelos *mpl*

biography *n* (**-phies**) biografía *f*

biology *n* biología *f* — **biologist** *n* biólogo *m,* -ga *f*

birch *n* abedul *m*

bird *n* pájaro *m* (pequeño), ave *f* (grande)

birth *n* nacimiento *m,* parto *m;* **give ∼ to** dar a luz a — **birthday** *n* cumpleaños

m — **birthplace** *n* lugar *m* de nacimiento

biscuit *n* bizcocho *m*

bishop *n* obispo *m*

bit trozo *m*, pedazo *m*; bit *m* (de información); **a** ⁓ un poco

bite *v* (**bit; bitten**) morder; picar — **bite**
n picadura *f* (de un insecto), mordedura
f (de un animal); bocado *m*

bitter *adj* amargo

black *adj* negro — **black** *n* negro *m*
(color); negro *m*, -gra *f* (persona) —
blackberry *n* (**-ries**) mora *f* — **black-
bird** *n* mirlo *m* — **blackboard** *n*
pizarra *f*, pizarrón *m* — **blackout** *n*
apagón *m* (de poder eléctrico); desmayo
m

bladder *n* vejiga *f*

blade *n* hoja *f* (de un cuchillo), cuchilla *f*
(de un patín)

blame *v* culpar, echar la culpa a —
blame *n* culpa *f* — **blameless** *adj* inocente

blank *adj* en blanco (de un papel), liso
(de una pared); vacío — **blank** *n* espacio *m* en blanco

blanket *n* manta *f*, cobija *f* — **blanket** *v*
cubrir

blazer *n* chaqueta *f* deportiva

bleach *n* lejía *f*, blanqueador *m*

bleed *v* (**bled**) sangrar

blend *v* mezclar, combinar — **blend** *n*
mezcla *f*, combinación *f* — **blender** *n*
licuadora *f*

bless *v* bendecir — **blessed** *or* **blest**
adj bendito — **blessing** *n* bendición *f*

blindness *n* ceguera *f*

blink *v* parpadear — **blink** *n* parpadeo *m*

bliss *n* dicha *f*, felicidad *f* (absoluta) —
blissful *adj* feliz

blister *n* ampolla *f*

blizzard *n* ventisca *f* (de nieve)

block *n* bloque *m*; obstrucción *f*; manzana *f*, cuadra *f* (de edificios) — **block**
v obstruir, bloquear

blond *or* **blonde** *adj* rubio — **blond** *or*
blonde *n* rubio *m*, -bia *f*

blood *n* sangre *f* — **blood pressure** *n*
tensión *f* (arterial) — **bloodstream** *n*
sangre *f*, torrente *m* sanguíneo —
bloody *adj* ensangrentado, sangriento

blossom *n* flor *f* — **blossom** *v* florecer

blouse *n* blusa *f*

blow *v* (**blew; blown**) soplar; sonar; ⁓
out fundirse (dícese de un fusible eléctrico), reventarse (dícese de una llanta)
— **blow** *n* golpe *m* — **blow up** *v* estallar, hacer explosión; volar; inflar

blue *adj* azul; triste — **blue** *n* azul *m* —
blueberry *n* (**-ries**) arándano *m* —
bluebird *n* azulejo *m* — **blues** *npl* tristeza *f*

bluff *n* farol *m*

blur *n* imágen *f* borrosa — **blur** *v* hacer
borroso

blurb *n* nota *f* publicitaria

blush *n* rubor *m* — **blush** *v* ruborizarse

boar *n* cerdo *m* macho

board *n* tabla *f*, tablón *m*; junta *f*, consejo
m; tablero *m* (de juegos); **room and** ⁓
comida y alojamiento — **board** *v* subir
a bordo de (una nave, un avión, etc.),
subir a (un tren); hospedar — **boarder**
n huésped *mf*

boast *n* jactancia *f* — **boast** *v* alardear,
jactarse

boat *n* barco *m* (grande), barca *f* (pequeña)

body *n* (**bodies**) cuerpo *m*; cadáver *m*;
conjunto *m* — **bodily** *adj* corporal —
bodyguard *n* guardaespaldas *mf*

boil *v* hervir

bold *adj* audaz; descarado — **boldness**
n audacia *f*

Bolivian *adj* boliviano *m*, -na *f*

bolt *n* cerrojo *m*; tornillo *m* — **bolt** *v*
atornillar; echar el cerrojo a

bomb *n* bomba *f* — **bombardment** *n*
bombardeo *m*

bond *n* vínculo *m*, lazo *m*; fianza *f*; bono
m (en finanzas) — **bond** *v* adherirse

bone *n* hueso *m*

bonfire *n* hoguera *f*

bonus *n* prima *f*; beneficio *m* adicional

bony *adj* huesudo; lleno de espinas (dícese de pescados)

book *n* libro *m*; libreta *f*, cuaderno *m* — **book** *v* reservar — **bookcase** *n* estantería *f* — **bookkeeping** *n* teneduría *f* de libros, contabilidad *f* — **booklet** *n* folleto *m* — **bookmark** *n* marcador *m* de libros — **bookseller** *n* librero *m*, -ra *f* — **bookstore** *n* librería *f*

boom *v* tronar, resonar; estar en auge, prosperar

boost *v* levantar; aumentar — **boost** *n* aumento *m*; estímulo *m*

boot *n* bota *f*, botín *m*

booth *n* cabina *f* (de teléfono, de votar), caseta *f* (de información)

border *n* borde *m*, orilla *f*

bore *v* aburrir — **bore** *n* pesado *m*, -da *f* (persona), lata *f* (cosa, situación) — **boredom** *n* aburrimiento *m* — **boring** *adj* aburrido, pesado

born *adj* nacido; **be** ~ nacer

borrow *v* pedir prestado, tomar prestado

Bosnian *adj* bosnio *m*, -nia *f*

bosom *n* pecho *m*, seno *m* (de una mujer); **bosom friend** amigo *m* íntimo

boss *n* jefe *m*, -fa *f*; patrón *m*, -trona *f* — **boss** *v* dirigir

botany *n* botánica *f*

both *adj* ambos, los dos, las dos — **both** *pron* ambos *m*, -bas *f*; los dos, las dos

bother *v* preocupar; molestar, fastidiar; ~ **to** molestarse en — **bother** *n* molestia *f*

bottle *n* botella *f*, frasco *m*; **baby** ~ biberón *m* — **bottle** *v* embotellar — **bottleneck** *n* embotellamiento *m*

bottom *n* fondo *m* (de una caja, del mar, etc.), pie *m* (de una escalera, una montaña, etc.), final *m* (de una lista); nalgas *fpl*, trasero *m* — **bottom** *adj* más bajo, inferior

bough *n* rama *f*

bound[1] *adj* **be** ~ **for** ir rumbo a

bound[2] *adj* obligado; decidido; **be** ~ **to** tener que

boundary *n* (**-aries**) límite *m*

bow[1] *v* inclinarse; ~ **one's head** inclinar la cabeza — **bow** *n* reverencia *f*, inclinación *f*

bow[2] *n* arco *m*

bowels *npl* intestinos *mpl*; entrañas *fpl*

bowl[1] *n* tazón *m*, cuenco *m*

bowl[2] *v* jugar a los bolos — **bowling** *n* bolos *mpl*

box[1] *v* boxear — **boxer** *n* boxeador *m*, -dora *f* — **boxing** *n* boxeo *m*

box[2] *n* caja *f*, cajón *m* — **box** *v* empaquetar — **box office** *n* taquilla *f*, boletería *f*

boy *n* niño *m*, chico *m*

boyfriend *n* novio *m*

brace *n* abrazadera *f*; ~**s** *npl* aparatos *mpl* (para dientes)

bracket *n* corchete *m* (marca de puntuación) — **bracket** *v* poner entre corchetes; catalogar

braille *n* braille *m*

brain *n* cerebro *m*; ~**s** *npl* inteligencia *f* — **brainy** *adj* inteligente, listo

brake *n* freno *m* — **brake** *v* frenar

branch *n* rama *f* (de una planta)

brand *n* or ~ **name** marca *f* de fábrica — **brand** *v* tachar, tildar

brassiere *n* sostén *m*, brasier *m*

brave *adj* valiente, valeroso — **brave** *v* afrontar, hacer frente a — **bravery** *n* valor *m*, valentía *f*

Brazilian *adj* brasileño *m*, -ña *f*

bread *n* pan *m*; ~ **crumbs** migajas *fpl*

breadth *n* anchura *f*

break *v* (**broke**; **broken**) romper, quebrar; infringir, violar; interrumpir; ~ **down** estropearse (dícese de una máquina), fallar (dícese de un sistema, etc.); ~ **into** entrar en; ~ **off** interrumpirse; ~ **out of** escaparse de; ~ **up** separarse — **break** *n* ruptura *f*, fractura *f*; **take a break** tomar(se) un descanso — **breakdown** *n* avería *f* (de máquinas), interrupción *f* (de comunicaciones), fracaso *m* (de negociaciones); **nervous breakdown** crisis *f* nerviosa

breakfast *n* desayuno *m*

breast *n* seno *m* (de una mujer); pecho *m*

breath *n* aliento *m*, respiración *f* — **breathe** *v* respirar

breed *v* (**bred**) criar (animales); engendrar, producir — **breed** *n* raza *f*

breeze *n* brisa *f*

brevity *n* brevedad *f*

brewery *n* (**-eries**) cervecería *f*

bribe *n* soborno *m* — **bribe** *v* sobornar

brick *n* ladrillo *m* — **bricklayer** *n* albañil *mf*

bride *n* novia *f* — **bridal** *adj* nupcial, de novia — **bridegroom** *n* novio *m*

bridge *n* puente *m* — **bridge** *v* tender un puente sobre

brief *adj* breve — **brief** *n* resumen *m*, sumario *m* — **briefcase** *n* portafolio *m*, maletín *m* — **briefly** *adv* brevemente

bright *adj* brillante, claro; alegre, animado; listo, inteligente — **brighten** *v* hacerse más brillante; iluminar; alegrar, animar

brilliant *adj* brillante — **brilliance** *n* resplandor *m*, brillantez *f*; inteligencia *f*

bring *v* (**brought**) traer; ~ **about** ocasionar; ~ **back** devolver; ~ **down** derribar; ~ **out** sacar; ~ **to an end** terminar (con); ~ **up** criar; sacar

British *adj* británico

broad *adj* ancho; general

broadcast *v* (**-cast**) emitir — **broadcast** *n* emisión *f*

broaden *v* ampliar, ensanchar; ensancharse — **broadly** *adv* en general — **broad–minded** *adj* de miras amplias, tolerante

broccoli *n* brócoli *m*, brécol *m*

brochure *n* folleto *m*

broil *v* asar a la parrilla

broken *adj* roto, quebrado

bronchitis *n* bronquitis *f*

brook *n* arroyo *m*

broom *n* escoba *f*

broth *n* caldo *m*

brother *n* hermano *m* — **brotherhood** *n* fraternidad *f* — **brother–in–law** *n* (**brothers–** . . .) cuñado *m*

brow *n* frente *f*; cima *f* (de una colina)

brown *adj* marrón, castaño (del pelo), moreno (de la piel) — **brown** *n* marrón *m* — **brown** *v* dorar (en cocinar)

brunet *or* **brunette** *adj* moreno — **brunet** *or* **brunette** *n* moreno *m*, -na *f*

brush *n* cepillo *m*, pincel *m* (de artista), brocha *f* (de pintor); maleza *f* — **brush** *v* cepillar

bubble *n* burbuja *f*

buck *n* dólar *m*

bucket *n* cubo *m*

buckle *n* hebilla *f* — **buckle** *v* abrochar

Buddhism *n* budismo *m* — **Buddhist** *adj* budista — **Buddhist** *n* budista *mf*

buddy *n* (**-dies**) compañero *m*, -ra *f*

budge *v* moverse; ceder

budget *n* presupuesto *m* — **budget** *v* presupuestar

buffalo *n* (**-lo** *or* **-loes**) búfalo *m*

buffet *n* bufé *m* (comida)

bug *n* bicho *m*, insecto *m* — **bug** *v* fastidiar, molestar; ocultar micrófonos en (una habitación, etc.)

build *v* (**built**) construir; desarrollar; ~ **up** aumentar, intensificar — **builder** *n* constructor *m*, -tora *f* — **building** *n* edificio *m*; construcción *f*

bulb *n* bombilla *f*

bulk *n* volumen *m*, bulto *m*

bull *n* toro *m*; macho *m*

bullet *n* bala *f*

bulletin *n* boletín *m* — **bulletin board** *n* tablón *m* de anuncios

bullfight *n* corrida *f* (de toros) — **bullfighter** *n* torero *m*, -ra *f*; matador *m*

bully *n* (**-lies**) matón *m* — **bully** *v* intimidar

bump *n* bulto *m*, protuberancia *f*; golpe

m; sacudida *f* — **bump** *v* chocar contra — **bumper** *n* parachoques *mpl*

bunch *n* grupo *m* (de personas), racimo *m* (de frutas, etc.), ramo *m* (de flores), manojo *m* (de llaves) — **bunch up** *v phr* amontarse, agruparse

bunny *n* (**-nies**) conejo *m*, -ja *f*

burden *n* carga *f* — **burden** *v* ~ ... **with** cargar . . . con

bureau *n* departamento *m* (del gobierno); agencia *f*

burglar *n* ladrón *m*, -drona *f* — **burglarize** *v* robar — **burglary** *n* (**-glaries**) robo *m*

burial *n* entierro *m*

burn *v* (**burned** *or* **burnt**) quemar; ~ **down** incendiar; ~ **up** consumir — **burn** *n* quemadura *f*

burst *v* (**burst** *or* **bursted**) reventarse; reventar — **burst** *n* estallido *m*, explosión *f*; arranque *m*, arrebato *m*

bury *v* enterrar; esconder

bus *n* (**buses** *or* **busses**) autobús *m*, bus *m* — **bus** *v* (**bused** *or* **bussed**) transportar en autobús

bush *n* arbusto *m*, mata *f*

busily *adv* afanosamente

business *n* negocios *mpl*, comercio *m*; empresa *f*, negocio *m*; **it's none of your** ~ no es asunto tuyo — **businessman** *n* (**-men**) empresario *m*, hombre *m* de negocios — **businesswoman** *n* (**-women**) empresaria *f*, mujer *f* de negocios

busy *adj* ocupado; concurrido

but *conj* pero; **not one** ~ **two** no uno sino dos — **but** *prep* excepto, menos

butcher *n* carnicero *m*, -ra *f* — **butcher** *v* matar

butter *n* mantequilla *f* — **butter** *v* untar con mantequilla

butterfly *n* (**-flies**) mariposa *f*

buttocks *npl* nalgas *fpl*

button *n* botón *m* — **button** *v* abotonar — **buttonhole** *n* ojal *m*

buy *v* (**bought**) comprar — **buy** *n* compra *f* — **buyer** *n* comprador *m*, -dora *f*

buzz *v* zumbar — **buzz** *n* zumbido *m* — **buzzer** *n* timbre *m*

by *prep* cerca de; por, por delante de; de, durante; para; de, a — **by** *adv* **by and by** poco después; **go by** pasar

bypass *v* evitar

bystander *n* espectador *m*, -dora *f*

byte *n* byte *m*, octeto *m*

byword *n* **be a** ~ **for** estar sinónimo de

C

c *n* (**c's** *or* **cs**) c, tercera letra del alfabeto inglés

cab *n* taxi *m*; cabina *f* (de un camión, etc.)

cabin *n* cabaña *f*; cabina *f* (de un avión, etc.), camarote *m* (de un barco)

cable *n* cable *m* — **cable television** *n* televisión *f* por cable

cactus *n* (**cacti** *or* **-tuses**) cactus *m*

cadet *n* cadete *mf*

café *n* café *m*, cafetería *f* — **cafeteria** *n* restaurante *m* autoservicio, cantina *f*

cage *n* jaula *f* — **cage** *v* enjaular

cake *n* pastel *m*, torta *f*

calcium *n* calcio *m*

calculate *v* calcular — **calculation** *n* cálculo *m* — **calculator** *n* calculadora *f*

calendar *n* calendario *m*

calf *n* (**calves**) pantorrilla *f* (de la pierna)

call *v* llamar; pasar, hacer (una) visita; ~ **for** requerir; ~ **off** cancelar — **call** *n* llamada *f*

calm *n* calma *f*, tranquilidad *f* — **calm** *v* calmar; **calm down** calmarse — **calm** *adj* tranquilo, en calma

calorie *n* caloría *f*

camel *n* camello *m*

camera *n* cámara *f*

camp *n* campamento *m* — **camp** *v* acampar, ir de camping

campaign *n* campaña *f* — **campaign** *v* hacer (una) campaña

camping *n* camping *m*

campus *n* ciudad *f* universitaria

can[1] *v aux* (**could**) poder; saber

can[2] *n* lata *f* — **can** *v* enlatar

Canadian *adj* canadiense

canal *n* canal *m*

canary *n* (**-naries**) canario *m*

cancel *v* (**-celed** *or* **-celled**) cancelar — **cancellation** *n* cancelación *f*

cancer *n* cáncer *m*

candid *adj* franco

candidate *n* candidato *m*, -ta *f* — **candidacy** *n* (**-cies**) candidatura *f*

candle *n* vela *f* — **candlestick** *n* candelero *m*

candy *n* (**-dies**) dulce *m*, caramelo *m*

cane *n* bastón *m* (para andar), vara *f* (para castigar); caña *f*, mimbre *m*

canine *n* ∼ *or* ∼ **tooth** colmillo *m*, diente *m* canino — **canine** *adj* canino

cannibal *n* caníbal *mf*

cannon *n* (**-nons** *or* **-non**) cañón *m*

canoe *n* canoa *f*, piragua *f* — **canoe** *v* ir en canoa

canon *n* canon *m*

can opener *n* abrelatas *m*

canteen *n* cantimplora *f*; cantina *f*

canvas *n* lona *f* (tela); lienzo *m* (de pintar)

cap *n* gorro *m*, -ra *f*; tapa *f*, tapón *m* (de botellas) — **cap** *v* tapar, cubrir

capable *adj* capaz, competente — **capability** *n* (**-ties**) capacidad *f*

capacity *n* (**-ties**) capacidad *f*

capital *adj* capital; mayúsculo (de las letras) — **capital** *n* **capital** *or* **capital city** capital *f*; **capital letter** mayúscula *f* — **capitalism** *n* capitalismo *m* — **capitalize** *v* escribir con mayúscula

capitol *n* capitolio *m*

capsule *n* cápsula *f*

captain *n* capitán *m*, -tana *f*

caption *n* subtítulo *m*

captivate *v* cautivar, encantar

capture *n* captura *f*, apresamiento *m* — **capture** *v* capturar, apresar

car *n* automóvil *m*, coche *m*, carro *m*; **railroad** ∼ vagón *m*

caramel *n* caramelo *m*

caravan *n* caravana *f*

card *n* tarjeta *f*; ∼ *or* **playing** ∼ carta *f*, naipe *m* — **cardboard** *n* cartón *m*

cardiac *adj* cardíaco

cardinal *n* cardenal *m* —

care *n* cuidado *m*; preocupación; **take** ∼ **of** cuidar (de) — **care** *v* preocuparse, inquietarse; **care for** cuidar (de), atender, querer; **I don't care** no me importa

career *n* carrera *f*

carefree *adj* despreocupado

careful *adj* cuidadoso — **carefully** *adv* con cuidado, cuidadosamente — **careless** *adj* descuidado — **carelessness** *n* descuido *m*

caress *n* caricia *f* — **caress** *v* acariciar

caricature *n* caricatura *f* — **caricature** *v* caricaturizar

caring *adj* solícito, afectuoso

carnival *n* carnaval *m*

carol *n* villancico *m*

carpenter *n* carpintero *m*, -ra *f* — **carpentry** *n* carpintería *f*

carpet *n* alfombra *f*

carriage *n* transporte *m* (de mercancías); porte *m*; **baby** ∼ cochecito *m*

carrot *n* zanahoria *f*

carry *v* (**-ried**) llevar; transportar; ∼ **oneself** portarse — **carry on** *v* realizar; portarse inapropiadamente; seguir, continuar — **carry out** *v* llevar a cabo, realizar; cumplir

carton *n* caja *f* (de cartón)

cartoon *n* caricatura *f*; historieta *f*; **animated** ∼ dibujos *mpl* animados

case *n* caso *m*; caja *f*; **in any** ∼ en todo caso

cash *n* efectivo *m,* dinero *m* en efectivo — **cash** *v* convertir en efectivo, cobrar

cashier *n* cajero *m,* -ra *f*

cash register *n* caja *f* registradora

casino *n* casino *m*

cassette *n* cassette *mf*

castle *n* castillo *m*; torre *f* (en ajedrez)

casual *adj* casual, fortuito; informal

cat *n* gato *m,* -ta *f*

catalog *or* **catalogue** *n* catálogo *m* — **catalog** *v* (**-loged** *or* **-logued**) catalogar

catastrophe *n* catástrofe *f*

catch *v* (**caught**) capturar, atrapar; sorprender; agarrar, captar — **catching** *adj* contagioso

category *n* (**-ries**) categoría *f*

cater *v* proveer comida

cathedral *n* catedral *f*

catholic *adj* universal; **Catholic** católico — **catholicism** *n* catolicismo *m*

cattle *npl* ganado *m* (vacuno)

cause *n* causa *f*; motivo *m* — **cause** *v* causar

caution *n* advertencia *f*; precaución *f*, cautela *f* — **caution** *v* advertir

cave *n* cueva *f*

cavern *n* caverna *f*

cavity *n* (**-ties**) cavidad *f*; caries *f* (dental)

CD *n* CD *m,* disco *m* compacto

cease *v* dejar de; cesar

ceiling *n* techo *m*

celebrate *v* celebrar — **celebrated** *adj* célebre — **celebration** *n* celebración *f*; fiesta *f* — **celebrity** *n* (**-ties**) celebridad *f*

celery *n* apio *m*

cell *n* célula *f*; celda *f* (en una cárcel, etc.) — **cell phone** *or* **cellular phone** teléfono celular *m*

cellar *n* sótano *m*

cellular *adj* celular

cement *n* cemento *m*

cemetery *n* (**-teries**) cementerio *m*

cent *n* centavo *m*

center *n* centro *m* — **center** *v* centrar

centigrade *adj* centígrado

centimeter *n* centímetro *m*

central *adj* central

century *n* (**-ries**) siglo *m*

ceramics *npl* cerámica *f*

cereal *n* cereal *m*

ceremony *n* (**-nies**) ceremonia *f*

certain *adj* cierto; **be** ～ **of** estar seguro de; **for** ～ seguro, con toda seguridad — **certainly** *adv* desde luego, por supuesto — **certainty** *n* certeza *f,* seguridad *f*

certify *v* (**-fied**) certificar — **certificate** *n* certificado *m,* partida *f,* acta *f*

chain *n* cadena *f*

chair *n* silla *f*; cátedra *f* (en una universidad) — **chairman** *n* (**-men**) presidente *m*

chalk *n* tiza *f,* gis *m*

challenge *v* disputar, poner en duda; desafiar — **challenge** *n* reto *m,* desafío *m*

champagne *n* champaña *m,* champán *m*

champion *n* campeón *m,* -peona *f* — **championship** *n* campeonato *m*

chance *n* azar *m,* suerte *f*; oportunidad *f*; **by** ～ por casualidad; **take a** ～ arriesgarse — **chance** *v* arriesgar

change *v* cambiar; cambiar de — **change** *n* cambio *m*

channel *n* canal *m*

chaos *n* caos *m*

chapel *n* capilla *f*

chapter *n* capítulo *m*

character *n* carácter *m*; personaje *m* (en una novela, etc.) — **characteristic** *adj* característico — **characteristic** *n* característica *f* — **characterize** *v* caracterizar

charge *n* carga *f* (eléctrica); precio *m*; **in** ～ **of** encargado de; **take** ～ **of** hacerse cargo de

charity *n* (**-ties**) organización *f* benéfica; caridad *f*

charm *n* encanto *m* — **charm** *v* encantar, cautivar — **charming** *adj* encantador

charter *n* carta *f* — **charter** *v* alquilar, fletar

chat *v* charlar — **chat** *n* charla *f*

cheap *adj* barato — **cheaply** *adv* barato, a precio bajo

cheat *v* hacer trampa(s); ~ *or* **cheater** *n* tramposo *m*, -sa *f*

check *n* inspección *f*, comprobación *f*; cheque *m*; cuenta *f* — **check** *v* revisar; comprobar; dar jaque (en ajedrez); **check in** enregistrarse (en un hotel)

checkers *n* damas *fpl*

checkup *n* chequeo *m*, examen *m* médico

cheek *n* mejilla *f*

cheer *n* alegría *f*; ~**s!** ¡salud! — **cheerful** *adj* alegre

cheese *n* queso *m*

chef *n* chef *m*

chemist *n* químico *m*, -ca *f* — **chemistry** *n* (**-tries**) química *f*

cherish *v* querer, apreciar

cherry *n* (**-ries**) cereza *f*

chess *n* ajedrez *m*

chest *n* pecho *m* (del cuerpo)

chestnut *n* castaña *f*

chew *v* masticar, mascar — **chewing gum** *n* chicle *m*

chic *adj* elegante

chicken *n* pollo *m*

chief *adj* principal — **chief** *n* jefe *m*, -fa *f* — **chiefly** *adv* principalmente

child *n* (**children**) niño *m*, -ña *f*; hijo *m*, -ja *f* — **childbirth** *n* parto *m* — **childhood** *n* infancia *f*, niñez *f* — **childish** *adj* infantil — **childlike** *adj* infantil, inocente

Chilean *adj* chileno

chili *or* **chile** *or* **chilli** *n or* ~ **pepper** chile *m*; ~ chile *m* con carne

chill *n* frío *m* — **chill** *v* enfriar — **chilly** *adj* **chillier; -est** fresco, frío

chimney *n* (**-neys**) chimenea *f*

chin *n* barbilla *f*

Chinese *adj* chino — **Chinese** *n* chino *m* (idioma)

chip *n or* **computer** ~ chip *m*

chocolate *n* chocolate *m*

choice *n* elección *f*, selección *f*; preferencia *f*

choir *n* coro *m*

choke *v* asfixiar, estrangular; atascar; asfixiarse, atragantarse (con comida)

choose *v* (**chose; chosen**) escoger, elegir; decidir

chop *v* cortar, picar (carne, etc.) — **chop** *n* chuleta *f* (de cerdo, etc.) — **choppy** *adj* picado, agitado

chopsticks *npl* palillos *mpl*

chorus coro *m* (grupo de personas); estribillo *m*

christening *n* bautizo *m*

Christian *n* cristiano *m*, -na *f* — **Christian** *adj* cristiano — **Christianity** *n* cristianismo *m*

Christmas *n* Navidad *f*

chronic *adj* crónico

chronology *n* (**-gies**) cronología *f* — **chronological** *adj* cronológico

chubby *adj* regordete, rechoncho

chunk *n* trozo *m*, pedazo *m*

church *n* iglesia *f*

chute *n* vertedor *m*; tobogán *m*

cigarette *n* cigarrillo *m*, cigarro *m*

cinema *n* cine *m*

cinnamon *n* canela *f*

cipher *n* cero *m*; cifra *f*

circle *n* círculo *m* — **circle** *v* dar vueltas (alrededor de); trazar un círculo alrededor de (un número, etc.)

circuit *n* circuito *m*

circular *adj* circular — **circular** *n* circular *f*

circulate *v* hacer circular; circular — **circulation** *n* circulación *f*; tirada *f* (de una publicación)

circumference *n* circunferencia *f*

circumstance *n* circunstancia *f*

circus *n* circo *m*

cite *v* citar

citizen *n* ciudadano *m*, -na *f* — **citizenship** *n* ciudadanía *f*

city *n* (**cities**) ciudad *f*
civic *adj* cívico
civil *adj* civil — **civilization** *n* civilización *f*
claim *v* reclamar; afirmar, sostener — **claim** *n*; demanda *f*, reclamación *f*; afirmación *f*
clap *v* aplaudir
clarify *v* (**-fied**) aclarar — **clarification** *n* clarificación *f*
clarinet *n* clarinete *m*
clarity *n* claridad *f*
clash *v* chocar, enfrentarse — **clash** *n* choque *m*
class *n* clase *f*
classic *or* **classical** *adj* clásico
classify *v* (**-fied**) clasificar — **classification** *n* clasificación *f*
classmate *n* compañero *m*, -ra *f* de clase
classroom *n* aula *f*, salón *m* de clase
claw *n* garra *f*, uña *f* (de un gato), pinza *f* (de un crustáceo) — **claw** *v* arañar
clean *adj* limpio — **clean** *v* limpiar — **cleaner** *n* limpiador *m*, -dora *f*; tintorería *f* — **cleanliness** *n* limpieza *f*
clear *adj* claro; transparente — **clear** *v* despejar (una superficie), desatascar (un tubo, etc.); **clear the table** levantar la mesa; **clear up** aclarar, resolver — **clearing** *n* claro *m* — **clearly** *adv* claramente; obviamente
clef *n* clave *f*
clerk *n* oficinista *mf*; empleado *m*, -da *f* de oficina; dependiente *m*, -ta *f*
clever *adj* ingenioso, hábil; listo, inteligente — **cleverly** *adv* ingeniosamente — **cleverness** *n* ingenio *m*; inteligencia *f*
click *v* chasquear; llevarse bien — **click** *n* chasquido *m*
client *n* cliente *m*, -ta *f*
climate *n* clima *m*
climax *n* clímax *m*, punto *m* culminante
climb *v* escalar, subir a, trepar a; $\sim$ *or* $\sim$ **up** subirse, treparse — **climb** *n* subida *f*
clinic *n* clínica *f* — **clinical** *adj* clínico

clip *v* cortar, recortar; sujetar (con un clip) — **clip** *n* clip *m* — **clipper** *n* *or* **nail** $\sim$ cortauñas *m*
clock *n* reloj *m* (de pared); **around the** $\sim$ las veinticuatro horas
clockwork *n* **like** $\sim$ con precisión
close[1] *v* cerrar; cerrarse; $\sim$ **in** acercarse
close[2] *adj* cercano, próximo; íntimo — **close** *or* **closely** *adv* cerca, de cerca — **closeness** *n* cercanía *f*
closet *n* armario *m*, clóset *m*
cloth *n* tela *f*
clothe *v* vestir — **clothes** *npl* ropa *f*; **put on one's clothes** vestirse — **clothing** *n* ropa *f*
cloud *n* nube *f* — **cloud** *v* nublar — **cloudy** *adj* nublado
clover *n* trébol *m*
clown *n* payaso *m*, -sa *f* — **clown around** *v* payasear
club *n* club *m*
clue *n* pista *f*, indicio *m*
clumsy *adj* torpe
clutch *n* embrague *m*, clutch *m* (de un automóvil)
coach *n* vagón *m* de pasajeros (de un tren); autobús *m*; entrenador *m*, -dora *f* — **coach** *v* entrenar (un atleta), dar clases particulares a (un alumno)
coal *n* carbón *m*
coast *n* costa *f*
coastline *n* litoral *m*
coat *n* abrigo *m* — **coating** *n* capa *f*
cobweb *n* telaraña *f*
cockroach *n* cucaracha *f*
cocoa *n* cacao *m*; chocolate *m* (bebida)
coconut *n* coco *m*
cod *ns* & *pl* bacalao *m*
code *n* código *m*
coffee *n* café *m* — **coffeepot** *n* cafetera *f*
coffin *n* ataúd *m*, féretro *m*
coherent *adj* coherente
coil *v* enrollar; enrollarse
coin *n* moneda *f*

coincide v coincidir — **coincidence** n coincidencia f, casualidad f

cold adj frío; **be** ~ tener frío — **cold** n frío m; resfriado m (en medicina)

coleslaw n ensalada f de col

collaborate v colaborar — **collaboration** n colaboración f

collapse v derrumbarse, hundirse; sufrir un colapso (físico o mental) — **collapse** n derrumbamiento m; colapso m

collar n cuello m (de camisa, etc.) — **collarbone** n clavícula f

collect v reunir; coleccionar, juntar (timbres, etc.); acumularse, juntarse — **collect** adv **call collect** llamar a cobro revertido, llamar por cobrar — **collection** n colección f; colecta f (de contribuciones) — **collector** n coleccionista mf

college n universidad f

cologne n colonia f

Colombian adj colombiano

colon n (**colons**) dos puntos mpl (signo de puntuación)

color n color m — **color** v colorear, pintar — **colored** adj de color — **colorful** adj de vivos colores — **colorless** adj incoloro

column n columna f — **columnist** n columnista mf

coma n coma m

comb n peine m — **comb** v peinar

combat n combate m

combine v combinar — **combination** n combinación f

come v (**came; come**) venir; llegar; ~ **about** suceder; ~ **back** regresar, volver; ~ **from** venir de, provenir de; ~ **in** entrar; ~ **out** salir; ~ **to** volver en sí; ~ **on!** ¡ándale!; ~ **up** surgir **how** ~? ¿por qué? — **comeback** n retorno m

comedy n (**-dies**) comedia f — **comedian** n cómico m, -ca f

comet n cometa m

comfortable adj cómodo

comic or **comical** adj cómico — **comic** n cómico m, -ca f; **comic book** revista f de historietas, cómic m — **comic strip** n tira f cómica, historieta f

command v ordenar, mandar — **command** n orden f; mando m

commemorate v conmemorar — **commemoration** n conmemoración f

comment n comentario m, observación f — **comment** v hacer comentarios — **commentary** n (**-taries**) comentario m

commerce n comercio m — **commercial** adj comercial — **commercial** n anuncio m, aviso m — **commercialize** v comercializar

commission n comisión f — **commission** v encargar (una obra de arte)

commit v confiar; cometer (un crimen) — **commitment** n compromiso m

committee n comité m, comisión f

common adj común; ordinario, común y corriente — **commonly** adv comúnmente — **common sense** n sentido m común

communicate v comunicar; comunicarse — **communication** n comunicación f — **communicative** adj comunicativo

communion n comunión f

Communism n comunismo m — **Communist** adj comunista

community n (**-ties**) comunidad f

compact adj compacto — **compact** n or **powder compact** polvera f — **compact disc** n disco m compacto

company n (**-nies**) compañía f; visita f

compare v comparar — **comparable** adj comparable — **comparative** adj comparativo, relativo — **comparison** n comparación f

compass n compás m

compassion n compasión f

compel v obligar — **compelling** adj convincente

compensate v ~ **for** compensar

compete *v* competir — **competition** *n* competencia *f*; concurso *m*

complain *v* quejarse — **complaint** *n* queja *f*

complement *n* complemento *m* — **complement** *v* complementar — **complementary** *adj* complementario

complete *adj* completo, entero; terminado; total — **complete** *v* completar — **completion** *n* conclusión *f*

complex *adj* complejo

complexion *n* cutis *m*, tez *f*

complicate *v* complicar — **complicated** *adj* complicado

compliment *v* felicitar

comply *v* (-plied) ~ **with** cumplir, obedecer

compose *v* componer; ~ **oneself** serenarse — **composer** *n* compositor *m*, -tora *f* — **composition** *n* composición *f*; ensayo *m*

compound *v* componer — **compound** *adj* compuesto

comprehend *v* comprender — **comprehension** *n* comprensión *f* — **comprehensive** *adj* inclusivo; amplio

compromise *n* acuerdo *m*, arreglo *m* — **compromise** *v* comprometer

computer *n* computadora *f*, computador *m*, ordenador *m* — **computerize** *v* informatizar

conceal *v* ocultar

concede *v* conceder, admitir

concentrate *v* concentrar; concentrarse — **concentration** *n* concentración *f*

concept *n* concepto *m* — **conception** *n* concepción *f*

concern *v* ~ **oneself about** preocuparse por — **concern** *n* asunto *m*; preocupación *f* — **concerning** *prep* con respecto a

concert *n* concierto *m*

conclude *v* concluir — **conclusion** *n* conclusión *f*

concrete *adj* concreto

condemn *v* condenar

condiment *n* condimento *m*

condition *n* condición *f* — **conditional** *adj* condicional

condolences *npl* pésame *m*

conduct *n* conducta *f* — **conduct** *v* conducir, dirigir; llevar a cabo

cone *n* cono *m*; **ice-cream** ~ cucurucho *m*, barquillo *m*

conference *n* conferencia *f*

confess *v* confesar — **confession** *n* confesión *f*

confidence *n* confianza *f*; confidencia *f*

confirm *v* confirmar — **confirmation** *n* confirmación *f*

conflict *n* conflicto *m* — **conflict** *v* oponerse

conform *v* ~ **with** corresponder a — **conformity** *n* (-ties) conformidad *f*

confuse *v* confundir — **confusing** *adj* confuso, desconcertante — **confusion** *n* confusión *f*, desconcierto *m*

congested *adj* congestionado — **congestion** *n* congestión *f*

congratulate *v* felicitar — **congratulations** *npl* felicitaciones *fpl*

congress *n* congreso *m* — **congressman** *n* (-men) congresista *mf*

conjunction *n* conjunción *f*

connect *v* conectarse — **connection** *n* conexión *f*; enlace *m* (como con un tren)

conscience *n* conciencia *f*

conscious *adj* consciente — **consciousness** *n* consciencia *f*

consequence *n* consecuencia *f*; **of no** ~ sin importancia

conservative *adj* conservador — **conservative** *n* conservador *m*, -dora *f*

consider *v* considerar — **considerate** *adj* considerado — **consideration** *n* consideración *f* — **considering** *prep* teniendo en cuenta

consist *v* ~ **in** consistir en — **consistency** *n* (-cies) consistencia *f*

console *v* consolar — **consolation** *n* consuelo *m*

constant *adj* constante — **constantly** *adv* constantemente

constitute *v* constituir — **constitution** *n* constitución *f*

constraint *n* restricción *f*, limitación *f*

construct *v* construir — **construction** *n* construcción *f*

consulate *n* consulado *m*

consult *v* consultar — **consultation** *n* consulta *f*

consume *v* consumir — **consumer** *n* consumidor *m*, -dora *f* — **consumption** *n* consumo *m*

contact *n* contacto *m* — **contact lens** *n* lente *mf* (de contacto)

contain *v* contener — **container** *n* recipiente *m*, envase *m*

contaminate *v* contaminar — **contamination** *n* contaminación *f*

contemporary *adj* contemporáneo

content[1] *n* contenido *m*; **table of ∼s** índice *m* de materias

content[2] *adj* contento — **content oneself with** *v phr* contentarse con

contest *v* disputar — **contest** *n* concurso *m*, competencia *f*

context *n* contexto *m*

continent *n* continente *m*

continue *v* continuar

contract *n* contrato *m*

contradiction *n* contradicción *f* — **contradict** *v* contradecir

contrary *n* (**-traries**) contrario — **contrary** *adj* contrario, opuesto

contribute *v* contribuir — **contribution** *n* contribución *f* — **contributor** *n* contribuyente *mf*

control *v* controlar — **control** *n* control *m*; **controls** *npl* mandos *mpl*

convene *v* convocar; reunirse

conversation *n* conversación *f*

convert *v* convertir

convex *adj* convexo

conviction *n* condena *f* (de un acusado); convicción *f*

convince *v* convencer — **convincing** *adj* convincente

convoke *v* convocar

cook *n* cocinero *m*, -ra *f* — **cook** *v* cocinar, guisar; preparar (comida)

cookie *or* **cooky** *n* (**-ies**) galleta *f* (dulce)

cooking *n* cocina *f*

cool *adj* fresco; tranquilo — **cool** *v* enfriar — **cooler** *n* nevera *f* portátil

cooperate *v* cooperar — **cooperation** *n* cooperación *f* — **cooperative** *adj* cooperativo

coordinate *v* coordinar — **coordination** *n* coordinación *f*

cope *v* arreglárselas; **∼ with** hacer frente a, poder con

copier *n* fotocopiadora *f*

copy *v* (**copied**) hacer una copia de; copiar — **copyright** *n* derechos *mpl* de autor

cord *n* cuerda *f*; *or* **electric ∼** cable *m* (eléctrico)

cordial *adj* cordial

core *n* corazón *m* (de una fruta); núcleo *m*, centro *m*

corn *n* grano *m* — **corncob** *n* mazorca *f*

corner *n* ángulo *m*, rincón *m* (en una habitación); esquina *f* (de una intersección)

coronary *n* (**-naries**) trombosis *f* coronaria

coronation *n* coronación *f*

corps *n* (**corps**) cuerpo *m*

corpse *n* cadáver *m*

correct *v* corregir — **correct** *adj* correcto — **correction** *n* corrección *f*

correspond *v* **∼ to** corresponder a — **correspondence** *n* correspondencia *f*

corridor *n* pasillo *m*

corruption *n* corrupción *f*

cosmetic *n* cosmético *m*

cosmopolitan *adj* cosmopolita

cosmos *n* cosmos *m*

cost *n* costo *m*, coste *m* — **cost** *v* (**cost**) costar

Costa Rican *adj* costarricense

costume *n* traje *m*; disfraz *m*

cottage *n* casita *f* (de campo)

cotton *n* algodón *m*

couch *n* sofá *m*

cough *v* toser — **cough** *n* tos *f*

councillor *or* **councilor** *n* concejal *m*, -jala *f*

counsel *n* consejo *m* — **counselor** *or* **counsellor** *n* consejero *m*, -ra *f*

count *v* contar — **count** *n* cuenta *f*; recuento *m*

counter *n* mostrador *m* (de un negocio)

countless *adj* incontable, innumerable

country *n* (**-tries**) país *m*; campo *m* — **country** *adj* campestre, rural — **countryman** *n* (**-men**) compatriota *mf*

couple *n* pareja *f* (de personas); **a ∼ of** un par de

courage *n* valor *m*

course *n* curso *m*; **of ∼** desde luego, por supuesto

court *n* cancha *f*, pista *f* (en deportes)

courtesy *n* (**-sies**) cortesía *f*

courtyard *n* patio *m*

cousin *n* primo *m*, -ma *f*

cover *v* cubrir — **cover** *n* cubierta *f*; abrigo *m*, refugio *m*; tapa *f*; portada *f* (de una revista); **covers** *npl* mantas *fpl*, cobijas *fpl* ; **take cover** ponerse a cubierto

cow *n* vaca *f*

coward *n* cobarde *mf* — **cowardice** *n* cobardía *f* — **cowardly** *adj* cobarde

cowboy *n* vaquero *m*

crab *n* cangrejo *m*, jaiba *f*

crack *v* rajar, partir

cracker *n* galleta *f* (de soda, etc.)

cradle *n* cuna *f*

craft *n* oficio *m*; (**craft**) embarcación *f* — **craftsman** *n* (**-men**) artesano *m*, -na *f* — **craftsmanship** *n* artesanía *f*, destreza *f*

cramp *n* calambre *m*, espasmo *m* (de los músculos)

crane *n* grúa *f* (máquina)

crash *v* estrellar; estrellarse, chocar — **crash** *n* estrépito *m*; choque *m*

crawl *v* arrastrarse, gatear (de un bebé)

crayon *n* lápiz *m* de cera

crazy *adj* **-zier; -est** loco

cream *n* crema *f*, nata *f* — **cream cheese** *n* queso *m* crema — **creamy** *adj* cremoso

create *v* crear — **creation** *n* creación *f* — **creator** *n* creador *m*, -dora *f*

creature *n* criatura *f*, animal *m*

credence *n* **lend ∼ to** dar crédito a

credit *n* crédito *m* — **credit card** *n* tarjeta *f* de crédito

creek *n* arroyo *m*, riachuelo *m*

creep *v* (**crept**) **creeping** arrastrarse

crew *n* tripulación *f* (de una nave); equipo *m*

crib *n* cuna *f* (de un bebé)

cricket *n* grillo *m* (insecto); críquet *m* (juego)

crime *n* crimen *m*

crinkle *v* arrugar

cripple *v* lisiar, dejar inválido; inutilizar, paralizar

crisis *n* (**crises**) crisis *f*

crisp *adj* crujiente; frío y vigorizante (del aire) — **crispy** *adj* **crispier; -est** crujiente

criterion *n* (**-ria**) criterio *m*

critic *n* crítico *m*, -ca *f* — **critical** *adj* crítico — **criticism** *n* crítica *f* — **criticize** *v* criticar

crocodile *n* cocodrilo *m*

crop *n* cosecha *f*

cross *n* cruz *f*; cruzar, atravesar; cruzar; *or* **∼ out** tachar — **cross** *adj* que atraviesa — **cross–eyed** *adj* bizco — **crossing** *n* cruce *m*, paso *m*; travesía *f* (del mar) *f* — **crossroads** *n* cruce *m* — **crosswalk** *n* cruce *m* peatonal, paso *m* de peatones — **crossword puzzle** *n* crucigrama *m*

crow *n* cuervo *m*

crowd *v* amontonarse; atestar, llenar — **crowd** *n* multitud *f*, muchedumbre *f*

crucial *adj* crucial
crucifix *n* crucifijo *m*
crude *adj* crudo
cruel *adj* cruel — **cruelty** *n* crueldad *f*
cruet *n* vinagrera *f*
cruise *n* crucero *m* — **cruiser** *n* crucero *m*; patrulla *f* (de policía)
crumb *n* miga *f*, migaja *f*
crumble *v* desmenuzar
crunch *v* ronzar (con los dientes), hacer crujir (con los pies, etc.) — **crunchy** *adj* crujiente
crush *v* aplastar, apachurrar
crutch *n* muleta *f*
cry *v* (**cried**) gritar; llorar — **cry** *n* (**cries**) grito *m*
crystal *n* cristal *m*
Cuban *adj* cubano
cube *n* cubo *m* — **cubic** *adj* cúbico
cucumber *n* pepino *m*
cue *n* señal *f*
cuff puño *m* (de una camisa)
cultivate *v* cultivar — **cultivation** *n* cultivo *m*
culture *n* cultura *f* — **cultural** *adj* cultural — **cultured** *adj* culto
cunning *adj* astuto, taimado
cup *n* taza *f*; copa *f*
cupboard *n* alacena *f*, armario *m*
curb *n* freno *m*; borde *m* de la acera

cure *n* cura *f*, remedio *m* — **cure** *v* curar
curious *adj* curioso — **curiosity** *n* (**-ties**) curiosidad *f*
curl *n* rizo *m* — **curler** *n* rulo *m*
currency *n* (**-cies**) moneda *f*
current *adj* actual — **current** *n* corriente *f*
curriculum *n* (**-la**) plan *m* de estudios
curtain *n* cortina *f* (de una ventana), telón *m* (en un teatro)
curve *v* hacer una curva; encorvar — **curve** *n* curva *f*
cushion *n* cojín *m*
custom *n* costumbre *f* — **customary** *adj* habitual, acostumbrado — **customer** *n* cliente *m*, -ta *f* — **customs** *npl* aduana *f*
cut *v* (**cut**) cortar; reducir, rebajar; ∼ **oneself** cortarse; ∼ **up** cortar en pedazos; ∼ **in** interrumpir — **cut** *n* corte *m*
cute *adj* lindo
cutlery *n* cubiertos *mpl*
cutlet *n* chuleta *f*
cutting *adj* cortante, mordaz
cycle *n* ciclo *m*; bicicleta *f* — **cycle** *v* ir en bicicleta — **cyclist** *n* ciclista *mf*
cynic *n* cínico *m*, -ca *f* — **cynicism** *n* cinismo *m*
Czech *adj* checo — **Czech** *n* checo *m* (idioma)

D

d *n* (**d's** *or* **ds**) d *f*, cuarta letra del alfabeto inglés
dad *n* papá *m*
daily *adj* diario
daisy *n* (**-sies**) margarita *f*
damage *n* daño *m*, perjuicio *m* — **damage** *v* dañar
damn *v* condenar
damp *adj* húmedo — **dampen** *v* humedecer — **dampness** *n* humedad *f*

dance *v* bailar — **dance** *n* baile *m* — **dancer** *n* bailarín *m*, -rina *f*
dandruff *n* caspa *f*
danger *n* peligro *m*
Danish *adj* danés — **Danish** *n* danés *m* (idioma)
daring *adj* atrevido, audaz — **daring** *n* audacia *f*
dark *adj* oscuro; moreno (del pelo o de la piel) — **darken** *v* oscurecer; oscurecerse — **darkness** *n* oscuridad *f*

dart *n* dardo *m*

dash *n* guión *m* largo (signo de puntuación)

data *ns & pl* datos *mpl* — **database** *n* base *f* de datos

date[1] *n* dátil *m* (fruta)

date[2] *n* fecha *f* cita *f*

daughter *n* hija *f* — **daughter–in–law** *n* (**daughters–** . . .) nuera *f*

dawn *v* amanecer — **dawn** *n* amanecer *m*

day *n* día *m; or* **working** ∼ jornada *f*; **the** ∼ **before** el día anterior; **the** ∼ **before yesterday** anteayer; **the** ∼ **after** el día siguiente; **the** ∼ **after tomorrow** pasada mañana — **daybreak** *n* amanecer *m*

daze *v* aturdir — **daze** *n* **in a daze** aturdido

dead *adj* muerto — **deadline** *n* fecha *f* límite — **deadlock** *n* punto *m* muerto — **deadly** *adj* mortal, letal

deaf *adj* sordo — **deafen** *v* ensordecer — **deafness** *n* sordera *f*

deal *v* (**dealt**) ∼ **with** tratar con — **dealer** *n* comerciante *mf*

death *n* muerte *f*

debate *n* debate *m*, discusión *f* — **debate** *v* debatir, discutir

debt *n* deuda *f* — **debtor** *n* deudor *m*, -dora *f*

decade *n* década *f*

decal *n* calcomanía *f*

decanter *n* licorera *f*

deceive *v* engañar — **deceit** *n* engaño *m* — **deceitful** *adj* engañoso

December *n* diciembre *m*

decent *adj* decente — **decency** *n* (**-cies**) decencia *f*

deception *n* engaño *m* — **deceptive** *adj* engañoso

decide *v* decidir; decidirse

decimal *adj* decimal — **decimal** *n* número *m* decimal

decision *n* decisión *f* — **decisive** *adj* decisivo

deck *n or* ∼ **of cards** baraja *f* (de naipes)

declare *v* declarar

decorate *v* decorar — **decoration** *n* decoración *f*

decrease *v* disminuir — **decrease** *n* disminución *f*

decree *n* decreto *m* — **decree** *v* decretar

dedicate *v* dedicar ∼ **oneself to** consagrarse a — **dedication** *n* dedicación *f*; dedicatoria *f*

deduce *v* deducir; concluir

deduct *v* deducir — **deduction** *n* deducción *f*

deed *n* acción *f*, hecho *m*

deep *adj* hondo, profundo — **deep** *adv* **deep down** en el fondo — **deepen** *v* ahondar

deer *ns & pl* ciervo *m*

defeat *v* vencer, derrotar — **defeat** *n* derrota *f*

defect *n* defecto *m* — **defective** *adj* defectuoso

defend *v* defender — **defendant** *n* acusado *m*, -da *f* — **defense** *n* defensa *f* — **defenseless** *adj* indefenso

defer *v* diferir, aplazar; ∼ **to** deferir a

defiance *n* desafío *m* — **defiant** *adj* desafiante

define *v* definir — **definite** *adj* definido; seguro, incuestionable — **definition** *n* definición *f* — **definitive** *adj* definitivo

deflect *v* desviar; desviarse

deformity *n* (**-ties**) deformidad *f*

defy *v* (**-fied**) desafiar

degree *n* grado *m; or* **academic** ∼ título *m*

dehydrate *v* deshidratar

delay *n* retraso *m* — **delay** *v* aplazar; retrasar; demorar

delegate *n* delegado *m*, -da *f* — **delegate** *v* delegar — **delegation** *n* delegación *f*

delicacy *n* (**-cies**) delicadeza *f*; manjar *m*, exquisitez *f* — **delicate** *adj* delicado

delicatessen *n* charcutería *f*

delicious *adj* delicioso

delightful *adj* delicioso, encantador

delinquent *adj* delincuente — **delinquent** *n* delincuente *mf*

deliver *v* entregar, repartir; liberar; asistir en el parto de (un niño); pronunciar (un discurso, etc.); asestar (un golpe, etc.) — **delivery** *n* (**-eries**) entrega *f*, reparto *m*; liberación *f*; parto *m*, alumbramiento *m*

demise *n* fallecimiento *m*

democracy *n* (**-cies**) democracia *f* — **democratic** *adj* democrático

demon *n* demonio *m*

demonstrate *v* demostrar; manifestarse — **demonstration** *n* demostración *f*; manifestación *f*

denial *n* negación *f*, rechazo *m*

denounce *v* denunciar

dentist *n* dentista *mf* — **dentures** *npl* dentadura *f* postiza

deny *v* negar

deodorant *n* desodorante *m*

department *n* sección *f* (de una tienda, etc.), departamento *m* (de una empresa, etc.), ministerio *m* (del gobierno) — **department store** *n* grandes almacenes *mpl*

depend *v* ~ **on** depender de; contar con; **that** ~**s** eso depende — **dependence** *n* dependencia *f* — **dependent** *adj* dependiente

deplete *v* agotar, reducir

deplorable *adj* lamentable

deposit *v* depositar — **deposit** *n* depósito *m*; entrega *f* inicial

depress *v* deprimir — **depression** *n* depresión *f*

deprive *v* privar

depth *n* profundidad *f*

deranged *adj* trastornado

descendant *n* descendiente *mf* — **descent** *n* descenso *m*; descendencia *f*

describe *v* describir — **description** *n* descripción *f* — **descriptive** *adj* descriptivo

deserve *v* merecer

design *v* diseñar; proyectar — **design** *n* diseño *m*; plan *m*, proyecto *m*

designate *v* nombrar, designar

designer *n* diseñador *m*, -dora *f*

desire *v* desear — **desire** *n* deseo *m*

desk *n* escritorio *m*, pupitre *m* (en la escuela)

despair *v* desesperar — **despair** *n* desesperación *f*

desperation *n* desesperación *f*

despondent *adj* desanimado

dessert *n* postre *m*

destination *n* destino *m* — **destined** *adj* destinado; **destined for** con destino a — **destiny** *n* destino *m*

destroy *v* destruir — **destruction** *n* destrucción *f* — **destructive** *adj* destructivo

detergent *n* detergente *m*

deteriorate *v* deteriorarse — **deterioration** *n* deterioro *m*

determine *v* determinar — **determined** *adj* decidido — **determination** *n* determinación *f*

deterrent *n* medida *f* disuasiva

detest *v* detestar

devalue *v* devaluar

devastation *n* devastación *f*

develop *v* aparecer; desarrollar; desarrollarse; ~ **an illness** contraer una enfermedad — **development** *n* desarrollo *m*

deviation *n* desviación *f*

device *n* dispositivo *m*, mecanismo *m*

devil *n* diablo *m*, demonio *m*

devise *v* idear, concebir

devoid *adj* desprovisto

dexterity *n* (**-ties**) destreza *f*

diagnosis *n* (**-noses**) diagnóstico *m* — **diagnose** *v* diagnosticar — **diagnostic** *adj* diagnóstico

diagonal *adj* diagonal — **diagonal** *n* diagonal *f*

diagram *n* diagrama *m*

dial *v* marcar

dialect *n* dialecto *m*

dialogue *n* diálogo *m*

diamond *n* diamante *m*; **baseball** ～ cuadro *m*, diamante *m*

diaper *n* pañal *m*

diaphragm *n* diafragma *m*

diary *n* (**-ries**) diario *m*

dice *ns & pl* dados *mpl* (juego)

dictate *v* dictar — **dictation** *n* dictado *m*

dictionary *n* (**-naries**) diccionario *m*

die *v* morir; ～ **down** amainar, disminuir; ～ **out** extinguirse; **be dying for** morirse por

differ *v* diferir, ser distinto; no estar de acuerdo — **difference** *n* diferencia *f* — **different** *adj* distinto, diferente

difficult *adj* difícil — **difficulty** *n* (**-ties**) dificultad *f*

dig *v* (**dug**) cavar

digest digerir — **digestible** *adj* digerible — **digestion** *n* digestión *f*

digit *n* dígito *m*, número *m*; dedo *m* — **digital** *adj* digital

digress *v* desviarse del tema, divagar — **digression** *n* digresión *f*

dilate *v* dilatar; dilatarse

dilemma *n* dilema *m*

dimension *n* dimensión *f*

dinner *n* cena *f*, comida *f*

dint *n* **by** ～ **of** a fuerza de

diploma *n* (**-mas**) diploma *m*

diplomacy *n* diplomacia *f* — **diplomat** *n* diplomático *m*, -ca *f* — **diplomatic** *adj* diplomático

direct *v* dirigir; mandar — **direct** *adj* directo; franco — **direct** *adv* directamente — **direction** *n* dirección *f*; **ask directions** pedir indicaciones — **director** *n* director *m*, -tora *f*

dirty *adj* sucio; obsceno, cochino

disability *n* (**-ties**) minusvalía *f*, invalidez *f* — **disable** *v* incapacitar — **disabled** *adj* minusválido

disadvantage *n* desventaja *f*

disagreeable *adj* desagradable

disappear *v* desaparecer — **disappearance** *n* desaparición *f*

disaster *n* desastre *m*

discharge *v* descargar; liberar, poner en libertad; despedir; cumplir con (una obligación) — **discharge** *n* descarga *f* (de electricidad), emisión *f* (de humo, etc.); despido *m*; alta *f* (de un paciente), puesta *f* en libertad (de un preso); supuración *f* (en medicina)

disciple *n* discípulo *m*, -la *f*

discipline *n* disciplina *f*; castigo *m* — **discipline** *v* disciplinar; castigar

disclose *v* revelar

discomfort *n* incomodidad *f*; malestar *m*; inquietud *f*

disconnect *v* desconectar

discount *n* descuento *m*, rebaja *f* — **discount** *v* descontar (precios); descartar

discourage *v* desalentar, desanimar

discover *v* descubrir

discreet *adj* discreto

discretion *n* discreción *f*

discriminate *v* ～ **against** discriminar; ～ **between** distinguir entre — **discrimination** *n* discriminación *f*; discernimiento *m*

discuss *v* hablar de, discutir — **discussion** *n* discusión *f*

disdain *n* desdén *m* — **disdain** *v* desdeñar

disease *n* enfermedad *f*

disgust *n* asco *m*, repugnancia *f*

dish *n* plato *m*; *or* **serving** ～ fuente *f*; **wash the** ～**es** lavar los platos — **dish** *vt or* **dish up** servir

disheveled *or* **dishevelled** *adj* desaliñado, despeinado (del pelo)

dishonest *adj* deshonesto

dishwasher *n* lavaplatos *m*, lavavajillas *m*

disillusion *v* desilusionar — **disillusionment** *n* desilusión *f*

disk *or* **disc** *n* disco *m*

dislike *n* aversión *f*, antipatía *f* — **dislike** *v* tener aversión a

disloyal *adj* desleal

dismiss *v* despedir, destituir

disorder *n* desorden *m*

disorganize *v* desorganizar

dispel *v* disipar

dispense *v* repartir, distribuir; ～ **with** prescindir de

disperse *v* dispersar; dispersarse

displace *v* desplazar; reemplazar

display *v* exponer, exhibir — **display** *n* muestra *f*, exposición *f*

displease *v* desagradar

disposal *n* **have at one's** ～ tener a su disposición — **disposition** *n* temperamento *m*, carácter *m*

dispute *v* cuestionar; discutir — **dispute** *n* disputa *f*, conflicto *m*

disqualification *n* descalificación *f* — **disqualify** *v* (**-fied**) descalificar

disrespectful *adj* irrespetuoso

disruption *n* trastorno *m*

dissolve *v* disolver; disolverse

dissuade *v* disuadir

distance *n* distancia *f*; **in the** ～ a lo lejos — **distant** *adj* distante

distinct *adj* distinto; claro — **distinction** *n* distinción *f*

distinguish *v* distinguir

distract *v* distraer

distress *n* angustia *f*, aflicción *f*; **in** ～ en peligro — **distress** *v* afligir — **distressing** *adj* penoso

distribute *v* distribuir, repartir — **distribution** *n* distribución *f* — **distributor** *n* distribuidor *m*, -dora *f*

district *n* distrito *m* (zona política)

distrust *n* desconfianza *f* — **distrust** *v* desconfiar de

disturbance *n* alboroto *m*, disturbio *m*; interrupción *f*

disuse *n* **fall into** ～ caer en desuso

ditto *n* ～ **marks** comillas *fpl*

diverse *adj* diverso — **diversify** *v* (**-fied**) diversificar; diversificarse

diversity *n* diversidad *f*

divert *v* desviar

divide *v* dividir; dividirse

dividend *n* dividendo *m*

division *n* división *f*

divorce *n* divorcio *m* — **divorce** *v* divorciar; divorciarse — **divorcée** *n* divorciada *f*

divulge *v* revelar, divulgar

dizzy *adj* mareado — **dizziness** *n* mareo *m*, vértigo *m*

DNA *n* ADN *m*

do *v* (**did; done**) hacer; preparar; estar, ir, andar; ser suficiente; ～ **away with** abolir, eliminar; **how are you doing?** ¿cómo estás? — **do** *v aux* **do you know her?** ¿la conoces? **I don't know** yo no se; **do you speak English?** ¿habla inglés?

doctor *n* médico *m*, -ca; doctor *m*, -tora *f*

doctrine *n* doctrina *f*

document *n* documento *m* — **document** *v* documentar — **documentary** *n* (**-ries**) documental *m*

dodge *v* esquivar, eludir

dog *n* perro *m*, -rra *f*

dogma *n* dogma *m* — **dogmatic** *adj* dogmático

doll *n* muñeco *m*, -ca *f*

dollar *n* dólar *m*

dolphin *n* delfín *m*

domain *n* dominio *m*; campo *m*, esfera *f*

domination *n* dominación *f* — **dominate** *v* dominar

donate *v* donar, hacer un donativo de — **donation** *n* donativo *m*

done *adj* terminado, hecho; cocido

donkey *n* (**-keys**) burro *m*

donor *n* donante *mf*

door *n* puerta *f* — **doorway** *n* entrada *f*, portal *m*

dormitory *n* (**-ries**) dormitorio *m*

dose *n* dosis *f* — **dosage** *n* dosis *f*

dot *n* punto *m*; **on the** ～ en punto

double *adj* doble — **double** *v* doblar; doblarse — **double** *adv* (el) doble — **double** *n* doble *mf* — **double bass** *n* contrabajo *m*

doubt *v* dudar; desconfiar de, dudar de — **doubt** *n* duda *f* — **doubtful** *adj* dudoso

dough *n* masa *f*

dove *n* paloma *f*

down *adv* hacia abajo; **come/go** ～ bajar; ～ **here** aquí abajo; **fall** ～ caer; **lie** ～ acostarse; **sit** ～ sentarse — **down** *prep* a lo largo de; a través de; **down the hill** cuesta abajo — **down** *adj* de bajada — **downhearted** *adj* desanimado — **downstairs** *adv* abajo — **downstairs** *adj* de abajo — **downtown** *n* centro *m* (de la ciudad) — **downtown** *adv* al centro, en el centro — **downtown** *adj* del centro

dozen *n* docena *f*

draft *n or* **rough** ～ borrador *m*; conscripción *f* (militar) — **draft** *v*; hacer el borrador de; reclutar

drag *v* arrastrar; arrastrarse

drain escurrir(se) (de los platos); alcantarilla *f*; agotamiento *m* — **drainpipe** *n* tubo *m* de desagüe

drama *n* drama *m* — **dramatic** *adj* dramático — **dramatist** *n* dramaturgo *m*, -ga *f* — **dramatize** *v* dramatizar

drastic *adj* drástico

draw *v* (**drew; drawn**) tirar de; dibujar, trazar; ～ **a conclusion** llegar a una conclusión; ～ **up** redactar — **draw** *n* empate *m*; atracción *f* — **drawer** *n* gaveta *f*, cajón *m* (en un mueble)

dread *v* temer — **dread** *n* pavor *m*, temor *m*

dream *n* sueño *m* — **dream** *v* (**dreamed** *or* **dreamt**) soñar; **dream up** idear — **dreamy** *adj* soñador

dress *v* vestir; vestirse — **dress** *n* ropa *f*; vestido *m* (de mujer)

drill *n* taladro *m* — **drill** *v* perforar, taladrar

drink *v* (**drank; drunk** *or* **drank**) beber — **drink** *n* bebida *f*

drive *v* (**drove; driven**) conducir; manejar; impulsar; ～ **one to** (**do . . .**) llevar a algún a (hacer . . .) — **drive** *n* paseo *m* (en coche); energía *f*; instinto *m*

driver *n* conductor *m*, -tora *f*; chofer *m*

drizzle *n* llovizna *f* — **drizzle** *v* lloviznar

drool *v* babear — **drool** *n* baba *f*

drop *n* gota *f* (de líquido); caída *f* — **drop** *v* caer(se); bajar, descender; abandonar, dejar; **drop off** dejar

drown *v* ahogar; ahogarse

drugstore *n* farmacia *f*

drum *n* tambor *m*

drunk *adj* borracho

dry *adj* seco — **dry** *v* (**dried**) secar; secarse — **dryer** *n* secadora *f* — **dryness** *n* sequedad *f*, aridez *f*

duck *n* (**duck** *or* **ducks**) pato *m*, -ta *f*

due *adj* esperado; debido — **dues** *npl* cuota *f*

duel *n* duelo *m*

dull *adj* torpe — **dull** *v* entorpecer (los sentidos), aliviar (el dolor)

duplicate *adj* duplicado — **duplicate** *v* duplicar, hacer copias de — **duplicate** *n* duplicado *m*, copia *f*

durable *adj* duradero

duration *n* duración *f*

during *prep* durante

dusk *n* anochecer *m*, crepúsculo *m*

dust *n* polvo *m* — **dustpan** *n* recogedor *m*

Dutch *adj* holandés — **Dutch** *n* holandés *m* (idioma)

dwarf *n* (**dwarfs**) enano *m*, -na *f*

dynamic *adj* dinámico

E

e *n* (**e's** *or* **es**) e *f*, quinta letra del alfabeto inglés

each *adj* cada — **each** *pron* cada uno *m*, cada una *f*; **each other** el uno al otro — **each** *adv* cada uno, por persona

eager *adj* entusiasta; impaciente — **eagerness** *n* entusiasmo *m*, impaciencia *f*

eagle *n* águila *f*

ear *n* oreja *f*

early *adv* temprano — **early** *adj* primero; **be early** llegar temprano

earn *v* ganar

earnings *npl* ingresos *mpl*; ganancias *fpl*

earphone *n* audífono *m*

earring *n* pendiente *m*, arete *m*

earth *n* tierra *f* — **earthquake** *n* terremoto *m* — **earthworm** *n* lombriz *f* (de tierra)

ease *n* facilidad *f*; comodidad *f*

easily *adv* fácilmente, con facilidad

east *adv* al este — **east** *n* este *m*; **the East** el Oriente

easy *adj* fácil — **easygoing** *adj* tolerante, relajado

eat *v* (**ate; eaten**) comer

eccentricity *n* excentricidad *f*

echo *n* (**echoes**) eco *m*

eclipse *n* eclipse *m*

ecology *n* ecología *f* — **ecological** *adj* ecológico

economy *n* economía *f* — **economic** *or* **economical** *adj* económico — **economics** *n* economía *f* — **economist** *n* economista *mf* — **economize** *v* economizar

Ecuadoran *or* **Ecuadorean** *or* **Ecuadorian** *adj* ecuatoriano

edge *n* borde *m*; filo *m* (de un cuchillo)

edit *v* editar, redactar, corregir — **edition** *n* edición *f* — **editor** *n* director *m*, -tora *f* (de un periódico); redactor *m*, -tora *f* (de un libro) — **editorial** *n* editorial *m*

educate *v* educar, instruir; informar — **education** *n* educación *f* — **educator** *n* educador *m*, -dora *f*

effect *n* efecto *m*; **go into** ~ entrar en vigor — **effective** *adj* eficaz; efectivo, vigente — **effectiveness** *n* eficacia *f*

efficient *adj* eficiente — **efficiency** *n* eficiencia *f*

effort *n* esfuerzo *m*

egg *n* huevo *m* — **eggplant** *n* berenjena *f*

eight *n* ocho *m* — **eight** *adj* ocho — **eight hundred** *n* ochocientos *m*

eighteen *n* dieciocho *m* — **eighteen** *adj* dieciocho

eighth *n* octavo *m*, -va *f* (en una serie)

eighty *n* (**eighties**) ochenta *m* — **eighty** *adj* ochenta

either *adj* cualquiera (de los dos); ninguno; cada — **either** *pron* cualquiera *mf* (de los dos); ninguno *m*, -na *f* (de los dos); **either** *or* **either one** algún *m*, alguna *f* — **either** *conj* o; ni

eject *v* expulsar, expeler

elaborate *adj* detallado — **elaborate** *v* elaborar

elastic *adj* elástico — **elastic** *n* elástico *m*; goma *f* (elástica) — **elasticity** *n* elasticidad *f*

elbow *n* codo *m*

elder *adj* mayor — **elder** *n* mayor *mf*; anciano *m*, -na *f* (de un tribu, etc.) — **elderly** *adj* mayor, anciano

elect *v* elegir — **election** *n* elección *f* — **electoral** *adj* electoral — **electorate** *n* electorado *m*

electricity *n* electricidad *f* — **electrician** *n* electricista *mf* — **electrify** *v* (**-fied**) electrificar

electronic *adj* electrónico — **electronic mail** *or* **E-mail** *n* correo *m* electrónico
elegant *adj* elegante — **elegance** *n* elegancia *f*
element *n* elemento *m* — **elementary school** *n* escuela *f* primaria
elephant *n* elefante *m*, -ta *f*
elevate *v* elevar — **elevator** *n* ascensor *m*
eleven *n* once *m* — **eleven** *adj* once — **eleventh** *adj* undécimo — **eleventh** *n* undécimo *m*, -ma *f* (en una serie); onceavo *m*, onceava parte *f*
eliminate *v* eliminar — **elimination** *n* eliminación *f*
elliptical *or* **elliptic** *adj* elíptico
elm *n* olmo *m*
else[1] *adv* **how ～ ?** ¿de qué otro modo?; **where ～ ?** ¿en qué otro sitio?; **or ～** si no, de lo contrario — **elsewhere** *adv* en otra parte
else[2] *adj* **everyone ～** todos los demás; **nobody ～** ningún otro, nadie más; **nothing ～** nada más
embark *v* embarcar
embarrass *v* avergonzar — **embarrassing** *adj* embarazoso — **embarrassment** *n* vergüenza *f*
embellish *v* adornar, embellecer — **embellishment** *n* adorno *m*
embrace *v* abrazar — **embrace** *n* abrazo *m*
embryo *n* (**embryos**) embrión *m*
emerald *n* esmeralda *f*
emerge *v* salir, aparecer
emergency *n* (**-cies**) emergencia *f*; **～ exit** salida *f* de emergencia; **～ room** sala *f* de urgencias, sala *f* de guardia
emigrant *n* emigrante *mf* — **emigrate** *v* emigrar — **emigration** *n* emigración *f*
emotion *n* emoción *f* — **emotional** *adj* emocional; emotivo
emphasis *n* (**-phases**) énfasis *m* — **emphasize** *v* subrayar — **emphatic** *adj* enérgico, categórico
employ *v* emplear — **employee** *n* empleado *m*, -da *f* — **employer** *n* patrón *m*, -trona *f;* empleador *m*, -dora *f* — **employment** *n* trabajo *m*, empleo *m*
empty *adj* vacío — **empty** *v* (**-tied**) vaciar — **emptiness** *n* vacío *m*
enable *v* hacer posible, permitir
enclose *v* encerrar, cercar — **enclosure** *n* anexo *m* (con una carta)
encourage *v* animar, alentar — **encouragement** *n* aliento *m*; fomento *m*
encyclopedia *n* enciclopedia *f*
end *n* fin; extremo *m*, punta *f* — **end** *v* terminar
endeavor *v* **～ to** esforzarse por — **endeavor** *n* esfuerzo *m*
ending *n* final *m*, desenlace *m*
endless *adj* interminable; innumerable
endure *v* soportar, aguantar; durar
enemy *n* (**-mies**) enemigo *m*, -ga *f*
energy *n* energía *f* — **energetic** *adj* enérgico
engage *v* captar, atraer (la atención, etc.) — **engagement** *n* cita *f*, hora *f;* compromiso *m* — **engaging** *adj* atractivo
engine *n* motor *m* — **engineer** *n* ingeniero *m*, -ra *f;* maquinista *mf* (de locomotoras) — **engineering** *n* ingeniería *f*
English *adj* inglés — **English** *n* inglés *m* (idioma) — **Englishman** *n* (**-men**) inglés *m* — **Englishwoman** *n* (**-women**) inglesa *f*
enhance *v* aumentar, mejorar
enjoy *v* disfrutar, gozar de — **enjoyable** *adj* agradable — **enjoyment** *n* placer *m*
enlarge *v* agrandar, agrandarse; ampliar — **enlargement** *n* ampliación *f*
enlist *v* alistar
enormous *adj* enorme
enough *adj* bastante, suficiente — **enough** *adv* bastante — **enough** *pron* (lo) suficiente, (lo) bastante; **not enough** no basta
enrage *v* enfurecer
enrich *v* enriquecer
enroll *v* matricular, inscribir
ensure *v* asegurar

entail *v* suponer, conllevar

entangle *v* enredar — **entanglement** *n* enredo *m*

enter *v* entrar (en); ~ **into** firmar (un acuerdo), entablar (negociaciones, etc.)

enterprise *n* empresa *f* — **enterprising** *adj* emprendedor

entertain *v* entretener, divertir; considerar — **entertainment** *n* entretenimiento *m*, diversión *f*

enthrall *or* **enthral** *v* cautivar, embelesar

enthusiasm *n* entusiasmo *m* — **enthusiast** *n* entusiasta *mf* — **enthusiastic** *adj* entusiasta

entire *adj* entero, completo — **entirely** *adv* completamente

entitle *v* titular

entity *n* (**-ties**) entidad *f*

entrance¹ *v* encantar, fascinar

entrance² *n* entrada *f*

entrust *v* confiar

entry *n* (**-tries**) entrada *f*; entrada *f*, anotación *f*

envelop *v* envolver — **envelope** *n* sobre *m*

envious *adj* envidioso

environment *n* medio *m* ambiente

envy *n* envidia *f* — **envy** *v* (**-vied**) envidiar

enzyme *n* enzima *f*

epidemic *n* epidemia *f*

episode *n* episodio *m*

epoch *n* época *f*

equal *adj* igual; **be** ~ **to** estar a la altura de (una tarea, etc.) — **equal** *n* igual *mf* — **equal** *v* igualar — **equality** *n* igualdad *f*

equation *n* ecuación *f*

equator *n* ecuador *m*

equilibrium *n* (**-riums** *or* **-ria**) equilibrio *m*

equipment *n* equipo *m*

equivalent *adj* equivalente — **equivalent** *n* equivalente *m*

era *n* era *f*, época *f*

erase *v* borrar — **eraser** *n* goma *f* de borrar, borrador *m*

errand *n* mandado *m*, recado *m*

error *n* error *m* — **erroneous** *adj* erróneo

eruption *n* erupción *f*

escalator *n* escalera *f* mecánica

escape *v* escapar a, evitar; escaparse, fugarse — **escape** *n* fuga *f*; **escape from reality** evasión *f* de la realidad

Eskimo *adj* esquimal

especially *adv* especialmente

espresso *n* (**-sos**) café *m* exprés

essay *n* ensayo *m* (literario), composición *f* (académica)

essence *n* esencia *f* — **essential** *adj* esencial

establish *v* establecer — **establishment** *n* establecimiento *m*

estimate *v* calcular, estimar — **estimate** *n* cálculo *m* (aproximado); **estimate of costs** presupuesto *m* — **estimation** *n* juicio *m*; estima *f*

eternal *adj* eterno — **eternity** *n* (**-ties**) eternidad *f*

ethics *ns & pl* ética *f*, moralidad *f*

ethnic *adj* étnico

euphemism *n* eufemismo *m*

European *adj* europeo

evaluate *v* evaluar

eve *n* víspera *f*

even *adj* regular, constante; igual; ~ **number** número *m* par — **even** *adv* hasta, incluso

evening *n* tarde *f*, noche *f*

event *n* acontecimiento *m*, suceso *m*; prueba *f* (en deportes); **in the** ~ **of** en caso de

ever *adv* siempre

every *adj* cada; ~ **month** todos los meses; ~ **other day** cada dos días — **everybody** *pron* todos *mpl*, -das *fpl*; todo el mundo — **everyday** *adj* cotidiano, de todos los días — **everything** *pron* todo — **everywhere** *adv* en todas partes, por todas partes

evidence *n* pruebas *fpl*; testimonio *m*, declaración *f*

evil *adj* malvado, malo — **evil** *n* mal *m*, maldad *f*

evolution *n* evolución *f*, desarrollo *m*

exact *adj* exacto, preciso — **exact** *v* exigir — **exactly** *adv* exactamente

exaggerate *v* exagerar — **exaggeration** *n* exageración *f*

examine *v* examinar — **exam** *n* examen *m* — **examination** *n* examen *m*

example *n* ejemplo *m*

excellent *adj* excelente

except *prep or* ∼ **for** excepto, menos, salvo — **except** *v* exceptuar — **exception** *n* excepción *f* — **exceptional** *adj* excepcional

excess *n* exceso *m* — **excess** *adj* excesivo, de sobra

exchange *n* intercambio *m* — **exchange** *v* cambiar, intercambiar

excite *v* excitar, emocionar — **excited** *adj* excitado, entusiasmado — **excitement** *n* entusiasmo *m*, emoción *f*

exclaim *v* exclamar — **exclamation** *n* exclamación *f* — **exclamation point** *n* signo *m* de admiración

excluding *prep* excepto, con excepción de — **exclusion** *n* exclusión *f* — **exclusive** *adj* exclusivo

excuse *v* perdonar; ∼ **me** perdóne, perdón — **excuse** *n* excusa *f*

execute *v* **-cuted; -cuting** ejecutar

executive *adj* ejecutivo — **executive** *n* ejecutivo *m*, -va *f*

exemplify *v* (**-fied**) ejemplificar

exercise *n* ejercicio *m* — **exercise** *v* hacer ejercicio

exhaust *v* agotar — **exhaustive** *adj* exhaustivo

exhibit *v* exponer; mostrar — **exhibition** *n* exposición *f*

exist *v* existir — **existence** *n* existencia *f*

exit *n* salida *f* — **exit** *v* salir

expect *v* esperar; contar con

expedition *n* expedición *f*

expend *v* gastar — **expense** *n* gasto *m*; **expenses** *npl* gastos *mpl*, expensas *fpl* — **expensive** *adj* caro

experience *n* experiencia *f* — **experience** *v* experimentar — **experiment** *n* experimento *m*

expert *adj* experto — **expert** *n* experto *m*, -ta *f* — **expertise** *n* pericia *f*, competencia *f*

expire *v* caducar, vencer — **expiration** *n* vencimiento *m*, caducidad *f*

explain *v* explicar — **explanation** *n* explicación *f*

explicit *adj* explícito

export *v* exportar — **export** *n* exportación *f*

expose *v* exponer; descubrir, revelar

express *adj* expreso, rápido — **express** *adv* por correo urgente — **express** *v* expresar — **expression** *n* expresión *f*

extend *v* extender; prolongar; ampliar — **extension** *n* extensión *f*; **extension cord** alargador, extensión *m*

exterior *adj* exterior — **exterior** *n* exterior *m*

external *adj* externo

extra *adj* suplementario, de más — **extra** *n* extra *m* — **extra** *adv* extra, más

extraordinary *adj* extraordinario

extreme *adj* extremo — **extremity** *n* (**-ties**) extremidad *f*

extrovert *n* extrovertido *m*, -da *f* — **extroverted** *adj* extrovertido

eye *n* ojo *m*; visión *f*, vista *f*; mirada *f* — **eye** *v* mirar — **eyebrow** *n* ceja *f* — **eyeglasses** *npl* anteojos *mpl*, lentes *mpl* — **eyelash** *n* pestaña *f* — **eyelid** *n* párpado *m* — **eyesight** *n* vista *f*, visión *f*

F

f *n* (**f's** *or* **fs**) f, sexta letra del alfabeto inglés

fable *n* fábula *f*

fabric *n* tela *f*, tejido *m*

fabulous *adj* fabuloso

facade *n* fachada *f*

face *n* cara *f*, rostro *m* (de una persona); fisonomía *f*, aspecto *m*; cara *f* (de una moneda), fachada *f* (de un edificio); ~ **value** valor *m* nominal; **in the ~ of** en medio de, ante — **face** *v* estar frente a; enfrentarse a; dar a — **facedown** *adv* boca abajo — **faceless** *adj* anónimo

facial *adj* de la cara, facial

facetious *adj* gracioso, burlón

facility *n* (**-ties**) facilidad *f*

facsimile *n* facsímile *m*, facsímil *m*

fact *n* hecho *m*; **in ~** en realidad

faction *n* facción *m*, bando *m*

factor *n* factor *m*

factory *n* (**-ries**) fábrica *f*

faculty *n* (**-ties**) facultad *f*

fad *n* moda *f* pasajera, manía *f*

fail *v* fracasar (de una empresa, un matrimonio, etc.); fallar; ~ **in** faltar a, no cumplir con; suspender, ser reprobado ~ **to do** no hacer; reprobar — **fail** *n* **without fail** sin falta — **failure** *n* fracaso *m*; falla *f*

faint *v* desmayarse — **faint** *n* desmayo *m* — **faintly** *adv* débilmente

fair¹ *n* feria *f*

fair² *adj* justo — **fair** *adv* **play fair** jugar limpio — **fairly** *adv* bastante — **fairness** *n* justicia *f*

fairy *n* (**fairies**) hada; ~ **tale** cuento *m* de hadas

faith *n* fe *f* — **faithful** *adj* fiel — **faithfulness** *n* fidelidad *f*

fall *v* (**fell; fallen**) caer, bajar (de los precios), descender (de la temperatura); ~ **asleep** dormirse; ~ **in love** enamorarse; ~ **through** fracasar — **fall** *n* caída *f*, bajada *f* (de precios), descenso *m* (de temperatura); otoño *m*

false *adj* falso; ~ **teeth** dentadura *f* postiza

fame *n* fama *f*

familiar *adj* familiar — **familiarity** *n* familiaridad *f*

family *n* (**-lies**) familia *f*

famous *adj* famoso

fan *n* ventilador *m*, abanico *m*; aficionado *m*, -da *f* (a un pasatiempo); admirador *m*, -dora *f* (de una persona) — **fan** *v* avivar (un fuego)

fantasy *n* (**-sies**) fantasía *f* — **fantastic** *adj* fantástico

far *adv* (**farther** *or* **further; farthest** *or* **furthest**) lejos; **as ~ as** hasta (un lugar), con respecto a (un tema); ~ **away** a lo lejos; ~ **from it!** ¡todo lo contrario!; **so ~** hasta ahora, todavía — **far** *adj* (**farther** *or* **further; farthest** *or* **furthest**) lejano — **faraway** *adj* remoto, lejano

farewell *n* despedida *f*

farm *n* granja *f*, hacienda *f* — **farm** *v* cultivar (la tierra), criar (animales); ser agricultor — **farmer** *n* agricultor *m*, -tora *f*; granjero *m*, -jera *f* — **farmhand** *n* peón *m* — **farming** *n* agricultura *f*, cultivo *m* (de plantas), crianza *f* (de animales)

fascinate *v* fascinar — **fascination** *n* fascinación *f*

fashion *n* manera *f*; moda *f*; **out of ~** pasada de moda

fast *adj* rápido; ~ **friends** amigos *mpl* leales — **fast** *adv* firmemente; rápidamente; **fast asleep** profundamente dormido

fasten *v* sujetar (papeles, etc.), abrochar (una blusa, etc.), abrocharse; cerrar (una maleta, etc.) — **fastener** n cierre m

fat adj gordo — **fat** n grasa f

fatal adj mortal — **fatality** n (-ties) víctima f mortal

fate n suerte f

father n padre m — **fatherhood** n paternidad f — **father–in–law** n (**fathers– . . .**) suegro m — **fatherly** adj paternal

fatigue n fatiga f

fatten v engordar

faucet n grifo m

fault n defecto m; culpa f; falla f (geológica) — **faulty** adj defectuoso

fauna n fauna f

favor n favor m; in ∼ of a favor de — **favor** v favorecer; estar a favor de — **favorable** adj favorable — **favorite** n favorito m, -ta f — **favorite** adj favorito

fear n miedo m, temor m — **fear** v temer — **fearful** adj temeroso

feasible adj viable, factible

feast n fiesta f — **feast** v **feast upon** darse un festín de

feat n hazaña f

feather n pluma f

feature n rasgo m (de la cara); ∼ **film** largometraje m

February n febrero m

fed up adj harto

fee n honorarios mpl

feeble adj débil

feed v (**fed**) dar de comer a, alimentar(se); comer

feel v (**felt**) sentir (una sensación, etc.); tocar, palpar — **feel** n tacto m, sensación f — **feeling** n sensación f; sentimiento m

feign v fingir

female adj femenino — **female** n mujer f (persona); hembra f (animal)

feminine adj femenino — **feminism** n feminismo m

fence n cerco m, -ca f; valla f — **fence** v

hacer esgrima — **fencing** n esgrima m (deporte)

fender n guardabarros mpl

ferment v fermentar — **fermentation** n fermentación f

fertility n fertilidad f — **fertilize** v fecundar (un huevo), abonar (el suelo)

festive adj festivo — **festivity** n (-ties) festividad f

fever n fiebre f

few adj pocos; **a** ∼ **times** varias veces — **few** pron pocos; **a few** algunos, unos cuantos — **fewer** adj or pron menos

fiber or **fibre** n fibra f

fiction n ficción f — **fictional** or **fictitious** adj ficticio

fidelity n fidelidad f

field n campo m

fifteen n quince m — **fifteen** adj quince

fifth n quinto m, -ta f (en una serie); quinto m (en matemáticas) — **fifth** adj quinto

fifty n (-ties) cincuenta m — **fifty** adj cincuenta

fight v (**fought**) luchar (contra); pelear — **fight** n lucha f; pelea f — **fighter** n luchador m, -dora f

figure n número m, cifra f; figura f; **watch one's** ∼ cuidar la línea — **figure** v figurar

file[1] n lima f (instrumento) — **file** v limar

file[2] v archivar (documentos) — **file** n archivo m

file[3] n fila f

fill v llenar, rellenar

film n película f — **film** v filmar

filter n filtro m — **filter** v filtrar

fin n aleta f

final adj final — **final** n final f (en deportes) — **finalist** n finalista mf — **finalize** v finalizar

finance n finanzas fpl; ∼**s** npl recursos mpl financieros — **finance** v financiar — **financial** adj financiero

find v (**found**) encontrar; darse cuenta

de; ~ **out** enterarse — **find** *n* hallazgo
m — **finding** *n* hallazgo *m*

fine[1] *n* multa *f* — **fine** *v* multar

fine[2] *adj* fino; sutil — **fine** *adv* bien —
fine arts *npl* bellas artes *fpl* — **finely**
adv fino, menudo

finger *n* dedo *m* — **fingernail** *n* uña *f* —
fingerprint *n* huella *f* digital

finish *v* acabar, terminar

finite *adj* finito

fire *n* fuego *m*; incendio *m*; **catch** ~ incendiarse (de bosques, etc.), prenderse
(de fósforos, etc.) — **firearm** *n* arma *f*
de fuego — **firefighter** *n* bombero *m*,
-ra *f* — **firefly** *n* (**-flies**) luciérnaga *f* —
fireplace *n* hogar *m*, chimenea *f* —
firewood *n* leña *f* — **fireworks** *npl*
fuegos *mpl* artificiales

firm[1] *n* empresa *f*

firm[2] *adj* firme — **firmness** *n* firmeza *f*

first *adj* primero; **at** ~ **sight** a primera
vista; **for the** ~ **time** por primera vez
— **first** *adv* primero; **first of all** en
primer lugar — **first** *n* primero *m*, -ra *f*
— **first aid** *n* primeros auxilios *mpl*

fiscal *adj* fiscal

fish *n* (**fish**) pez *m* (vivo), pescado *m*
(para comer) — **fish** *v* pescar — **fisherman** *n* (**-men**) pescador *m*, -dora *f* —
fishing *n* pesca *f* — **fish market** *n*
pescadería *f*

fit[1] *n* ataque *m*

fit[2] *adj* en forma — **fit** *v* quedar bien a (de
la ropa); caber (en una caja, etc.), enca-
jar (en un hueco, etc.) — **fitness** *n*
salud *f*

five *n* cinco *m* — **five** *adj* cinco — **five
hundred** *n* quinientos *m* — **five hundred** *adj* quinientos

fix *v* fijar, sujetar; arreglar — **fixed** *adj*
fijo

flag *n* bandera *f* — **flagpole** *n* asta *f*

flame *n* llama *f*

flammable *adj* inflamable

flap *n* solapa *f* (de un sobre, un libro,
etc.), tapa *f* (de un recipiente) — **flap** *v*
batir, agitar

flash *n* ~ **of lightning** relámpago *m*; **in
a** ~ de repente — **flashlight** *n* linterna
f

flatter *v* halagar — **flattering** *adj* halagador — **flattery** *n* halagos *mpl*

flavor *n* gusto *m*, sabor *m*

flaw *n* defecto *m*

flea *n* pulga *f*

flee *v* (**fled**) huir (de)

fleet *n* flota *f*

fleeting *adj* fugaz

Flemish *adj* flamenco

flexibility *n* flexibilidad *f* — **flexible** *adj*
flexible

flier *n* folleto *m*

flight *n* vuelo *m*

flipper *n* aleta *f*

float *n* flotador *m* — **float** *v* flotar; hacer
flotar

flock *n* rebaño *m* (de ovejas), bandada *f*
(de pájaros)

flood *n* inundación *f* — **flood** *v* inundar
— **floodlight** *n* foco *m*

floor *n* suelo *m*, piso *m*; **dance** ~ pista *f*
de baile

floppy disk *n* diskette *m*, disquete *m*

flour *n* harina *f*

flourish *v* florecer

flow *v* fluir, correr

flower *n* flor *f* — **flower** *v* florecer —
flowerpot *n* maceta *f*

flu *n* gripe *f*

fluctuate *v* fluctuar — **fluctuation** *n*
fluctuación *f*

fluency *n* fluidez *f* — **fluent** *adj* fluido

fluid *adj* fluido

flush *n* rubor *m*, sonrojo *m*

flute *n* flauta *f*

fly[1] *v* (**flew; flown**) volar; ir en avión;
correr — **flyer** *n* volante *m*

fly[2] *n* (**flies**) mosca *f* (insecto)

foamy *adj* espumoso

focus *n* (**-ci**) foco *m*; **be in** ~ estar enfo-
cado; ~ **of attention** centro *m* de

atención — **focus** v v enfocar; centrar (la atención, etc.); **focus on** enfocar (con los ojos), concentrarse en (con la mente)

fog n niebla f

fold v doblar, plegar; or ~ **up** doblarse, plegarse — **fold** n pliegue m — **folder** n carpeta f

folklore n folklore m

follow v seguir; ~ **up on** seguir con — **following** adj siguiente — **following** n seguidores mpl

fondness n afición f

food n comida f, alimento m

fool v bromear — **foolishness** n tontería f

foot n (**feet**) pie m — **football** n fútbol m americano — **footprint** n huella f — **footwear** n calzado m

for prep para; por; durante; con respecto a — **for** conj puesto que, porque

forage v ~ **for** buscar

forbid v (**-bade**; **-bidden**) prohibir

force n fuerza f; **by** ~ por la fuerza; **in** ~ en vigor, en vigencia; **armed** ~s fuerzas fpl armadas — **force** v forzar

forearm n antebrazo m

forecast v (**-cast**) predecir, pronosticar — **forecast** n predicción f, pronóstico m

forefinger n índice m, dedo m índice

forefront n **at/in the** ~ a la vanguardia

forehead n frente f

foreign adj extranjero — **foreigner** n extranjero m, -ra f

forest n bosque m

foretell v (**-told**) predecir

forever adv para siempre

forfeit n prenda f (en un juego)

forge n herrería — **forge** v forjar (metal, etc.); falsificar

forget v (**-got**; **-gotten** or **-got**) olvidar(se), olvidarse de — **forgetful** adj olvidadizo

forgive v (**-gave**; **-given**) perdonar — **forgiveness** n perdón m

form n forma f; formulario m — **form** v formar(se)

formal adj formal — **formality** n formalidad f

formation n forma f

former adj antiguo, anterior

formula n (**-las** or **-lae**) fórmula f

fortunate adj afortunado — **fortunately** adv afortunadamente — **fortune** n fortuna f

forty n (**forties**) cuarenta m — **forty** adj cuarenta

forward adj hacia adelante (en dirección), delantero (en posición) — **forward** adv (hacia) adelante — **forward** n delantero m, -ra f (en deportes)

foul n falta f (en deportes) — **foul** v cometer faltas (en deportes)

found v fundar, establecer — **foundation** n fundamento m; cimientos mpl (de un edificio)

fountain n fuente f

four n cuatro m — **four** adj cuatro — **four hundred** adj cuatrocientos — **four hundred** n cuatrocientos m

fourteen n catorce m — **fourteen** adj catorce

fourth n cuarto m, -ta f (en una serie); cuarto m, cuarta parte f — **fourth** adj cuarto

fox n zorro m, -ra f

foyer n vestíbulo m

fraction n fracción f

fracture n fractura f — **fracture** v fracturar

fragile adj frágil

fragment n fragmento m

fragrance n fragancia f, aroma m

frail adj débil, delicado

frame n marco m (de un cuadro, una puerta, etc.); or ~s npl montura f (para anteojos) — **frame** v enmarcar; formular

frank adj franco

fraternal adj fraterno, fraternal — **fraternity** n (**-ties**) fraternidad f

freckle n peca f

free adj libre; or ~ **of charge** gratuito, gratis; suelto — **free** v liberar, poner en libertad; soltar, desatar — **free** adv or **for free** gratis — **freedom** n libertad f — **free will** n libre albedrío m

freeze v (**froze; frozen**) congelar(se); helar(se) — **freezer** n congelador m — **freezing** adj helado

French adj francés — **French** n francés m (idioma) — **Frenchman** n francés m — **french fries** npl papas fpl fritas

frequent v frecuentar — **frequency** n frecuencia f — **frequently** adv a menudo, frecuentemente

fresh adj fresco; ~ **water** agua m dulce

friction n fricción f

Friday n viernes m

friend n amigo m, -ga f — **friendliness** n simpatía f — **friendship** n amistad f

fright n miedo m, susto m — **frighten** v asustar, espantar — **frightening** adj espantoso

frill n volante m

frisk v cachear, registrar

frivolous adj frívolo — **frivolity** n frivolidad f

frog n rana f

from prep de; desde; de, por; ~ **now on** a partir de ahora

front n parte f delantera — **front** vi or **front on** dar a, estar orientado a — **front** adj delantero, de adelante

frontier n frontera f

frost n helada f; escarcha f (en una superficie)

froth n espuma f — **frothy** adj espumoso

fruit n fruta f; fruto m — **fruitful** adj fructífero — **fruitless** adj infructuoso

frustrate v frustrar — **frustration** n frustración f

fry v (**fried**) freír — **frying pan** n sartén mf

fuel n combustible m

fugitive n fugitivo m, -va f

full adj lleno; completo, detallado; de lleno

fun n diversión f; **have** ~ divertirse — **fun** adj divertido

function n función f — **function** v funcionar — **functional** adj funcional

fund n fondo m; ~**s** npl fondos mpl — **fund** v financiar

fundamental adj fundamental — **fundamentals** npl fundamentos mpl

funeral adj funeral, fúnebre — **funeral** n funeral m, funerales mpl — **funeral home** or **funeral parlor** n funeraria f

fungus n (**fungi**) hongo m

funny adj divertido, gracioso

furious adj furioso

furnace n horno m

furnish v amueblar (una casa, etc.) — **furniture** n muebles mpl, mobiliario m

furry adj peludo (de un animal), de peluche (de un juguete, etc.)

furthermore adv además

fuse[1] n mecha f (de una bomba, etc.)

fuse[2] v fundir(se); fusionar(se) — **fusion** n fusión f

fuss n jaleo m, alboroto m

future adj futuro — **future** n futuro m

G

g n (**g's** or **gs**) g f, séptima letra del alfabeto inglés

gaiety n alegría f — **gaily** adv alegremente

gain n ganancia f; aumento m — **gain** v ganar, adquirir

galaxy n (**-axies**) galaxia f

gallery n (**-leries**) galería f

gallon *n* galón *m*

gallop *v* galopar — **gallop** *n* galope *m*

gamble *v* jugar; jugarse — **gamble** *n* apuesta *f* — **gambler** *n* jugador *m*, -dora *f*

game *n* juego *m*; partido *m*

gang *n* banda *f*, pandilla *f*

gap *n* espacio *m*; intervalo *m*; brecha *f*, distancia *f*

garage *n* garaje *m*

garbage *n* basura *f* — **garbage can** *n* cubo *m* de la basura

garden *n* jardín *m* — **gardener** *n* jardinero *m*, -ra *f*

garlic *n* ajo *m*

gas *n* (**gases**) gas *m*; gasolina *f*

gasoline *n* gasolina *f*

gasp *v* dar un grito ahogado

gas station *n* gasolinera *f*

gastronomy *n* gastronomía *f*

gate *n* puerta *f*; barrera *f* — **gateway** *n* puerta *f*

gather *v* reunir; recoger; deducir; reunirse (de personas), acumularse (de cosas) — **gathering** *n* reunión *f*

gauze *n* gasa *f*

gay *adj* alegre; gay, homosexual

gaze *v* mirar (fijamente) — **gaze** *n* mirada *f*

gear *n* equipo *m*; efectos *mpl* personales; marcha *f* (de un vehículo)

gelatin *n* gelatina *f*

gender *n* sexo *m*; género *m* (en la gramática)

gene *n* gen *m*, gene *m*

genealogy *n* genealogía *f*

general *adj* general — **general** *n* general *mf* (militar); **in general** en general, por lo general — **generalize** *v* generalizar — **generally** *adv* generalmente, en general

generate *v* generar — **generation** *n* generación *f*

generous *adj* generoso; abundante — **generosity** *n* generosidad *f*

genial *adj* afable, simpático

genius *n* genio *m*

gentle *adj* suave, dulce; ligero — **gentleman** *n* (**-men**) caballero *m*, señor *m* — **gentleness** *n* delicadeza *f*, ternura *f*

genuine *adj* verdadero, auténtico

geography *n* geografía *f*

geology *n* geología *f*

geometry *n* geometría *f*

geriatric *adj* geriátrico — **geriatrics** *n* geriatría *f*

German *adj* alemán — **German** *n* alemán *m* (idioma)

gesture *n* gesto *m*

get *v* (**got; got** *or* **gotten**) conseguir, obtener; recibir; ganar; traer; coger, agarrar; entender; preparar; ponerse, hacerse; ir; avanzar; **have got** tener; **have got to** tener que; **get up** levantarse

ghost *n* fantasma *f*, espectro *m* — **ghostly** *adv* fantasmal

giant *n* gigante *m*, -ta *f* — **giant** *adj* gigantesco

gift *n* regalo *m*; don *m*

gigantic *adj* gigantesco

gild *v* (**gilded** *or* **gilt**) dorar

ginger *n* jengibre *m*

giraffe *n* jirafa *f*

girl *n* niña *f*, muchacha *f*, chica *f* — **girlfriend** *n* novia *f*, amiga *f*

gist *n* essencia *f* **get the ~ of** comprender lo esencial de

give *v* (**gave; given**) dar; señalar; presentar; ceder; **~ out** repartir; agotarse; **~ up** rendirse — **given** *adj* determinado; dado, inclinado — **given name** *n* nombre *m* de pila

glad *adj* alegre, contento; **be ~** alegrarse; **~ to meet you!** ¡mucho gusto! — **gladden** *v* alegrar — **gladly** *adv* con mucho gusto — **gladness** *n* alegría *f*, gozo *m*

glance *v* **~ at** mirar, dar un vistazo a — **glance** *n* mirada *f*, vistazo *m*

glare *v* brillar, relumbrar

glass *n* vidrio *m*, cristal *m*; **a ~ of milk**

un vaso de leche; ~**es** *npl* anteojos *mpl*, lentes *fpl* — **glassware** *n* cristalería *f*

gleam *n* destello *m*

glide *v* deslizarse (en una superficie), planear (en el aire)

glimmer *n* luz *f* trémula, luz *f* tenue

globe *n* globo *m* — **global** *adj* global, mundial

gloom *n* oscuridad *f*; tristeza *f* — **gloomy** *adj* sombrío, tenebroso; deprimente, lúgubre; pesimista

glory *n* (**-ries**) gloria *f*

glossary *n* (**-ries**) glosario *m*

glove *n* guante *m*

glow *v* brillar, resplandecer — **glow** *n* resplandor *m*, brillo *m*

glue *n* pegamento *m*, cola *f* — **glue** *v* pegar

glum *adj* sombrío, triste

go *v* (**went; gone**) ir; irse, salir; ir, extenderse; venderse; funcionar, marchar; desaparecer — **go** *v aux* **be going to** ir a — **go** *n* (**goes**) **be on the** ~ no parar

goal *n* meta *m*, objetivo *m*; gol *m* (en deportes) — **goalkeeper** *or* **goalie** *n* portero *m*, -ra *f*; arquero *m*, -ra *f*

goat *n* cabra *f*

god *n* dios *m*; **God** Dios *m* — **godchild** *n* (**-children**) ahijado *m*, -da *f* — **godfather** *n* padrino *m* — **godmother** *n* madrina *f* — **godparents** *npl* padrinos *mpl*

gold *n* oro *m* — **golden** *adj* (hecho) de oro; dorado — **goldsmith** *n* orfebre *mf*

golf *n* golf *m* — **golf** *v* jugar (al) golf — **golfer** *n* golfista *mf*

gone *adj* ido, pasado; muerto; desaparecido

good *adj* (**better; best**) bueno; amable; ~ **afternoon** (**evening**) buenas tardes; **be** ~ **at** tener facilidad para; **feel** ~ sentirse bien; **have a** ~ **time** divertirse; ~ **morning** buenos días; ~ **night** buenas noches — **good** *n* bien *m*;

bondad *f*; **goods** *npl* bienes *mpl*; mercancías *fpl*, mercaderías *fpl* — **good** *adv* bien — **good–bye** *or* **good–by** *n* adiós *m* — **good–looking** *adj* bello, guapo — **goodness** *n* bondad *f* — **goodwill** *n* buena voluntad *f* — **goody** *n* (**goodies**) golosina *f*

goose *n* (**geese**) ganso *m*, -sa *f*; oca *f*

gorilla *n* gorila *m*

gossip *n* chismoso *m*, -sa *f* (persona); chisme *m* — **gossip** *v* chismear, contar chismes — **gossipy** *adj* chismoso

gourmet *n* gastrónomo *m*, -ma *f*

govern *v* gobernar — **government** *n* gobierno *m* — **governor** *n* gobernador *m*, -dora *f*

gown *n* vestido *m*

grace *n* gracia *f* — **graceful** *adj* grácil — **gracious** *adj* cortés, gentil

grade *n* grado *m*, año *m* (a la escuela); nota *f*

gradual *adj* gradual — **gradually** *adv* gradualmente, poco a poco

graduate *n* licenciado *m*, -da *f* (de la universidad), bachiller *mf* (de la escuela secundaria) — **graduate** *v* graduar; graduarse, licenciarse — **graduation** *n* graduación *f*

graffiti *npl* graffiti *mpl*

grain *n* grano *m*; cereales *mpl*; veta *f*, vena *f* (de madera)

gram *n* gramo *m*

grammar *n* gramática *f*

grand *adj* magnífico, espléndido; fabuloso, estupendo — **grandchild** *n* (**-children**) nieto *m*, -ta *f* — **granddaughter** *n* nieta *f* — **grandfather** *n* abuelo *m* — **grandmother** *n* abuela *f* — **grandparents** *npl* abuelos *mpl* — **grandson** *n* nieto *m*

grant *v* conceder; reconocer, admitir; **take for granted** dar (algo) por sentado — **grant** *n* subvención *f*; beca *f*

grape *n* uva *f*

grapefruit *n* toronja *f*, pomelo *m*

graph n gráfico m, -ca f — **graphic** adj gráfico

grasp v agarrar; comprender, captar — **grasp** n agarre m; comprensión f; alcance m

grass n hierba f (planta); césped m, pasto m — **grasshopper** n saltamontes m — **grassy** adj cubierto de hierba

grateful adj agradecido — **gratefully** adv con agradecimiento — **gratefulness** n gratitud f, agradecimiento m

gratify v (**-fied**) complacer; satisfacer

gratitude n gratitud f

grave[1] n tumba f, sepultura f

grave[2] adj grave

graveyard n cementerio m

gravity n gravedad f

gray adj gris; ~ **hair** pelo m canoso — **gray** n gris m — **gray** vi or **turn gray** encanecer, ponerse gris

grease n grasa f — **grease** v engrasar — **greasy** adj grasiento; graso, grasoso

great adj grande; estupendo, fabuloso — **great–grandchild** n (**-children**) bisnieto m, -ta f — **great–grandfather** n bisabuelo m — **great–grandmother** n bisabuela f — **greatly** adv mucho; muy — **greatness** n grandeza f

Greek adj griego — **Greek** n griego m (idioma)

green adj verde — **green** verde m (color); **greens** npl verduras fpl

greet v saludar; recibir — **greeting** n saludo m; ~**s** npl saludos mpl, recuerdos mpl

grid n red f

grief n dolor m, pesar m — **grieve** v entristecer

grill v asar a la parrilla — **grill** n parrilla f (para cocinar) — **grille** or **grill** n reja f, rejilla f

grim adj severo; sombrío

grime n mugre f, suciedad f — **grimy** adj **grimier; -est** mugriento, sucio

grinder n molinillo m

grip v agarrar, asir — **grip** n; agarre m; control m, dominio m

groan v gemir — **groan** n gemido m

groceries npl comestibles mpl — **grocer** n tendero m, -ra f

groggy adj atontado

groin n ingle f

groom n novio m — **groom** v almohazar (un animal); preparar

ground n suelo m, tierra f — **ground** v fundar, basar

group n grupo m — **group** v agrupar; **group together** agruparse

grove n arboleda f

grow v (**grew; grown**) cultivar; dejarse crecer (el pelo, etc.); crecer; aumentar; volverse, ponerse; ~ **dark** oscurecerse; ~ **up** hacerse mayor — **grower** n cultivador m, -dora f

growl v gruñir — **growl** n gruñido m

grown–up adj mayor — **grown–up** n persona f mayor

growth n crecimiento m; aumento m; desarrollo m

grumble v refunfuñar, rezongar

grunt v gruñir — **grunt** n gruñido m

guarantee n garantía f — **guarantee** v garantizar

guard n guardia f; protección f — **guard** v proteger, vigilar — **guardian** n guardián m, -diana f

guess v adivinar; suponer, creer; ~ **at** adivinar — **guess** n conjetura f, suposición f

guest n invitado m, -da f; huésped mf (a un hotel)

guide n guía mf (persona), guía f (libro, etc.) — **guide** v guiar — **guidance** n orientación f — **guidebook** n guía f — **guideline** n pauta f, directriz f

guilt n culpa f, culpabilidad f — **guilty** adj **guiltier; -est** culpable

guitar n guitarra f

gulf n golfo m; abismo m

gull n gaviota f

gulp vt or ~ **down** tragarse, engullir

gum[1] *n* encía *f* (de la boca)
gum[2] *n* goma *f* de mascar, chicle *m*
gun *n* arma *f* de fuego — **gun** ～ *v or* ～ **down** matar a tiros, asesinar — **gunman** *n* (-men) pistolero *m*
gut *n* intestino *m*

guy *n* tipo *m*
gym *or* **gymnasium** *n* (-siums) *or* -**sia** gimnasio *m* — **gymnast** *n* gimnasta *mf* — **gymnastics** *ns & pl* gimnasia *f*
gynecology *n* ginecología *f* — **gynecologist** *n* ginecólogo *m*, -ga *f*

H

h *n* (**h's** *or* **hs**) h *f*, octava letra del alfabeto inglés
habit *n* hábito *m*, costumbre *f*
habitual *adj* habitual
hack *v or* ～ **into** piratear (un sistema informático)
hail[1] *v* llamar (un taxi)
hail[2] *n* granizo *m* (en meteorología) — **hail** *v* granizar — **hailstone** *n* piedra *f* de granizo
hair *n* pelo *m*, cabello *m*; vello *m* (en las piernas, etc.) — **hairbrush** *n* cepillo *m* (para el pelo) — **haircut** *n* corte *m* de pelo; **get a haircut** cortarse el pelo — **hairdo** *n* (-dos) peinado *m* — **hairdresser** *n* peluquero *m*, -ra *f* — **hairless** *adj* calvo — **hair spray** *n* laca *f* (para el pelo) — **hairy** *adj* peludo, velludo
hale *adj* saludable, robusto
half *n* (**halves**) mitad *f*; *or* **halftime** tiempo *m* (en deportes); **in** ～ por la mitad — **half** *adj* medio; **half an hour** una media hora — **half** *adv* medio — **half brother** *n* medio hermano *m*, hermanastro *m* — **halfhearted** *adj* sin ánimo, poco entusiasta — **half sister** *n* media hermana *f*, hermanastra *f* — **halfway** *adv* a medio camino — **halfway** *adj* medio
hall *n* corredor *m*, pasillo *m*; sala *f*; vestíbulo *m*; residencia *f* universitaria
hallmark *n* sello *m* (distintivo)
Halloween *n* víspera *f* de Todos los Santos

hallucination *n* alucinación *f*
hallway *n* entrada *f*; corredor *m*, pasillo *m*
halt *n* **call a** ～ **to** poner fin a; **come to a** ～ pararse — **halt** *v* parar; pararse
halve *v* partir por la mitad; reducir a la mitad
ham *n* jamón *m*
hamburger *or* **hamburg** *n* hamburguesa *f*
hammer *n* martillo *m* — **hammer** *v* martillar, martillear
hammock *n* hamaca *f*
hamper[1] *v* obstaculizar, dificultar
hamper[2] *n* cesto *m*, canasta *f* (para ropa sucia)
hamster *n* hámster *m*
hand *n* mano *f*; manecilla *f*, aguja *f* (de un reloj, etc.); letra *f*, escritura *f*; obrero *m*, -ra *f*; **by** ～ a mano; **lend a** ～ echar una mano **on** ～ a mano, disponible; **on the other** ～ por otro lado — **hand** *v* pasar, dar; **hand out** distribuir; **hand over** entregar — **handbag** *n* cartera *f*, bolso *m* — **handbook** *n* manual *m*
handicap *n* minusvalía *f* (física) — **handicapped** *adj* minusválido
handicrafts *npl* artesanía(s) *f(pl)*
handkerchief *n* (-chiefs) pañuelo *m*
handle *n* asa *m* (de una taza, etc.), mango *m* (de un utensilio), pomo *m* (de una puerta), tirador *m* (de un cajón) — **handle** *v* tratar, manejar — **handlebars** *npl* manillar *m*, manubrio *m*
handout *n* dádiva *f*, limosna *f*

handrail *n* pasamanos *m*

handshake *n* apretón *m* de manos

handsome *adj* apuesto, guapo

handwriting *n* letra *f*, escritura *f*

hang *v* (**hung**) colgar; ahorcar; pender; caer (de la ropa, etc.); ~ **one's head** bajar la cabeza; ~ **up on . . .** colgar a . . . — **hang** *n* caída *f*

haphazard *adj* casual, fortuito

happen *v* pasar, suceder, ocurrir; **it so happens that . . .** da la casualidad de que . . . — **happening** *n* suceso *m,* acontecimiento *m*

happy *adj* feliz; **be** ~ alegrarse; **be** ~ **with** estar contento con — **happiness** *n* felicidad *f*

harass *v* acosar

harbor *n* puerto *m*

hard *adj* duro; difícil; **be a** ~ **worker** ser muy trabajador; ~ **liquor** bebidas *fpl* fuertes; ~ **water** agua *f* dura — **hard** *adv* fuerte; **work hard** trabajar duro; **take . . . hard** tomarse . . . muy mal — **harden** *v* endurecer — **hardly** *adv* apenas; **hardly ever** casi nunca — **hardness** *n* dureza *f*; dificultad *f* — **hardware** *n* hardware *m* (en informática) — **hardworking** *adj* trabajador

hardy *adj* fuerte (de personas), resistente (de las plantas)

harm *n* daño *m* — **harm** *v* hacer daño a (una persona), dañar (una cosa), perjudicar (la reputación de algún, etc.) — **harmful** *adj* perjudicial — **harmless** *adj* inofensivo

harmony *n* armonía *f*

harness *n* arnés *m* — **harness** *v* enjaezar; utilizar

harsh *adj* áspero; fuerte (dícese de una luz), discordante (dícese de sonidos)

harvest *n* cosecha *f* — **harvest** *v* cosechar

haste *n* prisa *f*, apuro *m*; **make** ~ darse prisa, apurarse — **hasten** *v* acelerar;

apresurarse, apurarse — **hasty** *adj* precipitado

hat *n* sombrero *m*

hatchet *n* hacha *f*

hate *n* odio *m* — **hate** *v* odiar, aborrecer — **hateful** *adj* odioso — **hatred** *n* odio *m*

haughty *adj* altanero, altivo

haul *v* tirar; arrastrar — **haul** *n* **a long haul** un trayecto largo

haunt *v* frecuentar, rondar; inquietar — **haunt** *n* sitio *m* predilecto

have *v* (**had**) tener; comer, tomar; permitir; dar (una fiesta, etc.), convocar (una reunión); ~ **one's hair cut** cortarse el pelo; ~ **something done** mandar hacer algo — **have** *v aux* haber

haven *n* refugio *m*

hawk *n* halcón *m*

hazard *n* peligro *m,* riesgo *m* — **hazard** *v* arriesgar, aventurar

haze *n* bruma *f,* neblina *f*

he *pron* él

head *n* cabeza *f*; cabeza *f* (de un clavo, etc.), cabecera *f* (de una mesa); jefe *m,* -fa *f*; **be out of one's** ~ estar loco; **come to a** ~ llegar a un punto crítico ~**s or tails** cara o cruz; **per** ~ por cabeza — **head** *adj* principal — **head** *v* encabeza; dirigirse — **headache** *n* dolor *m* de cabeza — **headline** *n* titular *m* — **headphones** *npl* auriculares *mpl,* audífonos *mpl*

heal *v* curar; cicatrizar

health *n* salud *f* — **healthy** *adj* sano, saludable

hear *v* (**heard**) oír; oír; ~ **about** enterarse de ~ **from** tener noticias de — **hearing** *n* oído *m* — **hearing aid** *n* audífono *m*

heart *n* corazón *m*; **at** ~ en el fondo; **by** ~ de memoria; **lose** ~ descorazonarse; **take** ~ animarse — **heart attack** *n* infarto *m*, ataque *m* al corazón

heat *v* calentar — **heat** *n* calor *m*;

calefacción f — **heated** adj acalorado
— **heater** n calentador m
heaven n cielo m
heavy adj pesado
Hebrew adj hebreo — **Hebrew** n hebreo
m (idioma)
heel n talón m (del pie), tacón m (de un
zapato)
height n estatura f (de una persona), altura f (de un objeto); cumbre f; **what is
your ～?** ¿cuánto mides?
heir n heredero m, -ra f — **heiress** n
heredera f
helicopter n helicóptero m
hello interj ¡hola!
helmet n casco m
help v ayudar; **～ oneself** servirse; **I
can't ～ it** no lo puedo remediar —
help n ayuda f; personal m; **help!** ¡so-
corro!, ¡auxilio! — **helper** n ayudante
mf — **helpful** adj servicial, amable; útil
— **helpless** adj incapaz; indefenso
hem n dobladillo m
hemisphere n hemisferio m
hemorrhage n hemorragia f
hen n gallina f
her adj su, sus — **her** pron la; le, se; ella
— **herself** pron se; ella misma
herb n hierba f
here adv aquí, acá; **～ you are!** ¡toma!
hero n (-roes) héroe m — **heroic** adj
heroico — **heroine** n heroína f —
heroism n heroísmo m
hers pron (el) suyo, (la) suya, (los)
suyos, (las) suyas; **some friends of ～**
unos amigos suyos, unos amigos de ella
heterosexual adj heterosexual — n heterosexual mf
hi interj ¡hola!
hiccup n hipo
hide¹ n piel f, cuero m
hide² v (**hid; hidden** or **hid**) esconderse;
esconder; ocultar (motivos, etc.) —
hide–and–seek n escondite m, escondidas fpl

hierarchy n (-chies) jerarquía f — **hierarchical** adj jerárquico
high adj alto; borracho, drogado — **high**
adv alto — **high** n récord m, máximo m
— **higher** adj superior; **higher education** enseñanza f superior — **high
school** n escuela f superior, escuela f
secundaria — **highway** n carretera f
hiker n excursionista mf
hill n colina f, cerro m; cuesta f — **hillside** n ladera f, cuesta f
hilt n puño m
him pron lo; le, se; él — **himself** pron se;
él mismo
Hindu adj hindú
hinge n bisagra f, gozne m
hip n cadera f
his adj su, sus, de él — **his** pron (el)
suyo, (la) suya, (los) suyos, (las) suyas;
some friends of ～ unos amigos
suyos, unos amigos de él
Hispanic adj hispano, hispánico
history n (-ries) historia f; historial m —
historian n historiador m, -dora f —
historic or **historical** adj histórico
hit v (**hit**) golpear, pegar; dar (con un
proyectil); afectar; alcanzar; chocar —
hit n golpe m; éxito m
HIV n VIH m, virus m del sida
hoarse adj ronco
hobby n (-bies) pasatiempo m
hockey n hockey m
hog n cerdo m
hold v (**held**) tener; sostener; contener;
considerar; or **～ back** detener; **～ up**
retrasar — **holdup** n atraco m; retraso
m, demora f
hole n agujero m, hoyo m
holiday n día m feriado, fiesta f
hollow n hueco m; hondonada f
holocaust n holocausto m
holy adj santo, sagrado
homage n homenaje m
home n casa f; hogar m; residencia f,
asilo m — **home** adv **go home** ir a

casa — **homemaker** *n* ama *f* de casa —
homework *n* tarea *f*, deberes *mpl*
homicide *n* homicidio *m*
homogeneous *adj* homogéneo
honest *adj* honrado; sincero — **honestly** *adv* sinceramente — **honesty** *n* honradez *f*
honey *n* miel *f* — **honeymoon** *n* luna *f* de miel
honor *n* honor *m* — **honor** *v* honrar — **honorable** *adj* honorable, honroso — **honorary** *adj* honorario
hook *n* gancho *m*; *or* ~ **and eye** corchete *m*; **off the** ~ descolgado — **hook** *v* enganchar; engancharse
hope *v* esperar que — **hope** *n* esperanza *f* — **hopeful** *adj* esperanzado
horizon *n* horizonte *m* — **horizontal** *adj* horizontal
hormone *n* hormona *f*
horn *n* cuerno *m* (de un animal); trompa *f* (instrumento musical); bocina *f*, claxon *m* (de un vehículo)
horoscope *n* horóscopo *m*
horror *n* horror *m* — **horrible** *adj* horrible — **horrify** *v* (**-fied**) horrorizar
horse *n* caballo *m* — **horseman** *n* (**-men**) jinete *m* — **horsepower** *n* caballo *m* de fuerza — **horseshoe** *n* herradura *f* — **horsewoman** *n* (**-women**) jinete *f*
hose *n* manguera *f*, manga *f*
hospital *n* hospital *m* — **hospitalize** *v* hospitalizar
host[1] *n* anfitrión *m*, -triona *f*; presentador *m*, -dora *f* (de televisión, etc.) — **host** *v* ofrecer; presentar (un programa de televisión, etc.)
host[2] *n* hostia *f*, Eucaristía *f*
hostage *n* rehén *m*
hostel *n or* **youth** ~ albergue *m* juvenil
hot *adj* caliente, caluroso (del tiempo), cálido (del clima)
hot dog *n* perro *m* caliente

hotel *n* hotel *m*
hound *n* perro de caza — *v* acosar, perseguir
hour *n* hora *f* — **hourglass** *n* reloj *m* de arena
house *n* casa *f*; cámara *f* (del gobierno) — **house** *v* albergar — **housewife** *n* (**-wives**) ama *f* de casa — **housing** *n* viviendas *fpl*; caja *f* protectora
how *adv* cómo; qué; ~ **are you?** ¿cómo está Ud.?; ~ **come** por qué; ~ **much** cuánto; ~ **do you do?** mucho gusto; ~ **old are you?** ¿cuántos años tienes? — **how** *conj* como
however[1] *conj* de cualquier manera que ~ **you like** como quieras
however[2] *adv* sin embargo, no obstante ~ **difficult it is** por díficil que sea ~ **hard I try** por más que me esfuerce
hug *v* abrazar — **hug** *n* abrazo *m*
human *adj* humano — **human** *n* (ser *m*) humano *m* — **humane** *adj* humano, humanitario — **humanitarian** *adj* humanitario — **humanity** *n* humanidad *f*
humble *v* humillar; ~ **oneself** humillarse — **humble** *adj* humilde
humid *adj* húmedo — **humidity** *n* humedad *f*
humiliate *v* humillar — **humiliation** *n* humillación *f* — **humility** *n* humildad *f*
humor *n* humor *m* — **humor** *v* seguir la corriente a, complacer
hundred *adj* cien, ciento — **hundred** *n* ciento *m*
Hungarian *adj* húngaro — **Hungarian** *n* húngaro *m* (idioma)
hunger *n* hambre *m* — **hungry** *adj* hambriento
hunt *v* cazar; ~ **for** buscar — **hunt** *n* caza *f*, cacería *f*; búsqueda *f*, busca *f* — **hunter** *n* cazador *m*, -dora *f* — **hunting** *n* caza *f*
hurdle *n* valla *f* (en deportes); obstáculo *m*
hurl *v* lanzar, arrojar

hurrah *interj* ¡hurra!
hurricane *n* huracán *m*
hurry *n* prisa *f*, apuro *f* — **hurry** *v* (**-ried**) darse prisa, apurarse; apurar, dar prisa a — **hurried** *adj* apresurado — **hurriedly** *adv* apresuradamente, de prisa
hurt *v* (**hurt**) hacer daño a, lastimar; ofender, herir; doler; **my foot hurts** me duele el pie
husband *n* esposo *m*, marido *m*
hut *n* cabaña *f*

hygiene *n* higiene *f* — **hygienic** *adj* higiénico
hymn *n* himno *m*
hyperactive *adj* hiperactivo
hyphen *n* guión *m*
hypocrisy *n* hipocresía *f* — **hypocrite** *n* hipócrita *mf* — **hypocritical** *adj* hipócrita
hypothesis *n* (**-eses**) hipótesis *f*
hysteria *n* histeria *f*, histerismo *m* — **hysterical** *adj* histérico

I

i *n* (**i's** *or* **is**) i *f*, novena letra del alfabeto inglés
I *pron* yo
ice *n* hielo *m* — **ice cream** *n* helado *m*
idea *n* idea *f*
ideal *adj* ideal — **ideal** *n* ideal *m* — **idealist** *n* idealista *mf* — **idealistic** *adj* idealista — **idealize** *v* idealizar
identity *n* identidad *f* — **identical** *adj* idéntico — **identify** *v* (**-fied**) identificar; **identify with** identificarse con — **identification** *n* identificación *f*; **identification card** carnet *m*, carné *m*
ideology *n* ideología *f* — **ideological** *adj* ideológico
idiocy *n* idiotez *f*
idiom *n* modismo *m* — **idiomatic** *adj* idiomático
idiot *n* idiota *mf* — **idiotic** *adj* idiota
idol *n* ídolo *m* — **idolize** *v* idolatrar
if *conj* si; aunque, si bien; ~ **so** si es así
ignore *v* ignorar, no hacer caso de — **ignorance** *n* ignorancia *f* — **ignorant** *adj* ignorante
ill *adj* (**worse; worst**) enfermo; malo — **ill** *adv* (**worse; worst**) mal
illegal *adj* ilegal
illegitimate *adj* ilegítimo
illiterate *adj* analfabeto — **illiteracy** *n* analfabetismo *m*

illogical *adj* ilógico
illuminate *v* iluminar — **illumination** *n* iluminación *f*
illusion *n* ilusión *f*
illustrate *v* ilustrar — **illustration** *n* ilustración *f*
illustrious *adj* ilustre, glorioso
ill will *n* animadversión *f*, mala voluntad *f*
image *n* imagen *f* — **imaginary** *adj* imaginario — **imagination** *n* imaginación *f* — **imagine** *v* imaginar(se)
imbalance *n* desequilibrio *m*
imitation *n* imitación *f* — **imitation** *adj* de imitación, artificial — **imitate** *v* imitar, remedar
immature *adj* inmaduro
immediate *adj* inmediato
immense *adj* inmenso
immigrant *n* inmigrante *mf* — **immigration** *n* inmigración *f*
imminent *adj* inminente
immobile *adj* inmóvil — **immobilize** *v* inmovilizar
immoral *adj* inmoral
impact *n* impacto *m*
impartial *adj* imparcial — **impartiality** *n* imparcialidad *f*
impatience *n* impaciencia *f* — **impatient** *adj* impaciente — **impatiently** *adv* con impaciencia

impeccable *adj* impecable
impede *v* dificultar — **impediment** *n* impedimento *m*, obstáculo *m*
impending *adj* inminente
impenetrable *adj* impenetrable
imperative *adj* imperativo
imperceptible *adj* imperceptible
imperfection *n* imperfección *f* — **imperfect** *adj* imperfecto
imperialism *n* imperialismo *m*
impersonal *adj* impersonal
impersonation *n* imitación *f* — **impersonator** *n* imitador *m*, -dora *f*
impetuous *adj* impetuoso, impulsivo
impetus *n* ímpetu *m*, impulso *m*
implement *n* instrumento *m*, implemento *m* — **implement** *v* poner en práctica
implicate *v* implicar
imply *v* (**-plied**) implicar
impolite *adj* descortés, maleducado
import *v* importar (mercancías) — **important** *adj* importante — **importance** *n* importancia *f* — **importation** *n* importación *f* — **importer** *n* importador *m*, -dora *f*
impose *v* imponer — **imposing** *adj* imponente
impossible *adj* imposible — **impossibility** *n* imposibilidad *f*
impostor *or* **imposter** *n* impostor *m*, -tora *f*
impotent *adj* impotente — **impotence** *n* impotencia *f*
impracticable *adj* impracticable
imprecise *adj* impreciso — **imprecision** *n* imprecisión *f*
impregnable *adj* impenetrable
impregnate *v* impregnar; fecundar
impress *v* impresionar — **impression** *n* impresión *f* — **impressive** *adj* impresionante
improbable *adj* improbable
improve *v* mejorar
improvise *v* improvisar — **improvisation** *n* improvisación *f*

impulse *n* impulso *m* — **impulsive** *adj* impulsivo
impure *adj* impuro — **impurity** *n* impureza *f*
in *prep* en; por; dentro de — **in** *adv* dentro, adentro — **in** *adj* de moda
inability *n* incapacidad *f*
inactive *n* inactivo — **inactivity** *n* inactividad *f*
inadequate *adj* insuficiente
inanimate *adj* inanimado
inappropriate *adj* impropio, inoportuno
inaugurate *v* investir (a un presidente, etc.); inaugurar — **inauguration** *n* investidura *f* (de una persona), inauguración *f* (de un edificio, etc.)
incalculable *adj* incalculable
incapable *adj* incapaz — **incapacitate** *v* incapacitar — **incapacity** *n* incapacidad *f*
incense *n* incienso *m*
inch *n* pulgada *f*
incidentally *adv* a propósito
incite *v* incitar, instigar
incline *v* inclinar; **be ～ed to** inclinarse a, tender a — **incline** *n* pendiente *f* — **inclination** *n* inclinación *f*; deseo *m*, ganas *fpl*
include *v* incluir — **inclusion** *n* inclusión *f*
incoherent *adj* incoherente — **incoherence** *n* incoherencia *f*
income *n* ingresos *mpl* — **income tax** *n* impuesto *m* sobre la renta
incomparable *adj* incomparable
incompetent *adj* incompetente — **incompetence** *n* incompetencia *f*
incomplete *adj* incompleto
incomprehensible *adj* incomprensible
inconceivable *adj* inconcebible
inconsiderate *adj* desconsiderado
inconvenient *adj* incómodo, inconveniente — **inconvenience** *n* incomodidad *f*, molestia *f*; inconveniente *m*
incorrect *adj* incorrecto

increase n aumento m — **increase** v aumentar

incredible adj increíble

incredulous adj incrédulo

indebted adj endeudado

indecisive adj indeciso

indefinite adj indefinido

indelible adj indeleble

independent adj independiente — **independence** n independencia f

index n (-**dexes** or -**dices**) índice m — **index finger** n dedo m índice

Indian adj indio m, -dia f

indication n indicio m, señal f — **indicate** v indicar — **indicative** adj indicativo

indifferent adj indiferente

indigenous adj indígena

indigestion n indigestión f

indirect adj indirecto

indiscreet adj indiscreto — **indiscretion** n indiscreción f

indiscriminate adj indiscriminado

indispensable adj indispensable, imprescindible

indisputable adj indiscutible

individual adj individual; particular — **individual** n individuo m — **individually** adv individualmente

induce v inducir; provocar

industry n industria f; diligencia f — **industrial** adj industrial

inequality n desigualdad f

inescapable adj ineludible

inevitable adj inevitable

inexplicable adj inexplicable

infallible adj infalible

infancy n infancia f

infect v infectar — **infection** n infección f — **infectious** adj contagioso

infer v deducir, inferir

inferior adj inferior — **inferior** n inferior mf

infidelity n infidelidad f

infinite adj infinito

infinitive n infinitivo m

infinity n infinito m

infirmary n enfermería f

inflame v inflamar — **inflammable** adj inflamable — **inflammation** n inflamación f

inflation n inflación f

inflexible adj inflexible

influential adj influyente

influx n afluencia f

inform v informar

informal adj informal; familiar (del lenguaje) — **informality** n falta f de ceremonia — **informally** adv de manera informal

information n información f — **informative** adj informativo

infrastructure n infraestructura f

infrequently adv raramente

infuse v infundir

ingenious adj ingenioso — **ingenuity** n ingenio

ingest v ingerir

ingratitude n ingratitud f

ingredient n ingrediente m

inhabit v habitar — **inhabitant** n habitante mf

inhale v aspirar

inherent adj inherente

inherit v heredar — **inheritance** n herencia f

inhibit v inhibir — **inhibition** n inhibición f

inhuman adj inhumano — **inhumane** adj inhumano

initial adj inicial — **initial** n inicial f — **initial** v poner las iniciales a

initiate v iniciar — **initiation** n iniciación f — **initiative** n iniciativa f

inject v inyectar — **injection** n inyección f

injure v herir; ~ **oneself** hacerse daño — **injury** n herida f

injustice n injusticia f

ink n tinta f

in–laws npl suegros mpl

inn n posada f, hostería f

innate *adj* innato

inner *adj* interior, interno

inning *n* entrada *f*

innocent *adj* inocente — **innocent** *n* inocente *mf* — **innocence** *n* inocencia *f*

innovate *v* innovar — **innovation** *n* innovación *f* — **innovative** *adj* innovador — **innovator** *n* innovador *m,* -dora *f*

innumerable *adj* innumerable

inoffensive *adj* inofensivo

input *n* contribución *f;* entrada *f* (de datos) — **input** *v* (**-putted** *or* **-put**) entrar (datos, etc.)

inquire *v* preguntar; ~ **about** informarse sobre; ~ **into** investigar — **inquisitive** *adj* curioso

insane *adj* loco — **insanity** *n* locura *f*

inscription *n* inscripción *f*

insecure *adj* inseguro, poco seguro — **insecurity** *n* inseguridad *f*

insensitive *adj* insensible

inseparable *adj* inseparable

insert *v* insertar (texto), introducir (una moneda, etc.)

inside *n* interior *m;* ~ **out** al revés — **inside** *adv* dentro, adentro — **inside** *adj* interior — **inside** *prep or* **inside of** dentro de

insignificant *adj* insignificante

insinuate *v* insinuar

insist *v* insistir — **insistent** *adj* insistente

insomnia *n* insomnio *m*

inspection *n* inspección *f*

inspire *v* inspirar — **inspiration** *n* inspiración *f* — **inspirational** *adj* inspirador

install *v* instalar — **installation** *n* instalación *f* — **installment** *n* plazo *m,* cuota *f;* entrega *f* (de una publicación o telenovela)

instance *n* ejemplo *m*

instant *n* instante *m* — **instantaneous** *adj* instantáneo

instead of *prep* en vez de, en lugar de

institute *n* instituto *m* — **institution** *n* institución *f*

instruct *v* instruir — **instruction** *n* instrucción *f*

instrument *n* instrumento *m* — **instrumental** *adj* instrumental; **be instrumental in** jugar un papel fundamental en

insufficient *adj* insuficiente

insular *adj* insular; estrecho de miras

insulate *v* aislar — **insulation** *n* aislamiento *m*

insure *v* asegurar — **insurance** *n* seguro *m*

insurmountable *adj* insuperable

intact *adj* intacto

intake *n* consumo *m* (de alimentos), entrada *f* (de aire, etc.)

intangible *adj* intangible

integral *adj* integral

integrate *v* integrar(se)

integrity *n* integridad *f*

intellectual *adj* intelectual — **intellectual** *n* intelectual *mf* — **intelligence** *n* inteligencia *f* — **intelligent** *adj* inteligente — **intelligible** *adj* inteligible

intend *v* **be** ~**ed for** ser para; ~ **to do** pensar hacer — **intended** *adj* intencionado, deliberado

intense *adj* intenso — **intensify** *v* (**-fied**) intensificar(se) — **intensity** *n* intensidad *f* — **intensive** *adj* intensivo

intent *n* intención *f* — **intent** *adj* atento, concentrado; **intent on doing** resuelto a hacer — **intention** *n* intención *f* — **intentional** *adj* intencional, deliberado

interact *v* interactuar; ~ **with** relacionarse con — **interaction** *n* interacción *f* — **interactive** *adj* interactivo

intercede *v* interceder

interest *n* interés *m* — **interest** *v* interesar — **interested** *adj* interesado — **interesting** *adj* interesante

interface *n* interfaz *mf* (de una computadora)

interior *adj* interior — **interior** *n* interior *m*

interjection *n* interjección *f*

interlude *n* intervalo *m*; interludio *m* (en música, etc.)

intermediate *adj* intermedio — **intermediary** *n* intermediario *m*, -ria *f*

intermission *n* intervalo *m*, intermedio *m*

intermittent *adj* intermitente

international *adj* internacional

interpret *v* interpretar — **interpretation** *n* interpretación *f* — **interpreter** *n* intérprete *mf*

interrogate *v* interrogar — **interrogation** *n* interrogatorio *m* — **interrogative** *adj* interrogativo

interrupt *v* interrumpir — **interruption** *n* interrupción *f*

intersect *v* cruzar (de calles), cruzarse; cortar (de líneas) — **intersection** *n* cruce *m*, intersección *f*

interval *n* intervalo *m*

intervene *v* intervenir; transcurrir, pasar — **intervention** *n* intervención *f*

interview *n* entrevista *f* — **interview** *v* entrevistar — **interviewer** *n* entrevistador *m*, -dora *f*

intimate *adj* íntimo — **intimacy** *n* intimidad *f*

into *prep* en, a; **bump** ∼ darse contra; **3** ∼ **12** 12 dividido por 3

intolerant *adj* intolerante

intoxicated *adj* embriagado; ∼ **with** ebrio de

intransitive *adj* intransitivo

intrinsic *adj* intrínseco

introduce *v* introducir; presentar (a una persona) — **introduction** *n* introducción *f*; presentación *f* (de una persona) — **introductory** *adj* introductorio

introvert *n* introvertido *m*, -da *f* — **introverted** *adj* introvertido

intuition *n* intuición *f* — **intuitive** *adj* intuitivo

invade *v* invadir

invalid[1] *adj* inválido

invalid[2] *n* inválido *m*, -da *f*

invariable *adj* invariable

invasion *n* invasión *f*

invention *n* invención *f* — **inventor** *n* inventor *m*, -tora *f*

inventory *n* inventario *m*

invert *v* invertir

invertebrate *adj* invertebrado — **invertebrate** *n* invertebrado *m*

investigator *n* investigador *m*, -dora *f*

investment *n* inversión *f*

invitation *n* invitación *f* — **invite** *v* invitar; buscar (problemas, etc.)

invoice *n* factura *f*

involuntary *adj* involuntario

involve *v* concernir, afectar; suponer

IOU *n* pagaré *m*, vale *m*

Iranian *adj* iraní

Iraqi *adj* iraquí

irate *adj* furioso

iris *n* (**irises**) lirio *m* (planta); (**irises** *or* **irides**) iris *m* (del ojo)

Irish *adj* irlandés

iron *n* hierro *m*, fierro *m* (metal); plancha *f* (para la ropa) — **iron** *v* planchar

ironic *adj* irónico

irony *n* ironía *f*

irrational *adj* irracional

irrefutable *adj* irrefutable

irregular *adj* irregular — **irregularity** *n* irregularidad *f*

irrelevant *adj* irrelevante

irresponsible *adj* irresponsable — **irresponsibility** *n* irresponsabilidad *f*

irreverent *adj* irreverente

irreversible *adj* irreversible, irrevocable

irrigate *v* irrigar, regar — **irrigation** *n* irrigación *f*, riego *m*

irritate *v* irritar — **irritating** *adj* irritante — **irritation** *n* irritación *f*

Islamic *adj* islámico

island *n* isla *f*

isolate *v* aislar — **isolation** *n* aislamiento *m*

Israeli *adj* israelí

issue *n* número *m* (de una revista, etc.)

isthmus *n* istmo *m*

it *pron* él, ella; le, se; lo, la; él, ella

Italian *adj* italiano — **Italian** *n* italiano *m* (idioma)

italics *n* cursiva *f*

item *n* punto *m* (en una agenda); **news ~** noticia *f*

itinerant *adj* ambulante

itinerary *n* itinerario *m*

its *adj* su, sus

itself *pron* se; (él) mismo, (ella) misma, sí (mismo); **by ~** solo

J

j *n* (**j's** *or* **js**) j *f*, décima letra del alfabeto inglés

jab *n* golpe *m* abrupto

jack *n* gato *m* (mecanismo) — **jack** *vt or* **~ up** levantar (con un gato); subir

jacket *n* chaqueta *f*

jail *n* cárcel *f* — *v* encarcelar

jam¹ *v* apiñar, embutir; atascar, atorar; atascarse, atrancarse — **jam** *n or* **traffic jam** embotellamiento *m* (de tráfico)

jam² *n* mermelada *f*

jangle *v* hacer un ruido metálico; hacer sonar

January *n* enero *m*

Japanese *adj* japonés — **Japanese** *n* japonés *m* (idioma)

jar *n* tarro *m*

jargon *n* jerga *f*

jaw *n* mandíbula *f* (de una persona), quijada *f* (de un animal)

jazz *n* jazz *m*

jealous *adj* celoso — **jealousy** *n* celos *mpl*, envidia *f*

jeans *npl* jeans *mpl*, vaqueros *mpl*

jersey *n* (**-seys**) jersey *m*

jet *n* chorro *m*; *or* **~ airplane** avión *m* a reacción, reactor *m*

jewel *n* joya *f* — **jeweler** *or* **jeweller** *n* joyero *m*, -ra *f* — **jewelry** *n* joyas *fpl*, alhajas *fpl*

Jewish *adj* judío

jiggle *v* sacudir, zarandear — **jiggle** *n* sacudida *f*

jingle *v* tintinear; hacer sonar — **jingle** *n* tintineo *m*

job *n* empleo *m*, trabajo *m*; trabajo *m*

jockey *n* (**-eys**) jockey *mf*

jog *v* hacer footing; **~ one's memory** refrescarle la memoria a algún — **jogging** *n* footing *m*

join *v* unir, juntar; reunirse con; *or* **~ together** unirse; hacerse socio (de una organización, etc.)

joint *n* articulación *f* (en anatomía); juntura *f*, unión *f* — **jointly** *adv* conjuntamente

joke *n* chiste *m*, broma *f* — **joke** *v* bromear — **joker** *n* bromista *mf*; comodín *m* (en los naipes)

jolly *adj* alegre, jovial

jot *v or* **~ down** anotar, apuntar

journal *n* diario *m*; revista *f* — **journalism** *n* periodismo *m* — **journalist** *n* periodista *mf*

journey *n* (**-neys**) viaje *m* — **journey** *v* (**-neyed**) viajar

jovial *adj* jovial

joy *n* alegría *f* — **joyful** *adj* alegre, feliz

Judaism *n* judaísmo *m*

judge *v* juzgar — *n* juez *mf* — **judgment** *or* **judgement** *n* fallo *m*, sentencia *f*; juicio *m*

judicial *adj* judicial — **judicious** *adj* juicioso

juice *n* jugo *m* — **juicy** *adj* jugoso

July *n* julio *m*

jumble *v* mezclar

jumbo *adj* gigante
jump *v* saltar; ~ **at** no dejar escapar (una oportunidad, etc.) — **jump** *n* salto *m*
June *n* junio *m*
jungle *n* selva *f*
junior *adj* más joven; subalterno — **junior** *n* persona *f* de menor edad; subalterno *m*, -na *f*; estudiante *mf* de penúltimo año

junk *n* trastos *mpl* (viejos) — **junk** *v* echar a la basura
jury *n* (-ries) jurado *m*
just *adj* justo — **just** *adv* apenas; exactamente; sólo, solamente; **just now** ahora mismo
justice *n* justicia *f*; juez *mf*
justify *v* (-fied) justificar — **justification** *n* justificación *f*

K

k *n* (**k's** *or* **ks**) k *f*, undécima letra del alfabeto inglés
kangaroo *n* (-roos) canguro *m*
karate *n* karate *m*
keen *adj* afilado; cortante, penetrante; entusiasta
keep *v* (**kept**) guardar; cumplir (una promesa), acudir a (una cita); hacer quedar, detener; impedir; ~ **up** mantener(se); conservarse; *or* ~ **on** no dejar — **keep n earn one's keep** ganarse el pan; **for keeps** para siempre — **keeper** *n* guarda *mf*
kernel *n* almendra *f*; meollo *m*
ketchup *n* salsa *f* de tomate
key *n* llave *f*; tecla *f* (de un piano o una máquina) — **key** *adj* clave — **key ring** *n* llavero *m*
kick *v* dar una patada a; ~ **out** echar a patadas; dar patadas (de una persona), cocear (de un animal) — **kick** *n* patada *f*, coz *f* (de un animal); placer *m*
kid *n* niño *m*, -ña *f*; chivo *m*, -va *f*; cabrito *m*; — **kid** *v or* ~ **around** bromear — **kidnap** *v* secuestrar, raptar
kidney *n* (-neys) riñón *m*
kill *v* matar; acabar con; ~ **time** matar el tiempo — **kill** *n* presa *f* — **killer** *n* asesino *m*, -na *f*
kilo *n* (-los) kilo *m* — **kilogram** *n* kilogramo *m* — **kilometer** *n* kilómetro *m*
kin *n* parientes *mpl*

kind *n* tipo *m*, clase *f* — **kind** *adj* amable — **kindness** *n* bondad *f*
kindergarten *n* jardín *m* infantil, jardín *m* de niños
kindle *v* encender (un fuego); despertar
kindly *adv* amablemente; **take** ~ **to** aceptar de buena gana
kinship *n* parentesco *m*
kiss *v* besar(se) — **kiss** *n* beso *m*
kit *n* **first–aid** ~ botiquín *m*
kitchen *n* cocina *f*
knapsack *n* mochila *f*
knead *v* amasar, sobar; masajear
knee *n* rodilla *f*
kneel *v* (**knelt** *or* **kneeled**) arrodillarse
knife *n* (**knives**) cuchillo *m*
knight *n* caballo *m* (en ajedrez)
knit *v* (**knit** *or* **knitted**) tejer — **knit** *n* prenda *f* tejida
knock *v* golpear; criticar; dar un golpe, llamar (a la puerta); darse, chocar — **knock** *n* golpe *m*, llamada *f* (a la puerta)
knot *n* nudo *m*
know *v* (**knew; known**) saber; conocer (a una persona, un lugar); ~ **how to** saber — **knowing** *adj* cómplice — **knowingly** *adv* de manera cómplice; a sabiendas — **knowledge** *n* conocimiento *m*; conocimientos *mpl*, saber *m* — **knowledgeable** *adj* informado, entendido

knuckle *n* nudillo *m*
Koran (the) *n* el Corán *m*

Korean *adj* coreano *m*, -na *f* — **Korean**
n coreano *m* (idioma)

L

l *n* (**l's** *or* **ls**) l *f*, duodécima letra del alfabeto inglés
label *n* etiqueta *f*; marca *f*
labor *n* trabajo *m* — **labor** *v* trabajar
laboratory *n* (**-ries**) laboratorio *m*
lace *n* encaje *m*; cordón *m* (de zapatos) — **lace** *v* atar
lack *v* carecer de, no tener; **be lacking** faltar — **lack** *n* falta *f*, carencia *f*
ladder *n* escalera *f*
lady *n* (**-dies**) señora *f*, dama *f*
lake *n* lago *m*
lamb *n* cordero *m*
lame *adj* cojo, renco
lament *v* lamentar — **lament** *n* lamento *m*
lamp *n* lámpara *f* — **lampshade** *n* pantalla *f*
land *n* tierra *f*; país *m* — **land** *v* desembarcar (pasajeros de un barco), hacer aterrizar (un avión); aterrizar (de un avión) — **landing** *n* aterrizaje *m* (de aviones) — **landscape** *n* paisaje *m*
lane *n* carril *m* (de una carretera); camino *m*
language *n* idioma *m*, lengua *f*; lenguaje *m*
laptop *adj* portátil
large *adj* grande — **largely** *adv* en gran parte
lasagna *n* lasaña *f*
laser *n* láser *m*
lash *n* pestaña *f*
last *v* durar — **last** *n* último *m*, -ma *f*; **at last** por fin, finalmente — **last** *adv* por última vez, en último lugar — **last** *adj*; último — **lastly** *adv* por último, finalmente
late *adj* tarde; avanzado (de la hora) —

late *adv* tarde — **lately** *adv* recientemente, últimamente
Latin–American *adj* latinoamericano
laugh *v* reír(se) — **laugh** *n* risa *f* — **laughter** *n* risa *f*, risas *fpl*
launch *v* lanzar — **launch** *n* lanzamiento *m*
launder *v* lavar y planchar (ropa) — **laundry** *n*, *pl* -**dries** ropa *f* sucia; lavandería *f* (servicio); **do the laundry** lavar la ropa
lavatory *n* (**-ries**) baño *m*, cuarto *m* de baño
law *n* ley *f*; derecho *m* (profesión, etc.) — **lawyer** *n* abogado *m*, -da *f*
lawn *n* césped *m*
lay *v* (**laid**) poner, colocar; **~ out** presentar, exponer
layer *n* capa *f*
lazy *adj* perezoso — **laziness** *n* pereza *f*
lead *v* (**led**) dirigir; encabezar, ir al frente de ; llevar, conducir (a algo) — **lead** *n* delantera *f* — **leader** *n* jefe *m*, -fa *f* — **leadership** *n* mando *m*, dirección *f*
leaf *n* (**leaves**) hoja *f* — **leaf** *v* **leaf through** hojear (un libro, etc.)
league *n* liga *f*
lean *v* inclinarse
leap *v* (**leapt** *or* **leaped**) saltar, brincar — **leap** *n* salto *m*, brinco *m* — **leap year** *n* año *m* bisiesto
learn *v* aprender — **learned** *adj* sabio, erudito — **learner** *n* principiante *mf*, estudiante *mf* — **learning** *n* erudición *f*, saber *m*
lease *n* contrato *m* de arrendamiento — **lease** *v* arrendar
least *adj* menor; más mínimo — **least** *n*

at least por lo menos — **least** *adv* menos

leather *n* cuero *m*

leave *v* (**left**) dejar; salir(se) de (un lugar); irse — **leave** *n or* **leave of absence** permiso *m*, licencia *f*

lecture *n* conferencia *f* — **lecture** *v* dar clase, dar una conferencia

left *adj* izquierdo — **left** *adv* a la izquierda — **left** *n* izquierda *f* — **left-handed** *adj* zurdo

leg *n* pierna *f* (de una persona, de ropa), pata *f* (de un animal, de muebles); etapa *f* (de un viaje)

legal *adj* legítimo, legal; legal, jurídico — **legality** *n* (**-ties**) legalidad *f* — **legalize** *v* legalizar

legible *adj* legible

legislate *v* legislar — **legislation** *n* legislación *f*

legitimate *adj* legítimo — **legitimacy** *n* legitimidad *f*

leisure *n* ocio *m*, tiempo *m* libre

lemon *n* limón *m* — **lemonade** *n* limonada *f*

lend *v* (**lent**) prestar

length *n* largo *m*; duración *f* — **lengthen** *v* alargar

lens *n* lente *mf* (de un instrumento)

less *adv or adj or pron or prep* menos

lesson *n* clase *f*, curso *m*

let *v* (**let**) dejar, permitir; alquilar; ∼**'s go!** ¡vamos!, ¡vámonos!

letter *n* carta *f*; letra *f* (del alfabeto)

lettuce *n* lechuga *f*

level *n* nivel *m* — **level** *v* nivelar

lever *n* palanca *f*

liable *adj* responsable; probable — **liability** *n* (**-ties**) responsabilidad *f*; desventaja *f*

liberal *adj* liberal — **liberal** *n* liberal *mf*

liberate *v* liberar — **liberation** *n* liberación *f*

liberty *n* (**-ties**) libertad *f*

library *n* (**-braries**) biblioteca *f* — **librarian** *n* bibliotecario *m*, -ria *f*

license *or* **licence** *n* licencia *f*; permiso *m* — **license** *v* autorizar

lie[1] *v* (**lay; lain**) acostarse; estar situado, encontrarse

lie[2] *v* (**lied**) mentir — **lie** *n* mentira *f*

life *n* (**lives**) vida *f* — **lifeboat** *n* bote *m* salvavidas — **lifeguard** *n* socorrista *mf* — **lifestyle** *n* estilo *m* de vida

lift *v* levantar — **lift** *n*; levantamiento *m*

light[1] *n* luz *f*; lámpara *f* — **light** *v* (**lit** *or* **lighted**) encender (un fuego); iluminar — **lightbulb** *n* bombilla *f*, bombillo *m* — **lighten** *v* iluminar — **lighter** *n* encendedor *m* — **lightning** *n* relámpago *m*, rayo *m*

light[2] *adj* ligero — **lighten** *v* aligerar — **lightly** *adv* suavemente

like[1] *v* gustarle (a uno); querer; **if you** ∼ si quieres

like[2] *adj* parecido — **like** *conj* como; como si — **likely** *adj* probable — **likewise** *adv* lo mismo; también

limb *n* miembro *m* (en anatomía); rama *f* (de un árbol)

limit *n* límite *m* — **limit** *v* limitar, restringir — **limitation** *n* limitación *f*, restricción *f* — **limited** *adj* limitado

limp *v* cojear — **limp** *n* cojera *f*

line *n* línea *f*; cuerda *f*; fila *f*; cola *f*

lingerie *n* ropa *f* íntima femenina, lencería *f*

linguistics *n* lingüística *f* — **linguist** *n* lingüista *mf* — **linguistic** *adj* lingüístico

link *n* eslabón *m* (de una cadena); lazo *m*; conexión *f* — **link** *v* enlazar, conectar

lion *n* león *m* — **lioness** *n* leona *f*

lip *n* labio *m*; borde *m* — **lipstick** *n* lápiz *m* de labios

liquid *adj* líquido — **liquid** *n* líquido *m* — **liquidate** *v* liquidar — **liquidation** *n* liquidación *f*

list *n* lista *f* — **list** *v* enumerar; incluir (en una lista)

listen *v* escuchar — **listener** *n* oyente *mf*

liter *n* litro *m*

literacy *n* alfabetismo *m*

literal *adj* literal — **literally** *adv* literalmente, al pie de la letra

literature *n* literatura *f* — **literary** *adj* literario

little *adj* (**littler** *or* **less** *or* **lesser; littlest** *or* **least**) pequeño; **a** ～ un poco de — **little** *adv* (**less; least**) poco — **little** *pron* poco *m*, -ca *f*

live *v* vivir; residir; llevar (una vida) — **live** *adj* vivo — **livelihood** *n* sustento *m*, medio *m* de vida — **lively** *adj* animado, alegre — **liven** *v* *or* **liven up** animar(se)

liver *n* hígado *m*

living *adj* vivo — **living room** *n* living *m*, sala *f* (de estar)

lizard *n* lagarto *m*

load *n* carga *f*; carga *f*, peso *m* — **load** *v* cargar

loaf *n* (**loaves**) pan *m*, barra *f* (de pan)

loan *n* préstamo *m* — **loan** *v* prestar

lobby *n* (**-bies**) vestíbulo *m*

lobster *n* langosta *f*

local *adj* local — **locality** *n* (**-ties**) localidad *f*

locate *v* situar, ubicar; localizar — **location** *n* situación *f*, lugar *m*

lock *n* cerradura *f* (de una puerta, etc.) — **lock** *v* cerrar (con llave); *or* **lock up** encerrar — **locker** *n* armario *m*

lodge *v* hospedar(se), alojar(se); presentar — **lodging** *n* alojamiento *m*

loft *n* desván *m* (en una casa) — **lofty** *adj* noble, elevado

log *n* ～ **on** entrar (en el sistema); ～ **off** salir (del sistema) — **logger** *n* leñador *m*, -dora *f*

logic *n* lógica *f*

loin *n* lomo *m*

lollipop *or* **lollypop** *n* pirulí *m*, chupete *m*

lone *adj* solitario — **loneliness** *n* soledad *f* — **lonely** *adj* solitario, solo — **loner** *n* solitario *m*, -ria *f*

long *adv* mucho tiempo; **as** ～ **as** mientras; **no** ～**er** ya no; **so** ～! ¡hasta luego!, ¡adiós! — **long** *adj* largo

longitude *n* longitud *f*

look *v* mirar; parecer; ～ **after** cuidar (de); ～ **for** esperar; ～ **for** buscar; ～ **into** investigar; ～ **out** tener cuidado; ～ **over** revisar — **look** *n* mirada *f*; aspecto *m*, aire *m* — **lookout** *n* puesto *m* de observación; vigía *mf*

loom *v* aparecer, surgir; ser inminente

loose *adj* flojo, suelto — **loosely** *adv* sin apretar; aproximadamente — **loosen** *v* aflojar

lord *n* señor *m*, noble *m*; **the Lord** el Señor

lose *v* (**lost**) perder; ～ **one's way** perderse; ～ **time** atrasarse (de un reloj) — **loser** *n* perdedor *m*, -dora *f* — **loss** *n* pérdida *f*; derrota *f* — **lost** *adj* perdido; **get lost** perderse

lot *n* suerte *f*; **a** ～ **of** *or* ～**s of** mucho, un montón de

lotion *n* loción *f*

lottery *n* (**-teries**) lotería *f*

loud *adj* alto, fuerte; ruidoso; llamativo — **loud** *adv* fuerte; **out loud** en voz alta — **loudly** *adv* en voz alta — **loudspeaker** *n* altavoz *m*

love *n* amor *m*; **fall in** ～ enamorarse — **love** *v* querer, amar — **lovable** *adj* adorable — **lovely** *adj* lindo, precioso — **lover** *n* amante *mf* — **loving** *adj* cariñoso

low *adj* bajo; escaso — **low** *adv* bajo — **lower** *adj* inferior, más bajo — **lower** *v* bajar

loyal *adj* leal, fiel — **loyalty** *n* (**-ties**) lealtad *f*

lubricate *v* lubricar — **lubricant** *n* lubricante *m* — **lubrication** *n* lubricación *f*

lucid *adj* lúcido — **lucidity** *n* lucidez *f*

luck *n* suerte *f*; **good** ～! ¡buena suerte! — **luckily** *adv* afortunadamente — **lucky** *adj* afortunado

luggage *n* equipaje *m*

lumber *n* madera *f*

luminous *adj* luminoso

lunar *adj* lunar

lunch *n* almuerzo *m*, comida *f* — **lunch**
  v almorzar, comer — **luncheon** *n* co-
  comida *f*, almuerzo *m*

lung *n* pulmón *m*

luxurious *adj* lujoso — **luxury** *n* (**-ries**)
  lujo *m*

M

m *n* (**m's** *or* **ms**) m *f*, decimotercera letra
  del alfabeto inglés

machine *n* máquina *f* — **machinery** *n*
  (**-eries**) maquinaria *f*; mecanismo *m*

mad *adj* loco; insensato; furioso

madam *n* (**mesdames**) señora *f*

madness *n* locura *f*

magazine *n* revista *f*

magic *n* magia *f* — **magician** *n* mago *m*,
  -ga *f*

magistrate *n* magistrado *m*, -da *f*

magnificent *adj* magnífico

magnifying glass *n* lupa *f*

mail *n* correo *m*; correspondencia *f* —
  mail *v* enviar por correo — **mailbox** *n*
  buzón *m* — **mailman** *n* (**-men**) cartero
  m

main *adj* principal

maintain *v* mantener — **maintenance** *n*
  mantenimiento *m*

majority *n* (**-ties**) mayoría *f*

make *v* (**made**) hacer; fabricar; constituir; preparar; poner; obligar; **~ a decision** tomar una decisión; **~ a living**
  ganar la vida; **~ do** arreglárselas; **~
  for** dirigirse a; **~ good** tener éxito —
  make *n* marca *f* — **make–believe** *n*
  fantasía *f* — **make–believe** *adj* imaginario — **make out** *v* hacer (un cheque,
  etc.); distinguir; comprender; **how did
  you make out?** ¿qué tal te fue? —
  makeup *n* maquillaje *m* — **make up** *v*
  preparar; inventar; formar; hacer las
  paces

male *n* macho *m* (de animales o plantas),
  varón *m* (de personas) — **male** *adj*
  macho; masculino

mainutrition *n* desnutrición *f*

mama *or* **mamma** *n* mamá *f*

mammal *n* mamífero *m*

man *n* (**men**) hombre *m*

manage *v v* manejar; administrar, dirigir
  — **management** *n* dirección *f* — **manager** *n* director *m*, -tora *f*; gerente *mf*

mandate *n* mandato *m* — **mandatory**
  adj obligatorio

maneuver *n* maniobra *f* — **maneuver** *v*
  maniobrar

mania *n* manía *f*

manipulate *v* manipular — **manipulation** *n* manipulación *f*

mankind *n* género *m* humano, humanidad *f*

manly *adj* viril

manner *n* manera *f*; clase *f*; **~s** *npl*
  modales *mpl*, educación *f*

mansion *n* mansión *f*

manual *adj* manual — **manual** *n* manual
  m

manufacture *v* fabricar — **manufacturer** *n* fabricante *mf*

many *adj* **more; most** muchos; **as ~**
  tantos; **how ~** cuántos; **too ~** de-
  masiados — **many** *pron* muchos *pl*,
  -chas *pl*

map *n* mapa *m* — **map** *v* trazar el mapa
  de; *or* **map out** planear, proyectar

march *n* marcha *f* — **march** *v* marchar,
  desfilar

March *n* marzo *m*

margarine *n* margarina *f*

margin *n* margen *m* — **marginal** *adj*
  marginal

mark *n* marca *f*; mancha *f*; huella *f*;

blanco *m*; nota *f* — **mark** *v* marcar; manchar; señalar; calificar (un examen, etc.); conmemorar; caracterizar; **mark off** delimitar — **marked** *adj* marcado, notable — **markedly** *adv* notablemente — **marker** *n* marcador *m*

market *n* mercado *m* — **market** *v* vender, comercializar — **marketplace** *n* mercado *m*

marriage *n* matrimonio *m*; casamiento *m*, boda *f* — **married** *adj* casado; **get married** casarse

marry *v* (**-ried**) casar(se) (con)

Mars *n* Marte *m*

martyr *n* mártir *mf*

marvel *n* maravilla *f* — **marvel** *v* maravillarse — **marvelous** *or* **marvellous** *adj* maravilloso

masculine *adj* masculino

mask *n* máscara *f* — **mask** *v* enmascarar

mass *n* masa *f*; cantidad *f*; **the ～es** las masas

Mass *n* misa *f*

massage *n* masaje *m* — **massage** *v* masajear

massive *adj* enorme, masivo

master *n* maestro *m*, -tra *f*; **～'s degree** maestría *f* — **master** *v* dominar — **masterful** *adj* magistral — **mastery** *n* maestría *f*

match *n* fósforo *m*, cerilla *f* (para encender); partido *m*, combate *m* (en boxeo); **be a good ～** hacer buena pareja — **match** *v* concordar, coincidir; igualar; combinar con, hacer juego con (ropa, colores, etc.); *or* **match up** emparejar

material *adj* material; importante — **material** *n* material *m*; tela *f*, tejido *m*

maternal *adj* maternal — **maternity** *n* maternidad *f* — **maternity** *adj* de maternidad; **maternity clothes** ropa *f* de futura mamá

mathematics *ns & pl* matemáticas *fpl* — **mathematical** *adj* matemático — **mathematician** *n* matemático *m*, -ca *f*

matter *n* materia *f*; asunto *m*, cuestión *f*;

as a ～ of fact en efecto, en realidad; for that ～ de hecho; to make ～s worse para colmo de males; what's the ～? ¿qué pasa? — **matter** *v* importar

mattress *n* colchón *m*

mature *adj* maduro — **mature** *v* madurar — **maturity** *n* madurez *f*

maximum *n* (**-ma** *or* **-mums**) máximo *m* — **maximum** *adj* máximo

may *v aux* (**might**) poder; **come what ～** pase lo que pase; **it ～ happen** puede pasar; **～ the best man win** que gane el mejor

May *n* mayo *m*

maybe *adv* quizás, tal vez

mayonnaise *n* mayonesa *f*

mayor *n* alcalde *m*, -desa *f*

me *pron* me; **for ～** para mí; **give it to ～!** ¡dámelo!; **it's ～** soy yo; **with ～** conmigo

mean¹ *v* (**meant**) querer decir; querer, tener la intención de; **be meant for** estar destinado a; **he didn't ～ it** no lo dijo en serio

mean² *adj* malo; mezquino, tacaño; humilde

mean³ *n* promedio *m*

meander *v* serpentear; vagar

meaning *n* significado *m*, sentido *m*

means *n* medio *m*; **by all ～** por supuesto; **by ～ of** por medio de; **by no ～** de ninguna manera

meanwhile *adv* mientras tanto

measure *n* medida *f* — **measure** *v* medir — **measurement** *n* medida *f* — **measure up** *v* **measure up to** estar a la altura de

meat *n* carne *f* — **meatball** *n* albóndiga *f*

mechanic *n* mecánico *m*, -ca *f* — **mechanical** *adj* mecánico — **mechanics** *ns & pl* mecánica *f*; **mechanism** *n* mecanismo *m*

media *or* **mass ～** *npl* medios *mpl* de comunicación

medical *adj* médico — **medicinal** *adj*

medicinal — **medicine** *n* medicina *f*; medicina *f*, medicamento *m*

meditate *v* meditar — **meditation** *n* meditación *f*

meet *v* (**met**) reunirse; conocerse; encontrarse (con); satisfacer; **pleased to ~ you** encantado de conocerlo — **meet** *n* encuentro *m* — **meeting** *n* reunión *f*

megabyte *n* megabyte *m*

melancholy *n* melancolía *f* — **melancholy** *adj* melancólico, triste

melody *n* (**-dies**) melodía *f*

melon *n* melón *m*

melt *v* derretir(se), fundirse

member *n* miembro *m*

memory *n* (**-ries**) memoria *f*; recuerdo *m*

menace *n* amenaza *f* — **menace** *v* amenazar

mental *adj* mental — **mentality** *n* mentalidad *f*

mention *n* mención *f* — **mention** *v* mencionar; **don't mention it!** ¡de nada!, ¡no hay de qué!

menu *n* menú *m*

merchant *n* comerciante *mf* — **merchandise** *n* mercancía *f*, mercadería *f*

merciful *adj* misericordioso, compasivo — **merciless** *adj* despiadado

Mercury *n* Mercurio *m*

merge *v* combinar; unir(se), fusionar(se) (de las compañías), confluir (de los ríos, las calles, etc.) — **merger** *n* unión *f*, fusión *f*

merit *n* mérito *m*

mess *n* desorden *m* — **mess** *v* **mess around** entretenerse; **mess up** desordenar; echar a perder; **mess with** meterse con

message *n* mensaje *m* — **messenger** *n* mensajero *m*, -ra *f*

metal *n* metal *m* — **metallic** *adj* metálico

metamorphosis *n* metamorfosis *f*

metaphor *n* metáfora *f*

meteorological *adj* meteorológico —

meteorologist *n* meteorólogo *m*, -ga *f* — **meteorology** *n* meteorología *f*

meter *n* metro *m*

method *n* método *m* — **methodical** *adj* metódico

metropolis *n* metrópoli *f* — **metropolitan** *adj* metropolitano

Mexican *adj* mexicano

microbe *n* microbio *m*

microphone *n* micrófono *m*

microscope *n* microscopio *m*

microwave *n* microonda *f*; *or* ~ **oven** microondas; un horno de microondas *m*

mid *adj* ~ **morning** a media mañana; **in ~-August** a mediados de agosto; **she is in her mid thirties** tiene alrededor de 35 años — **midair** *n* **in midair** en el aire — **midday** *n* mediodía *m*

middle *adj* de en medio, del medio — **middle** *n* medio *m*, centro *m*; **in the middle of** en medio de (un espacio), a mitad de (una actividad); **in the middle of the month** a mediados del mes — **middle–aged** *adj* de mediana edad — **Middle Ages** *npl* Edad *f* Media — **middle class** *n* clase *f* media

midnight *n* medianoche *f*

might *n* fuerza *f*, poder *m*

mile *n* milla *f* — **mileage** *n* distancia *f* recorrida (en millas), kilometraje *m*

military *adj* militar

milk *n* leche *f* — **milk** *v* ordeñar (una vaca, etc.)

millennium *n* (**-nia**) *or* **-niums** milenio *m*

millimeter *n* milímetro *m*

million *n* millón *m*; **a ~ people** un millón de personas — **millionaire** *n* millonario *m*, -ria *f*

mimic *v* (**-icked**) remedar — **mimicry** *n* imitación *f*

mind *n* mente *f*; capacidad *f* intelectual; opinión *f*; razón *f*; **have a ~ to** tener intención de — **mind** *v* cuidar; obedecer; tener cuidado con; **I don't mind** no me importa, me es igual; **I don't mind**

the heat no me molesta el calor —
mindful *adj* atento — **mindless** *adj*
sin sentido

mine¹ *pron* (el) mío, (la) mía, (los) míos,
(las) mías

mine² *n* mina *f* — **miner** *n* minero *m*, -ra
f — **mining** *n* minería *f*

mineral *n* mineral *m*

minimize *v* minimizar — **minimum** *adj*
mínimo — **minimum** *n* (**-ma** *or*
-mums) mínimo *m*

minister *n* ministro *m*, -tra *f* (en política)
— **minister** *v* **minister to** cuidar (de),
atender a — **ministry** *n* (**-tries**) ministerio *m*

minor *adj* menor; sin importancia —
minor *n* menor *mf* (de edad) — **minority** *n* (**-ties**) minoría *f*

mint *n* menta *f* (planta)

minus *prep* menos

minute¹ *n* minuto *m*; ~**s** *npl* actas *fpl*
(de una reunión)

minute² *adj* diminuto, minúsculo

miracle *n* milagro *m*

mirror *n* espejo *m*

mischief *n* travesuras *fpl* — **mischievous** *adj* travieso

miss *v* errar, faltar; perder (una oportunidad, un vuelo, etc.); **I ~ you** te echo
de menos

Miss *n* señorita *f*

missing *adj* perdido, desaparecido

mission *n* misión *f*

mist *n* neblina *f*, bruma *f*

mistake *v* (**mistook; mistaken**) entender mal; confundir — **mistake** *n* error
m; **make a mistake** equivocarse —
mistaken *adj* equivocado

mistreat *v* maltratar

misunderstanding *n* malentendido *m*

mix *v* mezclar(se); ~ **up** confundir —
mix *n* mezcla *f* — **mixture** *n* mezcla *f*

moan *n* gemido *m* — **moan** *v* gemir

mobile *adj* móvil — **mobile** *n* móvil *m*
— **mobility** *n* movilidad *f*

moccasin *n* mocasín *m*

model *n* modelo *m*; modelo *mf* (persona)
— **model** *adj* modelo

modem *n* módem *m*

moderate *adj* moderado — **moderate** *n*
moderado *m*, -da *f* — **moderate** *v* moderar

modern *adj* moderno

modest *adj* modesto

modify *v* (**-fied**) modificar

moist *adj* húmedo — **moisten** *v*
humedecer

molar *n* muela *f*

mom *n* mamá *f*

moment *n* momento *m*

Monday *n* lunes *m*

money *n* dinero *m* — **monetary** *adj*
monetario

monitor *v* controlar

monkey *n* (**-keys**) mono *m*, -na *f* —
monkey wrench *n* llave *f* inglesa

monologue *n* monólogo *m*

month *n* mes *m* — **monthly** *adv* mensu-
almente — **monthly** *adj* mensual

monument *n* monumento *m*

moon *n* luna *f*

mop *v* trapear, pasar la fregona a

moral *adj* moral — **moral** *n* moraleja *f*
(de un cuento, etc.); **morals** *npl* moral
f, moralidad *f*

more *adj* más — **more** *adv* más; **more
and more** cada vez más; **more or less**
más o menos; **once more** una vez más
— **more** *n* más *m* — **more** *pron* más —
moreover *adv* además

morning *n* mañana *f*; **good ~!** ¡buenos
días!; **in the ~** por la mañana

mortal *adj* mortal — **mortal** *n* mortal *mf*
— **mortality** *n* mortalidad *f*

mortgage *n* hipoteca *f* — **mortgage** *v*
hipotecar

mosque *n* mezquita *f*

most *adj* la mayoría de, la mayor parte
de; **(the) ~** más — **most** *adv* más —
most *n* más *m*, máximo *m* — **most**
pron la mayoría, la mayor parte

mother *n* madre *f* — **motherhood** *n*

maternidad *f* — **mother–in–law** *n* (**mothers–** . . .) suegra *f*

motion *n* movimiento *m*; moción *f*; **set in** ~ poner en marcha — **motion** *v* **motion to** hacer una señal a — **motionless** *adj* inmóvil — **motion picture** *n* película *f*

motive *n* motivo *m* — **motivate** *v* motivar — **motivation** *n* motivación *f*

motor *n* motor *m* — **motorcycle** *n* motocicleta *f* — **motorist** *n* automovilista *mf*, motorista *mf*

mount[1] *n* montura *f* — **mount** *v* subir (una escalera)

mount[2] *n* monte *m* — **mountain** *n* montaña *f* — **mountainous** *adj* montañoso

mourning *n* luto *m*

mouse *n* (**mice**) ratón *m* (animal); (**mice** *or* **mouses**) ratón *m* (de computador) — **mousetrap** *n* ratonera *f*

mouth *n* boca *f* (de una persona o un animal), desembocadura *f* (de un río) — **mouthful** *n* bocado *m*

move *v* ir; conmover; transportar, trasladar; proponer; mudarse; mover(se); tomar medidas — **move** *n* movimiento *m*; mudanza *f*; medida *f* — **movable** *or* **moveable** *adj* movible, móvil — **movement** *n* movimiento *m*

movie *n* película *f*; ~**s** *npl* cine *m*

Mr. *n* (**Messrs.**) señor *m*

Mrs. *n* (**Mesdames**) señora *f*

Ms. *n* señora *f*, señorita *f*

much *adj* (**more; most**) mucho —

much *adv* (**more; most**) mucho; **as much as** tanto como; **how much?** ¿cuánto?; **too much** demasiado — **much** *pron* mucho, -cha

mud *n* barro *m*, lodo *m*

muddy *adj* fangoso, lleno de barro

mug *v* asaltar, atracar

multimedia *adj* multimedia

multinational *adj* multinacional

multiple *adj* múltiple — **multiple** *n* múltiplo *m* — **multiplication** *n* multiplicación *f* — **multiply** *v* (**-plied**) multiplicar(se)

multitude *n* multitud *f*

municipal *adj* municipal — **municipality** *n* (**-ties**) municipio *m*

muscle *n* músculo *m* — **muscular** *adj* muscular; musculoso

museum *n* museo *m*

mushroom *n* hongo *m*, seta *f*; champiñón *m* (en la cocina)

music *n* música *f* — **musical** *adj* musical — **musician** *n* músico *m*, -ca *f*

Muslim *adj* musulmán — **Muslim** *n* musulmán *m*, -mana *f*

must *v aux* deber, tener que; **you** ~ **come** tienes que venir; **you** ~ **be tired** debes (de) estar cansado

mustache *n* bigote *m*, bigotes *mpl*

mute *adj* mudo — **mute** *n* mudo *m*, -da *f*

mutiny *n* (**-nies**) motín *m*

my *adj* mi

myself *pron* me; yo mismo; **by** ~ solo

mystery *n* (**-teries**) misterio *m* — **mysterious** *adj* misterioso

myth *n* mito *m*

N

n *n* (**n's** *or* **ns**) *nf*, decimocuarta letra del alfabeto inglés

nail *n* clavo *m*; uña *f* (de un dedo) — **nail** *vt or* **nail down** clavar — **nail file** *n* lima *f* de uñas

naive *or* **naïve** *adj* ingenuo

naked *adj* desnudo

name *n* nombre *m*; fama *f*; **first name** nombre *m*; **surname** apellido *m* — **name** *v* poner nombre a; nombrar —

nameless *adj* anónimo — **namely** *adv* a saber

nap *v* echarse una siesta — **nap** *n* siesta *f*

nape *n or* ~ **of the neck** nuca *f*

napkin *n* servilleta *f*

narrate *v* narrar — **narration** *n* narración *f* — **narrative** *n* narración *f* — **narrator** *n* narrador *m*, -dora *f*

narrow *adj* estrecho, angosto; limitado — **narrow** *v* estrecharse

nasal *adj* nasal

nasty *adj* malo, cruel; desagradable; asqueroso

nation *n* nación *f* — **national** *adj* nacional — **nationality** *n* (-ties) nacionalidad *f* — **nationalize** *v* nacionalizar

native *adj* natal (de un país, etc.); ~ **language** lengua *f* materna — **native** *n* nativo *m*, -va *f*; **be a native of** ser natural de — **nativity** *n* (-ties) **the Nativity** la Navidad

nature *n* naturaleza *f*; índole *f*, clase *f* — **natural** *adj* natural — **naturally** *adv* naturalmente

naughty *adj* travieso, pícaro

naval *adj* naval

navel *n* ombligo *m*

navigate *v* navegar; gobernar (un barco), pilotar (un avión); navegar por (un río, etc.) — **navigation** *n* navegación *f* — **navigator** *n* navegante *mf*

near *adv* cerca — **near** *prep* cerca de — **near** *adj* cercano, próximo — **near** *v* acercarse a —**nearby** *adv* cerca — **nearby** *adj* cercano —**nearly** *adv* casi — **nearsighted** *adj* miope

neat *adj* ordenado, limpio; pulcro — **neatly** *adv* muy arreglado; hábil, ingenioso hábilmente

necessary *adj* necesario — **necessarily** *adv* necesariamente — **necessity** *n* (-ties) necesidad *f*

neck *n* cuello *m* (de una persona o una botella), pescuezo *m* (de un animal); cuello *m* — **necklace** *n* collar *m*

need *n* necesidad *f* — **need** *v* necesitar, exigir; **need to** tener que — **need** *v aux* tener que

needle *n* aguja *f*

negative *adj* negativo — **negative** *n* negación *f* (en gramática); negativo *m* (en fotografía)

neglect *v* descuidar *m*

negotiate *v* negociar — **negotiable** *adj* negociable — **negotiation** *n* negociación *f*

Negro *n* (-groes) negro *m*, -gra *f*

neighbor *n* vecino *m*, -na *f* — **neighborhood** *n* barrio *m*, vecindario *m*; **in the neighborhood of** alrededor de

neither *conj* ~ . . . **nor** ni . . . ni; ~ **am/do I** yo tampoco — **neither** *pron* ninguno, -na — **neither** *adj* ninguno (de los dos)

nephew *n* sobrino *m*

nerve *n* nervio *m*; ~**s** *npl* nervios *mpl* — **nervous** *adj* nervioso — **nervousness** *n* nerviosismo *m*

nest *n* nido *m* — **nest** *v* anidar

net *n* red *f* — **net** *v* pescar, atrapar (con una red)

network *n* red *f*

neutral *adj* neutral — **neutrality** *n* neutralidad *f*

never *adv* nunca, jamás; no; ~ **mind** no importa — **nevermore** *adv* nunca jamás — **nevertheless** *adv* sin embargo, no obstante

new *adj* nuevo — **newborn** *adj* recién nacido — **newly** *adv* recién, recientemente — **news** *n* noticias *fpl* — **newscast** *n* noticiario *m*, noticiero *m* — **newscaster** *n* presentador *m*, -dora *f* (de un noticiario) — **newspaper** *n* periódico *m*, diario *m*

New Year's Day *n* día *m* del Año Nuevo

next *adj* próximo; siguiente — **next** *adv* la próxima vez; después, luego; ahora — **next to** *adv* casi — **next to** *prep* al lado de

Nicaraguan *adj* nicaragüense

nice *adj* agradable, bueno; amable — **nicely** *adv* bien; amablemente

nickname *n* apodo *m*, sobrenombre *m*

niece *n* sobrina *f*

night *n* noche *f*; **at ∼** de noche; **last ∼** anoche — **nightclub** *n* club *m* nocturno — **nightfall** *n* anochecer *m* — **nightgown** *n* camisón *m* (de noche) — **nightmare** *n* pesadilla *f*

nine *adj* nueve — **nine** *n* nueve *m* — **nine hundred** *adj* novecientos — **nine hundred** *n* novecientos *m* — **nineteen** *adj* diecinueve — **nineteen** *n* diecinueve *m* — **nineteenth** *adj* decimonoveno, decimonono — **nineteenth** *n* decimonoveno *m*, -na *f*; decimonono *m*, -na *f* (en una serie) — **ninetieth** *adj* nonagésimo — **ninetieth** *n* nonagésimo *m*, -ma *f* (en una serie); noventavo *m* (en matemáticas) — **ninety** *adj* noventa — **ninety** *n* (**-ties**) noventa *m* — **ninth** *adj* noveno — **ninth** *n* noveno *m*, -na *f* (en una serie); noveno *m* (en matemáticas)

nipple *n* pezón *m* (de una mujer)

no *adv* no — **no** *adj* ninguno — **no** *n* (**noes** *or* **nos**) no *m*

nobody *pron* nadie

nod *v* saludar con la cabeza; **∼ off** dormirse; *or* **∼ yes** asentir con la cabeza

noise *n* ruido *m*

nominate *v* proponer, postular; nombrar

none *pron* ninguno, ninguna

nonetheless *adv* sin embargo, no obstante

nonsense *n* tonterías *fpl*, disparates *mpl*

nonstop *adj* directo — **nonstop** *adv* sin parar

noodle *n* fideo *m*

noon *n* mediodía *m*

no one *pron* nadie

nor *conj* **neither . . . ∼** ni . . . ni

norm *n* norma *f* — **normal** *adj* normal

north *adv* al norte — **north** *adj* norte, del norte — **north** *n* norte *m* — **North**

American *adj* norteamericano — **northern** *adj* del norte, norteño

Norwegian *adj* noruego

nose *n* nariz *f* (de una persona), hocico *m* (de un animal)

nostalgia *n* nostalgia *f* — **nostalgic** *adj* nostálgico

not *adv* no

note *v* observar, notar; anotar — **note** *n* nota *f*; **take notes** apuntar — **notebook** *n* libreta *f*, cuaderno *m*

nothing *pron* nada

notice *n* letrero *m*, aviso *m* — **notice** *v* notar

notion *n* noción *f*, idea *f*

notwithstanding *prep* a pesar de, no obstante — **notwithstanding** *adv* sin embargo — **notwithstanding** *conj* a pesar de que

noun *n* nombre *m*, sustantivo *m*

nourish *v* nutrir — **nourishment** *n* alimento *m*

novel *adj* original — **novel** *n* novela *f* — **novelist** *n* novelista *mf* — **novelty** *n* (**-ties**) novedad *f*

November *n* noviembre *m*

now *adv* ahora; entonces; **from ∼ on** de ahora en adelante; **right ∼** ahora mismo — **now** *conj or* **now that** ahora que, ya que — **nowadays** *adv* hoy en día

nowhere *adv* por ninguna parte, por ningún lado; a ninguna parte, a ningún lado — **nowhere** *n* ninguna parte *f*

nuclear *adj* nuclear

nude *adj* desnudo — **nude** *n* desnudo *m*

number *n* número *m* — **number** *v*; numerar; contar, incluir

nun *n* monja *f*

nurse *n* enfermero *m*, -ra *f* — **nurse** *v* cuidar (de), atender; amamantar — **nursery** *n* (**-eries**) *or* **day nursery** guardería *f* — **nursing home** *n* asilo *m* de ancianos

nurture *v* nutrir

nut *n* nuez *f*; **∼s and bolts** tuercas y

tornillos — **nutcracker** *n* cascanueces
m

nutrition *n* nutrición *f*
nylon *n* nilón *m*

O

o *n* (**o's** *or* **os**) o *f*, decimoquinta letra del
alfabeto inglés; cero *m*

oak *n* (**oaks** *or* **oak**) roble *m*

oath *n* juramento *m*

oats *npl* avena *f* — **oatmeal** *n* harina *f* de
avena

obedient *adj* obediente

obey *v* obedecer

object *n* objeto *m*; objetivo *m*; complemento *m* (en gramática) — **objective**
adj objetivo — **objective** *n* objetivo *m*

obligation *n* obligación *f* — **obligatory**
adj obligatorio

obscurity *n* oscuridad *f* — **obscure** *adj*
oscuro — **obscure** *v* oscurecer; ocultar

observe *v* observar; mirar — **observation** *n* observación *f*

obsession *n* obsesión *f* — **obsessive**
adj obsesivo

obstacle *n* obstáculo *m*

obtain *v* obtener, conseguir

obvious *adj* obvio, evidente

occasion *n* ocasión *f* — **occasional** *adj*
poco frecuente, ocasional — **occa-
sionally** *adv* de vez en cuando

occult *adj* oculto

occupy *v* (**-pied**) ocupar — **occupant** *n*
ocupante *mf* — **occupation** *n* ocupación *f*

occur *v* ocurrir

ocean *n* océano *m*

o'clock *adv* at 6 ~ a las seis; **it's one**
~ es la una

October *n* octubre *m*

odd *adj* extraño, raro; ~ **number**
número *m* impar

of *prep* de; **five minutes** ~ **ten** las diez
menos cinco

off *adv* be ~ irse **cut** ~ cortar **day** ~

día *m* de descanso; **fall** ~ caerse; **shut**
~ apagar — **off** *prep* de — **off** *adj* can-
celado; apagado

offend *v* ofender — **offense** *or* **offence**
n ataque *m*; ofensiva *f* (en deportes);
delito *m* — **offensive** *adj* ofensivo

offer *v* ofrecer — **offer** *n* oferta *f*

office *n* oficina *f*; cargo *m* — **officer** *n*
oficial *mf*; *or* **police officer** agente *mf*
(de policía)

often *adv* muchas veces, a menudo, con
frecuencia; **every so** ~ de vez en
cuando

oh *interj* ¡oh!, ¡ah!

oil *n* aceite *m*; petróleo *m* — **oily** *adj*
aceitoso, grasiento

OK *or* **okay** *adv* muy bien; ~! ¡de
acuerdo!, ¡bueno! — *adj* bien

old *adj* viejo; antiguo; **be ten years** ~
tener diez años (de edad); ~ **man** anciano *m*; ~ **woman** anciana *f* — **old** *n*
the old los viejos, los ancianos —
old–fashioned *adj* anticuado

olive *n* aceituna *f* (fruta)

Olympic *adj* olímpico — **Olympics** *npl*
the Olympics las Olimpiadas, las
Olimpíadas

omit *v* omitir — **omission** *n* omisión *f*

on *prep* en; sobre; ~ **foot** a pie; ~
Monday el lunes — **on** *adv* **and so on**
etcétera; **keep on** seguir; **later on** más
tarde; **put on** ponerse (ropa), poner
(música, etc.); **turn on** encender (una
luz, etc.), abrir (una llave) — **on** *adj* encendido (de luces, etc.), abierto (de
llaves)

once *adv* una vez; antes — **once** *n* **at
once** al mismo tiempo; **at once** inmediatamente — *conj* una vez que

oncoming *adj* que viene

one *adj* un, uno; único — **one** *n*; uno *m* (número); **one by one** uno a uno — **one** *pron* uno, una; **that one** aquél, aquella; **which one?** ¿cuál? — **one-self** *pron* se; sí mismo, sí misma; uno mismo, una misma; **by oneself** solo — **one–way** *adj* de sentido único (de una calle)

ongoing *adj* en curso, corriente

onion *n* cebolla *f*

only *adj* único — **only** *adv* sólo, solamente; **if only** ojalá, por lo menos — **only** *conj* pero

onto *prep* sobre

open *adj* abierto; vacante, libre — **open** *v* abrir; comenzar — **open** *n* **in the open** al aire libre; sacado a la luz — **open–air** *adj* al aire libre — **opener** *n* **or can ~ abrelatas** *m* — **opening** *n* abertura *f*; comienzo *m*, apertura *f*

operate *v* funcionar; hacer funcionar (una máquina); dirigir, manejar — **operation** *n* operación *f* funcionamiento *m*

opinion *n* opinión *f*

opponent *n* adversario *m*, -ria *f*; contrincante *mf* (en deportes)

opportunity *n* (**-ties**) oportunidad *f* — **opportune** *adj* oportuno

oppose *v* oponerse a — **opposed** *adj* **opposed to** en contra de

opposite *adj* de enfrente; opuesto — **opposite** *n* **the opposite** lo contrario, lo opuesto — **opposite** *adv* enfrente — **opposite** *prep* enfrente de, frente a — **opposition** *n* oposición *f*; **in opposition to** en contra de

oppress *v* oprimir

optimism *n* optimismo *m* — **optimist** *n* optimista *mf* — **optimistic** *adj* optimista

option *n* opción *f*

or *conj* o; ni; **~ else** si no

oral *adj* oral

orange *n* naranja *f* (fruta); naranja *m* (color)

orchestra *n* orquesta *f*

orchid *n* orquídea *f*

order *v* ordenar; pedir (mercancías, etc.); hacer un pedido — **order** *n* orden *m*; orden *f*; pedido *m*; **in order that** para que; **in order to** para

ordinary *adj* normal, corriente; ordinario — **ordinarily** *adv* generalmente

organ *n* órgano *m* — **organic** *adj* orgánico — **organism** *n* organismo *m* — **organize** *v* organizar — **organization** *n* organización *f*

orgasm *n* orgasmo *m*

oriental *adj* del Oriente, oriental — **orientation** *n* orientación *f*

origin *n* origen *m* — **original** *n* original *m* — **original** *adj* original — **originality** *n* originalidad *f* — **originally** *adv* originariamente — **originate** *v* originar

ornament *n* adorno *m*

orphan *n* huérfano *m*, -na *f*

ostrich *n* avestruz *m*

other *adj* otro; **every ~ day** cada dos días; **on the ~ hand** por otra parte, por otro lado — **other** *pron* otro, otra; **the others** los otros, las otras, los demás, las demás — **otherwise** *adv* eso aparte, por lo demás; de otro modo; si no

ought *v aux* deber

ounce *n* onza *f*

our *adj* nuestro — **ours** *pron* (el) nuestro, (la) nuestra, (los) nuestros, (las) nuestras — **ourselves** *pron* nos; nosotros, nosotras; nosotros mismos, nosotras mismas

out *adv* fuera, afuera; **cry ~ gritar; go ~ salir; look ~ mirar para afuera; run ~ of** agotar; **turn ~** apagar (una luz); **take ~** sacar — **out** *adj* ausente; fuera de moda; apagado

outcome *n* resultado *m*

outdo *v* (**-did; -done**) superar

outdoor *adj* al aire libre — **outdoors** *adv* al aire libre

outer *adj* exterior

outgoing *adj* extrovertido

outlay *n* desembolso *m*

outlet *n* salida *f*; *or* **electrical** ∼ toma *f* de corriente

outline *n* contorno *m*; bosquejo *m*, boceto *m*; esquema *m* — **outline** *v* bosquejar; delinear, esbozar

outlook *n* perspectivas *fpl*; punto *m* de vista

out of *prep* de; por; sin

output *n* producción *f*, rendimiento *m*; salida *f* (informática) — **output** *v* (**-putted** *or* **-put**) producir

outrage *n* atrocidad *f*, escándalo *m*; ira *f*, indignación *f* — **outrageous** *adj* escandaloso

outright *adv* por completo; en el acto — **outright** *adj* completo, absoluto

outset *n* comienzo *m*, principio *m*

outside *n* exterior *m*; **from the** ∼ desde fuera, desde afuera — **outside** *adj* exterior, externo — **outside** *adv* fuera, afuera — **outsider** *n* forastero *m*, -ra *f*

outskirts *npl* afueras *fpl*, alrededores *mpl*

outspoken *adj* franco, directo

outstanding *adj* pendiente; excepcional

outward *adj* hacia afuera; externo, external — **outward** *or* **outwards** *adv* hacia afuera

oval *n* óvalo *m* — **oval** *adj* ovalado

ovary *n* (**-ries**) ovario *m*

oven *n* horno *m*

over *adv* por encima; otra vez, de nuevo; más; **all** ∼ por todas partes; **cross** ∼ cruzar; **fall** ∼ caerse; ∼ **and** ∼ una y otra vez; ∼ **here** aquí ∼ **there** allí — **over** *prep* encima de, sobre; por encima de, sobre; en, durante; **over \$5** más de \$5 — **over** *adj* terminado, acabado

overall *adv* en general — **overall** *adj* total, en conjunto — **overalls** *npl* overol *m*

overcoat *n* abrigo *m*

overcome *v* (**-came; -come**) vencer; agobiar

overdo *v* (**-did; -done**) hacer demasiado; exagerar

overdose *n* sobredosis *f*

overdraft *n* sobregiro *m*, descubierto *m*

overhand *adv* por encima de la cabeza

overhead *adv* por encima — **overhead** *adj* de arriba

overland *adv or adj* por tierra

overlook *v* dar a (un jardín, el mar, etc.); pasar por alto

overly *adv* demasiado

overnight *adv* por la noche; de la noche a la mañana — **overnight** *adj* de noche

overpass *n* paso *m* elevado

overseas *adv* en el extranjero — **overseas** *adj* extranjero, exterior

oversleep *v* (**-slept**) quedarse dormido

overt *adj* manifiesto

overtake *v* (**-took; -taken**) adelantar; superar

overtime *n* horas *fpl* extras (de trabajo)

overwhelm *v* agobiar; aplastar (a un enemigo)

owe *v* deber — **owing to** *prep* debido a

owl *n* búho *m*

own *adj* propio — **own** *v* poseer, tener — **own** *pron* (**my, your, his/her/their, our**) el mío, la mía; el tuyo, la tuya; el suyo, la suya; el nuestro, la nuestra; **be on one's own** estar solo; **to each his own** cada uno a lo suyo — **owner** *n* propietario *m*, -ria *f* — **ownership** *n* propiedad *f*

oxygen *n* oxígeno *m*

P

p *n* (**p's** *or* **ps**) p *f*, decimosexta letra del alfabeto inglés

pace *n* ritmo *m*; **keep ~ with** andar al mismo paso que

pacify *v* (**-fied**) apaciguar — **pacifier** *n* chupete *m* — **pacifist** *n* pacifista *mf*

pack *n* mochila *f*; paquete *m* — **pack** *v* empaquetar; llenar; hacer (una maleta) — **package** *v* empaquetar — **package** *n* paquete *m*

pact *n* pacto *m*, acuerdo *m*

pad *n* bloc *m* (de papel)

padlock *n* candado *m*

page *n* página *f* (de un libro, etc.)

pain *n* dolor *m*; pena *f* (mental); **~s** *npl* esfuerzos *mpl* — **pain** *v* doler — **painkiller** *n* analgésico *m*

paint *v* pintar — **paint** *n* pintura *f* — **paintbrush** *n* pincel *m* (de un artista), brocha *f* (para casas) — **painter** *n* pintor *m*, -tora *f* — **painting** *n* pintura *f*

pair *n* par *m*; pareja *f*

pajamas *npl* pijama *m*, piyama *mf*

Pakistani *adj* paquistaní

palace *n* palacio *m*

palate *n* paladar *m*

pale *adj* pálido — **pale** *v* palidecer

Palestinian *adj* palestino

palm[1] *n* palma *f* (de la mano)

palm[2] *or* **~ tree** palmera *f*

palpitate *v* palpitar — **palpitation** *n* palpitación *f*

pan *n* cacerola *f*; sartén *mf*

pancake *n* crepe *mf*, panqueque *m*

panic *n* pánico *m*

panorama *n* panorama *m*

panther *n* pantera *f*

panties *npl* bragas *fpl*, calzones *mpl*

pants *npl* pantalón *m*, pantalones *mpl*

papaya *n* papaya *f*

paper *n* papel *m* — **paperback** *n* libro *m* en rústica

paprika *n* pimentón *m*

parachute *n* paracaídas *m*

paradise *n* paraíso *m*

paragraph *n* párrafo *m*

Paraguayan *adj* paraguayo

paralysis *n* parálisis *f* — **paralyze** *v* paralizar

paraphrase *n* paráfrasis *f* — **paraphrase** *v* parafrasear

paraplegic *n* parapléjico *m*, -ca *f*

paratrooper *n* paracaidista *mf* (militar)

parcel *n* paquete *m*

pardon *n* perdón *m*

parent *n* madre *f*, padre *m*; **~s** *npl* padres *mpl*

parenthesis *n* (**-theses**) paréntesis *m*

parish *n* parroquia *f*

park *n* parque *m* — **park** *v* estacionar, parquear

parking *n* estacionamiento *m*

parliament *n* parlamento *m* — **parliamentary** *adj* parlamentario

parole *n* libertad *f* condicional

parrot *n* loro *m*, papagayo *m*

parsley *n* perejil *m*

part *n* parte *f*; pieza *f*

partial *adj* parcial

participate *v* participar

participle *n* participio *m*

particular *adj* particular; **in ~** en particular, en especial

partition *n* tabique *m*

partner *n* pareja *f* (en un juego, etc.)

party *n* (**-ties**) partido *m* (político); fiesta *f*

pass *v* pasar; aprobar (en) un examen, una ley, etc.); **~ down** transmitir — **passable** *adj* transitable (de un camino, etc.) — **passage** *n* pasillo *m* (dentro de un edificio), pasaje *m* (entre edificios)

passenger *n* pasajero *m*, -ra *f*

passion *n* pasión *f* — **passionate** *adj* apasionado
passive *adj* pasivo
Passover *n* Pascua *f* (en el judaísmo)
passport *n* pasaporte *m*
password *n* contraseña *f*
past *adj* pasado; anterior — **past** *prep* por delante de; más allá de; **half past two** las dos y media — **past** *n* pasado *m* — **past** *adv* por delante
paste *n* pasta *f* — **paste** *v* pegar
pastime *n* pasatiempo *m*
pastor *n* pastor *m*, -tora *f*
pasture *n* pasto *m*
paternal *adj* paternal — **paternity** *n* paternidad *f*
path *n* camino *m*, sendero *m*; trayectoria *f*
patience *n* paciencia *f* — **patient** *adj* paciente — **patient** *n* paciente *mf*
patio *n* (**-tios**) patio *m*
patriot *n* patriota *mf* — **patriotic** *adj* patriótico
patrol *n* patrulla *f* — **patrol** *v* patrullar
pattern *n* modelo *m*
paunch *n* panza *f*
pause *n* pausa *f*
pave *v* pavimentar — **pavement** *n* pavimento *m*
pavilion *n* pabellón *m*
paw *n* pata *f*
pawn *n* peón *m* (en ajedrez)
pay *v* (**paid**) pagar; ∼ **attention** prestar atención; ∼ **back** devolver — **payment** *n* pago *m*
pea *n* guisante *m*, arveja *f*
peace *n* paz *f* — **peaceful** *adj* pacífico
peach *n* melocotón *m*, durazno *m*
peak *n* cumbre *f*, cima *f*, pico *m* (de una montaña)
peanut *n* cacahuete *m*, maní *m*
pear *n* pera *f*
pearl *n* perla *f*
peasant *n* campesino *m*, -na *f*
pedal *n* pedal *m* — **pedal** *v or* **pedalling** pedalear

pedestrian *n* peatón *m*, -tona *f*
pediatrician *n* pediatra *mf*
peel *v* pelar (fruta, etc.) pelarse (de la piel), descharse (de la pintura) — **peel** *n* piel *f*, cáscara *f*
pelt *n* piel *f* (de un animal)
pelvis *n* (**-vises** *or* **-ves**) pelvis *f*
pen *n or* **ballpoint** ∼ bolígrafo *m*; *or* **fountain** ∼ pluma *f*
penal *adj* penal
penance *n* penitencia *f*
pencil *n* lápiz *m* — **pencil sharpener** *n* sacapuntas *m*
pending *adj* pendiente
penetrate *v* penetrar — **penetrating** *adj* penetrante — **penetration** *n* penetración *f*
penicillin *n* penicilina *f*
peninsula *n* península *f*
pension *n* pensión *m*, jubilación *f*
pensive *adj* pensativo
pentagon *n* pentágono *m*
people *ns & pl* **people** *npl* gente *f*, personas *fpl*; *pl* ∼**s** pueblo *m*
pepper *n* pimienta *f* (condimento); pimiento *m* (fruta)
peppermint *n* menta *f*
perceive *v* percibir
percent *adv* por ciento — **percentage** *n* porcentaje *m*
perception *n* percepción *f*
percussion *n* percusión *f*
perfect *adj* perfecto — **perfect** *v* perfeccionar — **perfection** *n* perfección *f* — **perfectionist** *n* perfeccionista *mf*
perforate *v* perforar
perform *v* representar (una obra teatral), interpretar (una obra musical); actuar — **performance** *n* representación *f* — **performer** *n* actor *m*, -triz *f;* intérprete *mf* (de música)
perfume *n* perfume *m*
perhaps *adv* tal vez, quizá, quizás
peril *n* peligro *m*
period *n* período *m* (de tiempo); punto *m*

(en puntuación); época *f* — **periodic** *adj* periódico

peripheral *adj* periférico

perish *v* perecer

permanent *adj* permanente — **permanent** *n* permanente *f*

permission *n* permiso *m* — **permit** *v* permitir — **permit** *n* permiso *m*

perpendicular *adj* perpendicular

persecute *v* perseguir — **persecution** *n* persecución *f*

person *n* persona *f* — **personality** *n* (**-ties**) personalidad *f* — **personnel** *n* personal *m*

perspective *n* perspectiva *f*

persuade *v* persuadir

Peruvian *adj* peruano

perverse *adj* obstinado

pessimist *n* pesimista *mf* — **pessimistic** *adj* pesimista

petal *n* pétalo *m*

petition *n* petición *f* — **petition** *v* dirigir una petición a

petroleum *n* petróleo *m*

phenomenon *n* (**-na** *or* **-nons**) fenómeno *m*

philanthropy *n* filantropía *f*

philosophy *n* (**-phies**) filosofía *f* — **philosopher** *n* filósofo *m*, -fa *f*

phobia *n* fobia *f*

phosphorus *n* fósforo *m*

photocopy *n* (**-copies**) fotocopia *f* — **photograph** *n* fotografía *f*, foto *f* — **photograph** *v* fotografiar — **photographer** *n* fotógrafo *m*, -fa *f* — **photography** *n* fotografía *f*

phrase *n* frase *f*

physical *adj* físico

physics *ns & pl* física *f* — **physicist** *n* físico *m*, -ca *f*

physiology *n* fisiología *f*

physique *n* físico *m*

piano *n* (**-anos**) piano *m* — **pianist** *n* pianista *mf*

pick *v* recoger — **pick** *n or* **pickax** pico *m*

pickle *n* pepinillo *m* (encurtido)

pick up *v* levantar

picnic *n* picnic *m*

picture *n* cuadro *m*; imagen *f*

pie *n* pastel *m* (con fruta o carne), empanada *f* (con carne)

piece *n* pieza *f*

piety *n* piedad *f*

pig *n* cerdo *m*, -da *f*; puerco *m*, -ca *f*

pigeon *n* paloma *f*

pigtail *n* coleta *f*, trenza *f*

pile *n* montón *m*, pila *f* — **pile** *v* amontonar, apilar

pill *n* pastilla *f*, píldora *f*

pillow *n* almohada *f*

pilot *n* piloto *mf*

pin *n* alfiler *m* — **pin** *v* prender, sujetar (con alfileres)

pinch *v* pellizcar — **pinch** *n* pellizco *m*

pineapple *n* piña *f*, ananás *m*

pink *n* rosa *m*, rosado *m* — **pink** *adj* rosa, rosado

pioneer *n* pionero *m*, -ra *f*

pipe *n* tubo *m*, caño *m*; pipa *f* (para fumar) — **pipeline** *n* conducto *m*, oleoducto *m* (para petróleo)

pistol *n* pistola *f*

piston *n* pistón *m*

pit *n* hoyo *m*, fosa *f*

pizza *n* pizza *f*

place *n* sitio *m*, lugar *m*; asiento *m*; puesto *m*; papel *m*; **take** ~ tener lugar; **take the** ~ **of** sustituir a — **place** *v* poner, colocar; identificar, recordar; **place an order** hacer un pedido — **placement** *n* colocación *f*

plagiarism *n* plagio *m*

plaid *adj* escocés

plain *adj n* llanura *f*, planicie *f*

plan *n* plan *m*, proyecto *m*; plano *m* — **plan** *v* planear, proyectar; tener planeado; hacer planes

plane *n* plano *m*, nivel *m*

planet *n* planeta *f*

plank *n* tabla *f*

planning *n* planificación *f*

plant *n* planta *f*

plantain *n* plátano *m* (grande)

plaque *n* placa *f*

plaster *n* yeso *m* — **plaster** *v* enyesar — **plaster cast** *n* escayola *f*

plastic *adj* de plástico; plástico, flexible — **plastic** *n* plástico *m*

plate *n* plato *m*

platform *n* andén *m* (de una estación de ferrocarril)

platter *n* fuente *f*

play *n* juego *m* — **play** *v* jugar; jugar (deportes, etc.), jugar a (juegos); tocar (música o un instrumento) — **player** *n* jugador *m*, -dora *f* — **playing card** *n* naipe *m*, carta *f* — **playwright** *n* dramaturgo *m*, -ga *f*

pleasant *adj* agradable, grato — **please** *v* complacer; satisfacer agradar — **please** *adv* por favor — **pleasure** *n* placer *m*, gusto *m*

pledge *n* prenda *f*

plot *n* argumento *m* (de una novela, etc.)

plug *n* enchufe *m* (eléctrico) — **plug** *v* **plug in** enchufar

plum *n* ciruela *f*

plumber *n* fontanero *m*, -ra *f*; plomero *m*, -ra *f*

plunge *v* sumergir; hundir

plural *adj* plural — **plural** *n* plural *m*

plus *prep* más

pocket *n* bolsillo *m* — **pocketbook** *n* cartera *f*, bolsa *f* — **pocketknife** *n* (**-knives**) navaja *f*

poem *n* poema *m* — **poet** *n* poeta *mf*

point *n* punto *m*; punta *f*; **be beside the** ∼ no venir al caso; **there's no** ∼ no sirve de nada — **point** *v* apuntar; *or* **point out** señalar, indicar; **point at** señalar (con el dedo)

poison *n* veneno *m* — **poison** *v* envenenar

poker *n* póquer *m* (juego de naipes)

polarize *v* polarizar

pole[1] *n* palo *m*, poste *m*

pole[2] *n* polo *m* (en geografía)

police *v* mantener el orden en — **police** *ns or pl* **the police** la policía — **policeman** *n* (**-men**) policía *m*

policy *n* (**-cies**) política *f*

polish *v* pulir; limpiar (zapatos) — **polish** *n* brillo *m*, lustre *m*; betún *m* (para zapatos), cera *f* (para suelos y muebles), esmalte *m* (para las uñas)

Polish *adj* polaco — **Polish** *n* polaco *m* (idioma)

polite *adj* cortés — **politeness** *n* cortesía *f*

political *adj* político — **politician** *n* político *m*, -ca *f* — **politics** *ns & pl* política *f*

poll *n* encuesta *f*, sondeo *m*; encuestar, sondear

pollute *v* contaminar — **pollution** *n* contaminación *f*

pool *n* billar *m*; *or* **swimming** ∼ piscina *f*

poor *adj* pobre; malo — **poorly** *adv* mal

popcorn *n* palomitas *fpl*

pope *n* papa *m*

popular *adj* popular — **popularity** *n* popularidad *f*

population *n* población *f*

porcelain *n* porcelana *f*

port *n* puerto *m*

portable *adj* portátil

porter *n* maletero *m*, mozo *m* (de estación)

portion *n* porción *f*

portrait *n* retrato *m*

portray *v* representar, retratar; interpretar (un personaje)

Portuguese *adj* portugués — **Portuguese** *n* portugués *m* (idioma)

pose *v* plantear (una pregunta, etc.), representar (una amenaza); posar; ∼ **as** hacerse pasar por

position *n* posición *f*; puesto *m*

positive *adj* positivo

possess *v* poseer — **possessive** *adj* posesivo

possible *adj* posible — **possibility** *n*
(**-ties**) posibilidad *f*

postal *adj* postal — **postcard** *n* tarjeta *f*
postal

poster *n* cartel *m*

posterity *n* posteridad *f*

posthumous *adj* póstumo

postpone *v* aplazar

postwar *adj* de (la) posguerra

pot *n* olla *f* (de cocina)

potato *n* (**-toes**) patata *f*, papa *f*

pottery *n* cerámica *f*

pound[1] *n* libra *f* (unidad de dinero o de
peso)

pound[2] *v* golpear

poverty *n* pobreza *f*

powder *v* empolvar — **powder** *n* polvo
m

power *n* poder *m*; fuerza *f*; potencia *f*
(política); energía *f* — **powerful** *adj*
poderoso — **powerless** *adj* impotente

practical *adj* práctico

practice *or* **practise** *v* practicar; practicar — **practice** *n* práctica *f*

prank *n* travesura *f*

pray *v* rezar; ~ **for** rogar — **prayer** *n*
oración *f*

preach *v* predicar

precaution *n* precaución *f*

precedent *n* precedente *m*

precious *adj* precioso

precipitation *n* precipitación *f*; preci-
pitaciones *fpl* (en meteorología)

precise *adj* preciso — **precision** *n* precisión *f*

precocious *adj* precoz

predict *v* pronosticar, predecir — **prediction** *n* pronóstico *m*, predicción *f*

predominant *adj* predominante

preface *n* prefacio *m*, prólogo *m*

prefer *v* preferir

prefix *n* prefijo *m*

pregnancy *n* (**-cies**) embarazo *m* —
pregnant *adj* embarazada

prehistoric *adj* prehistórico

prejudice *n* prejuicio *m*; perjuicio *m*

preliminary *adj* preliminar

premarital *adj* prematrimonial

premature *adj* prematuro

premise *n* premisa *f* (de un argumento);
~**s** *npl* recinto *m*, local *m*

premium *n* *or* **insurance** ~ prima *f* (de
seguro)

prepare *v* preparar; prepararse —
preparation *n* preparación *f*

preposition *n* preposición *f*

prescription *n* receta *f*

presence *n* presencia *f*

present[1] *adj* actual; **be** ~ **at** estar presente en — **present** *n* presente *m*; **at
present** actualmente

present[2] *n* regalo *m* — **presentation** *n*
presentación *f*

preserve *v* conservar; mantener

president *n* presidente *m*, -ta *f* — **presidency** *n* (**-cies**) presidencia *f*

press *v* apretar; presionar — **pressure** *n*
presión *f* — **pressure** *v* presionar,
apremiar

prestige *n* prestigio *m*

pretend *v* fingir

pretext *n* pretexto *m*

pretty *adj* lindo, bonito

prevent *v* impedir — **prevention** *n* prevención *f*

previously *adv* anteriormente

price *n* precio *m*

prickly *adj* espinoso

pride *n* orgullo *m*

priest *n* sacerdote *m*

primary *adj* primario; principal

primitive *adj* primitivo

principal *adj* principal

principle *n* principio *m*

print *v* imprimir (libros, etc.); escribir
con letra de molde — **printer** *n* impresora *f* (máquina) — **printing** *n* impresión *f*; imprenta *f* (profesión); letras
fpl de molde

priority *n* (**-ties**) prioridad *f*

prison *n* prisión *f*, cárcel *f* — **prisoner** *n*
preso *m*, -sa *f*

privacy *n* intimidad *f* — **private** *adj* privado

privilege *n* privilegio *m*

prize *n* premio *m*

pro *n* the ⁓s and cons los pros y los contras

probability *n* (-ties) probabilidad *f*

problem *n* problema *m*

procedure *n* procedimiento *m*

proceed *v* proceder — **proceedings** *npl* proceso *m* (en derecho)

process *n* proceso *m*; **in the** ⁓ **of** en vías de — **process** *v* procesar

proclaim *v* proclamar

produce *v* producir; causar; presentar, mostrar; poner en escena (una obra de teatro) — **produce** *n* productos *mpl* agrícolas — **product** *n* producto *m*

profession *n* profesión *f* — **professional** *adj* profesional — **professional** *n* profesional *mf* — **professor** *n* profesor *m*, -sora *f*

profile *n* perfil *m*

profit *n* beneficio *m*, ganancia *f* — **profit** *v* sacar provecho (de), beneficiarse (de) — **profitable** *adj* provechoso

profound *adj* profundo

prognosis *n* (-noses) pronóstico *m*

program *n* programa *m* — **program** *v* programar

progress *n* progreso *m*; avance *m* — **progress** *v* progresar, avanzar

prohibit *v* prohibir — **prohibition** *n* prohibición *f*

project *n* proyecto *m* — **projection** *n* proyección *f* — **projector** *n* proyector *m*

prologue *n* prólogo *m*

prolong *v* prolongar

promise *n* promesa *f* — **promise** *v* prometer

promote *v* ascender (a un alumno o un empleado); promover, fomentar; promocionar — **promoter** *n* promotor *m*, -tora *f*; empresario *m*, -ria *f* (en deportes) — **promotion** *n* ascenso *m* (de

un alumno o un empleado); publicidad *f*, propaganda *f*

prompt *v* apuntar (a un actor, etc.); puntual

prong *n* punta *f*, diente *m*

pronoun *n* pronombre *m*

pronounce *v* pronunciar — **pronouncement** *n* declaración *f* — **pronunciation** *n* pronunciación *f*

proof *n* prueba *f* — **proof** *adj* **proof against** a prueba de

propaganda *n* propaganda *f*

propeller *n* hélice *f*

property *n* (-ties) propiedad *f*; inmueble *m*

proportion *n* proporción *f*; parte *f* — **proportional** *adj* proporcional

proposal *n* propuesta *f*

propose *v* proponer; ⁓ **to do** pensar hacer; proponer matrimonio — **proposition** *n* proposición *f*

proprietor *n* propietario *m*, -ria *f*

prose *n* prosa *f*

prosecute *v* procesar

prospect *n* perspectiva *f*

prosper *v* prosperar — **prosperity** *n* prosperidad *f* — **prosperous** *adj* próspero

prostitute *n* prostituta *f*

protagonist *n* protagonista *mf*

protect *v* proteger — **protection** *n* protección *f* — **protective** *adj* protector — **protector** *n* protector *m*, -tora *f*

protest *n* protesta *f* — **protest** *v* protestar — **protester** *or* **protestor** *n* manifestante *mf*

protrude *v* sobresalir

proud *adj* orgulloso

prove *v* probar

proverb *n* proverbio *m*, refrán *m*

provide *v* proveer

provision *n* provisión *f*, suministro *m*; ⁓s *npl* víveres *mpl* — **provisional** *adj* provisional

provoke *v* provocar — **provocation** *n* provocación *f*

proximity n proximidad f
prudent adj prudente
prune n ciruela f pasa
pseudonym n seudónimo m
psychiatrist n psiquiatra mf
psychology n psicología f — **psychological** adj psicológico — **psychologist** n psicólogo m, -ga f
puberty n pubertad f
public adj público — **public** n público m — **publication** n publicación f — **publicity** n publicidad f
publish v publicar — **publisher** n editor m, -tora f (persona)
pudding n budín m, pudín m
puddle n charco m
Puerto Rican adj puertorriqueño
pull n tirón m — **pull** v tirar (de)
pulse n pulso m
pumpkin n calabaza f, zapallo m
punch v or **paper** ∼ perforadora f
punctual adj puntual — **punctuality** n puntualidad f
punctuation n puntuación f

punish v castigar — **punishment** n castigo m — **punitive** adj punitivo
pupil[1] n alumno m, -na f (de colegio)
pupil[2] n pupila f (del ojo)
puppet n títere m
puppy n (**-pies**) cachorro m, -rra f
purchase v comprar — **purchase** n compra f
pure adj puro
puree n puré m
purify v (**-fied**) purificar — **purification** n purificación f
purity n pureza f
purple n morado m
purpose n propósito m; determinación f; **on** ∼ a propósito
purse n or **change** ∼ monedero m
pursue v perseguir — **pursuit** n persecución f
push v empujar; apretar; presionar; empujar — **push** n empujón m
put v (**put**) poner; meter; decir; ∼ **one's mind to** proponerse hacer
puzzle v n rompecabezas m

Q

q n (**q's** or **qs**) q f, decimoséptima letra del alfabeto inglés
quack n charlatán m, -tana f
qualification n requisito m; ∼**s** npl capacidad f; **without** ∼ sin reservas — **qualify** v (**-fied**) clasificarse (en deportes) — **qualified** adj capacitado
quality n (**-ties**) calidad f; cualidad f
quantity n (**-ties**) cantidad f
quarrel n pelea f, riña f — **quarrel** v pelearse, reñir
quarter n cuarto m (en matemáticas); moneda f de 25 centavos; barrio m; ∼ **after three** las tres y cuarto; ∼**s** npl alojamiento m — **quarter** v dividir en cuatro partes — **quarterly** adv cada tres meses — **quarterly** adj trimestral

— **quarterly** n (**-lies**) publicación f trimestral
quartet n cuarteto m
queen n reina f
query n (**-ries**) pregunta f — **query** v (**-ried**) preguntar; cuestionar
quest n búsqueda f
question n pregunta f; cuestión f; **be out of the** ∼ ser indiscutible; **call into** ∼ poner en duda; **without** ∼ sin duda — **question** v preguntar; cuestionar; interrogar — **question mark** n signo m de interrogación — **questionnaire** n cuestionario m
quick adj rápido; agudo — **quick** n **to the quick** en lo vivo — **quickly** adv rápidamente

quiet *n* silencio *m*; tranquilidad *f* —
  quiet *adj* silencioso; tranquilo; callado;
  discreto (dícese de colores, etc.) —
  quiet *v* hacer callar; calmar; *or* **quiet**
  down calmarse

quit *v* (**quit**) parar; dimitir, renunciar; dejar,
  abandonar; **~ doing** dejar de hacer
quota *n* cuota *f*, cupo *m*
quotation *n* cita *f*; presupuesto *m* —
  quote *v* citar; cotizar (en finanzas)

R

r *n* (**r's** *or* **rs**) r *f*, decimoctava letra del alfabeto inglés
rabbit *n* conejo *m*, -ja *f*
race¹ *n* raza *f*; **human ~** género *m* humano
race² *n* carrera *f* (competitiva) — **race** *v*
  correr (en una carrera); ir corriendo —
  racehorse *n* caballo *m* de carreras
racial *adj* racial — **racism** *n* racismo *m*
  — **racist** *n* racista *mf*
rack *n* **luggage ~** portaequipajes *m*
  ~ed with atormentado por
racket *n* raqueta *f* (en deportes)
radar *n* radar *m*
radiance *n* resplandor *m* — **radiate** *v*
  irradiar
radio *n* (**-dios**) radio *mf* (aparato), radio *f*
  (medio) — **radio** *v* transmitir por radio
raft *n* balsa *f*
rag *n* trapo *m* — **ragged** *adj* irregular;
  andrajoso, harapiento
rage *n* cólera *f*, rabia *f* — **rage** *v* estar furioso
raid *n* invasión *f* (militar); asalto *m* (por
  delincuentes), redada *f* (por la policía)
  — **raid** *v* invadir; asaltar
rail *n* barra *f*; pasamanos *m*; riel *m*; **by ~**
  por ferrocarril — **railing** *n* baranda *f*
  (de un balcón), pasamanos *m* (de una
  escalera) — **railroad** *n* ferrocarril *m*
rain *n* lluvia *f* — **rain** *v* llover — **rain-**
  bow *n* arco *m* iris — **raincoat** *n* impermeable *m* — **rainfall** *n* precipitación *f*
  — **rainy** *adj* lluvioso

raise *v* levantar; criar; cultivar; aumentar
  — **raise** *n* aumento *m*
raisin *n* pasa *f*
rally *v* (**-lied**) unirse, reunirse — **rally** *n*
  (**-lies**) reunión *f*, mitin *m*
RAM *n* RAM *f*
ramble *v* pasear; *or* **~ on** divagar —
  ramble *n* paseo *m*, excursión *f*
ramp *n* rampa *f*
ranch *n* hacienda *f* — **rancher** *n* hacen-
  dado *m*, -da *f*
random *adj* aleatorio; **at ~** al azar
range *n* pradera *f*; cocina *f*; amplitud *f*; *or*
  mountain ~ cordillera *f* — **range** *v* extenderse — **ranger** *n or* **forest ranger**
  guardabosque *mf*
rank *n* fila *f*; rango *m* (militar); **~s** *npl*
  soldados *mpl* rasos — **rank** *v* clasi-
  ficar(se)
rap *n or* **~ music** rap *m*
rapid *adj* rápido
rapport *n* **have a good ~** entenderse
  bien
rare *adj* excepcional; raro; poco cocido
  (de la carne) — **rarely** *adv* raramente
  — **rarity** *n* (**-ties**) rareza *f*
rash¹ *adj* imprudente, precipitado
rash² *n* sarpullido *m*, erupción *f*
raspberry *n* (**-ries**) frambuesa *f*
rat *n* rata *f*
rate *n* velocidad *f*, ritmo *m*; tipo *m*, tasa
  m (de interés, etc.); tarifa *f*; **at any ~**
  de todos modos — **rate** *v* considerar;
  merecer

rather *adv* bastante **I'd ~ . . .** prefiero
. . . ; **or ~** o mejor dicho

rating *n* clasificación *f*; **~s** *npl* índice *m*
de audiencia

rational *adj* racional — **rationalize** *v*
racionalizar

raw *adj* crudo; inexperto; **~ materials**
materias *fpl* primas

ray *n* rayo *m*

razor *n* maquinilla *f* de afeitar — **razor
blade** *n* hoja *f* de afeitar

reach *v* alcanzar; extenderse; *or* **~ out**
extender; llegar a (un acuerdo, un
límite, etc.); contactar — **reach** *n* alcance *m*; **within reach** al alcance

reaction *n* reacción *f* — **reaction** *n*
(-aries) reaccionario *m*, -ria *f* — **reactor** *n* reactor *m*

read *v* (**read**) leer — **readable** *adj* legible — **reader** *n* lector *m*, -tora *f* —
reading *n* lectura *f*

readily *adv* de buena gana; fácilmente

ready *adj* listo, preparado; dispuesto;
get ~ prepararse — **ready** *v* (**read-
ied**) preparar

real *adj* verdadero, real; auténtico —
real *adv* muy — **realism** *n* realismo *m*
— **realist** *n* realista *mf* — **reality** *n*
(-ties) realidad *f*

realize *v* darse cuenta de; realizar

really *adv* verdaderamente

rear *n* parte *f* de atrás; trasero *m*

rearrange *v* reorganizar, cambiar

reason *n* razón *f*; razonar — **reason-
able** *adj* razonable — **reasoning** *n* ra-
zonamiento *m*

rebel *n* rebelde *mf* — **rebellion** *n* re-
belión *f*

rebuild *v* (**-built**) reconstruir

recall *v* llamar (al servicio, etc.); recordar

receipt *n* recibo *m*; **~s** *npl* ingresos *mpl*

receive *v* recibir — **receiver** *n* receptor
m (de radio, etc.); *or* **telephone receiver** auricular *m*

recent *adj* reciente — **recently** *adv* recientemente

receptacle *n* receptáculo *m*, recipiente *m*

reception *n* recepción *f* — **receptionist**
n recepcionista *mf*

recharge *v* recargar — **rechargeable**
adj recargable

recipe *n* receta *f*

recipient *n* recipiente *mf*

recite *v* recitar (un poema, etc.) —
recital *n* recital *m*

reckon *v* calcular; considerar

reclaim *v* reclamar; recuperar

recline *v* reclinarse

recognition *n* reconocimiento *m* — **rec-
ognizable** *adj* reconocible — **recognize** *v* reconocer

recommend *v* recomendar — **recommendation** *n* recomendación *f*

reconsider *v* reconsiderar

record *v* anotar, apuntar; registrar;
grabar (música, etc.) — **record** *n* documento *m*; registro *m*; disco *m* (de
música, etc.); **world record** récord *m*
mundial; *or* **tape record** grabadora *f*
— **recording** *n* disco *m* — **record
player** *n* tocadiscos *m*

recover *v* recobrar; recuperarse — **recovery** *n* recuperación *f*

rectangle *n* rectángulo *m* — **rectangular** *adj* rectangular

rector *n* parroco *m* (clérigo); rector *m*,
-tora *f* (de una universidad) — **rectory**
n (**-ries**) rectoría *f*

recuperate *v* recuperar(se) — **recuper-
ation** *n* recuperación *f*

recur *v* repetirse — **recurrence** *n*
repetición *f* — **recurrent** *adj* que se
repite

recycle *v* reciclar

red *adj* rojo — **red** *n* rojo *m* — **redhead**
n pelirrojo *m*, -ja *f*

redo *v* (**-did; -done**) hacer de nuevo

reduce *v* reducir; adelgazar — **reduction** *n* reducción *f*

refer *v* **~ to** referirse a — **reference** *n*
referencia *f*; consulta *f*

referee *n* árbitro *m*, -tra *f* — **referee** *v* arbitrar

refill *v* rellenar — **refill** *n* recambio *m*

reflect *v* reflejar(se) — **reflection** *n* reflexión *f*; reflejo *m* — **reflector** *n* reflector *m*

reflex *n* reflejo *m* — **reflexive** *adj* reflexivo

reform *v* reformar — **reform** *n* reforma *f*

refrain *v* ∼ **from** abstenerse de

refresh *v* refrescar — **refreshments** *npl* refrigerio *m*

refrigerate *v* refrigerar — **refrigeration** *n* refrigeración *f* — **refrigerator** *n* nevera *f*, refrigerador *m*, frigorífico *m*

refuel *v* llenar de carburante; repostar

refund *v* reembolsar — **refund** *n* reembolso *m*

refuse *v* rehusar, rechazar; negarse; ∼ **to do** negarse a hacer — **refusal** *n* negativa *f*

regain *v* recuperar, recobrar

regard *n* consideración *f*; estima *f*; **in this** ∼ en este sentido; ∼**s** *npl* saludos *mpl*; **regarding** *prep* respecto a — **regardless** *adv* a pesar de todo — **regardless of** *prep* sin tener en cuenta; a pesar de

region *n* región *f* — **regional** *adj* regional

register *n* registro *m* — **register** *v* registrar (a personas), matricular (vehículos); certificar (correo); inscribirse, matricularse — **registration** *n* inscripción *f*, matriculación *f* — **registry** *n* (**-tries**) registro *m*

regret *v* lamentar — **regret** *n* arrepentimiento *m*; pesar *m* — **regrettable** *adj* lamentable

regular *adj* regular; habitual — **regular** *n* cliente *mf* habitual — **regularity** *n* regularidad *f*

rehabilitate *v* rehabilitar — **rehabilitation** *n* rehabilitación *f*

rehearse *v* ensayar — **rehearsal** *n* ensayo *m*

reign *n* reinado *m* — **reign** *v* reinar

reinforce *v* reforzar — **reinforcement** *n* refuerzo *m*

reject *v* rechazar — **rejection** *n* rechazo *m*

relate *v* relatar; relacionar; ∼ **to** estar relacionado con — **relation** *n* relación *f*; pariente *mf*; **in relation to** en relación con — **relationship** *n* relación *f*; parentesco *m* — **relative** *n* pariente *mf* — **relative** *adj* relativo — **relatively** *adv* relativamente

relax *v* relajar(se) — **relaxation** *n* relajación *f*

release *v* liberar, poner en libertad; soltar (un freno, etc.); despedir

relevant *adj* pertinente — **relevance** *n* pertinencia *f*

reliable *adj* fiable (de personas), fidedigno (de información, etc.) — **reliability** *n* (**-ties**) fiabilidad *f* (de una cosa), responsabilidad *f* (de una persona) — **rely** *v* (**-lied**) **rely on** depender de; confiar (en)

relief *n* alivio *m*; ayuda *f*; relevo *m* — **relieve** *v* aliviar

religion *n* religión *f* — **religious** *adj* religioso

remain *v* quedar(se); seguir, continuar — **remainder** *n* resto *m*

remark *n* comentario *m*, observación *f* — **remark** *v or* **remark on** observar — **remarkable** *adj* extraordinario, notable

remedy *n* (**-dies**) remedio *m* — **remedy** *v* (**-died**) remediar

remember *v* recordar; acordarse (de) — **remembrance** *n* recuerdo *m*

remind *v* recordar — **reminder** *n* recordatorio *m*

remote *adj* remoto — **remote control** *n* control *m* remoto

remove *v* quitar(se); sacar — **removable** *adj* separable, de quita y pon

rendition *n* interpretación *f*

renew *v* renovar

renovate *v* renovar — **renovation** *n* renovación *f*

renown *n* renombre *m* — **renowned** *adj* célebre, renombrado

rent *n* alquiler *m*, arrendamiento *m*, renta *f*; **for** ∼ se alquila — **rent** *v* alquilar — **rental** *n* alquiler *m* — **rental** *adj* de alquiler — **renter** *n* arrendatario *m, -ria f*

repair *v* reparar, arreglar — **repair** *n* reparación *f*, arreglo *m*

repeat *v* repetir — **repeat** *n* repetición *f*

repetition *n* repetición *f*

replace *v* reponer; reemplazar, sustituir; cambiar — **replacement** *n* sustitución *f*; sustituto *m, -ta f* (persona); *or* **replacement part** repuesto *m*

reply *v* (**-plied**) contestar, responder — **reply** *n* (**-plies**) respuesta *f*

report *n* informe *m*; rumor *m*; *or* **news** ∼ reportaje *m*; **weather** ∼ boletín *m* meteorológico — **report** *v* anunciar; informar; **report for duty** presentarse — **reporter** *n* periodista *mf*; reportero *m, -ra f*

represent *v* representar; presentar — **representation** *n* representación *f*

repress *v* reprimir — **repression** *n* represión *f*

reproduce *v* reproducir(se) — **reproduction** *n* reproducción *f*

republic *n* república *f*

reputation *n* reputación *f*

request *n* petición *f* — **request** *v* pedir

require *v* requerir; necesitar — **requirement** *n* necesidad *f*; requisito *m*

rescue *v* rescatar, salvar — **rescue** *n* rescate *m*

research *n* investigación *f* — **research** *v* investigar — **researcher** *n* investigador *m, -dora f*

resemble *v* parecerse a — **resemblance** *n* parecido *m*

reserve *v* reservar — **reserve** *n* reserva *f* — **reserved** *adj* reservado

reset *v* (**-set**) volver a poner (un reloj, etc.)

residence *n* residencia *f* — **reside** *v* residir

resign *v* dimitir; renunciar; ∼ **oneself to** resignarse a

resistant *adj* resistente

resolve *v* resolver

resort *n* recurso *m*; *or* **tourist** ∼ centro *m* turístico

resource *n* recurso *m*

respect *n* respeto *m*; **in some** ∼**s** en algún sentido — **respect** *v* respetar

respiration *n* respiración *f* — **respiratory** *adj* respiratorio

response *n* respuesta *f* — **respond** *v* responder — **responsibility** *n* (**-ties**) responsabilidad *f* — **responsible** *adj* responsable

rest *n* descanso *m* — **rest** *v* descansar; **rest on** depender de

restaurant *n* restaurante *m*

restful *adj* tranquilo, apacible

restless *adj* inquieto, agitado

restore *v* devolver; restablecer

restrain *v* contener; ∼ **oneself** contenerse

restriction *n* restricción *f* — **restrict** *v* restringir — **restricted** *adj* restringido

result *v* resultar — **result** *n* resultado *m*; **as a result of** como consecuencia de

resume *v* reanudar; continuar

résumé *or* **resume** *or* **resumé** *n* currículum *m* (vitae)

retire *v* jubilarse, retirarse (de un trabajo) — **retirement** *n* jubilación *f*

retrieve *v* cobrar, recuperar

return *v* volver, regresar; devolver — **return** *n* regreso *m*, vuelta *f*; **in return for** a cambio de

reveal *v* revelar

reverse *adj* inverso, contrario — **reverse** *n* dorso *m*, revés *m*; *or* **reverse gear** marcha *f* atrás

review *n* revisión *f*; resumen *m*; repaso *m*

(para un examen) — **review** *v* examinar; repasar (una lección); reseñar

revise *v* revisar, corregir (una publicación) — **revision** *n* corrección *f*, modificación *f*

revival *n* reanimación *f*, reactivación *f*

revolution *n* revolución *f* — **revolutionary** *adj* revolucionario

reward *v* recompensar — **reward** *n* recompensa *f*

rewrite *v* (**-wrote; -written**) volver a escribir

rhyme *n* rima *f* — **rhyme** *v* rimar

rhythm *n* ritmo *m*

rib *n* costilla *f*

ribbon *n* cinta *f*

rice *n* arroz *m*

rich *adj* rico — **richness** *n* riqueza *f*

rid *v* (**rid**) librar; **get** ∼ **of** deshacerse de

riddle *n* adivinanza *f*

ride *v* (**rode; ridden**) montar (a caballo, en bicicleta), ir (en auto, etc.); recorrer — **ride** *n* paseo *m*, vuelta *f*; aparato *m* (en un parque de diversiones) — **rider** *n* jinete *mf* (a caballo); ciclista *mf*, motociclista *mf*

ridiculous *adj* ridículo — **ridicule** *n* burlas *fpl* — **ridicule** *v* ridiculizar

rifle *n* rifle *m*, fusil *m*

right *adj* bueno, justo; correcto; apropiado, adecuado; recto; **be** ∼ tener razón; bien *m*; **on the** ∼ a la derecha — **right** *adv* bien; inmediatamente — **right–hand** *adj* derecho — **right–handed** *adj* diestro — **rightly** *adv* justamente; correctamente

rigid *adj* rígido

ring[1] *v* (**rang; rung**) sonar (de un timbre, etc.); tocar (un timbre, etc.) — **ring** *n* llamada *f* (por teléfono)

ring[2] *n* anillo *m*, sortija *f*; aro *m*; círculo *m* — **ringlet** *n* rizo *m*, bucle *m*

rink *n* pista *f* (de patinaje)

rinse *n* enjuague *m*

ripe *adj* maduro; ∼ **for** listo por — **ripen** *v* madurar

rise *v* (**rose; risen**) levantarse; salir (del sol, etc.); subir — **rise** *n* subida *f*; aumento *m*

risk *n* riesgo *m* — **risk** *v* arriesgar — **risky** *adj* arriesgado, riesgoso

rival *n* rival *mf* — **rival** *adj* rival

river *n* río *m*

road *n* carretera *f*; calle *f*; camino *m* — **roadway** *n* carretera *f*

roast *v* asar(se) (carne, etc.), tostar (café, etc.) — **roast** *n* asado *m* — **roast beef** *n* rosbif *m*

robot *n* robot *m*

robust *adj* robusto

rock[1] *n or* ∼ **music** música *f* rock

rock[2] *n* roca *f* (sustancia); piedra *f* — **rocky** *adj* rocoso

rocking chair *n* mecedora *f*

role *n* papel *m*

roll *n* rollo *m* (de película, etc.); rodar; ∼ **around** revolcarse; ∼ **over** darse la vuelta; ∼ **up** enrollar (papel, etc.), arremangar (una manga) — **roller** *n* rodillo *m*; rulo *m* — **roller coaster** *n* montaña *f* rusa — **roller–skate** *v* patinar (sobre ruedas) — **roller skate** *n* patín *m* (de ruedas)

Roman Catholic *adj* católico

romance *n* romanticismo; novela *f* romántica

Romanian *adj* rumano — **Romanian** *n* rumano *m* (idioma)

romantic *adj* romántico

roof *n* tejado *m*, techo *m*; ∼ **of the mouth** paladar *m* — **rooftop** *n* tejado *m*, techo *m*

room *n* cuarto *m*, habitación *f*; dormitorio *m* — **roommate** *n* compañero *m*, -ra *f* de cuarto

rooster *n* gallo *m*

root *n* raíz *f*

rope *n* cuerda *f* — **rope** *v* atar (con cuerda)

rose *n* rosa *f* (flor), rosa *m* (color) — **rose** *adj* rosa — **rosebush** *n* rosal *m*

rotate *v* girar — **rotation** *n* rotación *f*

rough *adj* áspero; accidentado; agitado; duro; brusco; aproximado; ~ **draft** borrador *m* — **roughly** *adv* bruscamente; aproximadamente — **roughness** *n* aspereza *f*

round *adj* redondo — **round** *n* asalto *m* (en boxeo), vuelta *f* (en juegos) — **round** *v* doblar; *or* **round off** redondear — **round–trip** *n* viaje *m* de ida y vuelta

route *n* ruta *f*; *or* **delivery** ~ recorrido *m*

routine *n* rutina *f* — **routine** *adj* rutinario

row[1] *v* ~ **a boat** remar — **rowboat** *n* bote *m* de remos

row[2] *n* fila *f* (de gente o asientos), hilera *f* (de casas, etc.)

rowdy *adj* escandaloso, alborotador

rub *v* frotar; ~ **in** aplicar frotando

rubber *n* goma *f*, caucho *m*; ~**s** *npl* chanclos *mpl* — **rubber band** *n* goma *f* (elástica) — **rubber stamp** *n* sello *m* (de goma)

rubbish *n* basura *f*; tonterías *fpl*

rude *adj* grosero, mal educado; brusco — **rudely** *adv* groseramente — **rudeness** *n* grosería *f*, mala educación *f*

rug *n* alfombra *f*, tapete *m*

rugged *adj* fuerte

ruin *n* ruina *f* — **ruin** *v* arruinar

rule *n* regla *f*; dominio *m*; **as a** ~ por lo general — **rule** *v* gobernar — **ruler** *n* regla *f* (para medir)

rumor *n* rumor *m*

run *v* (**ran; run**) correr; funcionar; extenderse; ~ **away** huir; ~ **into** tropezar con; ~ **into** chocar contra ~ **out of** quedarse sin ~ **over** atropellar — **run** *n*; carrera *f*

runner *n* corredor *m*, -dora *f*

runway *n* pista *f* de aterrizaje

rupture *n* ruptura *f* — **rupture** *v* romper; reventar

rural *adj* rural

rush *v* apresurar, apurar; asaltar — **rush** *n* prisa *f*, apuro *m* — **rush** *adj* urgente

Russian *adj* ruso — **Russian** *n* ruso *m* (idioma)

S

s *n* (**s's** *or* **ss**) s *f*, decimonovena letra del alfabeto inglés

sacred *adj* sagrado

sacrifice *n* sacrificio *m* — **sacrifice** *v* sacrificar

sad *adj* triste — **sadden** *v* entristecer

sadness *n* tristeza *f*

safe *adj* seguro; ileso — **safe** *n* caja *f* fuerte — **safeguard** *n* salvaguarda *f* — **safely** *adv* sin peligro — **safety** *n* seguridad *f*

sail *n* vela *f* (de un barco); **go for a** ~ salir a navegar; **set** ~ zarpar — **sail** *v* navegar — **sailboat** *n* velero *m* — **sailor** *n* marinero *m*

saint *n* santo *m*, -ta *f*

sake *n* **for goodness'** ~! ¡por Dios!

salad *n* ensalada *f*

salary *n* (**-ries**) sueldo *m*

sale *n* venta *f*; **for** ~ se vende; **on** ~ de rebaja — **salesman** *n* (**-men**) vendedor *m*, dependiente *m* — **saleswoman** *n* (**-women**) vendedora *f*, dependienta *f*

saliva *n* saliva *f*

salt *n* sal *f* — **salt** *v* salar — **salty** *adj* salado

salvage *n* salvamento *m* — **salvage** *v* salvar

salvation *n* salvación *f*

same *adj* mismo; **be the** ~ **(as)** ser igual (que); **the** ~ **thing (as)** la misma cosa (que) — **same** *pron* **the same** lo mismo

sample *n* muestra *f*

sand *n* arena *f* — **sand** *v* lijar (madera) — **sandy** *adj* arenoso

sandal *n* sandalia *f*

sandwich *n* sandwich *m*, bocadillo *m*

sane *adj* cuerdo

sanitary *adj* sanitario; higiénico — **sanitary napkin** *n* compresa *f* (higiénica) — **sanitation** *n* sanidad *f*

Santa Claus *n* Papá *m* Noel

satellite *n* satélite *m*

satire *n* sátira *f* — **satiric** *or* **satirical** *adj* satírico

satisfaction *n* satisfacción *f* — **satisfactory** *adj* satisfactorio — **satisfy** *v* (**-fied**) satisfacer — **satisfying** *adj* satisfactorio

Saturday *n* sábado *m*

Saturn *n* Saturno *m*

sauce *n* salsa *f* — **saucepan** *n* cacerola *f* — **saucer** *n* platillo *m*

sauna *n* sauna *mf*

sausage *n* salchicha *f*

savage *adj* salvaje, feroz — **savage** *n* salvaje *mf*

save *v* salvar; guardar; ahorrar (dinero, tiempo, etc.) — **save** *prep* salvo

saw *n* sierra *f*

say *v* (**said**) decir; marcar (de relojes, etc.); **that is to ～** es decir — **saying** *n* refrán *m*

scale *v* escalar

scan *v* escanear (en informática)

scandal *n* escándalo *m*; habladurías *fpl*

Scandinavian *adj* escandinavo

scar *n* cicatriz *f*

scarce *adj* escaso — **scarcely** *adv* apenas — **scarcity** *n* escasez *f*

scare *v* asustar; **be ～d of** tener miedo a — **scare** *n* susto *m*; pánico *m* — **scary** *adj* que da miedo

scarf *n* (**scarves**) *or* **scarfs** bufanda *f*; pañuelo *m*

scene *n* escena *f* — **scenery** *n* decorado *m*; paisaje *m* — **scenic** *adj* pintoresco

schedule *n* programa *m*; horario *m* — **schedule** *v* planear, programar

scheme *n* plan *m*; esquema *f*

scholar *n* erudito *m*, -ta *f* — **scholarship** *n* beca *f*

school *n* escuela *f*

science *n* ciencia *f* — **scientific** *adj* científico — **scientist** *n* científico *m*, -ca *f*

scissors *npl* tijeras *fpl*

scoop *n* pala *f*

scoot *v* ir rápidamente — **scooter** *n* patinete *m*; *or* **motor scooter** escúter *m*

scope *n* alcance *m*; posibilidades *fpl*

score *n* (**scores**) puntuación *f*; resultado *m* — **score** *v* marcar, anotarse (un tanto); sacar (una nota); marcar (en deportes)

Scot *n* escocés *m*, -cesa *f* — **Scottish** *adj* escocés

scout *n* explorador *m*, -dora *f*

scramble *v* trepar; **～ for** pelearse por; mezclar — **scrambled eggs** *npl* huevos *mpl* revueltos

scrap *n* pedazo *m*

scrape *v* rascar; rasparse (la rodilla, etc.); *or* **～ off** raspar; **～ together** reunir — **scrape** *n* rasguño *m*

scratch *v* arañar; rayar; rascarse (la cabeza, etc.); **～ out** tachar — **scratch** *n* arañazo *m*

scream *v* gritar, chillar — **scream** *n* grito *m*, chillido *m*

screen *n* pantalla *f*

screw *n* tornillo *m* — **screw** *v* atornillar

script *n* escritura *f*; guión *m* (de cine, etc.)

scuff *v* raspar, rayar

sculpture *n* escultura *f*

sea *n* mar *mf* — **seafood** *n* mariscos *mpl* — **seagull** *n* gaviota *f* — **seashell** *n* concha *f* (marina) — **seashore** *n* orilla *f* del mar — **seasick** *adj* mareado; **be**

seasick marearse — **seasickness** *n* mareo *m*

seal[1] *n* foca *f* (animal)

seal[2] *n* sello *m*

search *v* registrar; ∼ **for** buscar — **search** *n* búsqueda *f*

season *n* estación *f* (del año) — **seasoning** *n* condimento *m*

seat *n* asiento *m* — **seat** *v* **be seated** sentarse — **seat belt** *n* cinturón *m* de seguridad

second *adj* segundo — **second** *or* **secondly** *adv* en segundo lugar — **second** *n* segundo *m*, -da *f*; segundo *m* — **secondary** *adj* secundario — **secondhand** *adj* de segunda mano

secret *adj* secreto — **secret** *n* secreto *m*

secretary *n* (**-taries**) secretario *m*, -ria *f*; ministro *m*, -tra *f* (del gobierno)

secretly *adv* en secreto

sect *n* secta *f*

section *n* sección *f*, parte *f*

sector *n* sector *m*

security *n* (**-ties**) seguridad *f*; garantía *f* — **secure** *adj* seguro — **secure** *v* asegurar

see *v* (**saw; seen**) ver; entender; ∼ **you later!** ¡hasta luego!

seed *n* semilla *f*; germen *m*

seek *v* (**sought**) *or* ∼ **out** buscar; pedir

seem *v* parecer

segregate *v* segregar — **segregation** *n* segregación *f*

seldom *adv* pocas veces, raramente

select *adj* selecto — **select** *v* seleccionar — **selection** *n* selección *f* — **selective** *adj* selectivo

self *n* (**selves**) ser *m* — **selfish** *adj* egoísta — **selfishness** *n* egoísmo *m* — **selfless** *adj* desinteresado — **self–service** *adj* de autoservicio

sell *v* (**sold**) vender(se) — **seller** *n* vendedor *m*, -dora *f*

semester *n* semestre *m*

semicolon *n* punto y coma *m*

semifinal *n* semifinal *f*

seminar *n* seminario *m*

senate *n* senado *m* — **senator** *n* senador *m*, -dora *f*

send *v* (**sent**) mandar, enviar; ∼ **away for** pedir; ∼ **back** devolver (mercancías, etc.); ∼ **for** mandar a buscar — **sender** *n* remitente *mf*

senior *n* superior *m*; estudiante *mf* de último año (en educación); *or* ∼ **citizen** persona *f* mayor

sensation *n* sensación *f* — **sensational** *adj* sensacional

sense *n* sentido *m*; sensación *f* — **sense** *v* sentir — **senseless** *adj* sin sentido; inconsciente — **sensible** *adj* sensato, práctico — **sensibility** *n* sensibilidad *f* — **sensitive** *adj* sensible; susceptible — **sensitivity** *n* sensibilidad *f* — **sensual** *adj* sensual

sentence *n* frase *f*; sentencia *f* — **sentence** *v* sentenciar

sentiment *n* sentimiento *m*; opinión *f* — **sentimental** *adj* sentimental — **sentimentality** *n* sentimentalismo *m*

separation *n* separación *f* — **separate** *v* separar(se); distinguir — **separate** *adj* separado; aparte

September *n* septiembre *m*

sequence *n* orden *m*; secuencia *f* (de números o escenas)

Serb *or* **Serbian** *adj* serbio

serene *adj* sereno — **serenity** *n* serenidad *f*

sergeant *n* sargento *mf*

series *n* (**series**) serie *f*

serious *adj* serio — **seriously** *adv* seriamente

sermon *n* sermón *m*

serve *v* servir — **server** *n* camarero *m*, -ra *f*; servidor *m* (en informática) — **serving** *n* porción *f*, ración *f*

service *n* servicio *m*; **armed** ∼**s** fuerzas *fpl* armadas — **service** *v* revisar (un vehículo, etc.) — **service station** *n* estación *f* de servicio

session *n* sesión *f*

set *v* (**set**) **setting** *v or* ⌐ **down** poner; ⌐ **up** montar, armar; ⌐ **up** establecer; ponerse (del sol, etc.); ⌐ **in** empezar — **set** *n* juego *m* (de platos, etc.); set *m* (en tenis, etc.) — **setting** *n* escenario *m*

settle *v* asentarse (de polvo, colonos, etc.); fijar, decidir; resolver; calmar; ⌐ **down** calmarse; ⌐ **in** instalarse — **settlement** *n* pago *m*; colonia *f*, poblado *m*; acuerdo *m*

seven *adj* siete — **seven** *n* siete *m* — **seven hundred** *adj* setecientos — **seventeen** *adj* diecisiete — **seventeenth** *adj* decimoséptimo — **seventh** *adj* séptimo — **seventieth** *adj* septuagésimo — **seventy** *adj* setenta — **seventy** *n* (**-ties**) setenta *m*

several *adj* varios — **several** *pron* varios, varias

sew *v* (**sewed; sewn** *or* **sewed**) coser

sewing *n* costura *f*

sex *n* sexo *m* — **sexism** *n* sexismo *m*

shade *n* sombra *f*; *or* **window** ⌐ persiana *f* — **shade** *v* proteger de la luz — **shadow** *n* sombra *f*

shake *v* (**shook; shaken**) sacudir; agitar; ⌐ **hands with** dar la mano a; temblar — **shake** *n* sacudida *f* — **shaker** *n*; **salt shaker** salero *m*; **pepper shaker** pimentero *m* — **shaky** *adj* tembloroso

shame *n* vergüenza *f*; **what a** ⌐! ¡qué lástima! — **shame** *v* avergonzar — **shameful** *adj* vergonzoso — **shameless** *adj* desvergonzado

shampoo *v* lavar (el pelo) — **shampoo** *n* (**-poos**) champú *m*

shape *v* formar; **be** ⌐**d like** tener forma de; *or* ⌐ **up** tomar forma — **shape** *n* forma *f*

share *n* porción *f* — **share** *v* compartir; dividir

shark *n* tiburón *m*

sharp *adj* afilado; puntiagudo; agudo — **sharp** *adv* **at two o'clock sharp** a las dos en punto — **sharpen** *v* afilar (un cuchillo, etc.), sacar punta a (un lápiz) — **sharpener** *n or* **pencil sharpener** sacapuntas *m*

shave *v* (**shaved; shaved** *or* **shaven**) afeitar(se); cortar — **shave** *n* afeitada *f* — **shaver** *n* máquina *f* de afeitar

she *pron* ella

sheet *n* sábana *f* (de la cama); hoja *f* (de papel)

shelf *n* (**shelves**) estante *m*

shell *n* concha *f*; caparazón *m* (de un crustáceo, etc.); cáscara *f* (de un huevo, etc.) — **shell** *v* pelar (nueces, etc.)

shepherd *n* pastor *m* — **shepherd** *v* conducir, guiar

shield *n* escudo *m* — **shield** *v* proteger

shift *v* cambiar; mover(se) — **shift** *n* cambio *m*; turno *m* (de trabajo) — **shifty** *adj* sospechoso

shimmer *v* brillar, relucir

shin *n* espinilla *f*

shine *v* (**shone** *or* **shined**) brillar; alumbrar (una luz) — **shine** *n* brillo *m* — **shiny** *adj* brillante

ship *n* barco *m*, buque *m*; ⌐ *v* transportar, enviar (por barco) — **shipbuilding** *n* construcción *f* naval — **shipment** *n* envío *m* — **shipping** *n* transporte *m*; barcos *mpl*

shirt *n* camisa *f*

shiver *v* temblar (del frío, etc.) — **shiver** *n* escalofrío *m*

shock *n* choque *m*; golpe *m* emocional; shock *m* (en medicina)

shoe *n* zapato *m* — **shoelace** *n* cordón *m* (de zapato) — **shoemaker** *n* zapatero *m*, -ra *f*

shoot *v* (**shot**) disparar (en deportes, caza, etc.)

shop *n* tienda *f*; taller *m* — **shop** *v* hacer compras; **go shopping** ir de compras — **shopkeeper** *n* tendero *m*, -ra *f* — **shopper** *n* comprador *m*, -dora *f*

shore *n* orilla *f*

short *adj* corto; bajo (de estatura); brusco; **a** ⌐ **time ago** hace poco —

shortcake *n* tarta *f* de fruta — **short-coming** *n* defecto *m* — **shorten** *v* acortar — **shortly** *adv* dentro de poco — **shortness** *n* lo corto (de una cosa), baja estatura *f* (de una persona) — **shorts** *npl* shorts *mpl*, pantalones *mpl* cortos

shot *n* disparo *m*, tiro *m* — **shotgun** *n* escopeta *f*

shoulder *n* hombro *m* — **shoulder blade** *n* omóplato *m*

shout *v* gritar — **shout** *n* grito *m*

shove *v* empujar — **shove** *n* empujón *m*

shovel *n* pala *f*

show *v* (**showed; shown** *or* **showed**) mostrar; enseñar; demostrar; proyectar (una película), dar (un programa de televisión); ~ **off** hacer alarde de; notarse, verse; lucirse; ~ **up** aparecer — **show** *n* demostración *f*; exposición *f*; espectáculo *m* (teatral), programa *m* (de televisión, etc.)

shower *n* ducha *f*; fiesta *f* — **shower** *v* regar; ducharse

shrink *v* (**shrank; shrunk** *or* **shrunken**) encoger(se) (de ropa), reducirse (de números, etc.); *or* ~ **back** retroceder

shrivel *v or* ~ **up** arrugarse, marchitarse

shuffle *v* barajar (naipes), revolver (papeles, etc.); caminar arrastrando los pies

shun *v* evitar, esquivar

shut *v* (**shut**) cerrar; ~ **up** encerrar; *or* ~ **down** cerrarse; ~ **up!** ¡cállate!

shy *adj* tímido — **shyness** *n* timidez *f*

sick *adj* enfermo

side *n* lado *m*; ~ **by** ~ uno al lado de otro — **sidewalk** *n* acera *f* — **sideways** *adj & adv* de lado

sigh *v* suspirar — **sigh** *n* suspiro *m*

sight *n* vista *f*; espectáculo *m*; lugar *m* de interés (turístico)

sign *n* signo *m*; letrero *m*; seña *f*, señal *f* — **sign** *v* firmar (un cheque, etc.)

signal *n* señal *f* — **signal** *v* hacer señas a; señalar; señalizar (en un vehículo)

signature *n* firma *f*

significance *n* significado *m*; importancia *f* — **significant** *adj* importante — **signify** *v* (**-fied**) significar

silence *n* silencio *m* — **silence** *v* silenciar — **silent** *adj* silencioso; callado

silk *n* seda *f* — **silky** *adj* sedoso

silly *adj* tonto, estúpido

silver *n* plata *f* — **silverware** *n* plata *f* — **silvery** *adj* plateado

similar *adj* similar, parecido — **similarity** *n* (**-ties**) semejanza *f*, parecido *m*

simple *adj* simple; sencillo — **simplicity** *n* simplicidad *f*, sencillez *f* — **simplify** *v* (**-fied**) simplificar — **simply** *adv* sencillamente; realmente

simultaneous *adj* simultáneo

sin *n* pecado *m* — **sin** *v* pecar

since *adv or* ~ **then** desde entonces — **since** *conj*; desde que; ya que, como — **since** *prep* desde

sincere *adj* sincero — **sincerely** *adv* sinceramente — **sincerity** *n* sinceridad *f*

sing *v* (**sang** *or* **sung; sung**) cantar

singer *n* cantante *mf*

single *adj* solo, único; soltero — **single** *n* soltero *m*, -ra *f*; *or* **single room** habitación *f* individual — **single** *v* **single out** escoger; señalar

singular *adj* singular — **singular** *n* singular *m*

sink *v* (**sank** *or* **sunk; sunk**) hundir(se) (en un líquido); bajar, caer — **sink** *n or* **kitchen sink** fregadero *m*; *or* **bathroom sink** lavabo *m*, lavamanos *m*

sinner *n* pecador *m*, -dora *f*

sir *n* sir *m* (en un título); señor *m* (tratamiento)

sister *n* hermana *f* — **sister–in–law** *n* (**sisters–** . . .) cuñada *f*

sit *v* (**sat**) *or* ~ **down** sentar(se); estar (ubicado)

site *n* sitio *m*, lugar *m*

situation *n* situación *f*

six *adj* seis — **six** *n* seis *m* — **six hundred** *adj* seiscientos — **sixteen** *adj* dieciséis — **sixteenth** *adj* decimosexto — **sixth** *adj* sexto — **sixtieth** *adj* sexagésimo — **sixtieth** *n* sexagésimo *m*, -ma *f* (en una serie) — **sixty** *adj* sesenta — **sixty** *n* (**-ties**) sesenta *m*

size *n* tamaño *m*, talla *f* (de ropa), número *m* (de zapatos); magnitud *f* — **size** *v* **size up** evaluar

skate *n* patín *m* — **skate** *v* patinar — **skateboard** *n* monopatín *m* — **skater** *n* patinador *m*, -dora *f*

skeleton *n* esqueleto *m*

sketch *n* esbozo *m*, bosquejo *m* — **sketch** *v* bosquejar

ski *n* (**skis**) esquí *m* — **ski** *v* esquiar — **skier** *n* esquiador *m*, -dora *f*

skill *n* habilidad *f*, destreza *f*; técnica *f* — **skilled** *adj* hábil

skillful *adj* hábil, diestro

skin *n* piel *f* — **skin** *v* despellejar — **skinny** *adj* flaco

skip *v* ir brincando; saltarse — **skip** *n* brinco *m*, salto *m*

skirt *n* falda *f*

skull *n* cráneo *m* (de una persona viva), calavera *f* (de un esqueleto)

sky *n* (**skies**) cielo *m* — **skylight** *n* claraboya *f*, tragaluz *m* — **skyline** *n* horizonte *m*

slacks *npl* pantalones *mpl*

slap *v* dar una bofetada a — **slap** *n* bofetada *f*, cachetada *f*

Slavic *adj* eslavo

sled *n* trineo *m*

sleep *n* sueño *m*; **go to ~** dormirse — **sleep** *v* (**slept**) dormir — **sleepy** *adj* somnoliento, soñoliento

sleeve *n* manga *f* — **sleeveless** *adj* sin mangas

slender *adj* delgado

slice *v* cortar — **slice** *n* trozo *m*, rebanada *f* (de pan, etc.), tajada *f* (de carne)

slide *v* (**slid**) deslizarse — **slide** *n* deslizamiento *m*; tobogán *m* (para niños); diapositiva *f* (fotográfica)

slight *adj* ligero, leve; delgado — **slightly** *adv* ligeramente, un poco

slim *adj* delgado — **slim** *v* adelgazar

slip *v* resbalarse; deslizar — **slip** *n* error *m*, desliz *m*

slipper *n* zapatilla *f*, pantufla *f*

slit *n* rendija *f*; corte *m*, raja *f* — **slit** *v* (**slit**) cortar

slot *n* ranura *f*

slow *adj* lento; **be ~** estar atrasado (de un reloj) — **slow** *v* retrasar, retardar; *or* **slow down** ir más despacio — **slowly** *adv* lentamente, despacio — **slowness** *n* lentitud *f*

small *adj* pequeño, chico

smart *adj* listo, inteligente; elegante — **smartly** *adv* elegantemente

smash *n* golpe *m*; choque *m* — **smash** *v* romper; aplastar; hacerse pedazos; **smash into** estrellarse contra

smell *v* (**smelled** *or* **smelt**) oler — **smell** *n* (sentido *m* del) olfato *m*; olor *m* — **smelly** *adj* maloliente

smile *v* sonreír — **smile** *n* sonrisa *f*

smoke *n* humo *m* — **smoke** *v* fumar — **smoker** *n* fumador *m*, -dora *f*

smooth *adj* liso (de superficies), suave (de movimientos), tranquilo (del mar) — **smooth** *v* alisar — **smoothly** *adv* suavemente — **smoothness** *n* suavidad *f*

snack *n* refrigerio *m*, tentempié *m*

snake *n* culebra *f*, serpiente *f*

snappy *adj* rápido; elegante

snarl *v* gruñir — **snarl** *n* gruñido *m*

sneakers *npl* tenis *mpl*, zapatillas *fpl*

sneaky *adj* solapado

sneeze *v* estornudar — **sneeze** *n* estornudo *m*

sniff *v* oler

snoop *v* husmear — **snoop** *n* fisgón *m*, -gona *f*

snooze v dormitar — **snooze** n siestecita f, siestita f

snore v roncar — **snore** n ronquido m

snow n nieve f — **snow** v nevar — **snowfall** n nevada f — **snowman** n muñeco m de nieve — **snowplow** n quitanieves m — **snowstorm** n tormenta f de nieve — **snowy** adj **a snowy day** un día nevoso

so adv también; así; por lo tanto; or ~ **much** tanto; or ~ **very** tan; **and** ~ **on** etcétera; **I think** ~ creo que sí — **so** conj; así que; or **so that** para que; **so what?** ¿y qué? — **so** adj cierto — **so** pron **or so** más o menos

soap n jabón m

soccer n fútbol m

social adj social — **social** n reunión f social — **sociable** adj sociable — **society** n (-eties) sociedad f — **sociology** n sociología f

sock n (**socks**) calcetín m

socket n or **electric** ~ enchufe m, toma f de corriente

soda n or ~ **pop** refresco m, gaseosa f; or ~ **water** soda f

sofa n sofá m

soft adj blando; suave — **softball** n softbol m — **soft drink** n refresco m — **soften** v ablandar(se); suavizar(se) — **softly** adv suavemente — **software** n software m

soggy adj empapado

soil v ensuciar — **soil** n tierra f

solar adj solar

soldier n soldado mf

sole[1] n planta f (del pie), suela f (de un zapato)

sole[2] adj único — **solely** adv únicamente, sólo

solid adj — **solid** n sólido m

solitary adj solitario — **solitude** n soledad f

solo n (**solos**) solo m

solution n solución f — **soluble** adj soluble — **solve** v resolver

some adj un; algo de, un poco de; unos; algunos — **some** pron algunos, unos; un poco, algo — **somebody** pron alguien — **someday** adv algún día — **somehow** adv de algún modo; **somehow or other** de alguna manera u otra — **someone** pron alguien

something pron algo; ~ **else** otra cosa — **sometime** adv algún día, en algún momento — **sometimes** adv a veces — **somewhat** adv algo — **somewhere** adv en alguna parte, en algún lado; **somewhere around** alrededor de

son n hijo m

song n canción f

son-in-law n (**sons-** . . .) yerno m

soon adv pronto; dentro de poco; **as** ~ **as** en cuanto; **as** ~ **as possible** lo más pronto posible

soothe v calmar

sophomore n estudiante mf de segundo año

sore adj ~ **throat** dolor m de garganta — **sore** n llaga f — **sorely** adv muchísimo

sorry adj lamentable; **feel** ~ **for** compadecer; **I'm** ~ lo siento — **sorrow** n pesar m, pena f

sort n tipo m, clase f; **a** ~ **of** una especie de — **of a** ~ de alguna clase — **sort** v clasificar — **sort of** adv algo; más o menos

SOS n SOS m

so-so adj or adv así así

soul n alma f

sound n sonido m — **sound** v hacer sonar, tocar (una trompeta, etc.); sonar; parecer

soundly adv sólidamente; profundamente

soup n sopa f

sour adj agrio

source n fuente f, origen m

south adv al sur — **south** adj (del) sur — **south** n sur m — **South African**

adj sudafricano — **South American** *adj* sudamericano — **southerly** *adv or adj* del sur — **southern** *adj* del sur, meridional

souvenir *n* recuerdo *m*

space *n* espacio *m*; sitio *m*, lugar *m* — **space** *v* espaciar — **spaceship** *n* nave *f* espacial

spaghetti *n* espaguetis *mpl*

Spaniard *n* español *m*, -ñola *f*

Spanish *adj* español — **Spanish** *n* español *m* (idioma)

spark *n* chispa *f* — **spark** *v* chispear, echar chispas; despertar (interés), provocar (crítica) — **sparkle** *v* destellar, centellear — **sparkle** *n* destello *m*, centelleo *m*

speak *v* (**spoke; spoken**) hablar; hablar (un idioma); decir; ~ **out against** denunciar; ~ **up** hablar más alto; ~ **up for** defender — **speaker** *n* orador *m*, -dora *f*; hablante *mf* (de un idioma); altavoz *m*

special *adj* especial — **specialist** *n* especialista *mf* — **specialization** *n* especialización *f* — **specialize** *v* especializarse — **specially** *adv* especialmente — **specialty** *n* (**-ties**) especialidad *f*

species *ns & pl* especie *f*

specify *v* (**-fied**) especificar — **specific** *adj* específico — **specifically** *adv* específicamente; expresamente — **specification** *n* especificación *f*

spectacle *n* espectáculo *m* — **spectacular** *adj* espectacular

speech *n* habla *f*; discurso *m*

speed *n* rapidez *f*; velocidad *f* — **speed** *v* (**sped** *or* **speeded**) conducir a exceso de velocidad; *or* **speed up** acelerar — **speed limit** *n* velocidad *f* máxima — **speedy** *adj* **speedier, -est** rápido

spell *v* escribir (las letras de); *or* ~ **out** deletrear; significar

spelling *n* ortografía *f*

spend *v* (**spent**) gastar (dinero); pasar (las vacaciones, etc.); ~ **time on** dedicar tiempo a

spice *n* especia *f* — **spice** *v* condimentar, sazonar — **spicy** *adj* picante

spider *n* araña *f*

spill *v* derramar(se)

spin *v* (**spun**) girar; hilar (lana, etc.) — **spin** *n* vuelta *f*, giro *m*

spinach *n* espinacas *fpl*

spine *n* columna *f* vertebral; espina *f*

spiral *adj* de espiral, en espiral

spirit *n* espíritu *m* — **spiritual** *adj* espiritual — **spirituality** *n* (**-ties**) espiritualidad *f*

spite *n* **in** ~ **of** a pesar de — **spite** *v* fastidiar

splash *v* salpicar — *n* salpicadura *f*; mancha *f* (de color, etc.)

splendor *n* esplendor *m* — **splendid** *adj* espléndido

split *v* (**split**) partir; *or* ~ **up** dividir(se); partirse, rajarse

spoil *v* estropear; consentir, mimar

sponge *n* esponja *f*

sponsor *n* patrocinador *m*, -dora *f* — **sponsor** *v* patrocinar — **sponsorship** *n* patrocinio *m*

spontaneous *adj* espontáneo

spoon *n* cuchara *f* — **spoonful** *n* cucharada *f*

sport *n* deporte *m* — **sportsman** *n* (**-men**) deportista *m* — **sportswoman** *n* (**-women**) deportista *f* — **sporty** *adj* deportivo

spot *n* mancha *f*; punto *m*; lugar *m*, sitio *m*; **in a tight** ~ en apuros — **spot** *v* manchar; ver, descubrir — **spotless** *adj* impecable — **spotlight** *n* foco *m*, reflector *m*; **be in the spotlight** ser el centro de atención

spouse *n* cónyuge *mf*

spray[1] *n* ramillete *m*

spray[2] *n* rocío *m*; *or* **aerosol** ~ **spray** *m*; *or* ~ **bottle** atomizador *m* — **spray**

v rociar (una superficie), pulverizar (un líquido)

spread *v* (**spread**) propagar(se) (enfermedades), difundir(se) (noticias, etc.); *or* ~ **out** extender(se); untar (con mantequilla, etc.) — **spread** *n* propagación *f*, difusión *f*; extensión

spring *v* (**sprang** *or* **sprung; sprung**) saltar; ~ **from** surgir de — **spring** *n* manantial *m* (de aguas); primavera *f* (estación); salto *m*; elasticidad *f* — **springtime** *n* primavera *f* — **springy** *adj* mullido

sprinkle *v* salpicar, rociar; espolvorear — **sprinkle** *n* llovizna *f*

sprint *v* correr

sprout *v* brotar

spy *v* (**spied**) ver, divisar; ~ **on** espiar a — **spy** *n* espía *mf*

squadron *n* escuadrón *m* (de soldados), escuadra *f* (de aviones o naves)

square *n* cuadrado *m*; plaza *f* (de una ciudad) — **square** *adj* cuadrado — **square root** *n* raíz *f* cuadrada

squeak *v* chillar — **squeak** *n* chillido *m*

squeeze *v* apretar; exprimir (frutas, etc.); extraer (jugo, etc.) — **squeeze** *n* apretón *m*

squirrel *n* ardilla *f*

stab *n* puñalada *f*

stable *n* establo *m* (para ganado) — **stable** *adj* estable — **stability** *n* estabilidad *f* — **stabilize** *v* estabilizar

stadium *n* (**-dia** *or* **-diums**) estadio *m*

staff *n* (**staffs** *or* **staves**) bastón *m*; (**staffs**) personal *m* — **staff** *v* proveer de personal

stage *n* escenario *m* (de un teatro); etapa *f* — **stage** *v* poner en escena

stagger *v* tambalearse — **stagger** *n* tambaleo *m*

stair *n* escalón *m*, peldaño *m*; ~**s** *npl* escalera(s) *f(pl)* — **staircase** *n* escalera(s) *f(pl)* — **stairway** *n* escalera(s) *f(pl)*

stalk *n* tallo *m* (de una planta)

stamp *n* timbre *m*; *or* **postage** ~ sello *m*, estampilla *f* — **stamp** *v* franquear (una carta); sellar

stand *v* (**stood**) estar de pie, estar parado; estar; seguir vigente; reposar; ~ **aside** *or* ~ **back** apartarse; ~ **out** sobresalir; *or* ~ **up** ponerse de pie, pararse; poner, colocar; soportar — **stand** *n* puesto *m*; posición *f*; **stands** *npl* tribuna *f* — **stand by** *v* mantener (una promesa, etc.) — **stand up** *v* **stand up for** defender

standard *n* norma *f*; criterio *m*; ~ **of living** nivel *m* de vida — **standard** *adj* estándar — **standardize** *v* estandarizar

standing *n* posición *f*

standpoint *n* punto *m* de vista

star *n* estrella *f* — **star** *v* estar protagonizado por; **star in** protagonizar

stare *v* mirar fijamente — **stare** *n* mirada *f* fija

starlight *n* luz *f* de las estrellas

starry *adj* estrellado

start *v* empezar, comenzar; salir; *or* ~ **up** arrancar; empezar, comenzar; provocar; *or* ~ **up** montar; *or* ~ **up** arrancar (un motor, etc.) — **start** *n* principio *m*

starve *v* morirse de hambre; privar de comida — **starvation** *n* inanición *f*, hambre *f*

state *n* estado *m*; **the States** los Estados Unidos — **state** *v* decir; exponer — **statement** *n* declaración *f*; *or* **bank statement** estado *m* de cuenta — **statesman** *n* (**-men**) estadista *mf*

station *n* estación *f* (de trenes, etc.); condición *f* (social); canal *m* (de televisión), emisora *f* (de radio)

statistic *n* estadística *f*

statue *n* estatua *f*

stature *n* estatura *f*, talla *f*

status *n* situación *f*; *or* **social** ~ estatus *m*; **marital** ~ estado *m* civil

stay *v* quedarse, permanecer; alojarse; ~ **awake** mantenerse despierto; ~ **in**

quedarse en casa — **stay** n estancia f, estadía f; suspensión f

steady adj firme, seguro; fijo; responsable; constante — **steady** v (**steadied**) mantener firme; calmar (los nervios) — **steadily** adv progresivamente; sin parar; fijamente

steak n bistec m, filete m

steal v (**stole; stolen**) robar

steam n vapor m — **steam** v echar vapor; cocer al vapor; **steam up** empañar

steel n acero m

steering wheel n volante

stem[1] n tallo m (de una planta), pie m (de una copa)

stem[2] v contener, detener

step n paso m; escalón m; ～ **by** ～ paso por paso; **take** ～**s** tomar medidas — **step** v dar un paso; **step back** retroceder; **step down** retirarse — **step up** v aumentar

stepbrother n hermanastro m — **stepdaughter** n hijastra f — **stepfather** n padrastro m — **stepmother** n madrastra f — **stepsister** n hermanastra f — **stepson** n hijastro m

stereo n (**stereos**) estéreo m — **stereo** adj estéreo

sterile adj estéril — **sterility** n esterilidad f — **sterilization** n esterilización f — **sterilize** v esterilizar

stern adj severo, adusto

stew n estofado m, guiso m — **stew** v estofar, guisar; cocer; preocuparse

stick[1] n palo m; bastón m

stick[2] v (**stuck**) pegar; clavar; poner; ～ **out** sacar (la lengua, etc.) — **sticky** adj pegajoso

stiff adj rígido, tieso; forzado

stigmatize v estigmatizar

still adj inmóvil; callado — **still** adv todavía, aún; de todos modos, aún así

stimulate v estimular — **stimulant** n estimulante m — **stimulation** n estimulación f — **stimulus** n (**-li**) estímulo m

sting v (**stung**) picar — **sting** n picadura f

stingy adj tacaño — **stinginess** n tacañería f

stink v (**stank** or **stunk; stunk**) apestar, oler mal — **stink** n hedor m, peste f

stir v remover, revolver; mover; incitar

stitch n puntada f — **stitch** v coser

stock n existencias fpl; acciones fpl; **out of** ～ agotado; **take** ～ **of** evaluar — **stock** v surtir, abastecer; **stock up on** abastecerse de

stocking n media f

stocky adj robusto, fornido

stomach n estómago m — **stomachache** n dolor m de estómago

stone n piedra f; hueso m (de una fruta), pepa — **stony** adj pedregoso

stop v tapar; impedir; parar, detener(se); dejar de — **stop** n parada f, alto m; **put a stop to** poner fin a — **stoplight** n semáforo m — **stoppage** n or **work stoppage** paro m

store v guardar (comida, etc.), almacenar (datos, mercancías, etc.) — **store** n reserva f; tienda f — **storage** n almacenamiento m — **storehouse** n almacén m — **storekeeper** n tendero m, -ra f

storm n tormenta f, tempestad f — **storm** v asaltar — **stormy** adj tormentoso

story n (**stories**) cuento m; historia f

stove n estufa f (para calentar); cocina f

straight adj recto, derecho; lacio (del pelo) — **straight** adv derecho — **straightaway** adv inmediatamente — **straightforward** adj franco; claro, sencillo

strain v forzar (la vista o la voz); ～ **a muscle** sufrir un esguince — **strain** n tensión f; esguince m

strand n hebra f

strange adj extraño, raro; desconocido — **strangely** adv de manera extraña — **stranger** n desconocido m, -da f

strap n correa f; or **shoulder** ～ tirante

m — **strap** *v* sujetar con una correa — **strapless** *n* sin tirantes

strategy *n* (**-gies**) estrategia *f* — **strategic** *adj* estratégico

strawberry *n* (**-ries**) fresa *f*

stream *n* arroyo *m*, riachuelo *m*; chorro *m*, corriente *f* — **stream** *v* correr

street *n* calle *f* — **streetlight** *n* farol *m*

strength *n* fuerza *f*; fortaleza *f*; resistencia *f*, solidez *f*; intensidad *f* — **strengthen** *v* fortalecer; reforzar

stress *n* tensión *f*; acento *m* (en lingüística) — **stress** *v* enfatizar; *or* **stress out** estresar — **stressful** *adj* estresante

stretch *v* estirar(se) (músculos, elástico, etc.); extender(se)

strict *adj* estricto — **strictly** *adv* **strictly speaking** en rigor

strike *v* (**struck**) **struck; striking** *v* golpear; *or* ~ **against** chocar contra; *or* ~ **out** tachar; dar (la hora); golpear; atacar; declararse en huelga — **strike** *n* golpe *m*; huelga *f*, paro *m* (de trabajadores); ataque *m* — **striker** *n* huelgista *mf*

string *n* cordel *m*; sarta *f* (de perlas, insultos, etc.), serie *f* (de eventos, etc.); ~**s** *npl* cuerdas *fpl* (en música)

strip[1] *v* quitar; desnudar

strip[2] *n* tira *f*

stripe *n* raya *f*, lista *f* — **striped** *adj* a rayas, rayado

stroke *v* acariciar

stroll *v* pasearse — **stroll** *n* paseo *m* — **stroller** *n* cochecito *m* (para niños)

strong *adj* fuerte — **strongly** *adv* profundamente; totalmente; enérgicamente

structure *n* estructura *f*

struggle *v* forcejear; luchar — **struggle** *n* lucha *f*

stubborn *adj* terco, obstinado

student *n* estudiante *mf;* alumno *m*, -na *f* (de un colegio) — **study** *n* (**studies**) estudio *m* — **study** *v* (**studied**) estudiar

stuff *n* cosas *fpl*; cosa *f* — **stuff** *v* re-

llenar; meter — **stuffing** *n* relleno *m* — **stuffy** *adj* pesado, aburrido

stumble *v* tropezar

stupid *adj* estúpido — **stupidity** *n* tontería *f*, estupidez *f*

style *n* estilo *m*; moda *f*; **be in** ~ estar de moda — **style** *v* peinar (pelo), diseñar (vestidos, etc.) — **stylist** *n* estilista *mf*

subconscious *adj* subconsciente — **subconscious** *n* subconsciente *m*

subject *n* sujeto *m*; tema *m* — **subjective** *adj* subjetivo

subordinate *adj* subordinado — **subordinate** *n* subordinado *m*, -da *f* — **subordinate** *v* subordinar

subscribe *v* ~ **to** suscribirse a (una revista, etc.), suscribir (una opinión, etc.) — **subscriber** *n* suscriptor *m*, -tora *f* (de una revista, etc.); abonado *m*, -da *f* (de un servicio) — **subscription** *n* suscripción *f*

substance *n* sustancia *f*

substitute *n* sustituto *m*, -ta *f* (de una persona); sucedáneo *m* (de una cosa) — **substitute** *v* sustituir — **substitution** *n* sustitución *f*

subterranean *adj* subterráneo

subtitle *n* subtítulo *m*

subtle *adj* sutil — **subtlety** *n* (**-ties**) sutileza *f*

subtraction *n* resta *f* — **subtract** *v* restar

suburb *n* barrio *m* residencial, suburbio *m*; **the** ~**s** las afueras

subway *n* metro *m*

succeed *v* tener éxito (de personas), dar resultado (de planes, etc.) — **success** *n* éxito *m* — **successfully** *adv* con éxito

such *adj* tal; ~ **as** como — **such** *pron* tal; **and such** y cosas por el estilo; **as such** como tal — **such** *adv* muy

suck *v* *or* ~ **on** chupar — **sucker** *n* chupón *m* — **suction** *n* succión *f*

sudden *adj* repentino — **suddenly** *adv* de repente

suffer *v* sufrir; tolerar — **suffering** *n* sufrimiento *m*

sufficient *adj* suficiente — **sufficiently** *adv* (lo) suficientemente

sugar *n* azúcar *mf* — **sugary** *adj* azucarado

suggestion *n* sugerencia *f*; indicio *m* — **suggest** *v* sugerir; indicar

suicide *n* suicidio *m* (acto); suicida *mf* (persona)

suit *n* traje *m* (ropa) — **suit** *v* adaptar; ser apropiado para; convenir a (de fechas, etc.), quedar bien a (de ropa) — **suitable** *adj* apropiado — **suitcase** *n* maleta *f*, valija *f*

suite *n* suite *f* (de habitaciones); juego *m* (de muebles)

sulky *adj* malhumorado

sum *n* suma *f* — **sum** *v* **sum up** resumir — **summarize** *v* resumir — **summary** *n* (**-ries**) resumen *m*

summer *n* verano *m*

summon *v* llamar (a algún), convocar (una reunión); citar (en derecho)

sun *n* sol *m* — **sunbeam** *n* rayo *m* de sol — **sunburn** *n* quemadura *f* de sol — **sunlight** *n* sol *m* (luz *f* del) — **sunny** *adj* soleado — **sunrise** *n* salida *f* del sol — **sunset** *n* puesta *f* del sol — **sunshine** *n* sol *m*, luz *f* del sol

Sunday *n* domingo *m*

superior *adj* superior — **superior** *n* superior *m* — **superiority** *n* superioridad *f*

superlative *adj* superlativo (en gramática); excepcional — **superlative** *n* superlativo *m*

supermarket *n* supermercado *m*

supervisor *n* supervisor *m*, -sora *f*

supper *n* cena *f*, comida *f*

supplement *n* suplemento *m* — **supplement** *v* complementar — **supplementary** *adj* suplementario

supply *v* (**-plied**) suministrar; ~ **with** proveer de — **supply** *n* (**-plies**) suministro *m*; **supply and demand** oferta y demanda; **supplies** *npl* provisiones *fpl*, víveres *mpl* — **supplier** *n* proveedor *m*, -dora *f*

support *v* apoyar; mantener (una familia, etc.); sostener — **support** *n* apoyo *m* (moral), ayuda *f* (económica); soporte *m*

suppose *v* suponer; **be** ~**d to** tener que — **supposedly** *adv* supuestamente

suppress *v* reprimir; suprimir (noticias, etc.) — **suppression** *n* supresión *f* (de información)

supreme *adj* supremo — **supremacy** *n* (**-cies**) supremacía *f*

sure *adj* seguro — **sure** *adv* por supuesto, claro — **surely** *adv* seguramente

surface *n* superficie *f*

surgeon *n* cirujano *m*, -na *f* — **surgery** *n* (**-geries**) cirugía *f*

surname *n* apellido *m*

surpass *v* superar

surprise *n* sorpresa *f*; **take by** ~ sorprender — **surprise** *v* sorprender — **surprising** *adj* sorprendente

surrender *v* entregar, rendir(se) — **surrender** *n* rendición *m* (de una ciudad, etc.), entrega *f* (de posesiones)

surround *v* rodear — **surroundings** *npl* ambiente *m*

survey *v* medir (un solar); inspeccionar

survive *v* sobrevivir (a) — **survival** *n* supervivencia *f* — **survivor** *n* superviviente *mf*

susceptible *adj* ~ **to** propenso a — **susceptibility** *n* (**-ties**) propensión *f* (a enfermedades, etc.)

suspect *adj* sospechoso — **suspect** *n* sospechoso *m*, -sa *f* — **suspect** *v* sospechar (algo), sospechar de (algún) — **suspicion** *n* sospecha *f* — **suspicious** *adj* sospechoso; suspicaz

suspend *v* suspender — **suspense** *n* incertidumbre *m*; suspenso *m*, suspense *m* (en el cine, etc.) — **suspension** *n* suspensión *f*

sustain *v* sostener; sufrir

swallow *v* tragar —**swallow** *n* trago *m*

swamp *n* pantano *m*, ciénaga *f* — **swamp** *v* inundar — **swampy** *adj* pantanoso, cenagoso

swan *n* cisne *f*

swap *v* intercambiar — **swap** *n* cambio *m*

swarm *n* enjambre *m*

sway *n* balanceo *m* — **sway** *v* balancearse; influir en

swear *v* (**swore; sworn**) jurar; decir palabrotas — **swearword** *n* palabrota *f*

sweat *v* (**sweat** *or* **sweated**) sudar — **sweat** *n* sudor *m* — **sweater** *n* suéter *m* — **sweatshirt** *n* sudadera *f* — **sweaty** *adj* sudado

Swedish *adj* sueco — **Swedish** *n* sueco *m* (idioma)

sweep *v* (**swept**) barrer; ~ **aside** apartar; ~ **through** extenderse por — **sweeping** *adj* amplio; extenso

sweet *adj* dulce; agradable — **sweet** *n* dulce *m* — **sweeten** *v* endulzar — **sweetener** *n* endulzante *m* — **sweetheart** *n* novio *m*, -via *f*; cariño *m* — **sweetness** *n* dulzura *f*

swell *v* (**swelled; swelled** *or* **swollen**) *or* ~ **up** hincharse; aumentar, crecer — **swell** *n* oleaje *m* (del mar) — **swelling** *n* hinchazón *f*

swift *adj* rápido — **swiftly** *adv* rápidamente

swim *v* (**swam; swum**) **swimming** nadar; dar vueltas — **swim** *n* baño *m*; **go for a swim** ir a nadar — **swimmer** *n* nadador *m*, -dora *f*

swindle *v* estafar, timar

swing *v* (**swung**) balancear(se), oscilar; girar; hacer oscilar; arreglar — **swing** *n* vaivén *m*, balanceo *m*; cambio *m*; columpio *m* (para niños)

swirl *v* arremolinarse — **swirl** *n* remolino *m*; espiral *f*

Swiss *adj* suizo

switch *n* cambio *m*; interruptor *m*, llave *f* (de la luz, etc.) — **switch** *v* cambiar de; intercambiar; **switch on** encender, prender; **switch off** apagar; sacudir (la cola, etc.); cambiar; intercambiarse — **switchboard** *n* centralita *f*, conmutador *m*

swivel *v* girar (sobre un pivote)

swoon *v* desvanecerse

sword *n* espada *f*

syllable *n* sílaba *f*

symbol *n* símbolo *m* — **symbolic** *adj* simbólico — **symbolism** *n* simbolismo *m* — **symbolize** *v* simbolizar

symmetry *n* simetría *f*

sympathy *n* comprensión *f*; **sympathies** *npl* simpatías *fpl* — **sympathize** *v* **sympathize with** compadecerse de; comprender

symptom *n* síntoma *m*

synonym *n* sinónimo *m* — **synonymous** *adj* sinónimo

synthesis *n* (**-theses**) síntesis *f* — **synthesize** *v* sintetizar — **synthetic** *adj* sintético

Syrian *adj* sirio

syrup *n* jarabe *m*

system *n* sistema *m*; organismo *m*; **digestive** ~ aparato *m* digestivo — **systematic** *adj* sistemático

T

t *n* (**t's** *or* **ts**) t *f*, vigésima letra del alfabeto inglés

table *n* mesa *f*; tabla *f*; ~ **of contents** índice *m* de materias — **tablecloth** *n* mantel *m* — **tablespoon** *n* cuchara *f* grande; cucharada *f* (cantidad)

tablet *n* pastilla *f*

taboo *adj* tabú — **taboo** *n* tabú *m*

tacit *adj* tácito

tact *n* tacto *m* — **tactful** *adj* diplomático, discreto

tactical *adj* táctico — **tactic** *n* táctica *f*

tag *n* etiqueta *f* — **tag** *v* etiquetar

tail *n* cola *f*

tailor *n* sastre *m*, -tra *f*

take *v* (**took; taken**) tomar; llevar; sacar; ∼ **a bath** bañarse; ∼ **a walk** dar un paseo; ∼ **off** quitar, quitarse (ropa); ∼ **on** asumir (una responsabilidad, etc.); ∼ **out** sacar; ∼ **place** tener lugar; ∼ **off** despegar (de aviones, etc.)

talcum powder *n* polvos *mpl* de talco

tale *n* cuento *m*

talent *n* talento *m* — **talented** *adj* talentoso

talk *v* hablar; ∼ **about** hablar de; discutir — **talk** *n* conversación *f*; charla *f* — **talkative** *adj* hablador

tall *adj* alto; **how** ∼ **are you?** ¿cuánto mides?

tally *n* (**-lies**) cuenta *f*; concordar, cuadrar

tampon *n* tampón *m*

tan *v* broncearse — **tan** *n* bronceado *m*

tangle *v* enredar — **tangle** *n* enredo *m*

tank *n* tanque *m*, depósito *m*; tanque *m* (militar) — **tanker** *n* buque *m* tanque; *or* **tanker truck** camión *m* cisterna

tape *n* cinta *f* — **tape** *v* pegar con cinta; grabar

target *n* blanco *m*; objetivo *m*

tariff *n* tarifa *f*, arancel *m*

tart *n* pastel *m*

tartan *n* tartán *m*

task *n* tarea *f*

taste *v* probar; saber — **taste** *n* gusto *m*, sabor *m*; **in good/bad taste** de buen/mal gusto — **tasteful** *adj* de buen gusto — **tasteless** *adj* sin sabor

tax *v* gravar; poner a prueba — **tax** *n* impuesto *m* — **taxation** *n* impuestos *mpl* — **tax–exempt** *adj* libre de impuestos

taxi *n* (**taxis**) taxi *m*

tea *n* té *m* — **teacup** *n* taza *f* de té — **teapot** *n* tetera *f*

teach *v* (**taught**) enseñar, dar clases (de una asignatura) — **teacher** *n* profesor *m*, -sora *f*; maestro *m*, -tra *f* (de niños pequeños) — **teaching** *n* enseñanza *f*

team *n* equipo *m* — **team** *vi or* **team up** asociarse — **teammate** *n* compañero *m*, -ra *f* de equipo — **teamwork** *n* trabajo *m* de equipo

tear[1] *v* (**tore; torn**) romper, rasgar; ∼ **down** derribar; ∼ **up** romper (papel, etc.); romperse, rasgarse; ir a toda velocidad

tear[2] *n* lágrima *f* — **tearful** *adj* lloroso

tease *v* tomar el pelo a, burlarse de; fastidiar

teaspoon *n* cucharita *f*

technical *adj* técnico — **technician** *n* técnico *m*, -ca *f*

technique *n* técnica *f*

technological *adj* tecnológico — **technology** *n* (**-gies**) tecnología *f*

teddy bear *n* oso *m* de peluche

teenage *or* **teenaged** *adj* adolescente — **teenager** *n* adolescente *mf* — **teens** *npl* adolescencia *f*

telecommunication *n* telecomunicación *f*

telephone *n* teléfono *m* — **telephone** *v* llamar por teléfono

televise *v* televisar — **television** *n* televisión *f*

tell *v* (**told**) decir; contar; saber — **teller** *n or* **bank teller** cajero *m*, -ra *f*

temper *n* **have a bad** ∼ tener mal genio; **lose one's** ∼ perder los estribos — **temperament** *n* temperamento *m*

temperature *n* temperatura *f*; **have a** ∼ tener fiebre

tempest *n* tempestad *f*

temple *n* templo *m*; sien *f* (en anatomía)

temporarily *adv* temporalmente — **temporary** *adj* temporal

tempt *v* tentar — **temptation** *n* tentación *f*

ten *adj* diez — **ten** *n* diez *m*

tend[1] *v* cuidar

tend[2] *v* ~ **to** tender a — **tendency** *n* (-**cies**) tendencia *f*

tender *adj* tierno; dolorido

tenderness *n* ternura *f*

tennis *n* tenis *m*

tense *n* tiempo *m* — **tense** *adj* tenso — **tension** *n* tensión *f*

tent *n* tienda *f* de campaña

tenth *adj* décimo — **tenth** *n* décimo *m*, -ma *f* (en una serie)

term *n* término *m*; período *m*; **be on good** ~**s** tener buenas relaciones

terminate *v* terminar(se); poner fin a — **termination** *n* terminación *f*

terrain *n* terreno *m*

terrible *adj* espantoso, terrible — **terribly** *adv* terriblemente

terrific *adj* tremendo; estupendo

terrify *v* (-**fied**) aterrar, aterrorizar — **terrifying** *adj* aterrado

territory *n* (-**ries**) territorio *m*

terror *n* terror *m* — **terrorism** *n* terrorismo *m* — **terrorist** *n* terrorista *mf* — **terrorize** *v* aterrorizar

test *n* examen *m*, prueba *f*; análisis *m* (en medicina) — **test** *v* probar; examinar; analizar (la sangre, etc.)

testament *n* testamento *m*

testify *v* (-**fied**) testificar

testimony *n* (-**nies**) testimonio *m*

text *n* texto *m* — **textbook** *n* libro *m* de texto

than *conj* & *prep* que, de

thank *v* agradecer, dar (las) gracias a; ~ **you!** ¡gracias! — **thankful** *adj* agradecido — **thanks** *npl* gracias

Thanksgiving *n* día *m* de Acción de Gracias

that *pron* (**those**) ése, ésa, eso; aquél, aquélla, aquello; **like that** así; **that is** es decir — **that** *conj* que — **that** *adj* (**those**) ese, esa; aquel, aquella; **that one** ése, ésa — **that** *adv* tan

the *art* el, la, los, las; por — ~ *adv*

theater *or* **theatre** *n* teatro *m*

their *adj* su, sus, de ellos, de ellas — **theirs** *pron* (el) suyo, (la) suya, (los) suyos, (las) suyas

them *pron* los, las; les, se; ellos, ellas

theme *n* tema *m*; trabajo *m* (escrito)

themselves *pron* se; ellos mismos, ellas mismas; sí (mismos), sí (mismas)

then *adv* entonces; luego, después; además — **then** *adj* entonces

thence *adv* de ahí (en adelante)

theology *n* (-**gies**) teología *f* — **theological** *adj* teológico

theoretical *adj* teórico — **theory** *n* (-**ries**) teoría *f*

therapeutic *adj* terapéutico — **therapist** *n* terapeuta *mf* — **therapy** *n* (-**pies**) terapia *f*

there *adv* *or* **over** ~ allí, allá; *or* **right** ~ ahí; **who's** ~? ¿quién es? — **there** *pron* **there is/are** hay — **thereafter** *adv* después — **thereby** *adv* así — **therefore** *adv* por lo tanto

thermometer *n* termómetro *m*

thermos *n* termo *m*

thesaurus *n* (-**sauri** *or* -**sauruses**) diccionario *m* de sinónimos

thesis *n* (**theses**) tesis *f*

they *pron* ellos, ellas

thick *adj* grueso; espeso — **thickness** *n* grosor *m*, espesor *m*

thief *n* (**thieves**) ladrón *m*, -drona *f*

thigh *n* muslo *m*

thin *adj* delgado; claro, aguado; fino

thing *n* cosa *f*; **for one** ~ en primer lugar

think *v* (**thought**) pensar; creer; ~ **about** *or* ~ **of** pensar en; ~ **of** acordarse de; **what do you** ~ **of it?** ¿qué te parece?

third *adj* tercero — **third** *n* tercero *m*, -ra *f* (en una serie) — **Third World** *n* Tercer Mundo *m*

thirst *n* sed *f* — **thirsty** *adj* sediento

thirteen *adj* trece — **thirteen** *n* trece *m* — **thirteenth** *adj* décimo tercero treceavo *m* (en matemáticas)

thirty *adj* treinta — **thirty** *n* (**thirties**) treinta *m* — **thirtieth** *adj* trigésimo treintavo *m* (en matemáticas)

this *pron* (**these**) éste, ésta, esto; **like** ∼ así — **this** *adj* (**these**) este, esta

thorn *n* espina *f*

though *conj* aunque — **though** *adv* sin embargo; **as though** como si

thought *n* pensamiento *m*; idea *f* — **thoughtful** *adj* pensativo

thousand *adj* mil — **thousand** *n* mil *m* — **thousandth** *adj* milésimo

thread *n* hilo *m*; rosca *f* (de un tornillo)

threat *n* amenaza *f* — **threaten** *v* amenazar

three *adj* tres — **three** *n* tres *m* — **three hundred** *adj* trescientos — **three hundred** *n* trescientos *m*

thrill *v* emocionar — **thrill** *n* emoción *f* — **thriller** *n* película *f* de suspenso

throat *n* garganta *f*

through *prep* por, a través de; entre; a causa de; durante — **through** *adv* de un lado a otro (en el espacio), de principio a fin (en el tiempo); completamente — **throughout** *prep* por todo (un lugar), a lo largo de (un período de tiempo)

throw *v* (**threw; thrown**) tirar, lanzar; ∼ **away** *or* ∼ **out** tirar, botar

thumb *n* (dedo *m*) pulgar *m* — **thumb** *vt or* **thumb through** hojear

thunder *n* truenos *mpl* — **thunderbolt** *n* rayo *m*

Thursday *n* jueves *m*

thus *adv* así; por lo tanto

tic *n* tic *m* (nervioso)

tick *n* tictac *m* (sonido)

ticket *n* pasaje *m* (de avión), billete *m* (de tren, avión, etc.), boleto *m* (de tren o autobús); entrada *f* (al teatro, etc.); multa *f*

tie *n* atadura *f*, cordón *m*; lazo *m*; empate *m* (en deportes); corbata *f* — **tie** *v* atar, amarrar

tiger *n* tigre *m*

tight *adj* apretado; ajustado, ceñido — **tighten** *v* apretar; tensar — **tightly** *adv* bien, fuerte

time *n* tiempo *m*; época *f*; **at** ∼**s** a veces; **at this** ∼ en este momento; **for the** ∼ **being** por el momento; **have a good** ∼ pasarlo bien; **many** ∼**s** muchas veces **on** ∼ a tiempo — **time** *v* tomar el tiempo a (algún), cronometrar (una carrera, etc.) — **timeless** *adj* eterno — **timely** *adj* oportuno — **timer** *n* temporizador *m*, avisador *m* (de cocina) — **times** *prep*; **3 times 4 is 12** 3 por 4 son 12 — **timetable** *n* horario *m*

tiny *adj* diminuto, minúsculo

tip[1] *v* inclinar

tip[2] *n* punta *f*

tip[3] *n* consejo *m* — **tip** *v* **tip off** avisar

tip[4] *v* dar una propina a — **tip** *n* propina *f*

tire[1] *n* neumático *m*, llanta *f*

tire[2] *v* cansar(se) — **tired** *adj* **tired of** cansado de, harto de; **tired out** agotado — **tireless** *adj* incansable

tissue *n* pañuelo *m* de papel; tejido *m* (en biología)

title *n* título *m* — **title** *v* titular

to *prep* a; hacia; para; hasta; **a quarter** ∼ **seven** las siete menos cuarto

toast *v* tostar (pan, etc.); brindar por (una persona) — **toast** *n* pan *m* tostado, tostadas *fpl*; brindis *m* — **toaster** *n* tostador *m*

today *adv* hoy — **today** *n* hoy *m*

toe *n* dedo *m* (del pie)

together *adv* juntos; ∼ **with** junto con

toilet *n* baño *m*, servicio *m*; inodoro *m* (instalación) — **toilet paper** *n* papel *m* higiénico

token *n* ficha *f* (para un tren, etc.)

tolerance *n* tolerancia *f* — **tolerant** *adj* tolerante — **tolerate** *v* tolerar

toll *n* peaje *m*

tomato *n* (**-toes**) tomate *m*

tomb *n* tumba *f*, sepulcro *m* — **tombstone** *n* lápida *f*

tomorrow *adv* mañana — **tomorrow** *n* mañana *m*

ton *n* tonelada *f*

tongue *n* lengua *f*

tonight *adv* esta noche — **tonight** *n* esta noche *f*

too *adv* también; demasiado

tool *n* herramienta *f* — **toolbox** *n* caja *f* de herramientas

tooth *n* (**teeth**) diente *m* — **toothache** *n* dolor *m* de muelas — **toothbrush** *n* cepillo *m* de dientes — **toothpaste** *n* pasta *f* de dientes, pasta *f* dentífrica

top[1] *n* parte *f* superior; cima *f*, cumbre *f*; tapa *f*, cubierta *f*; **on ~ of** encima de — **top** *adj* de arriba, superior; mejor

top[2] *n* trompo *m* (juguete)

topic *n* tema *m*

torment *n* tormento *m*

tornado *n* (**-does** *or* **-dos**) tornado *m*

tortilla *n* tortilla *f*

tortoise *n* tortuga *f* (terrestre)

torture *n* tortura *f* — **torture** *v* torturar

total *adj* total — **total** *n* total *m*

touch *v* tocar — **touch** *n*; tacto *m* (sentido); toque *m*; pizca *f*; **keep in touch** mantenerse en contacto

tough *adj* duro; fuerte; severo; difícil — **toughen** *vt or* **toughen up** endurecer — **toughness** *n* dureza *f*

tour *n* viaje *m* (por un país, etc.), visita *f* (a un museo, etc.); gira *f* (de un equipo, etc.) — **tour** *v* viajar; hacer una gira (de equipos, etc.); viajar por, recorrer — **tourist** *n* turista *mf*

toward *or* **towards** *prep* hacia

towel *n* toalla *f*

tower *n* torre *f*

town *n* pueblo *m*; ciudad *f*

toxic *adj* tóxico

toy *n* juguete *m* — **toy** *v* **toy with** juguetear con

trace *n* rastro *m*, señal *f*

track *n* pista *f*; sendero *m*; *or* **railroad ~** vía *f* (férrea)

trade *n* oficio *m*; comercio *m*; industria *f*; cambio *m* — **trade** *v* comerciar; **trade something with** cambiar algo a — **trademark** *n* marca *f* registrada

tradition *n* tradición *f* — **traditional** *adj* tradicional

traffic *n* tráfico *m* — **traffic** *v* **traffic in** traficar con — **traffic light** *n* semáforo *m*

tragedy *n* (**-dies**) tragedia *f* — **tragic** *adj* trágico

trailer *n* remolque *m*; caravana *f* (vivienda)

train *n* tren *m* — **train** *v* adiestrar, entrenar (atletas, etc.); apuntar; prepararse, entrenarse (en deportes, etc.) — **trainer** *n* entrenador *m*, -dora *f*

traitor *n* traidor *m*, -dora *f*

trampoline *n* trampolín *m*

tranquillity *or* **tranquility** *n* tranquilidad *f* — **tranquil** *adj* tranquilo — **tranquilize** *v* tranquilizar — **tranquilizer** *n* tranquilizante *m*

transaction *n* transacción *f*

transatlantic *adj* transatlántico

transfer *v* transferir (fondos, etc.) — **transfer** *n* transferencia *f* (de fondos, etc.), traslado *m* (de una persona); boleto *m* (para hacer transbordo); calcomanía *f*

transform *v* transformar — **transformation** *n* transformación *f*

transit *n* tránsito *m*; transporte *m* — **transition** *n* transición *f* — **transitive** *adj* transitivo — **transitory** *adj* transitorio

translate *v* traducir — **translation** *n* traducción *f* — **translator** *n* traductor *m*, -tora *f*

transmit *v* transmitir — **transmission** *n* transmisión *f*

transparent *adj* transparente — **transparency** *n* (**-cies**) transparencia *f*

transport *v* transportar — **transport** *n* transporte *m*

trap *n* trampa *f* — **trap** *v* atrapar

trash *n* basura *f*

trauma *n* trauma *m* — **traumatic** *adj* traumático

travel *v* viajar — **travel** *n* viajes *mpl* — **traveler** *or* **traveller** *n* viajero *m*, -ra *f*

tray *n* bandeja *f*

treachery *n* traición *f* — **treacherous** *adj* traidor

treason *n* traición *f* (a la patria)

treasure *n* tesoro *m* — **treasure** *v* apreciar — **treasurer** *n* tesorero *m*, -ra *f*

treat *v* tratar; considerar

treatment *n* tratamiento *m*

treaty *n* (**-ties**) tratado *m*

tree *n* árbol *m*

tremble *v* temblar

tremendous *adj* tremendo

trend *n* tendencia *f*; moda *f*

trial *n* juicio *m*, proceso *m*; prueba *f*

triangle *n* triángulo *m*

tribe *n* tribu *f*

trick *n* trampa *f*; broma *f*; truco *m* — **trick** *v* engañar — **trickery** *n* engaño *m*

tricky *adj* **trickier; -est** astuto, taimado

tricycle *n* triciclo *m*

trillion *n* billón *m*

trim *v* recortar; adornar — **trim** *adj* esbelto; arreglado — **trim** *n* adornos *mpl*

trio *n* (**trios**) trío *m*

trip *n* viaje *m*

triumph *n* triunfo *m* — **triumph** *v* triunfar — **triumphal** *adj* triunfal

trivial *adj* trivial

troop *n* escuadrón *m* (de caballería), compañía *f* (de soldados) — **trooper** *n* soldado *m*; *or* **state trooper** policía *mf* estatal

tropic *n* trópico *m*

trot *n* trote *m* — **trot** *v* trotar

trouble *v* preocupar; molestar — **trouble** *n* problemas *mpl*; molestia *f*; **be in trouble** estar en apuros

trousers *npl* pantalón *m*, pantalones *mpl*

truck *n* camión *m*; carro *m* — **trucker** *n* camionero *m*, carro *m*

true *adj* verdadero; fiel; auténtico

truly *adv* verdaderamente

trumpet *n* trompeta *f*

trunk *n* tronco *m*; baúl *m* (equipaje); maletero *m* (de un auto)

trust *n* confianza *f*; esperanza *f*; crédito *m* — **trust** *v* confiar (en); esperar; fiarse de (en frases negativas)

truth *n* verdad *f*

try *v* (**tried**) tratar (de), intentar

T–shirt *n* camiseta *f*

tub *n* cuba *f*, tina *f*; envase *m*; bañera *f*

tube *n* tubo *m*

tuberculosis *n* tuberculosis *f*

tubing *n* tubería *f*

Tuesday *n* martes *m*

tuition *n* enseñanza *f*; *or* ～ **fees** matrícula *f*

tulip *n* tulipán *m*

tumble *v* caerse — **tumble** *n* caída *f*

tumor *n* tumor *m*

tumult *n* tumulto *m*

tuna *n* (**-na** *or* **-nas**) atún *m*

tune *n* melodía *f* — **tune** *v* afinar; **tune in** sintonizar

tunnel *n* túnel *m*

turkey *n* (**-keys**) pavo *m*

turn *v* hacer girar (una rueda, etc.), volver (la cabeza, una página, etc.); dar la vuelta a (una esquina); torcer; ～ **down** rechazar; bajar; ～ **in** entregar; ～ **off** cerrar (una llave), apagar (la luz, etc.); ～ **on** abrir (una llave), encender, prender (la luz, etc.); ～ **out** echar; producir; *or* ～ **over** dar la vuelta a, voltear; ～ **over** entregar; girar, dar vueltas; *or* ～ **around** darse la vuelta, volverse; ～ **into** convertirse en; ～ **out** resultar; ～ **up** aparecer — **turn** *n* vuelta *f*; cambio *m*; curva *f*

turtle *n* tortuga *f* (marina) — **turtleneck** *n* cuello *m* de tortuga

twelve *adj* doce — **twelve** *n* doce *m* —
twelfth *adj* duodécimo — **twelfth** *n*
duodécimo *m*, -ma *f* (en una serie); do-
ceavo *m* (en matemáticas)
twenty *adj* veinte — **twenty** *n* (**-ties**)
veinte *m* — **twentieth** *adj* vigésimo —
twentieth *n* vigésimo *m*, -ma *f* (en una
serie); veinteavo *m* (en matemáticas)
twice *adv* dos veces
twilight *n* crepúsculo *m*
twin *n* gemelo *m*, -la *f*; mellizo *m*, -za *f* —
twin *adj* gemelo, mellizo

twinkle *v* brillar (de los ojos) — **twinkle**
n centelleo *m*, brillo *m* (de los ojos)
twist *v* retorcer; girar; torcerse — **twist** *n*
vuelta *f*; giro *m*
two *adj* dos — **two** *n* (**twos**) dos *m* —
twofold *adj* doble — **twofold** *adv* al
doble — **two hundred** *adj* doscientos
— **two hundred** *n* doscientos *m*
type *n* tipo *m* — **type** *v* escribir a
máquina — **typewriter** *n* máquina *f* de
escribir
typical *adj* típico, característico

U

u *n* (**u's** *or* **us**) u *f*, vigésima primera letra
del alfabeto inglés
UFO *n* (**UFO's** *or* **UFOs**) ovni *m*, OVNI
m
ugly *adj* feo
ultimate *adj* final, último; máximo; fundamental
umbrella *n* paraguas *m*
umpire *n* árbitro *m*, -tra *f* — **umpire** *v* arbitrar
unacceptable *adj* inaceptable
unafraid *adj* sin miedo
unattached *adj* suelto; soltero
unattractive *adj* poco atractivo
unauthorized *adj* no autorizado
unavailable *adj* no disponible
unavoidable *adj* inevitable
unaware *adj* inconsciente; **be ~ of** ignorar — **unawares** *adv* **catch . . . unawares** agarrar a . . . desprevenido
unbalanced *adj* desequilibrado
unbearable *adj* inaguantable, insoportable
unbelievable *adj* increíble
unbending *adj* inflexible
unborn *adj* aún no nacido
unbreakable *adj* irrompible
unbroken *adj* intacto; continuo
unbutton *v* desabrochar, desabotonar

uncalled–for *adj* inapropiado, innecesario
uncertain *adj* incierto; **in no ~ terms**
de forma vehemente — **uncertainty** *n*
(**-ties**) incertidumbre *f*
unchanged *adj* igual, sin alterar — **un-
changing** *adj* inmutable
uncivilized *adj* incivilizado
uncle *n* tío *m*
unclear *adj* poco claro
uncomfortable *adj* incómodo; inquietante, desagradable
uncommon *adj* raro
unconcerned *adj* indiferente
unconditional *adj* incondicional
unconscious *adj* inconsciente
unconventional *adj* poco convencional
uncover *v* destapar; descubrir
undecided *adj* indeciso
undeniable *adj* innegable
under *adv* debajo; menos; *or* **~ anesthetic** bajo los efectos de la anestesia
~ 20 minutes menos de 20 minutos;
~ the circumstances dadas las cir-
cunstancias
underdeveloped *adj* subdesarrollado
underground *adv* bajo tierra; **go ~**
pasar a la clandestinidad — **underground** *adj* subterráneo; secreto, clan-

destino — **underground** n movimiento m clandestino

underneath adv debajo, abajo — **underneath** prep debajo de, abajo de

underpants npl calzoncillos mpl, calzones mpl

undershirt n camiseta f

understand v (**-stood**) comprender, entender

understatement n that's an ~ decir sólo eso es quedarse corto

underwater adj submarino — **underwater** adv debajo (del agua)

underwear n ropa f interior

undo v (**-did; -done**) deshacer, desatar; reparar (daños, etc.)

undress v desnudar(se)

uneasy adj incómodo; inquieto; agitado

uneducated adj inculto

unemployed adj desempleado — **unemployment** n desempleo m

unexpected adj inesperado

unfair adj injusto — **unfairness** n injusticia f

unfaithful adj infiel

unfasten v desabrochar (ropa, etc.); desatar (una cuerda, etc.)

unfavorable adj desfavorable

unfeeling adj insensible

unfit adj impropio; no apto, incapaz

unfold v extenderse; desarrollarse; desplegar(se), desdoblar; revelar (un plan, etc.)

unforgettable adj inolvidable

unforgivable adj imperdonable

unfortunate adj desgraciado, desafortunado; inoportuno

ungrateful adj desagradecido

unharmed adj salvo, ileso

uniform adj uniforme — **uniform** n uniforme m

unilateral adj unilateral

uninhabited adj deshabitado, despoblado

union n unión f; or **labor** ~ sindicato m, gremio m

unique adj único

unit n unidad f; módulo m (de un mobiliario)

unite v unir(se) — **unity** n unidad f; acuerdo m

universe n universo m — **universal** adj universal

university n (**-ties**) universidad f

unjust adj injusto

unkempt adj despeinado (del pelo)

unknown adj desconocido

unless conj a menos que, a no ser que

unlike adj diferente — **unlike** prep a diferencia de

unlimited adj ilimitado

unlock v abrir (con llave)

unlucky adj de mala suerte (de un número, etc.)

unmarried adj soltero

unmistakable adj inconfundible

unnatural adj anormal; afectado, forzado

unnecessary adj innecesario

unpleasant adj desagradable

unreal adj irreal

unsanitary adj antihigiénico

unsettled adj inestable; agitado, inquieto; variable (del tiempo)

unstable adj inestable

untidy adj desordenado (de una sala, etc.), desaliñado (de una persona)

untie v desatar

until prep hasta — **until** conj hasta que

untimely adj prematuro; inoportuno

untroubled adj tranquilo; be ~ by no estar afectado por

untrue adj falso

unused adj nuevo; be ~ to no estar acostumbrado a

unusual adj poco común, insólito

unwanted adj superfluo (de un objeto), no deseado (de un niño, etc.)

unwieldy adj difícil de manejar

unwilling adj poco dispuesto — **unwillingly** adv de mala gana

unworthy *adj* be ∼ of no ser digno de

up *adv* arriba; hacia arriba; ∼ **here/ there** aquí/allí arriba; ∼ **until** hasta — **up** *adj* levantado; terminado; **be up against** enfrentarse con; **be up on** estar al corriente de; **it's up to you** depende de tí; **the sun is up** ha salido el sol — **up** *prep* **go up the river** ir río arriba

update *v* poner al día, actualizar — **update** *n* puesta *f* al día

upgrade *v* elevar la categoría de (un puesto, etc.), mejorar (una facilidad, etc.)

uphill *adv* cuesta arriba — **uphill** *adj* en subida; **be an uphill battle** ser muy difícil

upon *prep* en, sobre; ∼ **leaving** al salir

upper *adj* superior — **upper** *n* parte *f* superior (del calzado, etc.)

uppercase *adj* mayúsculo

upper class *n* clase *f* alta

upright *adj* vertical; derecho; recto, honesto — **upright** *n* montante *m*, poste *m*

upset *v* (-set) volcar; alterar, inquietar; trastornar — **upset** *adj* alterado; **have an upset stomach** estar mal del estómago — **upset** *n* trastorno *m*

upside down *adv* al revés; **turn** ∼ volver — **upside–down** *adj* al revés

upstairs *adv* arriba — **upstairs** *adj* de arriba — **upstairs** *ns* & *pl* piso *m* de arriba

upward *adj* ascendente, hacia arriba

urban *adj* urbano

urgency *n* urgencia *f* — **urgent** *adj* urgente; **be urgent** urgir

Uruguayan *adj* uruguayo

us *pron* nos; nosotros, nosotras; **both of** ∼ nosotros dos; **it's** ∼**!** ¡somos nosotros!

usage *n* uso *m*

use *v* usar; ∼ **up** agotar, consumir — **use** *n* uso *m* — **used** *adj* usado; **be used to** estar acostumbrado a — **useful** *adj* útil, práctico — **usefulness** *n* utilidad *f* — **useless** *adj* inútil — **user** *n* usuario *m*, -ria *f*

usher *v* acompañar, conducir; ∼ **in** hacer entrar — **usher** *n* acomodador *m*, -dora *f*

usual *adj* habitual, usual; **as** ∼ como de costumbre

utility *n* (-ties) utilidad *f*; *or* **public** ∼ empresa *f* de servicio público

utilize *v* utilizar

V

v *n* (**v's** *or* **vs**) v *f*, vigésima segunda letra del alfabeto inglés

vacant *adj* libre; desocupado; vacante (dícese de un puesto); ausente (dícese de una mirada) — **vacancy** *n* (-cies) (puesto *m*) vacante *f*; habitación *f* libre (en un hotel, etc.)

vacate *v* desalojar, desocupar

vacation *n* vacaciones *fpl*

vaccine *n* vacuna *f*

vacuum *n* vacío *m* — **vacuum cleaner** *n* aspiradora *f*

vain *adj* vanidoso; **in** ∼ en vano

valid *adj* válido

valley *n* (-leys) valle *m*

value *n* valor *m* — **value** *v* valorar — **valuable** *adj* valioso

van *n* furgoneta *f*, camioneta *f*

vanguard *n* vanguardia *f*

vanilla *n* vainilla *f*

vanity *n* (-ties) vanidad *f*; *or* ∼ **table** tocador *m*

vapor *n* vapor *m*

variable *adj* variable — **variable** *n* variable *f* — **variant** *n* variante *f* — **variety** *n* (-ties) variedad *f*; surtido *m*; clase *f*

vary *v* (**varied**) variar
vase *n or* **flower** ~ florero *m*
VCR *or* **videocassette recorder** *n* vídeo *m*, videograbadora *f*
vegetable *adj* vegetal — **vegetable** *n* vegetal *m* (planta); **vegetables** *npl* verduras *fpl* — **vegetarian** *n* vegetariano *mf* — **vegetation** *n* vegetación *f*
vehicle *n* vehículo *m*
veil *n* velo *m* — **veil** *v* cubrir con un velo; velar
vein *n* vena *f*; veta *f* (de un mineral, etc.)
velocity *n* velocidad *f*
venetian blind *n* persiana *f* veneciana
Venezuelan *adj* venezolano
vengeance *n* venganza *f*; **take** ~ **on** vengarse de
ventilate *v* ventilar — **ventilation** *n* ventilación *f* — **ventilator** *n* ventilador *m*
venture *v* arriesgar; aventurar (una opinión, etc.); atreverse — **venture** *n or* **business venture** empresa *f*
Venus *n* Venus *m*
verb *n* verbo *m* — **verbal** *adj* verbal
verify *v* (**-fied**) verificar
versatile *adj* versátil
verse *n* verso *m*; poesía *f*; versículo *m* (en la Biblia)
version *n* versión *f*
vertical *adj* vertical — **vertical** *n* vertical *f*
vertigo *n* vértigo *m*
very *adv* muy; **the** ~ **same thing** la misma cosa ~ **much** mucho; ~ **well** muy bien — **very** *adj* mismo; solo, mero
veteran *n* veterano *m*, -na *f*
veterinarian *n* veterinario *m*, -ria *f* — **veterinary** *adj* veterinario
veto *n* (**-toes**) veto *m* — **veto** *v* vetar
vibrate *v* vibrar — **vibration** *n* vibración *f*
vice *n* vicio *m*
vice president *n* vicepresidente *m*, -ta *f*
victim *n* víctima *f*
victory *n* (**-ries**) victoria *f*
video *n* video *m*, vídeo *m* — **video** *adj*

de video — **videocassette** *n* videocasete *m*
Vietnamese *adj* vietnamita
view *n* vista *f*; opinión *f*; **come into** ~ aparecer; **in** ~ **of** en vista de (que) — **view** *v* ver; considerar — **viewer** *n or* **television viewer** televidente *mf* — **viewpoint** *n* punto *m* de vista
vigil *n* vela *f* — **vigilance** *n* vigilancia *f* — **vigilant** *adj* vigilante
vigor *n* vigor *m* — **vigorous** *adj* vigoroso; enérgico
vinegar *n* vinagre *m*
violate *v* violar — **violation** *n* violación *f*
violence *n* violencia *f* — **violent** *adj* violento
violet *n* violeta *f* (flor), violeta *m* (color)
violin *n* violín *m* — **violinist** *n* violinista *mf*
VIP *n* (**VIPs**) VIP *mf*
virtual *adj* virtual
virtue *n* virtud *f*; **by** ~ **of** en virtud de
virus *n* virus *m*
visible *adj* visible; evidente
vision *n* visión *f*; **have** ~**s of** imaginarse — **visionary** *adj* visionario
visit *v* visitar; hacer una visita — **visit** *n* visita *f*
visor *n* visera *f*
vista *n* vista *f*
visual *adj* visual
vital *adj* vital; esencial — **vitality** *n* vitalidad *f*, energía *f*
vitamin *n* vitamina *f*
vocabulary *n* (**-laries**) vocabulario *m*
vocal *adj* vocal; vociferante — **vocal cords** *npl* cuerdas *fpl* vocales — **vocalist** *n* cantante *mf*, vocalista *mf*
vocation *n* vocación *f*
vogue *n* moda *f*, boga *f*; **in** ~ de moda, en boga
voice *n* voz *f* — **voice** *v* expresar
volley *n* (**-leys**) descarga *f* (de tiros); torrente *m* (de insultos, etc.); volea *f* (en deportes) — **volleyball** *n* voleibol *m*

volume *n* volumen *m*

voluntary *adj* voluntario — **volunteer** *n* voluntario *m*, -ria *f* — **volunteer** *v* ofrecer(se) (a)

vomit *n* vómito *m* — **vomit** *v* vomitar

vote *n* voto *m*; derecho *m* al voto — **vote** *v* votar

vow *n* voto *m*, promesa *f* — **vow** *v* jurar

vulnerable *adj* vulnerable

W

w *n* (**w's** *or* **ws**) .w *f*, vigésima tercera letra del alfabeto inglés

wade *v* caminar por el agua; *or* ~ **across** vadear

waft *v* llevar por el aire; flotar

wage *n or* **wages** *npl* salario *m*

wager *n* apuesta *f* — **wager** *v* apostar

waist *n* cintura *f*

wait *v* esperar — **wait** *n* espera *f* — **waiter** *n* camarero *m*, mozo *m* — **waiting room** *n* sala *f* de espera

wake *v* (**woke; woken** *or* **waked**) despertar; *or* ~ **up** despertarse

waken *v* despertar(se)

walk *v* caminar, andar; pasear; caminar por; sacar a pasear (a un perro) — **walk** *n* paseo *m*; camino *m*; andar *m* — **walker** *n* paseante *mf*; excursionista *mf*

wall *n* muro *m* (exterior), pared *f* (interior), muralla *f* (de una ciudad)

wallet *n* billetera *f*, cartera *f*

want *v* querer; necesitar; carecer de — **want** *n* necesidad *f*; falta *f*; deseo *m*

war *n* guerra *f*

wardrobe *n* armario *m*; vestuario *m*

warehouse *n* almacén *m*, bodega *f*

warm *adj* caliente; tibio; cariñoso; **I feel** ~ tengo calor — **warm** *vt or* **warm up** calentar(se); **warm to** tomar simpatía a (algún), entusiasmarse con (algo)

warn *v* advertir, avisar — **warning** *n* advertencia *f*, aviso *m*

warranty *n* (**-ties**) garantía *f*

wash *v* lavar(se); arrastrar; ~ **away** llevarse; ~ **over** bañar — **wash** *n* lavado *m*; ropa *f* sucia — **washing machine** *n* máquina *f* de lavar, lavadora *f* — **washroom** *n* servicios *mpl* (públicos), baño *m*

wasp *n* avispa *f*

waste *v* desperdiciar, derrochar, malgastar; ~ **time** perder tiempo — **waste** *adj* de desecho — **waste** *n* derroche *m*, desperdicio *m*; desechos *mpl* — **wastebasket** *n* papelera *f*

watch *v* mirar; ~ **out!** ¡ten cuidado!, ¡ojo!; *or* ~ **over** vigilar, cuidar; reloj; velar — **watch** *n* vigilancia *f*; guardia *mf* — **watchful** *adj* vigilante — **watchman** *n* (**-men**) vigilante *m*, guarda *m*

water *n* agua *f* — **water** *v* regar (el jardín, etc.); **water down** diluir, aguar; lagrimar (de los ojos) — **waterfall** *n* cascada *f*, salto *m* de agua — **watermelon** *n* sandía *f* — **waterpower** *n* energía *f* hidráulica — **waterproof** *adj* impermeable — **watery** *adj* aguado, diluido; desvaído (de colores)

wave *v* agitar; ondular — **wave** *n* ola *f* (de agua); onda *f*

wax *n* cera *f* (para pisos, etc.) — **wax** *v* encerar

way *n* camino *m*; manera *f*, modo *m*; **by the** ~ a propósito, por cierto; **by** ~ **of** vía, pasando por; **come a long** ~ hacer grandes progresos **get in the** ~ meterse en el camino

we *pron* nosotros, nosotras

weak *adj* débil; aguado — **weakness** *n* debilidad *f*; flaqueza *f*, punto *m* débil

wealth *n* riqueza *f* — **wealthy** *adj* rico

weapon *n* arma *f*

wear *v* (**wore; worn**) llevar (ropa, etc.),

calzar (zapatos); ∼ out gastar — **wear** *n* uso *m*

weariness *n* cansancio *m*

weave *v* (**wove** *or* **weaved; woven** *or* **weaved**) tejer (tela); entretejer — **weave** *n* tejido *m*

web *n* red *f*

wedding *n* boda *f,* casamiento *m*

wedge *n* cuña *f;* porción *f,* trozo *m* — **wedge** *v* apretar (con una cuña); meter

Wednesday *n* miércoles *m*

week *n* semana *f* — **weekend** *n* fin *m* de semana — **weekly** *adv* semanalmente — **weekly** *adj* semanal — **weekly** *n* (**-lies**) semanario *m*

weep *v* (**wept**) llorar

weigh *v* pesar; sopesar; ∼ **down** sobrecargar (con una carga), abrumar (con preocupaciones, etc.)

weight *n* peso *m;* **gain** ∼ engordar; **lose** ∼ adelgazar

welcome *v* dar la bienvenida a, recibir — **welcome** *adj* bienvenido; **you're welcome** de nada — **welcome** *n* bienvenida *f,* acojida *f*

welfare *n* bienestar *m;* asistencia *f* social

well[1] *adv* (**better; best**) bien; bastante; **as** ∼ también; **as** ∼ **as** además de — **well** *adj* bien — **well** *interj* bueno; ¡vaya!

well[2] *n* pozo *m* — **well** *vi or* **well up** brotar, manar

well–being *n* bienestar *m* — **well–done** *adj* bien hecho; bien cocido (de la carne, etc.) — **well–off** *adj* acomodado

Welsh *adj* galés — **Welsh** *n* galés *m* (idioma); **the Welsh** los galeses

west *adv* al oeste — **west** *adj* oeste, del oeste — **west** *n* oeste *m*

wet *adj* mojado; lluvioso; ∼ **paint** pintura *f* fresca — **wet** *v* (**wet** *or* **wetted**) mojar, humedecer

whale *n* ballena *f*

what *adj* qué; cualquier — **what** *pron* qué; lo que; **what for?** ¿por qué?; **what if** y si — **whatever** *adj* cualquier; **there's no chance whatever** no hay ninguna posibilidad; **nothing whatever** nada en absoluto — **whatever** *pron* lo que; qué; **whatever it may be** sea lo que sea

wheat *n* trigo *m*

wheel *n* rueda *f; or* **steering** ∼ volante *m* (de automóviles, etc.), timón *m* (de barcos) — **wheel** *v* empujar (algo sobre ruedas); *or* **wheel around** darse la vuelta *f* — **wheelchair** *n* silla *f* de ruedas

when *adv* cuándo — **when** *conj* cuando — **when** *pron* cuándo — **whenever** *adv* cuando sea — **whenever** *conj* cada vez que; **whenever you like** cuando quieras

where *adv* dónde; ∼ **are you going?** ¿adónde vas? — **where** *conj or pron* donde — **wherever** *adv* en cualquier parte; dónde, adónde — **wherever** *conj* dondequiera que

whether *conj* si; ∼ **you like it or not** tanto si quieras como si no

which *adj* qué, cuál; **in** ∼ **case** en cuyo caso — **which** *pron* cuál; que, el (la) cual — **whichever** *adj* cualquier — **whichever** *pron* el (la) que, cualquiera que

while *n* rato *m;* **be worth one's** ∼ valer la pena; **in a** ∼ dentro de poco — **while** *conj* mientras; mientras que; aunque — **while** *v* **while away the time** matar el tiempo

whim *n* capricho *m,* antojo *m* —**whimsical** *adj* caprichoso, fantasioso

whine *v* gimotear; quejarse — **whine** *n* quejido *m,* gemido *m*

whip *v* azotar; batir (huevos, crema, etc.); agitarse; ∼ **up** avivar, despertar — **whip** *n* látigo *m*

whirlwind *n* torbellino *m*

whisper *v* cuchichear, susurrar — **whisper** *n* susurro *m*

whistle *v* silbar, chiflar; pitar (de un tren, etc.) — **whistle** *n* silbido *m,* chiflido *m* (sonido); silbato *m,* pito *m* (instrumento)

white *adj* blanco — **white** *n* blanco *m*

(color); clara *f* (de huevos) — **white-ness** *n* blancura *f*

who *pron* quién; que, quien — **whoever** *pron* quienquiera que, quien; quién

whole *adj* entero; intacto; **a ~ lot** muchísimo — **whole** *n* todo *m*; **as a whole** en conjunto; **on the whole** en general — **wholesaler** *n* mayorista *mf*

whom *pron* a quién; de quién, con quién, en quién; que, a quien

whose *adj* de quién; cuyo — **whose** *pron* de quién·

why *adv* por qué — **why** *n* (**whys**) porqué *m* — **why** *conj* por qué — **why** *interj* ¡vaya!, ¡mira!

wide *adj* ancho; amplio, extenso; *or* **~ of the mark** desviado — **wide** *adv* **wide apart** muy separados; **far and wide** por todas partes; **wide open** abierto de par en par — **widespread** *adj* extendido

widow *n* viuda *f* — **widow** *v* dejar viuda — **widower** *n* viudo *m*

width *n* ancho *m*, anchura *f*

wife *n* (**wives**) esposa *f*, mujer *f*

wig *n* peluca *f*

wild *adj* salvaje; agreste; desenfrenado; al azar; frenético; extravagante — **wild** *adv* **run wild** volver al estado silvestre (de las plantas), desmandarse (de los niños) — **wildlife** *n* fauna *f*

will[1] *v* (**would**) querer — **will** *v aux* **tomorrow we will . . .** mañana iremos de . . . ; **you will do as I say** harás lo que digo

will[2] *n* voluntad *f*; testamento *m*; **free ~** libre albedrío *m*

win *v* (**won**) ganar; conseguir; **~ over** ganarse a — **win** *n* triunfo *m*, victoria *f*

wind[1] *n* viento *m*; aliento *m*; flatulencia *f*; **get ~ of** enterarse de

wind[2] *v* (**wound**) serpentear; enrollar; **~ a clock** dar cuerda a un reloj

window *n* ventana *f* (de un edificio o una computadora), ventanilla *f* (de un vehículo), vitrina *f* (de una tienda)

windpipe *n* tráquea *f*

windshield *n* parabrisas *m*; **~ wiper** limpiaparabrisas *m*

wing *n* ala *f*; **under one's ~** bajo el cargo de algún — **winged** *adj* alado

wink *v* guiñar — **wink** *n* guiño *m*

winner *n* ganador *m*, -dora *f* — **winning** *adj* ganador; encantador

winter *n* invierno *m* — **winter** *adj* invernal, de invierno

wipe *v* limpiar; **~ away** enjugar (lágrimas), borrar (una memoria); **~ out** aniquilar, destruir — **wipe** *n* pasada *f* (con un trapo, etc.)

wire *n* alambre *m*; cable *m* (eléctrico o telefónico); telegrama *m* — **wire** *v* instalar el cableado en (una casa, etc.); atar con alambre; enviar un telegrama a — **wireless** *adj* inalámbrico

wisdom *n* sabiduría *f*

wise *adj* sabio; prudente

wit *n* ingenio *m*; agudeza *f*

with *prep* con; **~ you** contigo

withdraw *v* (**-drew; -drawn**) retirar; apartarse

within *adv* dentro — **within** *prep* dentro de; a menos de; dentro de, en menos de; **within reach** al alcance de la mano

without *adv* **do ~** pasar sin algo — **without** *prep* sin

withstand *v* (**-stood**) aguantar; resistir

witness *n* testigo *mf*; testimonio *m* — **witness** *v* ser testigo de; atestiguar (una firma, etc.)

witticism *n* agudeza *f*, ocurrencia *f*

witty *adj* ingenioso, ocurrente

wolf *n* (**wolves**) lobo *m*, -ba *f*

woman *n* (**women**) mujer *f*

wonder *n* maravilla *f*; asombro *m* — **wonder** *v* preguntarse — **wonderful** *adj* maravilloso, estupendo

wood *n* madera *f* (materia); leña *f*; *or* **~s** *npl* bosque *m* — **wood** *adj* de madera

wool *n* lana *f* — **woolen** *or* **woollen** *adj* de lana — **woolen** *n* lana *f* (tela) — **woolly** *adj* lanudo

word *n* palabra *f*; noticias *fpl*; **~s** *npl* letra *f* (de una canción, etc.) — **word**

processing n procesamiento m de textos — **word processor** n procesador m de textos

work n trabajo m; empleo m; obra f (de arte, etc.) — **work** v trabajar — **worker** n trabajador m, -dora f; obrero m, -ra f — **working** adj que trabaja (de personas), de trabajo (de la ropa, etc.); **be in working order** funcionar bien — **working class** n clase f obrera — **workingman** n (**-men**) obrero m — **workman** n (**-men**) obrero m; artesano m — **workshop** n taller m

world n mundo m; **think the ∼ of someone** tener a algún en alta estima — **world** adj mundial, del mundo — **worldwide** adv en todo el mundo — **worldwide** adj global, mundial

worm n gusano m, lombriz f; **∼s** npl lombrices fpl (parásitos)

worry v (**-ried**) preocupar(se), inquietar(se) — **worry** n (**-ries**) preocupación f — **worried** adj preocupado — **worrisome** adj inquietante

worse adv peor — **worse** adj peor; **from bad to worse** de mal en peor; **get worse** empeorar — **worse** n **the worse** el (la) peor, lo peor; **take a turn for the worse** ponerse peor — **worsen** v empeorar

worship v adorar; practicar una religión — **worship** n adoración f, culto m

worst adv peor — **worst** adj peor — **worst** n **the worst** lo peor, el (la) peor

worth n valor m (monetario); mérito m, valía f; **ten dollars' ∼ (of)** diez dólares de — **worth** prep **it's worth $10** vale $10; **it's worth doing** vale la pena hacerlo — **worthless** adj sin valor; inútil — **worthy** adj **-thier; -est** digno

would past of **will** **he ∼ often take his children to the park** solía llevar a sus hijos al parque; **∼ you kindly help me with this?** ¿tendría la bondad de ayudarme con esto?

wound n herida f — **wound** v herir

wrap v envolver; **∼ up** dar fin a — **wrap** n prenda f que envuelve (como un chal); envoltura f — **wrapper** n envoltura f, envoltorio m — **wrapping** n envoltura f, envoltorio m

wreck n **be a nervous ∼** tener los nervios destrozados — **wreck** v destrozar (un automóvil), naufragar (un barco)

wrench v arrancar (de un tirón); torcerse — **wrench** n tirón m, jalón m; torcedura f; or **monkey wrench** llave f inglesa

wrestle v luchar — **wrestler** n luchador m, -dora f — **wrestling** n lucha f

wretch n desgraciado m, -da f — **wretched** adj despreciable; desdichado **wretched weather** tiempo m espantoso

wrinkle n arruga f — **wrinkle** v arrugar(se)

wrist n muñeca f

write v (**wrote; written**) escribir — **writer** n escritor m, -tora f — **writing** n escritura f

wrong n injusticia f, mal m; agravio m (en derecho); **be in the ∼** haber hecho mal — **wrong** adj malo; inadecuado, inapropiado; incorrecto, equivocado; **be wrong** no tener razón — **wrong** adv mal, incorrectamente — **wrong** v ofender, ser injusto con — **wrongful** adj injusto; ilegal

X

x n (**x's** or **xs**) — x f, vigésima cuarta letra del alfabeto inglés

X ray n rayo m X; or **∼ photograph** radiografía f — **x–ray** v radiografiar

Y

y *n* (**y's** *or* **ys**) y *f*, vigésima quinta letra del alfabeto inglés

yard *n* yarda *f* (medida)

yawn *v* bostezar — **yawn** *n* bostezo *m*

year *n* año *m*; **she's ten ～s old** tiene diez años; **I haven't seen them in ～s** hace siglos que no los veo — **yearbook** *n* anuario *m* — **yearling** *n* animal *m* menor de dos años — **yearly** *adv* anualmente; **three times yearly** tres veces al año — **yearly** *adj* anual

yearn *v* anhelar — **yearning** *n* anhelo *m*, ansia *f*

yellow *adj* amarillo — **yellow** *n* amarillo *m*

yes *adv* sí; **say ～** decir que sí — **yes** *n* sí *m*

yesterday *n* ayer *m*; **the day before ～** anteayer — **yesterday** *adv* ayer

yet *adv* aún, todavía; sin embargo; **has he come ～?** ¿ya ha venido?; **not ～** todavía no; **～ more problems** más problemas aún — **yet** *conj* pero

yield *v* producir; **～ the right of way** ceder el paso; ceder — **yield** *n* rendimiento *m*, rédito *m* (en finanzas)

yoga *n* yoga *m*

yogurt *n* yogur *m*, yogurt *m*

yolk *n* yema *f* (de un huevo)

you *pron* tú; vos; ustedes *pl*; vosotros, vosotras *pl*; usted, ustedes *pl*; te, les *pl* (*se* before *lo, la, los, las*), os *pl*; lo, la; los, las *pl*; ti; vos; ustedes *pl*; vosotros, vosotras *pl*; usted, ustedes *pl*; **with ～** contigo; con ustedes *pl*; con vosotros, con vosotras *pl*; **with ～** con usted, con ustedes *pl*; **～ never know** nunca se sabe

young *adj* joven; **my ～er brother** mi hermano menor; **she is the ～est** es la más pequeña; **the ～** los jóvenes — **young** *npl* jóvenes *mfpl* (de los humanos), crías *fpl* (de los animales) — **youngster** *n* chico *m*, -ca *f*; joven *mf*

your *adj* tu; su; vuestro; su; **on ～ left** a la izquierda

yours *pron* (el) tuyo, (la) tuya, (los) tuyos, (las) tuyas; (el) suyo, (la) suya, (los) suyos, (las) suyas; (el) vuestro, (la) vuestra, (los) vuestros, (las) vuestras; (el) suyo, (la) suya, (los) suyos, (las) suyas

yourself *pron* (**yourselves**) te, se *pl*, os *pl*; se; tú mismo, tú misma; usted mismo, usted misma; ustedes mismos, ustedes mismas *pl*; vosotros mismos, vosotras mismas *pl*

youth *n* juventud *f*; joven *m* — **youthful** *adj* juvenil, de juventud; joven

yucca *n* yuca *f*

Yugoslavian *adj* yugoslavo

Z

z *n* (**z's** *or* **zs**) z *f*, vigésima sexta letra del alfabeto inglés

zeal *n* fervor *m*, celo *m*

zero *n* (**-ros**) cero *m*

zigzag *n* zigzag *m* — **zigzag** *v* zigzaguear

zip code *n* código *m* postal

zipper *n* cremallera *f*, cierre *m*

zone *n* zona *f*

zoology *n* zoología *f*

Common Spanish Abbreviations

SPANISH ABBREVIATION AND EXPANSION		ENGLISH EQUIVALENT	
abr.	abril	Apr.	April
A.C., a.C.	antes de Cristo	BC	before Christ
a. de J.C.	antes de Jesucristo	BC	before Christ
ago.	agosto	Aug.	August
Apdo., Aptdo.	apartado (de correos)	—	P.O. box
aprox.	aproximadamente	approx.	approximately
A.T.	Antiguo Testamento	O.T.	Old Testament
atte.	atentamente	—	sincerely
atto., atta.	atento, atenta	—	kind, courteous
av., avda.	avenida	ave.	avenue
a/v.	a vista	—	on receipt
Bo	banco	—	bank
c/, C/	calle	st.	street
C	centígrado, Celsius	C	centigrade, Celsius
C.	compañía	Co.	company
CA	corriente alterna	AC	alternating current
cap.	capítulo	ch., chap.	chapter
c.c.	centímetros cúbicos	cu. cm	cubic centimeters
CC	corriente continua	DC	direct current
Cd.	ciudad	—	city
CE	Comunidad Europea	EC	European Community
cf.	confróntese	cf.	compare
cg.	centígramo	cg	centigram
CI	coeficiente intelectual *or* de inteligencia	IQ	intelligence quotient
Cía.	compañía	Co.	company
cm.	centímetro	cm	centimeter
Cnel.	coronel	Col.	colonel
col.	columna	col.	column
Com.	comandante	Cmdr.	commander
comp.	compárese	comp.	compare
Cor.	coronel	Col.	colonel
C.P.	código postal	—	zip code
cta.	cuenta	ac., acct.	account
cte.	corriente	cur.	current
c/u	cada uno, cada una	ea.	each
CV	caballo de vapor	hp	horsepower
d.C.	después de Cristo	AD	anno Domini (in the year of our Lord)
dcha.	derecha	—	right
d. de J.C.	después de Jesucristo	AD	anno Domini (in the year of our lord)
dep.	departamento	dept.	department
dic.	diciembre	Dec.	December
dir.	director, directora	dir.	director
dir.	dirección	—	address

Common Spanish Abbreviations 214

do.	domingo	Sun.	Sunday
dpto.	departamento	dept.	department
Dr., Dra.	doctor, doctora	Dr.	doctor
dto.	descuento	—	discount
E, E.	Este, este	E	East, east
Ed.	editorial	—	publishing house
Ed., ed.	edición	ed.	edition
edif.	edificio	bldg.	building
edo.	estado	st.	state
EEUU, EE.UU	Estados Unidos	US, U.S.	United States
ej.	por ejemplo	e.g.	for example
E.M.	esclerosis multiple	MS	multiple sclerosis
ene.	enero	Jan.	January
etc.	etcétera	etc.	et cetera
ext.	extensión	ext.	extension
F	Fahrenheit	F	Fahrenheit
FC	ferrocarril	RR	railroad
feb.	febrero	Feb.	February
FF AA, FF.AA.	Fuerzas Armadas	—	armed forces
g., gr.	gramo	g., gm, gr.	gram
G.P.	giro postal	M.O.	money order
Gral.	general	gen.	general
h.	hora	hr.	hour
Hnos.	hermanos	Bros.	brothers
i.e.	esto es, es decir	i.e.	that is
incl.	inclusive	incl.	inclusive, inclusively
Ing.	ingeniero, ingeniera	eng.	engineer
izq.	izquierda	l	left
juev.	jueves	Thurs.	Thursday
jul.	julio	Jul.	July
jun.	junio	Jun.	June
kg.	kilogramo	kg	kilogram
km.	kilómetro	km	kilometer
km/h	kilómetros por hora	kph	kilometers per hour
kv, kV	kilovatio	kw, kW	kilowatt
l.	litro	l, lit.	liter
Lic.	licenciado, licenciada	—	*usually indicates a college graduate*
Ltda.	limitada	Ltd.	limited
lun.	lunes	Mon.	Monday
m	masculino	m	masculine
m	metro	m	meter
m	minuto	m	minute
mar.	marzo	Mar.	March

SPANISH ABBREVIATION AND EXPANSION		ENGLISH EQUIVALENT	
mart.	martes	**Tues.**	Tuesday
mg.	miligramo	**mg**	milligram
miérc.	miércoles	**Wed.**	Wednesday
min	minuto	**min.**	minute
mm.	milímetro	**mm**	millimeter
Mons.	monseñor	**Msgr.**	monsignor
N, N.	Norte, norte	**N, no.**	North, north
n/	nuestro	—	our
n.º	número	**no.**	number
N. de (la) R.	nota de la redacción	—	editor's note
NE	nordeste	**NE**	northeast
NN.UU.	Naciones Unidas	**UN**	United Nations
NO	noroeste	**NW**	northwest
nov.	noviembre	**Nov.**	November
N.T.	Nuevo Testamento	**N.T.**	New Testament
ntra., ntro.	nuestra, nuestro	—	our
NU	Naciones Unidas	**UN**	United Nations
núm.	número	**num.**	number
O, O.	Oeste, oeste	**W**	West, west
oct.	octubre	**Oct.**	October
OEA, O.E.A.	Organización de Estados Americanos	**OAS**	Organization of American States
OMS	Organización Mundial de la Salud	**WHO**	World Health Organization
ONG	organización no gubernamental	**NGO**	non-governmental organization
ONU	Organización de las Naciones Unidas	**UN**	United Nations
OTAN	Organización del Tratado del Atlántico Norte	**NATO**	North Atlantic Treaty Organization
p.	página	**p.**	page
P, P.	padre (*in religion*)	**Fr.**	father
pág.	página	**pg.**	page
pat.	patente	**pat.**	patent
PCL	pantalla de cristal líquido	**LCD**	liquid crystal display
P.D.	post data	**P.S.**	postscript
p. ej.	por ejemplo	**e.g.**	for example
PNB	Producto Nacional Bruto	**GNP**	gross national product
p°	paseo	**Ave.**	avenue
p.p.	porte pagado	**ppd.**	postpaid
PP, p.p.	por poder, por poderes	**p.p.**	by proxy
prom.	promedio	**av., avg.**	average
ptas., pts.	pesetas	—	
q.e.p.d.	que en paz descanse	**R.I.P.**	may he/she rest in peace
R, R/	remite	—	sender
ref., ref.ª	referencia	**ref.**	reference
rep.	república	**rep.**	republic

SPANISH ABBREVIATION AND EXPANSION   ENGLISH EQUIVALENT

r.p.m.	revoluciones por minuto	**rpm.**	revolutions per minute
rte.	remite, remitente	—	sender
s.	siglo	**c., cent.**	century
s/	su, sus	—	his, her, your, their
S, S.	Sur, sur	**S, so.**	South, south
S.	santa, santo	**St.**	saint
S.A.	sociedad anónima	**Inc.**	incorporated (company)
sáb.	sábado	**Sat.**	Saturday
SE	sudeste, sureste	**SE**	southeast
seg., sept.	segundo, segundos	**sec.**	second, seconds
sep., sept.	septiembre	**Sept.**	September
s.e.u.o.	salvo error u omisión	—	errors and omissions excepted
Sgto.	sargento	**Sgt.**	sergeant
S.L.	sociedad limitada	**Ltd.**	limited (corporation)
S.M.	Su Majestad	**HM**	His Majesty, Her Majesty
s/n	sin número	—	no (street) number
s.n.m.	sobre el nivel de mar	**a.s.l.**	above sea level
SO	sudoeste/suroeste	**SW**	southwest
Sr.	Señor	—	Mr.
Sra.	Señora	—	Mrs., Ms.
Srta.	señorita	—	Miss
S.R.C.	se ruega contestación	**R.S.V.P.**	please reply
ss.	siguientes	—	the following ones
SS, S.S.	Su Santidad	**H.H.**	His Holiness
Sta., Sto.	santa, santo	**St.**	saint
t, t.	tonelada	**t., tn.**	ton
TAE	tasa anual efectiva	**APR**	annual percentage rate
tb.	también	—	also
tel., Tel.	teléfono	**tel.**	telephone
Tm.	tonelada métrica	**MT**	metric ton
Tn.	tonelada	**t., tn**	ton
trad.	traducido	**tr., trans., transl.**	translated
UE	Unión Europea	**EU**	European Union
Univ.	universidad	**Univ., U.**	university
UPC	unidad procesadora central	**CPU**	central processing unit
Urb.	urbanización	—	residential area
v	versus	**v., vs.**	versus
v	verso	**v., ver., vs.**	verse
v.	véase	**vid.**	see
Vda.	viuda	—	widow
v.g., v.gr.	verbigracia	**e.g.**	for example
vier., viern.	viernes	**Fri.**	Friday
V.M.	Vuestra Majestad	—	Your Majesty
V°B°, V.°B.°	visto bueno	—	OK, approved
vol, vol.	volumen	**vol.**	volume
vra., vro.	vuestra, vuestro	—	your